Thinking

Thinking

An Invitation to Cognitive Science

Volume 3

edited by Daniel N. Osherson and Edward E. Smith

The MIT Press
Cambridge, Massachusetts
London, England

Second Printing, 1990

This book was set in Palatino by Asco Trade Typesetting Ltd., Hong Kong and printed and bound by Halliday Lithograph in the United States of America.

Library of Congress Cataloging-in-Publication Data
(Revised for vol. 3)

An Invitation to cognitive science.

  Vol. 3, edited by Daniel N. Osherson and Edward E. Smith.
  Includes indexes.
  Contents: v. 3. Thinking.
  1. Cognition. 2. Cognitive science. I. Osherson, Daniel N. II. Smith, Edward E.,
1940–
BF311.I68   1990   153   89-30868
ISBN 0-262-15037-9 (v. 3)
ISBN 0-262-65035-5 (v. 3: pbk.)

Contents

Epilogue

List of Contributors

Ned Block
Department of Linguistics and
Philosophy
Massachusetts Institute of
Technology

Susan Carey
Department of Brain and Cognitive
Sciences
Massachusetts Institute of
Technology

Paul M. Churchland
Department of Philosophy
University of California, San Diego

Keith J. Holyoak
Department of Psychology
University of California, Los
Angeles

R. C. Lewontin
Museum of Comparative Zoology
Harvard University

Daniel N. Osherson
Department of Brain and Cognitive
Sciences
Massachusetts Institute of
Technology

Mary C. Potter
Department of Brain and Cognitive
Sciences
Massachusetts Institute of
Technology

Paul Slovic
Decision Research
Eugene, Oregon

Edward E. Smith
Department of Psychology
University of Michigan

Stephen P. Stich
Department of Philosophy
University of California, San Diego

Foreword

The book you are holding is the third of a three-volume introduction to contemporary cognitive science. The thirty chapters that make up the three volumes have been written by thirty-one authors, including linguists, psychologists, philosophers, computer scientists, biologists, and engineers. The topics range from arm trajectories to human rationality, from acoustic phonetics to mental imagery, from the cerebral locus of language to the categories that people use to organize experience. Topics as diverse as these require distinctive kinds of theories, tested against distinctive kinds of data, and this diversity is reflected in the style and content of the thirty chapters.

As the authors of these volumes, we are united by our fascination with the mechanisms and structure of biological intelligence, especially human intelligence. Indeed, our principal goal in this introductory work is to reveal the vitality of cognitive science, to share the excitement of its pursuit, and to help you reflect upon its interest and importance. You may think of these volumes, then, as an invitation—namely, our invitation to join the ongoing adventure of research into human cognition.

The topics that we explore fall into four parts: "Language," whose nine chapters are found in volume 1, along with an introductory chapter for the volumes as a whole; "Visual Cognition" and "Action," which make up volume 2; and "Thinking," whose seven chapters belong to volume 3, along with an epilogue devoted to three supplementary topics. Each volume ends with a listing of the chapters in the other two.

Since each part is self-contained, the four parts may be read in any order. On the other hand, it is easiest to read the chapters within a given part in the order indicated. Each chapter concludes with suggestions for further reading and questions for further thought.

The artwork at the beginning of each chapter was provided by Todd Siler. We hope that it enhances your enjoyment of the work.

Paul M. Churchland

K. Dowling

Merrill F. Garrett

Innis Harl

John M. Hollerbach

Howard Lasnik

Joanne L. Miller

Daniel N. Osherson

Mary C. Potter

Edward E. Smith

Stephen P. Stich

Charles E. Wright

Edgar Zurif

Fred Dretske

H. L. Galiana

Alvin I. Goldman

James Higginbotham

Keith Holyoak

Richard K. Larson

Richard Lewontin

Ferdinand Vanderhoff

Steven Pinker

Paul Horr

Elizabeth Spelke

Shimon Ullmann

Al Yuille

Thinking

Thinking: Introduction

Edward E. Smith

The ability to think is perhaps the most distinctive of human capacities. Typically, thinking involves mentally representing some aspects of the world (including aspects of ourselves) and manipulating these representation or beliefs so as to yield new beliefs, where the latter may aid in accomplishing a goal.

The nature of *memory*, as discussed in chapter 1, provides a natural starting point for an analysis of thinking. Memory is the repository of many of the beliefs and representations that enter into thinking, and the retrievability of these representations can limit the quality of our thought.

Basic aspects of thought processes themselves are the concerns of the next four chapters, which deal with progressively more complex forms of thought. Chapter 2 takes up *categorization*, or the assignment of objects and events to categories. Categorization is fundamental to other thought processes because often the latter operate on categories rather than on individual experiences. Chapter 3 focuses on *judgment*, particularly how we judge the probabilities of uncertain events. Such probability judgments figure critically in determining the extent to which our behavior is rational. Chapter 4 takes up a closely related form of thought, namely *choice*, the means by which we decide among options. Again, the relation to rationality is central. Chapter 5 is explicitly concerned with *problem solving*. Although categorization, judgment, and choice are in some sense all instances of "problem solving," the bulk of chapter 5 is concerned with more complex situations than those encountered in previous chapters. These complex situations range from selecting a move in chess to planning how to paint a room.

The final two chapters in this part offer somewhat different perspectives on thought. Chapter 6 presents the *developmental perspective*, asking how knowledge and thought processes develop from birth to maturity, as well as in adulthood in moving from novicehood to expertise. Chapter 7 offers a *philosophical perspective*. The emphasis is on the notion of rationality, which has figured centrally in a number of the earlier chapters.

Chapter 1

Remembering

Mary C. Potter

Most of the time we take memory for granted: we keep track of the day's activities, recall (when asked) what we did last summer, know who's president, come up with the right words to express our thoughts, and know how to drive a car, all without any special effort to remember. On the other hand, some things are easily forgotten: the name of the person you've just been introduced to, the telephone number you have to look up each time you call it, the course material you read last week. Is memory simply erratic? If, as we will see, memory is actually highly structured and predictable, why does it function as it does? That is, why might it have evolved to work the way it does—and what are the costs and benefits of this design?

In this chapter we will look at three main phases of memory: registering or encoding information, retrieving or remembering it, and forgetting it. We will then consider short-term and longer-term memories and find evidence for multiple types of short-term memory.

Preparation of this chapter was supported by NSF grant BNS86-19053. I thank Virginia Valian and Judith Kroll for their comments and Michael Jordan for his comments on the section on connectionism.

1.1 Encoding, Retrieving, and Forgetting

1.1.1 The Functions of Memory

The purpose of having a memory is to store information for later use—sometimes for almost immediate use (as when you look up a telephone number and remember it only long enough to dial it), and sometimes for use at some undefined later time (as when you study a subject in school). What properties should a good memory system have to accomplish these functions? Let us start with an overview of the components of a memory system.

A first requirement of a memory system is that the information to be remembered should be put into an appropriate form for later use. This process is called *encoding*. Consider the form in which you might want to remember the information in this book. Although many people think of the ideal memory as being "photographic," a complete record of the experience of reading this book would be of limited usefulness because of the time that would be required to retrieve any particular piece of information in it—you would not want to reread a mental textbook each time you wanted to remember something. Even if you could go directly to the right "page" in memory, you would not usually want all the detail of the original experience. Therefore, encoding should reduce and transform information, retaining the important material (such as the main points in a chapter) and eliminating the trivial (such as the wording of individual sentences).

To be used later, the information must be capable of being *retrieved*—a second major requirement. (Between encoding and retrieval, information is *stored*.) The ability to retrieve a memory depends on just how it was encoded, on what other information is in storage, and on the circumstances of the retrieval attempt. Retrieval needs to be selective, so that wanted information is recovered without a flood of unwanted memories.

A third function of a memory system is to *forget* unneeded information; although forgetting often represents a failure of the system, it is also an essential component. Forgetting often has the effect of merging information about similar events, resulting in a more abstract and general representation of experience.

1.1.2 Encoding: Abstracting and Interpreting Experience

Before continuing, read this brief story about the telescope:

> In Holland a man named Lippershey was an eyeglass maker. One day his children were playing with some lenses, and they discovered that things seemed very close if two lenses were held about a foot apart.

Lippershey began experimenting, and his "spyglass" attracted much attention. He sent a letter about it to Galileo, the great Italian scientist. Galileo built his own instrument, took it out on the first clear night, and was amazed to find the empty dark spaces in the sky filled with stars!

Without looking back, decide which of the following three sentences was in the text you just read:

(1)   Galileo, the great Italian scientist, sent him a letter about it.

(2)   He sent Galileo, the great Italian scientist, a letter about it.

(3)   He sent a letter about it to Galileo, the great Italian scientist.

This example is taken from an experiment by Sachs (1967), who found that subjects could accept or reject a test sentence quite accurately if it came immediately after they had heard (or read: see Sachs 1974) the target sentence. But if the test was delayed for one or two sentences (as here), subjects rarely remembered the form of the target sentence (test sentence (2) was hard to reject), although they were easily able to reject test sentences in which the meaning was changed (as in sentence (1)).

Sachs's experiments show that information used during initial processing, such as the surface syntactic structure of a sentence, is not necessarily encoded in long-term memory, whereas the meaning is likely to be retained.

Levels of Processing

The kind of encoding we do makes a major difference in how much we remember, so one way to study the effects of encoding on memory is to give subjects different tasks to perform using the same materials. In an experiment by Craik and Tulving (1975) subjects made one of three types of yes-no judgments about a series of words. For example: Is TABLE in capital letters? Does MARKET rhyme with *weight*? Would FRIEND fit in the sentence *He met a _____ on the street*? The capital-letters task (which required the subject to pay attention to the word's visual appearance) was associated with very poor later memory for the words; the rhyme task (which required the subject to recall the sound of the word) led to somewhat better memory; but the sentence task (which required the subject to think about the word's meaning) produced the best results.

In Craik and Tulving's experiment each task oriented the subject toward a different aspect of the word. The resulting difference in memory has been called the *levels of processing* effect (Craik and Lockhart 1972). Paying attention to the visual appearance or sound of a word results in a shallow level of encoding that is easily forgotten, whereas paying attention to meaning results in a deeper and richer representation. For this reason, rote rehearsal of a word or string of words ("saying" them over and over) is an ineffective way of learning them, whereas thinking of meaning-based relationships among them is highly effective. Because encoding happens automatically as we perceive, think, and act, it makes surprisingly little difference whether we *intend* to remember something; what does matter is what kind of encoding we do.

One particularly effective form of encoding is to have the subject generate the word to be remembered. For example, subjects in an experiment of Slamecka and Graf (1978) generated a word in the same category as *ruby* that began with *d------*, a synonym for *sea* that began with *o----*, and so on. Subjects later remembered that *diamond* and *ocean* had been on the list better than they remembered word pairs they had seen but not generated themselves. The *generation effect* has been studied extensively; see Hirshman and Bjork 1988 for a recent review and theory.

Effects of encoding are not restricted to memory of verbal materials. Wiseman and Neisser (1974) presented subjects with a series of silhouettes of faces; examples are shown in figure 1.1. Some of these strange figures are difficult to see as faces. When subjects did succeed in "seeing" the face, they were more likely to recognize that picture as familiar on a later memory test, presumably because encoding the picture as an organized face was deeper (and so more memorable) than encoding it as an arbitrary pattern of black blobs. A similar point is made by experiments of Bower, Karlin, and Dueck (1975), some of whose "droodles" are also shown in figure 1.1. Subjects were better able to recognize or recall droodles if told what they represent; for example, figure 1.1c is a midget playing a trombone in a phone booth, and figure 1.1d is an early bird who caught a very strong worm.

Not only do we remember meaning rather than surface form, we also tend to retain the more important information, such as the fact that the Sachs paragraph was about the discovery of the telescope, better than details, such as the fact that the telescope was first called a spyglass. One explanation for selective remembering is that the "important" information is connected with more of the ideas or propositions in the text and is therefore processed repeatedly as the text is comprehended.[1] For example, having been told in advance that the paragraph is about the telescope, the

1. A proposition is a simple conceptual relationship or "idea unit" such as that Lippershey was an eyeglass maker or that Lippershey sent a letter to Galileo. It is assumed by most theorists that the meanings of sentences and texts are represented abstractly rather than in words and that the abstract, propositional representation omits certain kinds of information, such as the difference between sentences (2) and (3) in the Lippershey example, and adds other kinds of information, such as the fact that lenses were what Lippershey was experimenting with. See Kintsch 1974 for more about propositions and the representation of texts.

Figure 1.1
(a) and (b) are examples of highlight faces from Mooney 1957. (c) and (d) are droodles used in Bower, Karlin, and Dueck 1975.

reader is likely to connect the lenses mentioned in the second sentence with telescopes, and also the spyglass, Galileo, the "instrument," and looking at the stars—even though the word *telescope* is not used in the paragraph. (Even if you had not been told that the paragraph was about the telescope, you would probably have inferred that by the end of the paragraph.) To understand the paragraph, you interpret what is stated explicitly and also make inferences that flesh out the story. Work by Kintsch (1974, chap. 7) and other investigators has shown that the likelihood of remembering a given idea in a text (and also the likelihood that readers will rate it as important) is highly correlated with ,he number of times it appears in the underlying structure of ideas or propositions that readers build as they interpret the text.

In the telescope paragraph the relative importance of the ideas (and therefore their centrality in the resulting propositional structure) was inherent in the story. But importance may also be determined by the reader's goals. Anderson and Pichert (1978) had college students read a story about the activities of two boys at home either from the point of view of a burglar "casing" the house or from the point of view of an interested homebuyer. The perspective adopted during reading affected what subjects recalled later: for example, "homebuyers" were more likely to remember that the basement was musty, "burglars" were more likely to remember the coin collection and color TV. When the subjects were instructed to switch to the other point of view and recall the story a second time, they were able to recall details related to the new perspective that they had omitted the first time—but not as many as the subjects who had adopted that perspective during reading.

Anderson and Pichert's study illustrates a central principle of encoding: an object or event will be encoded differently in different contexts. The term *context* refers to any perceptions, sensations, or thoughts that are active at the time a given stimulus is encoded. Here, the context that was experimentally varied was the perspective the subject took (burglar or homebuyer), and the story was the stimulus whose encoding was studied. The reader's point of view determined the importance attached to details of the story: valuable, portable items versus house qualities.

One explanation for our better memory for important information, then, is that the important information is well connected. Another reason we remember some ideas better than others is that we give them more attention during encoding, perhaps because they are of special interest to us or because they are surprising or novel. A speaker or writer may signal which information is to be considered new, and which is already assumed or given, by the form in which it is expressed. *It is the girl who is petting the cat* implies that the new information is about the girl, whereas *It is the cat that the girl is petting* implies that the news is about the cat. Hornby (1974) showed that listeners do attend more carefully to the supposedly new information in such sentences than to the assumed information. Hornby's task required subjects to decide whether or not the sentence was true of a picture they were shown briefly. After the *It is the girl* ... sentence subjects were more likely to detect that a boy (not a girl) was pictured, whereas after the *It is the cat* ... sentence they were more likely to detect that a dog (not a cat) was being petted.

The experiments we have been discussing show that our memories are in large measure hostage to the form in which the remembered experience is encoded. Rather than being a complete record of the experience, a kind of mental videotape, memories are "contaminated" by processes that are part of perceiving and thinking: objects are recognized, scenes are interpreted, sentences are understood. Although the result is an imperfect record of the original event, the bias of the encoding process toward meaning, toward the most important ideas in a scene or text, and toward context-relevant interpretations solves two major design problems of memory: how to reduce the total amount of material to be remembered, and how to package it in the form in which we are likely to need it later.

Principles of Association: Contiguity and Frequency

What are the elementary processes of encoding? An ancient insight (going back at least to Aristotle) is that a new memory consists of a relationship or *association* between previously known entities. When you read the telescope story, the words and individual concepts were already known to you; it was the combination of ideas that was new. Before discussing how ideas become associated during encoding, consider another example.

Do you remember the moment when you found out that you were admitted to the college you decided to go to? The moment when you learned of the *Challenger* shuttle disaster? Can you remember any details of these occasions, such as exactly where you were, who you were with, what form the news came in, what you did next? Most people report that there are unusual occasions on which they can remember irrelevant details such as the clothes they were wearing and exactly where they were standing— a phenomenon that has been termed a *flashbulb memory* by Brown and Kulik (1977; see also McCloskey, Wible, and Cohen 1988). For many Americans, hearing of President Kennedy's assassination produced a flashbulb memory. On such an occasion all one's concurrent thoughts, actions, and perceptual experiences (even seemingly trivial ones) seem to become associated with the occasion, perhaps because the emotional impact of the event provides a physiological boost to memory.

Flashbulb memories are an extreme example of the principle of *association by contiguity*. The principle states that perceptions, thoughts, and other mental contents that occur at the same time are likely to become linked in memory, so that when one member of the pair or cluster occurs at a later time, the others are then recalled. Why should contiguous mental entities (thoughts, perceptions, and the like, occurring at more or less the same time) be bound together in memory? Many cooccurring experiences have nothing to do with each other—like the scenery you are driving past and the conversation you are having with your passenger. But the automatic creation of such associations, however arbitrary, may serve a useful function. We need to learn numerous arbitrary connections, such as the sounds of words and their meanings, the appearance and taste of foods, the places in the environment where given items are located, the fact that a growl may be followed by a bite. The principle of contiguity allows for this kind of arbitrariness in memory; any two mental events that cooccur tend to become linked (with exceptions that we will come to in a moment).

The formation of an association only when objects or events are in close temporal proximity has two advantages. Things that happen together are more likely to share some intrinsic or causal relationship than are things that happen at different times, increasing the likelihood that the association will be useful in discovering patterns and predicting events. Also, the principle of temporal proximity restricts the number of associations made; imagine the mental chaos that would result if all the thoughts that passed through your mind within any one-hour interval were fully interconnected in memory, so that each one reminded you of all the others!

Although temporal contiguity lays the groundwork for the formation of an association, the actual likelihood of making the association depends on what Seligman (1970) called *preparedness*. Seligman and others had noted in research on animal learning that a given species of animal may readily learn some associations but have great difficulty learning others. For example, a rat can readily associate a light with a shock, or a taste with the experience of becoming nauseated, but has great difficulty associating the taste with shock or the light with nausea (Garcia and Koelling 1966). This type of innate bias in what can readily become associated is widespread among animals (see Schwartz 1984, chap. 12), and it seems to be true also of humans (see, for example, chapter 6 on conceptual development). Notice that these innate constraints will generally select useful associations and avoid unprofitable ones; for example, learning the taste of a poisonous food will help the animal to avoid it in the future.

Surprisingly enough, temporal contiguity is not always essential to the learning of an association. In rats and other animals, the association between a foodstuff and getting sick may be made even though the sickness does not begin until hours after the food has been eaten (the Garcia effect). The association is more readily made if the food is different from the animal's usual diet. Therefore, an animal can be tricked into developing a dislike for an innocent but novel food, if it happens to get sick within a few hours of eating that food. (Humans report similar experiences that result in food aversions.) Even though this very specific innate learning mechanism sometimes associates unrelated events, it undoubtedly has survival value.

It is plain that we do not automatically remember all the connections among cooccurring ideas (even those that do not violate innate constraints). If we did, we could learn the vocabulary of a foreign language (in relation to the corresponding English words) in a few hours, and in general we could remember events and thoughts in much greater detail than we normally do. Evidently association by contiguity is a relatively weak form of learning and remembering. A second important principle is that of *frequency* or *practice*: each time two items appear contiguously, the association between them is strengthened (see Crowder 1976, chap. 9, for a discussion of the experimental evidence and related theoretical questions). This supplementary principle increases the likelihood that valid associations (such as causal relationships) will be strengthened at the expense of chance associations that do not reflect regularities in the world.

Other factors also work together with contiguity and frequency to strengthen useful associations selectively. As mentioned earlier, attention-directed learning aids memory; presumably attention maintains the to-be-associated ideas in contiguity for a longer time, strengthening the link between them. The added time both increases the strength of the asssociation directly and permits the retrieval of relevant information that may buttress the new association. For example, studying the vocabulary pair *dog-chien*, you might note that *chien* looks like *chain* and think of a chained dog. This extra association may help in the early stage of learning the French word (see Atkinson and Raugh's (1975) keyword method).

Nodes, Links, and Connectionism

The idea that memory consists of associations between mental entities underlies *associative models* of human memory. In such models the contents of memory consist of mental representations of items and their associative connections. Using the terminology of graph theory, items are commonly called *nodes* and connections between them are called *links*. Figure 1.2 illustrates a small fragment of such an associative network, representing knowledge about some animals. Notice that some of the links are labeled *is a* for the relationship "X is an instance of Y"; all the unlabeled links are property-of relationships such as "a robin has a red breast."

A basic assumption common to associative models of memory is that activation in one part of the network spreads over time to associated (linked) items. This spread of association constitutes memory retrieval. For example, activating *robin* leads to the activation of *eats worms, has a red breast*, and *is a bird*, each connected to *robin* by just one link. Thus, if this

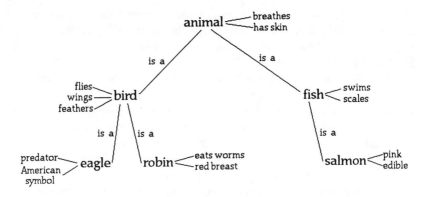

Figure 1.2
An associative semantic network (after Collins and Quillian 1969).

network is asked whether it "knows" that a robin has a red breast, it will find the connection more rapidly than it will find out whether a robin has wings (two links). (To answer such questions, the network representation must be augmented with a mechanism for making inferences such as that if a robin is bird, then it has all the properties of a bird.) Experiments by Collins and Quillian (1969) on the time subjects took to verify such statements supported their hypothesis that people encode information in hierarchical networks of this kind (see, however, Collins and Loftus 1975 and Smith 1978 for a more complete account, including some conflicting results).

Chapter 1 of the epilogue describes a recent approach to the modeling of cognitive processes that is called *connectionism* or *parallel distributed processing* (see also chapter 5). Connectionist models of memory have a number of interesting properties (see, for example, McClelland and Rumelhart 1986, chap. 17; the model described in that chapter is the one discussed here). These models employ nodes or *units* and associative links (*connections*), but the links are not labeled and the units do not correspond to single concepts as in the kind of network illustrated in figure 1.2. Instead, information in memory is distributed over a network consisting of a large number of units.

What corresponds to a given idea in memory (such as "cat") is a particular pattern of activity or state of the units in the network. Other ideas in memory (patterns) may be represented by the same network and many of the very same units, just as the pixels on a television screen can be turned on and off in different patterns to represent a huge number of different objects. But, unlike the TV screen, the units in a connectionist model are interconnected, and the strength (weights) of these connections can be modified by experience.

A pattern is learned through repeated experiences with the same or similar entities (such as cats) and with contrasting types of entities (such as dogs, lions, and toy cats). Each time a cat is seen, its particular stimulus properties are fed into the network, and activation then spreads out in accordance with the current weights on the connections between those initial units and other units in the network. The activity gradually "settles" to the most stable, lowest "energy" state consistent with the input pattern. The weights of the network are then modified to increase the likelihood that the same state will result when that stimulus or similar stimuli are encountered: in this way the network "recognizes" a stimulus.

After appropriate learning, a given pattern or state may be activated by an incomplete stimulus: seeing the silhouette of a cat's head may be sufficient to activate the full cat pattern. In effect, the network settles toward the pattern among those it already "knows" that is the best fit to the input. That is, these models embody a form of content-addressable memory (discussed in the next section): if you have some of the content (a profile of the cat's head), you can retrieve the complete concept in memory. If you have encountered many different cats, the model builds up an average or "prototype" concept of a cat, because the weights on the connections are continually adjusted to give the best fit to all the instances encountered. A cat you have seen just once or twice is likely to be remembered as more typical than it really was, because a single experience results in only small adjustments to the previous weights. (See chapter 2 for more on prototypes and categorization.)

Because a basic characteristic of these models is to converge on an existing pattern in memory that best fits the stimulus, the model has difficulty learning to distinguish stimuli that are highly similar—they tend to be classified as the same. If there is independent information about whether the stimulus actually was a cat or was something else, then that information can be incorporated in the learning rule so that the network can eventually learn to generate distinctive patterns for any two categories that have even slightly different inputs. In effect, the network comes to give more weight to the properties that distinguish between the categories. Thus, along with the representation of a prototype cat, the model can represent a particular familiar cat such as your cat Ginger, even if Ginger is unusual. In effect, enough experience with Ginger creates a special subcategory for him. Finally, because the weights on connections gradually decay to a neutral resting level over a long period of time, the most recent cat you have seen has more influence on the weights than earlier encounters with cats and is therefore likely to be remembered more accurately.

All these properties of a connectionist model of memory—the ability to recognize an object when supplied with only a part of it, the creation of prototype representations and distortions of memory toward the prototype, interference from similar categories, the ability to learn special instances, and the special salience of recent experiences—are at least qualitatively like those of human memory.[2]

What is the relationship between connectionist models of memory and semantic networks of the type illustrated in figure 1.2? Two very different suggestions have been made. One is that each node in a semantic network model would correspond to a connectionist module consisting of many units, perhaps thousands. In this manner, distributed connectionist models represent the fine-grain structure of the system, and semantic network models represent the macrostructure. The other suggestion is that the relations represented spatially in a diagram such as figure 1.2 are represented as temporal sequences in the network. Thought does not travel from one place in the network (such as the "bird" location) to another (such as the "robin" location), but rather the whole network shifts from the "bird" state to the "robin" state, given a nudge such as the query "What's a typical bird?" The temporal shifts in state that the network can make are learned in a manner analogous to the learning of each state; in effect, the network learns associations between states. A third possibility combines elements of the spatial and temporal hypotheses. When one concept is focal in the network (say, "bird"), exemplars or parts of that concept (say, "robin" or "wings") are also represented as subpatterns (Hinton 1988). If attention shifts to one of those subpatterns, the full pattern for that concept is generated and in turn its subpatterns are represented. Thus, attention can zoom in from wholes to parts and parts can be expanded to wholes.

Both the semantic network model of the type illustrated in figure 1.2 and connectionist representations of memory exemplify the close relationship between the form in which information is encoded and the way in which it is recovered. That brings us to the next phase of the memory system, retrieval.

1.1.3   Retrieval from Memory

A memory system has two main phases: acquisition of information (encoding) and later retrieval of the information. Just as the principle of temporal contiguity plays a basic role in the acquisition of a memory, another major principle, the principle of *content addressing*, is central in memory retrieval.

Can you think of a kind of bird that is yellow? Usually people come up with an instance almost immediately. The seemingly direct retrieval of the needed information is an example of content-addressed memory. *Content*

---

2. Although we have used visual pattern recognition to illustrate a connectionist model, the principles of the model can be applied to more abstract categorization, such as classifying a nation as a democracy. The input in that case might be from other connectionist "modules" rather than directly from the senses.

addressing (a term from computer science) means starting retrieval with part of the content of the to-be-remembered material (say, bird), which provides an "address" to the place in memory where identical or similar material is located.[3] If more than one item is found at that address, then further processing will be necessary to obtain the best memory match. Once a match has been made, associated information will be retrieved (such as the name or appearance of the object). An analogy is looking up a piece of information in an encyclopedia. Suppose you want to find out where Napoleon and Josephine got married. You might start by looking up "Napoleon," and then look for some heading like "marriage," and then read more carefully.

This way of getting into memory, by matching the current contents of experience to similar contents in memory and then retrieving associated information, is apparently the primary and perhaps the only way we remember.[4] But it is important to note that there are some kinds of information that cannot be used as a retrieval address, even though the information is in memory. For example, what word for a family relationship (for instance, *grandmother, cousin*) ends in *w*? Because you never encoded that piece of information explicitly, you are probably having trouble thinking of the word (hint: not *niece*).

Loftus (1972) had college subjects list instances of a superordinate object category such as "bird" or items that typically have a given property such as "yellow"; the subjects had one minute to make each list. On the average, subjects came up with 12 category members, but only 9 property exemplars. More interesting was that in producing exemplars of a property (say, yellow things), subjects tended to list several instances from one object category (say, yellow birds), then several from another, and so on. The implication is that we cannot readily address our memory for objects by a property such as "yellow" but instead must retrieve object categories and

3. Most computers do not have content-addressed memories but store information in arbitrary locations that are labeled by numbers; to retrieve a piece of information, its numbered location must be known. Unlike content-addressed memory, such arbitrary addressing systems do not degrade gracefully: if any of the address is forgotten, the partial address does not take the user to the "neighborhood" of the target information.

4. One alternative to content-addressed memory is *temporally organized memory*: one searches memory by starting with the present or some other arbitrary time point and searching backward or forward. This form of retrieval seems to be used in some instances, such as repeating what someone just said or recalling the day's activities. Even in such cases, however, the mechanism may be to start with a time tag ("this morning"), retrieve an associated item, and then retrieve the rest of the day's events by a chain of associations. This would be essentially the same mechanism as content addressing. Another search scheme is *random search*, which may be used when a small subset of memory has been selected by some other process such as content addressing. Here again, however, the basis for selecting the particular next item from the set in memory may be one's idiosyncratic associations.

scan them for instances exhibiting the property. Consistent with that interpretation, Freedman and Loftus (1971) found that subjects could come up with an instance (say, "canary") of a property-object combination such as "yellow bird" faster when given the category name before the property ("bird . . . yellow") than when given the property before the category name. Presumably, the way we are able to address a given memory depends on what characteristics were used in encoding it, and object categories are more fundamental to encoding than are properties.

Try another exercise in memory retrieval. Answer this series of questions as rapidly as possible: What month follows March? What year did Columbus set sail for America? How many animals of each kind did Moses take on the ark? Who was the American president before the present one? . . . It is possible that you mistakenly answered "two" to the question about the ark because you (your memory retrieval mechanism) thought of Noah when Moses was mentioned. (You may think that you just didn't see the word *Moses*, but subjects do not make the same mistake when *Nixon* is substituted for *Moses*.) This example, from an experiment by Erickson and Mattson (1981), illustrates the kind of imprecision that one might expect from a content-addressed retrieval system coupled with spreading activation. "Animals-on-the-ark" and "Moses" (Biblical figure) converge on the story of Noah and the ark; because Moses and Noah share several properties (male, major figure in Biblical stories, positive leaders), activation of "Moses" in the question will overlap with information about Noah, supporting the reader's impression that the correct address has been reached. The fact that such errors are uncommon in ordinary experience suggests that normally the retrieval process is subject to mental editing, so that only relevant information comes into awareness.

Thus, retrieval may be a two-stage process in which the first stage provides a large amount of material much of which is only marginally related to the initial stimulus or query; the second stage then selects according to some additional criteria, before passing the result to a third (conscious) stage.

Remembering is not restricted to deliberate reminiscence; rather, it is a continuous and essential accompaniment to thought. It is even doubtful that we *can* directly and deliberately recall something. What we do when trying to remember is to set the stage for the memory to be evoked by content addressing and by association. Efforts to recall have much in common with problem solving: we keep thinking about the question we are trying to answer (which contains some of the content of the to-be-remembered material) or about the person whose name we are trying to recall, which brings associated material to mind and may lead to the wanted memory. Or we think of the setting in which we acquired the information; and so on. Some problem-solving failures are instances of retrieval failure, even when the relevant knowledge is in memory. In chapter 5 experiments are reported in which subjects fail to recognize the formal similarity of a new problem to one solved earlier. That may happen because the subject did not explicitly encode the formal structure of the first problem, so it could not be addressed.

Just as we may fail to retrieve a relevant memory, we may also retrieve memories unintentionally. More precisely, a previous experience may have an influence on a current activity without our realizing it. Jacoby and Witherspoon (1982) had subjects respond to instructions such as "Name a musical instrument that employs a reed" and later asked them to write down a series of dictated words. The trick was that some of the dictated words were homonyms (*read/reed*) whose less common meaning had been used in the earlier instructions. There was a significant increase in the number of dictated words spelled according to the less common meaning when that meaning had been used in the earlier instructions. Yet the subjects were not aware of the connection between the two parts of the experiment: the retrieval of the earlier word was *implicit*.

Still more interesting was the finding that a group of patients with Korsakoff's syndrome gave the same results. Korsakoff patients are amnesic: they appear not to remember new information. Yet with this test of implicit memory, their memories seemed to be normal. Following Jacoby and Witherspoon's study, many instances of preserved implicit memory in amnesic patients have been reported, leading theorists to propose that there may be two fundamentally different long-term memory systems. One allows the retrieval of explicit memories of particular episodes or experiences, and it is this system that is damaged in amnesia. The other system simply makes certain items or connections between items more available, and it is relatively preserved in amnesia. For recent reviews and comments on these ideas, see Schacter 1987 and Humphreys, Bain, and Pike 1989.

1.1.4   Forgetting: Planned Obsolescence?

As already suggested, the ideal human memory system would not retain all the information that was ever experienced. Some of this raw information is lost during encoding. Now we consider how, subsequent to encoding, a memory system might continue to discard the less important information, retaining only what is essential.

As everyone knows, memories *decay* over time. We can think of a given memory as varying in strength: the stronger the memory, the greater the probability that it will be retrieved and the faster it will be retrieved. As time passes, memory strength is reduced, increasing the probability of forgetting. However, recalling or recognizing something boosts its memory strength once more, slowing the rate of forgetting. These two properties—strengthening by reactivating the memory and weakening with disuse—ensure the retention of material that was learned well originally or that is retrieved frequently. Like library books, material that is retrieved frequently is usually more useful or important than material that is retrieved rarely, so this is a simple but appropriate way of selecting information to be retained versus forgotten. The first way in which the forgetting process selects appropriate material to discard, then, is by disuse: use it or lose it.

The second way in which information is forgotten is by *interference* between memories. Surprisingly, this is the way most forgetting takes place—interference is more important than the mere passage of time (see Crowder 1976, chap. 7). Suppose, for example, that you meet someone named Susan Brown at a party, and she tells you that she grew up in Illinois, went to college at Stanford where she majored in computer science, and is now doing graduate work in cognitive science at MIT. Several weeks later you run into her again and recognize her face. Very possibly you remember little of what she told you about herself. (Without looking back, can you recall her name and the other information about her? Note what you remember, and then look back to check its accuracy.) Experiments have shown that most memory failures or memory distortions result from the activation of related or overlapping information that becomes mixed with or substitutes for the original information. For example, you may have "remembered" that Susan Brown studied computer science at MIT (because you may have retrieved the fact that MIT is a place where many students study computer science).

Memory changes occur when new information is merged with or mixed up with previously known information; sometimes the new information becomes distorted (as in the Susan Brown example), but sometimes the older information is changed. For example, if you later met someone else who went to Stanford, you might retrieve her biography when trying to recall Susan's, even though the information about Susan was acquired earlier. Notice once more that this is the kind of mistake that a content-addressed memory system would be expected to make: you see Susan's face, recall Stanford, and retrieve the wrong information at the Stanford address. Content addressing also explains why information that was stored *before* you encountered Susan Brown (such as your knowledge about MIT) can interfere with your memory for her. Both kinds of interference—from earlier memories and from subsequent information—tend to increase with elapsed time.

There are two ways in which this interference can actually be of benefit. The first is by promoting the development of general memories that summarize experience and the second is by updating memory as revised information is obtained. A general memory summing up your experience of (say) cats is created when you remember previous encounters with cats each time you come across a cat. The most frequent and most "important" characteristics of these encounters are the ones that will survive in memory, although at the cost of forgetting the detail of the individual episodes.

The second way in which interference may be useful can be illustrated by the parking problem: where did you park your car (or bike)? In this case only the most recent instance of parking is important, so it is helpful to have the most recent occasion dominate memory for previous instances. Indeed, people exhibit such a recency effect for where they parked their car (Pinto and Baddeley, as reported in Baddeley 1986) as well as for many other categories of information. The recency effect consists of enhanced memory for the most recent instance of a category, not total forgetting of all other instances; this makes it easy to retrieve the most recent instance when that is the relevant one (as in finding your car), without necessarily causing you to forget everything about earlier instances (as in remembering in which parking spots you got ticketed). Baddeley speculates that the role of the recency mechanism is to orient us in time and space: where we are and how we got there, what we have done recently, and the like. More broadly, it serves to tell us about "where we left off" in a conversation, a book, a train of thought, an activity.

To sum up, the main "problem" with memory—forgetting—turns out to be an important component of a memory system (at least one with realistic limitations on storage and processing capacity). Although the principles of forgetting appear to work beneficially in many cases, there are times when we need to remember information that we suspect will be easy to forget. Fortunately, knowledge of the way memory works can arm us with strategies for encoding and retrieving such information, strategies that include embedding the information in a meaningful context, thinking during encoding of the situations in which the information will later be wanted, and retrieving the information at frequent intervals.

1.2   The Temporal Architecture of Memory

We have talked about the rapid loss of "unimportant" information during encoding and the sources of subsequent forgetting through decay and interference. In this section we will look more closely at the temporal characteristics of memory.[5] At least four major temporal phases of memory

5. In textbooks since 1970 the division of memory systems is usually made somewhat differently: (1) sensory memory, including iconic and "echoic" memory; (2) short-term memory, with many of the properties of the present short-term verbal memory; and (3) long-term memory. But problems with this division have mounted (see Crowder 1982), leading me to adopt the division in the present chapter.

have been suggested, each dedicated to a different type of information: (1) *iconic (visual) memory*, which supports initial perception and may last less than half a second; (2) *very short-term conceptual memory*, which supports understanding and thought and may also last less than a second; (3) *short-term verbal memory*, which supports language comprehension and holds verbal information for about 2 seconds, losing it over the next 30 seconds; and (4) *long-term memory*, the stable form of encoded information that we focused on in the first part of this chapter.

It may seem surprising that the major division in the temporal architecture of memory occurs as early as 2 to 30 seconds after acquisition, separating long-term memory from the various forms of short-term or "working" memory. In the initial second or two after new visual or auditory information arrives it is actively processed: attended to, recognized, interpreted, related to other information. After this initial intensive processing, some of the information remains on hand for rapid retrieval if it becomes relevant again during the next few seconds. But after about 30 seconds without reactivation the information is no longer in working memory and has either been forgotten or has stabilized in long-term memory. Information continues to be forgotten, but once it has survived the marked loss of the first few seconds, the rate of forgetting is very much slower. Further loss follows a slowly decelerating function through minutes, days, and years. (For studies of long-term forgetting, see Bahrick, Bahrick, and Wittlinger 1975 on memory for high-school classmates and Squire 1989 on memory for one-season television programs.)

1.2.1   Iconic Memory

In order for us to recognize a scene, the visual pattern must continue to be available until it has been analyzed. Ordinarily we continue to look at the same point for 200 or 300 milliseconds, which is enough time to recognize most objects and scenes. But even if the lights went out a few milliseconds after the scene was presented, we would be able to recognize it, because our visual system is able to store the full perceptual information for about 200 milliseconds, a capacity called *iconic memory* (Neisser 1967).

Sperling (1960) studied iconic memory by having subjects view a brief 4 × 3 array of letters, followed by a blank screen. To demonstrate visual persistence, he signaled which row of letters to report only *after* the letters were removed. The subjects were able to report the letters in the designated row almost perfectly, if the experimenter signaled the row immediately after the array disappeared, whereas if the signal was delayed for 500 milliseconds, accuracy was no better for the signaled row than for the other rows. The initial capacity of iconic memory seems to be as great as that of perception itself, since any particular part of the visual field can be reported perfectly if the signal comes in time.

This brief iconic memory is wiped out by a new stimulus (an effect called *backward masking*), so it would not be of much use in normal viewing, when we look at one thing after another (Haber 1983). It is well that the next stimulus does mask the last one, or we would see double images. The only blanks in normal viewing occur when we blink, or during the 30 milliseconds or so that it takes to move our eyes from one spot to the next; iconic memory may help to bridge those gaps.

1.2.2   Very Short-term Conceptual Memory

It is easy to see why a visual representation of information would be needed only briefly, because the main goal of vision is to understand what is happening, and understanding involves encoding the perceptual information into an abstract conceptual form. What may be less obvious is that information at the conceptual level may also be needed only briefly during processing and might therefore be quickly forgotten. We will first review some evidence that conceptual information is indeed retrieved and forgotten rapidly, and we will then ask why the memory system might be designed in this way.

One source of evidence for a short-term conceptual memory comes from research with rapid sequences of pictures and words. The picture research was inspired by the everyday experience of looking around at the environment, in which a viewer fixates a new location every third of a second on the average. Since we may see a new scene with each fixation (for example, when we are in a moving vehicle), does that mean that we can understand the scene in 333 milliseconds? Do we also remember those scenes? People have an excellent memory for scenes they have viewed for 1 or 2 seconds (Shepard 1967; Standing 1973); but could we actually be storing the 10,000 or so snapshots lasting *one-third* of a second that our eyes deliver each hour? To be sure, many of these snapshots are redundant, but if we are taking a walk or driving or shopping, there could easily be 1,000 different scenes per hour.

To investigate this question, Potter and Levy (1969) presented 16-picture sequences of color photographs of distinct scenes at rates between 125 and 2,000 milliseconds per picture and then tested the viewer's ability to recognize them, mixed with new pictures. They found that, as in earlier research, subjects did well when the pictures were presented for 1 or 2 seconds each (they remembered over 80 percent of the pictures); as the sequences were speeded up, however, performance dropped dramatically.[6]

6. To estimate the proportion of pictures actually remembered, it is necessary to consider not only how many of the "old" pictures subjects say they recognize but also how many "new" pictures subjects mistakenly say they recognize. The proportions given here are adjusted for such guessing.

At a typical eye-fixation duration (333 milliseconds) subjects could remember only 50 percent of the pictures, and when the duration was 125 milliseconds, they remembered only about 15 percent.

Was it possible that the "forgotten" pictures were not actually forgotten but just had not been seen and understood as they flew by? By using a search task with a specified target (for instance, "Look for the picture of a picnic"), Potter (1975, 1976) showed that even at durations as brief as 113 milliseconds per picture viewers could understand most of the pictures well enough to detect the target (see also Biederman 1972). Because the target specifications were too general to be matched on the basis of simple visual attributes such as color or shape (what is the shape or color of a picnic?), this result suggested that most of the scenes *were* understood momentarily before being forgotten (see also Intraub 1981).

Even though viewers can understand what they are looking at within 100 to 200 milliseconds, then, understanding is not enough by itself to produce a lasting memory; extra processing is required to retain a scene for even a few seconds. The brief memory for scenes is conceptual rather than visual: unlike iconic memory, it is not wiped out by a visual mask *unless the visual "mask" requires conceptual processing* (Intraub 1984; Loftus, Hanna, and Lester 1988; Potter 1976). What would be the use of such a brief memory in normal perception? In one view,

> this momentary conceptual memory permits the viewer to respond to relevant events (targets) even when visual events are changing too fast ... to remember much. The normal rate of eye fixations, three a second, represents a reasonable compromise between the need for rapid monitoring of the environment for significant events and the need to remember some portion of what one has seen. (Potter 1976, 521)

Similar research has been carried out with rapid sequences of words, such as the following:

(4)   Tardy students annoy inexperienced teachers.

(5)   Purple concrete trained imaginative alleys.

Plausible sentences such as (4) were understood and remembered well when presented at 100 milliseconds per word, whereas nonsensical sentences such as (5) were remembered much less well (Potter 1982; see also Forster 1970). Because this difference is found even when the strings consist of only five to seven words (within the memory span for words presented more slowly, as we will see in the next section), this finding supports the proposal that initial understanding of a word (like a picture) can be followed by rapid forgetting within a second, as more words arrive to be processed. What saves words in plausible sentences from being forgotten is the existence of a syntactic and interpretive structure into which the momentarily available information can be assimilated. That is, the meanings of the words are available briefly, but unless they generate a structure at a higher level, they quickly exceed the capacity of very short-term conceptual memory and all but two or three are forgotten.

It is clear why we would want to achieve an understanding of what we are seeing or hearing as rapidly as possible, but it may be less clear why we can afford to lose within a second so much of what we have understood. One use for the fleeting understanding of scenes was already suggested: it allows us to respond to important events. More speculatively, the brief availability of a quantity of conceptual information (from long-term memory as well as from the immediate recognition of a word or picture) may permit the construction of a line of thought, in working on a problem or understanding the implications of a scene or sentence. In such cases information may be retrieved from long-term memory and used briefly in a step in the mental computation, after which it becomes irrelevant. It would be desirable to sweep that information out of working memory immediately, to avoid interference with subsequent computations. Possibly that is why our memory system has evolved to provide a very short-term form of conceptual working memory.

1.2.3   Short-term Verbal Memory

If you look up a telephone number to call someone, you probably say the number to yourself while reading it and again while dialing it. Similarly, if someone tells you a number out loud, you "hear" the number as an inner voice as you dial it or write it down. You may also hear the sounds of words as you read, and sometimes you hear your thoughts. The remarkable thing about this inner voice is that it serves as a short-term memory, like a very short-loop tape recorder that you can replay at will. (It is sometimes called *echoic memory*.) This mental tape recorder registers any sounds, not just speech. A particularly persuasive instance is the striking-clock phenomenon: if a clock begins striking when you are thinking of something else, you may be able to "replay" the first several strikes and count them. Because the strikes are identical, the memory representation must have preserved the temporal sequence. Three characteristics of this specialized short-term memory are that (1) it preserves information in a speechlike or auditory form, (2) it is severely limited in how much information it can hold, and (3) continuous rehearsal (rehearing) can maintain the contents of the memory indefinitely. A common memory test, the digit span (the largest number of random digits a subject can repeat back perfectly half the time), reflects this specialized form of memory.

To study the inner voice, Conrad (1964) showed subjects written strings of six or seven letters that they were to remember briefly and write down. He discovered that the errors they made were substitutions of letters that sounded like the originals, rather than of ones that looked like them. For example, *B* was substituted for *V* more frequently than *U* was. Later work by Baddeley and others (reviewed in Baddeley 1986) showed that such confusions in short-term memory for written material depend in some way on speech mechanisms, because if people are prevented from mentally saying the letters to themselves, they do not make sound-based confusions (although they also remember less). Baddeley developed a model called the *articulatory loop* hypothesis to account for these and other results. He regarded the articulatory loop as a component in the whole short-term memory system.

The articulatory loop system has two components, one a phonological store (inner hearing) and the other the articulatory loop (inner speaking). The phonological store holds a short sequence of speech sounds; listening to speech automatically fills the store, or it can be filled when written material is silently converted to a phonological form. Thus, hearing irrelevant speech while attempting to use the articulatory-phonological loop to remember something tends to disrupt memory: the irrelevant speech enters the phonological store, dislodging its contents. (It is harder to remember a telephone number if a news station is playing as you look up the number and then dial it.) In contrast, little or no disruption is produced by meaningless noise, even if it is loud (Colle and Welsh 1976; Baddeley 1986). Irrelevant music has an intermediate effect (Salomé and Baddeley 1989).

The speech system is used in converting a written item into a phonological representation. Occupying the articulators with irrelevant speech (for example, having a subject repeat "da da da..." while reading the to-be-remembered material) disables the loop, so no phonological representation of written material is created. Therefore, no sound-based confusions occur and there is no *additional* interference from hearing irrelevant speech—although much less is remembered, because the loop system is not available to augment the other short-term memory systems.

The second function of the articulatory loop is to refresh information in the phonological store by "rearticulating" it: that is the kind of rehearsal we do when keeping a telephone number in mind. Baddeley and others found something very interesting about this system: its capacity is closely correlated with the rate of overt speech. This shows up in three ways: people who articulate faster have larger memory spans; we can hold more short words than long words in short-term memory; and, for bilinguals, the digit span is greater in the language with faster-to-pronounce digits (Chinese is faster than English and English is faster than Welsh). The memory span for digits or words can be estimated by measuring the time an individual takes to read the items aloud: the amount read aloud in about 1.3 to 1.7 seconds is the amount that you will remember accurately in a memory span test, because you can keep that amount of material in the phonological store refreshed by "respeaking" it before it decays.

What role might a short-term phonological representation play in cognition, apart from remembering phone numbers and such? One strong possibility is that having a phonological trailing edge, in reading or listening to speech, is important in language understanding. Sentence comprehension is normally accomplished by word-by-word processing to a more abstract level, but there are occasions on which mistakes are made—in word recognition, in the building of the phrase structure of a sentence, or in sentence interpretation. Then the phonological form of the original input is consulted in order to recover from the mistake. Consider the sentence *Rapid righting with his uninjured hand saved from loss the contents of the capsized canoe*. Now imagine *listening* to the same sentence; you might try reading it to some friends, to see whether they understand it. Most listeners think at first that the second word is *writing*, not *righting*. To recover from the mistake, they have to review the sentence in phonological form.

Not only does the phonological representation help with understanding misleading sentences like the one just given, it seems also to be useful in normal syntactic processing. Patients with impaired articulatory/phonological representations have difficulty understanding long or complex sentences, such as *The book the pencil is on is red* (Baddeley, Vallar, and Wilson 1987); the phonological window may help to maintain the order of the critical words while the relationships are being worked out. Similarly, it seems likely that the articulatory-phonological loop is important in learning language, both to hold a segment of speech during comprehension and also to compare one's own speech output with a phonological model.

1.2.4   Long-term Memory

How do the three short-term memory systems just discussed relate to long-term memory? Is long-term memory "written" in only one of the forms or codes of short-term memory? The evidence points to multiple forms of long-term memory corresponding to each of the short-term memories, but with marked differences in the readiness with which different codes are retained. The dominant form of information in long-term memory is conceptual, because that is ordinarily the most important information about events and therefore receives more attention and processing time than sounds or appearances. And because we do remember so much conceptual information, there are innumerable distinct niches for encoding still more. But we do also remember how familiar things look or sound, so long-term memories are registered in those codes also, at least with repeated experience. Thus, long-term memory is biased toward abstract, conceptual information, but any information capable of being experienced can also be stored, as far as we know.

1.2.5   Conclusions and Implications: The Temporal Architecture of Memory

Each of the three short-term memory systems has the function of holding a certain kind of information for a short time while processing continues: the visual icon for visual perception; the phonological store as a backup for language processing and for remembering short sequences such as telephone numbers (with the articulatory loop for maintaining the information); and very short-term conceptual memory for high-level perception and thought. The idea that there are multiple forms of short-term memory, including others not discussed here such as the imagery buffer, has replaced the earlier assumption that there was one form of short-term memory (Baddeley 1986; Monsell 1984; Potter 1983).

What both the new and the older idea share is that these working memory systems (with the exception of the icon) are extremely limited in capacity: at any one time the phonological store holds less than two seconds' worth of spoken information, and conceptual short-term memory holds only three or four items. But what counts as an item? A letter in a word, a word, a sentence? Miller (1956) proposed that a *memory chunk* (as he called it) is any unit already represented as such in long-term memory, so that *IFB* is three chunks, but *FBI* is one chunk. The limited capacity of conceptual short-term memory implies that the formation of new ideas, associations, inferences, plans, arguments, and decisions—all of conscious, innovative thought—requires the *simultaneous* activity of only a few items.

How can we get along with such a limited capacity in the active, thinking part of the cognitive system? Consider the process of encoding new information: if associations can be made only among simultaneous or near-simultaneous mental events, will having only four active items permit efficient chunking? It turns out that in a hierarchical arrangement of information (oak and maple are trees, trees and flowers are plants, plants and animals are living things, ...) the number of branches at each level in the hierarchy that produces the most efficient retrieval search is three or four: with four branches, the average number of nodes in the tree that one will have to search to locate a given item at the bottom of the tree is minimized, and with three branches, the maximal number of nodes searched is minimized (Dirlam 1972; see also MacGregor 1987).

This observation suggests that it may be optimal to make associative links among groupings no larger than four, which is within the limited capacity of the short-term memory processors. An experiment in which a college student was trained to recall extraordinarily long lists of digits—as many as 89—after a single hearing supports this suggestion (Ericcson, Chase, and Faloon 1980). The subject, a competitive runner, learned to group the digits into chunks of three or four that he could interpret as times to run a given race, or some other meaningful number, and then to group those groups into higher clusters of three or four, and so on. In recalling, he simply unpacked the tree structure. Thus, the limited capacity of working memory may be optimal for creating long-term memory structures.

Let us now consider the consequences for reasoning and decision making. Is our limited capacity for having multiple ideas in mind the weakest link in the cognitive machinery? Perhaps so, but how do we manage to solve problems, reason, make decisions, and carry out actions as well as we do? The explanation is that many cognitive processes do not require moment-to-moment decisions of the central processor, which is limited to the current contents of working memory. Instead, they involve lower-level, specialized processors that perform automatically, once set in motion. Perceptual processing is automatic in this sense: if you look at a written word, you can't help recognizing it. Actions we take can also be regulated automatically; for example, a skilled pianist may be able to look at a piece of music and play it while carrying on a conversation, although nonautomatic aspects of playing such as interpretation will suffer.

In both these cases what may have begun as a laborious, centrally controlled, capacity-limited process became with long practice a self-regulating, automatic skill. In other cases the specialized processor is innate, requiring relatively little experience to develop; an example is seeing an object in three-dimensional space and picking it up smoothly. The central processor's job is to decide whether you should pick the object up, and perhaps decide how carefully you should do so (if it's a full cup of coffee, for example), but once the decision is made, the rest is under automatic control. It is primarily the highest-level decisions and thoughts that require the central processor with its limited capacity; we escape its confines only by the automation of perceptual, intellectual, and motor skills through extensive practice.

1.3   Conclusions and New Directions

We noted at the beginning of this chapter that memory is highly structured and predictable, and we have seen how each component of memory contributes to the overall effectiveness of the system. In this overview many topics have been set aside. For instance, nothing has been said about memory for motor skills, which recent theories and findings have suggested may follow somewhat different principles from the cognitive forms of memory discussed in this chapter. "Procedural" memories for riding a bicycle may be like some perceptual skills such as reading, in that both are acquired gradually with practice, both become automatic, and both may be damaged by brain lesions without necessarily affecting cognitive memory. Memory for one's language is another important special case. The discussions of categorization in chapter 2, problem solving in chapter 5, and cognitive development in chapter 6 are also relevant. In fact, almost every chapter in this volume makes implicit or explicit reference to memory and learning.

In the next decade advances in the field of memory are likely to be made in three broad areas. One is in gaining a better understanding of the biological basis of associative memory, both short-term and long-term. A second is in developing formal models of learning and memory, including the study of formal constraints on learning (see, for example, Osherson and Weinstein 1984). Related to this second area will be the further development of computer-based models of memory such as connectionist models. A third area is in better understanding the processes of perception and thought, and the ways they draw on the types of short-term and long-term memory sketched in this chapter. Although the study of human memory is one of the oldest fields of cognitive science, there is still much to be learned.

Suggestions for Further Reading

In addition to the references provided in the text, see Klatzky 1980 for a more complete introductory account of theories and research on memory, or Crowder 1976 for an advanced account. A thoughtful set of papers on human memory and learning that evaluate the progress of research in the last 100 years is provided in Gorfein and Hoffman 1987. For the relationship between memory and attention, see Norman 1976. For a unified theory of cognition and memory, instantiated in a computer model, see Anderson 1983, but bear in mind that many theorists believe that such a unified model is premature.

Much of the experimental work on human memory makes use of simple materials such as word lists or even lists of nonsense syllables. Although such materials allow the kinds of experimental controls that make interpretation of the results relatively straightforward, there are important characteristics of memory that can only be studied with more natural materials such as sentences or stories. Bartlett carried out one of the earliest experimental studies of memory for such materials, and his influential book (Bartlett 1932) contains many fascinating observations. Kintsch 1974 contains a review of more recent work. For a collection of articles on remembering in nonlaboratory settings, see Neisser 1982 and Gruneberg, Morris, and Sykes 1978 and 1988. Linton's study of her memories of everyday events in her own life over a several-year period (reported in two of those books) is particularly interesting.

Many insights about normal memory have been provided by the study of impaired memory associated with brain lesions. For a recent review, see Squire 1987. Closely related to human memory is the study of animal learning; once focused primarily on the conditions under which associations are formed between stimuli and responses, recent theories of animal learning and memory have incorporated cognitive concepts. For an introduction, see Schwartz 1984; and, on the relations between animal learning and human memory, see Nilsson and Archer 1985.

Finally, studies of people with exceptional memories (for example, Luria 1968; see also part 7 in Neisser 1982) and of specialized methods for remembering (Yates 1966) make interesting reading, although you should be aware that memory "tricks" are more useful for memorizing verbatim information than for developing and retaining a good understanding of material. See Ericsson and Polson 1988 for an interesting example of a practical use of such a specialized memory skill.

Questions

1.1 If what you will remember later depends on how you encode material when learning it, what steps might you take to study course material so that it will be memorable not only when you are answering an exam question but also in other relevant professional and personal contexts?

1.2 In section 1.1.2 we noted that the bias of the encoding process toward meaning rather than exact form, toward important ideas, and toward context-relevant interpretations puts the information in a form that would usually be most useful later. Why would each of these biases produce useful memories? Can you think of circumstances in which each of these biases might produce inappropriate memories?

1.3 In section 1.1.2 it was stated that there are some innate constraints on what experiences are readily associated. One suggestion is that objects and their locations are more easily associated than are objects and other stimuli such as sounds or colors. Design an experiment to test that hypothesis. Why will it be important to take into account the ease of learning the set of locations versus the set of colors or sounds?

1.4 Try drawing a simple associative network to show how thinking of *chain* might help you remember that *chien* is the French word for *dog* (see section 1.1.2). Consider what kinds of links (relationships) you would have to specify to avoid learning that *chien* means "chain" and to know that *dog* and *chien* are both words that name dogs. Notice that the network in figure 1.2 omits such complexities.

1.5 It has sometimes been suggested that an experience, once in long-term memory, is never truly forgotten but simply becomes difficult or impossible to retrieve. In light of the principles of forgetting discussed in section 1.1.4, how might this claim be true, at least for some experiences? Is the claim likely to be true for any of the short-term memories?

1.6 Bellugi, Klima, and Siple (1975) designed an experiment in which deaf subjects whose native language was Amerian Sign Language (ASL) recalled short lists of up to seven ASL words; a group of hearing subjects recalled the same lists presented in spoken English. Both groups wrote down the (English) words in order, as soon as the list was presented. The deaf subjects had an average memory span of 4.9 items, compared with 5.9 items for the hearing subjects. The hearing subjects tended to make sound-based errors (such as *house* for *horse*), but the deaf subjects made errors based on the similarity of the ASL signs for the two words (such as *apple* for *candy*; the two signs differ only by one finger position). What do these results tell us about short-term verbal memory in hearing and deaf individuals? How would the description of short-term verbal memory given in this chapter need to be modified or added to, to account for these results?

References

Anderson, J. R. (1983). *The architecture of cognition*. Cambridge, MA: Harvard University Press.

Anderson, R. C., and J. W. Pichert (1978). Recall of previously unrecallable information following a shift in perspective. *Journal of Verbal Learning and Verbal Behavior* 17, 1−12.

Atkinson, R. C., and M. R. Raugh (1975). An application of the mnemonic keyword method to the acquisition of a Russian vocabulary. *Journal of Experimental Psychology: Human Learning and Memory* 104, 126−133.

Baddeley, A. (1986). *Working memory*. Oxford: Clarendon Press.

Baddeley, A., G. Vallar, and B. Wilson (1987). Sentence comprehension and phonological memory: Some neuropsychological evidence. In M. Coltheart, ed., *Attention and Performance 12: The psychology of reading*. Hillsdale, NJ: L. Erlbaum Associates.

Bahrick, H. P., P. O. Bahrick, and R. P. Wittlinger (1975). Fifty years of memory for names and faces: A cross-sectional approach. *Journal of Experimental Psychology: General* 104, 54−75.

Bartlett, F. C. (1932). *Remembering: A study in experimental and social psychology*. Cambridge: Cambridge University Press.

Bellugi, U., E. S. Klima, and P. Siple (1975). Remembering in signs. *Cognition* 3, 93−125.

Biederman, I. (1972). Perceiving real-world scenes. *Science* 177, 77−80.

Bower, G. H., M. B. Karlin, and A. Dueck (1975). Comprehension and memory for pictures. *Memory and Cognition* 3, 216−220.

Brown, R., and J. Kulik (1977). Flashbulb memories. *Cognition* 5, 73−99.

Colle, H. A., and A. Welsh (1976). Acoustic masking in primary memory. *Journal of Verbal Learning and Verbal Behavior* 15, 17−32.

Collins, A. M., and E. F. Loftus (1975). A spreading-activation theory of semantic processing. *Psychological Review* 82, 407−428.

Collins, A. M., and M. R. Quillian (1969). Retrieval times from semantic memory. *Journal of Verbal Learning and Verbal Behavior* 8, 240−247.

Conrad, R. (1964). Acoustic confusion in immediate memory. *British Journal of Psychology* 55, 75−84.

Craik, F. I. M., and R. S. Lockhart (1972). Levels of processing: A framework for memory research. *Journal of Verbal Learning and Verbal Behavior* 11, 671−684.

Craik, F. I. M., and E. Tulving (1975). Depth of processing and the retention of words in episodic memory. *Journal of Experimental Psychology: General* 104, 268−294.

Crowder, R. G. (1976). *Principles of learning and memory*. Hillsdale, NJ: L. Erlbaum Associates.

Crowder, R. G. (1982). The demise of short-term memory. *Acta Psychologica* 50, 291−323.

Dirlam, D. K. (1972). Most efficient chunk sizes. *Cognitive Psychology* 3, 355−359.

Erickson, T. D., and M. E. Mattson (1981). From words to meaning: A semantic illusion. *Journal of Verbal Learning and Verbal Behavior* 20, 540−551.

Ericsson, K. A., W. G. Chase, and S. Faloon (1980). Acquisition of a memory skill. *Science* 208, 1181−1182.

Ericsson, K. A., and P. G. Polson (1988). An experimental analysis of the mechanisms of a memory skill. *Journal of Experimental Psychology: Learning, Memory, and Cognition* 14, 305−316.

Forster, K. I. (1970). Visual perception of rapidly presented word sequences of varying complexity. *Perception and Psychophysics* 8, 215−221.

Freedman, J. L., and E. F. Loftus (1971). Retrieval of words from long-term memory. *Journal of Verbal Learning and Verbal Behavior* 10, 107−115.

Garcia, J., and R. A. Koelling (1966). The relation of cue to consequence in avoidance learning. *Psychonomic Science* 4, 123−124.

Gorfein, D. S., and R. R. Hoffman (1987). *Memory and learning: The Ebbinghaus Centennial Conference*. Hillsdale, NJ: L. Erlbaum Associates.

Gruneberg, M. M., P. E. Morris, and R. N. Sykes, (1978). *Practical aspects of memory*. London: Academic Press.

Gruneberg, M. M., P. E. Morris, and R. N. Sykes, eds. (1988). *Practical aspects of memory*, vol. 2. London: Wiley.

Haber, R. N. (1983). The impending demise of the icon: A critique of the concept of iconic storage in visual information processing (with commentary and reply). *Behavioral and Brain Sciences* 6, 1–54.

Hinton, G. E. (1988). Representing part-whole hierarchies in connectionist networks. In *Proceedings of the Tenth Annual Conference of the Cognitive Science Society*. Hillsdale, NJ: L. Erlbaum Associates.

Hirshman, E., and R. A. Bjork (1988). The generation effect: Support for a two-factor theory. *Journal of Experimental Psychology: Learning, Memory, and Cognition* 14, 484–494.

Hornby, P. A. (1974). Surface structure and presupposition. *Journal of Verbal Learning and Verbal Behavior* 13, 530–538.

Humphreys, M. S., J. D. Bain, and R. Pike (1989). Different ways to cue a coherent system: A theory for episodic, semantic, and procedural tasks. *Psychological Review* 96, 208–233.

Intraub, H. (1981). Rapid conceptual identification of sequentially presented pictures. *Journal of Experimental Psychology: Human Perception and Performance* 7, 604–610.

Intraub, H. (1984). Conceptual masking: The effects of subsequent visual events on memory for pictures. *Journal of Experimental Psychology: Learning, Memory, and Cognition* 10, 115–125.

Jacoby, L. L., and D. Witherspoon (1982). Remembering without awareness. *Canadian Journal of Psychology* 36, 300–324.

Kintsch, W. (1974). *The representation of meaning in memory*. Hillsdale, NJ: L. Erlbaum Associates.

Klatzky, R. L. (1980). *Human memory: Structures and processes*. 2nd ed. San Francisco: W. H. Freeman.

Loftus, E. F. (1972). Nouns, adjectives, and semantic memory. *Journal of Experimental Psychology* 96, 213–215.

Loftus, G. R., A. M. Hanna, and L. Lester (1988). Conceptual masking: How one picture captures attention from another picture. *Cognitive Psychology* 20, 237–282.

Luria, A. R. (1968). *The mind of a mnemonist*. (Translated by L. Solotaroff.) New York: Basic Books.

McClelland, J. L., D. E. Rumelhart, and the PDP Research Group (1986). *Parallel distributed processing: Explorations in the microstructure of cognition*. Vol. 2: *Psychological and biological models*. Cambridge, MA: MIT Press.

McCloskey, M., C. G. Wible, and N. J. Cohen (1988). Is there a special flashbulb-memory mechanism? *Journal of Experimental Psychology: General* 117, 171–181.

MacGregor, J. N. (1987). Short-term memory capacity: Limitation or optimization? *Psychological Review* 94, 107–108.

Miller, G. A. (1956). The magical number seven, plus or minus two: Some limits on our capacity for processing information. *Psychological Review* 63, 81–97.

Monsell, S. (1984). Components of working memory underlying verbal skills: A "Distributed Capacities" view. In H. Bouma and D. Bouwhuis, eds., *Attention and performance 10: Control of language processes*. Hillsdale, NJ: L. Erlbaum Associates.

Mooney, C. M. (1957). Age in the development of closure ability in children. *Canadian Journal of Psychology* 11, 219–226.

Neisser, U. (1967). *Cognitive psychology*. New York: Appleton-Century-Crofts.

Neisser, U. (1982). *Memory observed*. San Francisco: W. H. Freeman.

Nilsson, L.-G., and T. Archer, eds. (1985). *Perspectives on learning and memory*. Hillsdale, NJ: L. Erlbaum Associates.

Norman, D. A. (1976). *Memory and attention*. 2nd ed. New York: Wiley.

Osherson, D. N., and S. Weinstein (1984). Formal learning theory. In M. S. Gazzaniga, ed., *Handbook of cognitive neuroscience*. New York: Plenum Press.

Potter, M. C. (1975). Meaning in visual search. *Science* 187, 965–966.

Potter, M. C. (1976). Short-term conceptual memory for pictures. *Journal of Experimental Psychology: Human Learning and Memory* 2, 509–522.

Potter, M. C. (1982). Very short-term memory: In one eye and out the other. Paper presented at the Annual Meeting of the Psychonomic Society.

Potter, M. C. (1983). Representational buffers: The eye-mind hypothesis in picture perception, reading, and visual search. In K. Rayner, ed., *Eye movements in reading: Perceptual and language processes*. New York: Academic Press.

Potter, M. C., and E. I. Levy (1969). Recognition memory for a rapid sequence of pictures. *Journal of Experimental Psychology* 81, 10–15.

Sachs, J. S. (1967). Recognition memory for syntactic and semantic aspects of connected discourse. *Perception and Psychophysics* 2, 437–442.

Sachs, J. S. (1974). Memory in reading and listening to discourse. *Memory and Cognition* 2, 95–100.

Salomé, P., and A. Baddeley (1989). Effects of background music on phonological short-term memory. *Quarterly Journal of Experimental Psychology* 41A, 107–122.

Schacter, D. L. (1987). Implicit memory: History and current status. *Journal of Experimental Psychology: Learning, Memory, and Cognition* 13, 501–518.

Schwartz, B. (1984). *Psychology of learning and behavior*. New York: Norton.

Seligman, M. E. P. (1970). On the generality of the laws of learning. *Psychological Review* 77, 406–418.

Shepard, R. N. (1967). Recognition memory for words, sentences, and pictures. *Journal of Verbal Learning and Verbal Behavior* 6, 156–163.

Slamecka, N. J., and P. Graf (1978). The generation effect: Delineation of a phenomenon. *Journal of Experimental Psychology: Human Learning and Memory* 4, 592–604.

Smith, E. E. (1978). Theories of semantic memory. In W. K. Estes, ed., *Handbook of learning and cognitive processes*, vol. 6. Hillsdale, NJ: L. Erlbaum Associates.

Sperling, G. (1960). The information available in brief visual presentations. *Psychological Monographs* 74 (11, Whole No. 498).

Squire, L. R. (1987). *Memory and brain*. New York: Oxford University Press.

Squire, L. R. (1989). On the course of forgetting in very long-term memory. *Journal of Experimental Psychology: Learning, Memory, and Cognition* 15, 241–245.

Standing, L. (1973). Learning 10,000 pictures. *Quarterly Journal of Experimental Psychology* 25, 207–222.

Wiseman, S., and U. Neisser (1974). Perceptual organization as a determinant of visual recognition memory. *American Journal of Psychology* 87, 675–681.

Yates, F. A. (1966). *The art of memory*. Middlesex, England: Penguin.

Chapter 2

Categorization

Edward E. Smith

We are forever carving nature at its joints, dividing it into categories so that we can make sense of the world. If we see a particular child pet a particular dog at a particular time and a particular place, we code it as just another instance of "children like dogs." In doing this, we reduce a wealth of particulars to a simple relation between the categories "children" and "dogs" and free our mental capacities for other tasks.[1]

What exactly is a category? For now, let us take a *category* to be a class of objects that we believe belong together. (The word *believe* is critical here—we are dealing with the psychological sense of *category*, not the logical sense that is sometimes captured by linguistic theories.) Our major concern in this chapter is with the process by which people assign objects to categories, but this concern requires that we first consider the nature of categories. In section 2.1 we will analyze the nature of categories and consider three characteristics of a class of objects that make it into

Preparation of this chapter was supported by U.S. Public Health Service grant MH 37208.
I thank Daniel Osherson for helpful comments on an earlier version.
1. Quotation marks are used throughout the chapter to indicate categories.

a category. One characteristic is the similarity of the objects grouped together, and in section 2.2 we will discuss alternative means for measuring similarity. We will opt for a model in which the similarity of objects is measured in terms of their features. In section 2.3 we will apply this model to categorization tasks and see that it accounts for a variety of empirical findings. In section 2.4 we will briefly look at some other issues in research on categorization.

2.1   What Is a Category? Three Critical Characteristics

2.1.1   Classes and Categories

We take a category to be a class of objects that seem to belong together. The critical part of this definition is "seem to belong together," for there are an indefinite number of classes of objects in the world whose members do not seem to belong together. Thus, there is the class of all objects that weigh an even number of grams (or an odd number of grams, or a prime number of grams, etc.), the class of all things that are *not* green (or *not* round, or *not* democratic, etc.), the class of all things that can be scraped *or* worshiped (or tasted *or* mistrusted, or inflamed *or* envied, etc.), and so on. In all these cases the class of objects has some property in common yet the class is not treated as a category. What characteristics of a class give it the status of categoryhood? Three characteristics are discussed in the following sections.

2.1.2   Coding of Experience

Perhaps the most striking characteristic of a category is that we use it to code experience. We may perceive some complex object as a kind of "chair," remember it as a "chair," describe it to others as a *chair*, and reason about it in the same way. Coding by category is fundamental to mental life because it greatly reduces the demands on perceptual processes, storage space, and reasoning processes, all of which are known to be limited (see, for example, the discussion of short-term memories in chapter 1). This coding aspect of categories is presumably why human languages contain simple terms for categories, such as *tiger*, *chair*, and *mother*; that is, frequently used codes are associated with brief descriptions.

Categories vary in the extent to which they are used as codes. Categories are often structured into a *taxonomy*—a hierarchy in which successive levels refer to increasingly more specific objects—and categories at an intermediate level are more likely to be used to code experience than are categories at lower or higher levels (Rosch et al. 1976). Consider the taxonomy for fruits. The category "fruit" would be at a high or *superordinate* level, "apple" would be at an intermediate or *basic* level, and "McIntosh apple" would be at a relatively low or *subordinate* level. (For objects, the basic level may be identified with the most abstract level that is associated with a specific shape; the superordinate and subordinate levels are simply the levels above and below the basic one.) Here, *apple*, which is at the basic level, would be the preferred code, as witnessed by the facts that (1) people overwhelmingly prefer to name a particular object *apple* rather than *fruit* or *McIntosh apple*, and (2) they can decide that a particular apple is an "apple" faster than they can decide that it is a "fruit" or a "McIntosh apple" (Rosch et al. 1976).

Note that this coding aspect of categories does not apply to classes that are not categories. Thus, generally we do not code things as "objects that weigh an even number of grams" or as "objects that can be scraped or worshiped." Nor are there simple terms in the language for these classes.

2.1.3   Inductive Inferences

Whenever we use existing beliefs to generate new ones, we have drawn an inference. An inference can be either "deductive," in which case it is *impossible* for the new belief to be false if the old ones are true, or "inductive," in which case it is *improbable* for the new belief to be false if the old ones are true (see Skyrms 1986). There is an intimate relation between inductive inferences and categories; namely, categorization of an object licenses inductive inferences about that object.

An experimental demonstration used by Gelman and Markman (1986) illustrates this relation. On each trial of the experiment subjects were presented three pictures, where the third picture looked like one of the first two but was from the same category as the other picture. For example, on one trial the pictures were of a flamingo, a bat, and a blackbird, where the blackbird resembled the bat. New information was given about the first two pictures, then a question was asked about the third one. For example: regarding the flamingo, subjects were told, "This bird's heart has a right aortic arch only"; regarding the bat, they were told, "This bat's heart has a left aortic arch only"; and regarding the blackbird, they were asked, "What does this bird's heart have?" Subjects responded with "right aortic arch only" almost 90 percent of the time, thus basing their decision on common category membership rather than physical similarity. More surprisingly, when 4-year-old children were tested in the same paradigm (though with simpler properties), they based their decision on category membership almost 70 percent of the time. Very early on, we know that members of the same category are likely to share many invisible properties even if they do not resemble one another.

Different kinds of categories differ in the extent to which they support inductive inferences. For one thing, basic and subordinate categories support more inferences than do superordinate categories (Rosch et al. 1976). For example, people will attribute far more properties to an object classified as an "apple" or a "McIntosh apple" than to an object classified as a "fruit." (There is little difference, though, between the number of inductive inferences supported by basic categories and the number supported by subordinate categories.)

Another distinction among categories that has implications for induction is that between *natural kinds* like "tiger" and "daisy," which deal with naturally occurring species of flora and fauna, and *artifact kinds* like "chair" and "shirt," which deal with person-made objects (see, for example, Schwartz 1979). Natural kind categories seem to support more inductive inferences about invisible properties than do artifact kinds. Having been told, for example, that some chair has a particular nonvisible property—say, that is has lignin all through it—we may be hesitant to conclude that another chair has this property, at least compared to the ease with which we generalize from a flamingo's having a right-aortic-arch heart to another bird's having such a heart (Gelman and O'Reilly 1988).

Categories in general support more inductive inferences than do classes that are not categories. We draw more inferences, say, about "fruit" or "furniture" than about "objects that weigh an even number of grams."

2.1.4   Similarity

Another characteristic of many categories is that their members tend to be physically similar to one another while being physically dissimilar from members of contrasting categories. Of course, there are limits to this, as in the earlier example where one bird was less similar to another bird than to a bat. Still, in general we divide the world so as to maximize within-category similarity while minimizing between-category similarity.

The extent to which this characteristic is manifest again depends on the taxonomic level of the categories. At the superordinate level members of a category need not resemble one another; instances of "fruit," for example, may share few physical properties (consider a raisin and a watermelon). At the subordinate level members of a category closely resemble one another, but they also resemble members of contrasting categories (two McIntosh apples look very much alike, but they also resemble a Delicious apple). It is primarily at the basic level that members of a category resemble one another *and* look different from members of contrasting categories (two apples look like each other yet differ from oranges or peaches).

As usual, this characteristic of categories seems not to apply to classes that are not categories. On the average, there is little physical similarity among "objects that weigh an even number of grams," or among "objects that can be scraped or worshiped."[2]

2.1.5   Relations among the Three Characteristics

Two questions arise about the relations among the three characteristics. (1) Do they cohere; that is, do they pick out the same classes as categories? (2) Do they give the same kind of information about concepts?

With regard to coherence, there is substantial convergence among the three criteria, at least for basic categories. A basic category ("apple") is often used to code experience, affords numerous inductive inferences (particularly if it is a natural kind category), and tends to maximize within-category similarity while minimizing between-category similarity. For non-basic categories, there is less convergence. Although a subordinate category ("McIntosh apple") may be used to code experience in some contexts, the fact that it is rarely denoted by a single term suggests limits to its coding potential; further, although a subordinate category supports numerous inferences, it maximizes within-category similarity at the cost of substantial between-category similarity. In contrast, although a superordinate category ("fruit") also may be used to code experience in some contexts, it promotes few inductive inferences and clearly does not maximize within-category similarity.

With regard to the second question, the three characteristics seem to have different natures. Similarity represents a *guide* to categorization, whereas the other two characteristics generally reflect the *consequences* of categorization. To the extent that members of a category are similar to one another yet dissimilar from instances of other categories, we can decide whether or not a novel object belongs to the category by assessing its similarity to known category members (versus its dissimilarity from known nonmembers). Once this categorization is made, we can code the object in terms of the category (with a simple term) and infer hidden properties of the object.[3]

Because our primary interest lies in the process of categorization, and not in its products, we will focus on the similarity characteristic of categories. We will assume for the time being that assigning an object to a category rests on determining that the object is sufficiently similar either to known members of the category or to a summary of known members. Our

2. However, similarity considerations alone cannot explain why we have the categories that we do. For example, if the only criterion for categoryhood was to maximize within-class similarity, then all categories should have only one member (Medin 1983)!

3. I am oversimplifying here with regard to what is a guide versus what is a consequence of categorization. For example, knowing that two objects belong to the same category can make them seem more similar (Tversky 1977), in which case similarity is a consequence of categorization. Still, the basic distinction drawn in the text covers most cases.

next order of business is to find a means for measuring the similarity between a pair of objects or between an object and a summary of category members.[4]

2.2   Measurement of Similarity

There are two general approaches to the measurement of similarity: geometric and featural.

2.2.1   Geometric Approach

In the geometric approach, objects or items are represented as points in some multidimensional space such that the metric distance between two points corresponds to the *dissimilarity* between the two items. To illustrate, figure 2.1 represents 20 different fruits, as well as the category "fruit" itself, in a two-dimensional space. The shorter the metric distance between a pair of points, the more similar the corresponding fruits. For example, "apple" is more similar to "plum" than to "date," but more similar to "date" than to "coconut."

The space in figure 2.1 was constructed by a systematic procedure developed by Shepard (1962). First, a group of subjects rated the similarity between every possible pair of items ("apple"-"banana," "apple"-"plum," "apple"-"fruit," and so on—210 distinct pairs in all, for the items represented in figure 2.1). The similarity ratings were then input to a computer program that used an iterative procedure to position the items in a space (predetermined to have a certain dimensionality) so that the metric distance between items corresponded as closely as possible to the (inverse of) judged similarity between the items.

Crucial to the representation in figure 2.1 is the assumption that psychological distance is "metric" (just as ordinary physical space is). That is, it is assumed there is a function, d, that assigns to every pair of points a non-negative number, their "distance," in accord with the following three axioms:

(1)   *Minimality*
$$d(a, b) \geqslant d(a, a) = d(b, b) = 0$$

(2)   *Symmetry*
$$d(a, b) = d(b, a)$$

---

4. There is more to categorization than similarity. For one thing, sometimes categorization involves determining whether or not an object satisfies a definition. Although natural kind and artifact kind categories lack true definitions (see, for example, Putnam 1975), "nominal kind" categories like "uncle," "felony," and "even number" seem to have them (Schwartz 1979). Nominal kind categories are tailor-made for some specialized system, such as kinship, law, or arithmetic. Deciding that something fits in such a category presumably involves determining that it meets the definition, though even here factors like similarity may play some role (Armstrong, Gleitman, and Gleitman 1983). Another matter is that categorization sometimes involves inductive reasoning; this matter is discussed in section 2.3.3.

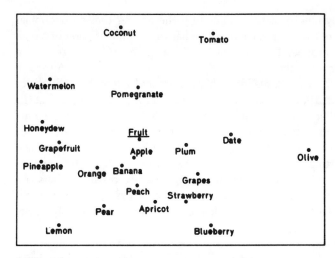

Figure 2.1
A two-dimensional space for representing the similarity relations among 20 instances of fruit and the category "fruit" itself. (From Tversky and Hutchinson 1986.)

(3)   *Triangle inequality*
$$d(a, b) + d(b, c) \geq d(a, c).$$

Minimality says that the distance between any item and itself is identical for all items, and is the mimimum possible. *Symmetry* says that the distance between two items is the same regardless of whether we start at one item or the other. And *triangle inequality* essentially says that the shortest distance between two points is a straight line. All three assumptions are evident in figure 2.1. For example, the distance between "peach" and "date" is (1) greater than that between "peach" and "peach," (2) equal to that between "date" and "peach," and (3) less than the sum of the distances between (a) "peach" and "apple" and (b) "apple" and "date."

The geometric approach has a history of success in representing perceptual objects (for a partial review, see Shepard 1974). Given a two-dimensional representation of color, for example, one can use the distances between the colors to accurately predict the likelihood that a subject in a memory experiment will confuse one color with another. However, the geometric approach works less well in representing conceptual items, such as categories and their instances. Indeed, for conceptual items, Tversky (1977) has produced evidence against each one of the metric axioms.

Minimality is compromised by the fact that the more we know about an item, the more similar it is judged to itself. The president of the United States, for example, seems more similar to himself than does some obscure member of the House or Senate. A familiar category like "apple" seems more similar to itself than does an unfamiliar category like "pomegranate."

The axiom of symmetry is undermined by the finding that an unfamiliar category is judged more similar to a familiar or prominent category than the other way around. For example, a "pomegranate" is judged more similar to an "apple" than an "apple" is to a "pomegranate." Although exact violations of the triangle inequality are harder to describe (though see Tversky and Gati 1982), we can capture the gist of them by noting that the axiom implies that if items a and b are similar to one another and so are items b and c, then a and c cannot be very dissimilar. One counterexample to this involves countries: Jamaica is similar to Cuba, and Cuba is similar to Russia, but Jamaica and Russia are very dissimilar. A milder counterexample is manifested in the similarity ratings used to construct the space of fruits in figure 2.1: "lemon" was judged similar to "orange," and "orange" was judged similar to "apricot," but "lemon" and "apricot" were rated quite dissimilar.

Another problem for the geometric approach involves the notion of a "nearest neighbor" (Tversky and Hutchinson 1986). If we obtain similarity ratings for pairs of items, as in the fruit example, then for each item we can refer to the item rated most similar to it as its "nearest neighbor." We can now characterize an item by how many other items it is the nearest neighbor to. When this was done with the similarity ratings for fruits, the category "fruit" turned out to be the nearest neighbor for 18 of the 20 other terms. This finding is problematic because it is impossible for one item in a metric space to be a nearest neighbor to so many other items as long as the space is of relatively low dimensionality. In fact, in a two-dimensional space the maximum number of items to which another item can serve as nearest neighbor is five (look at figure 2.1). At a minimum, a nine-dimensional space is needed to accommodate "fruit" being the nearest neighbor to 18 items. And once "fruit" is positioned in such a space so that it is the nearest neighbor to the appropriate 18 items, there is no guarantee that the distances between the 18 items themselves will adequately capture the similarity ratings for the relevant pairs of items. The general problem is that a category serves as the nearest neighbor to many of its instances, so many as to call into question the appropriateness of low-dimensional metric representations.

The above challenges to the geometric approach are not without their critics. Defenders of the geometric approach have argued, for example, that violations of symmetry and the triangle inequality arise more often when similarity is judged directly ("Rate the similarity of a to b") than when it is judged indirectly (say, by the frequency with which a and b are confused with one another). This suggests that direct judgments require complex decision processes that are the source of the asymmetries (Krumhansl 1978; Nosofsky 1986). Still, at this moment the weight of the evidence points away from geometric representations of categories.

2.2.2   Featural Approach

In the featural approach, an item is represented as a set of discrete features, such as "red", "round," and "hard," and the similarity between two items is assumed to be an increasing function of the features they have in common and a decreasing function of the features that they differ on. The best-known version of this approach is Tversky's (1977) contrast model. The similarity between the set of features characterizing item i (labeled I) and the set characterizing item j (labeled J) is given by (4):

(4) $\text{Sim}(I, J) = af(I \cap J) - bf(I - J) - cf(J - I).$

Here $I \cap J$ designates the set of features common to the two items, $I - J$ designates the set of features distinct to item i, and $J - I$ designates the set of features distinct to item j. In addition, f is a function that measures the salience of each set of features, and a, b, and c are parameters that determine the relative contribution of the three feature sets.

Table 2.1 illustrates the contrast model with examples drawn from the domain of fruits. Each panel of the table deals with a phenomenon that surfaced in our discussion of the geometric approach. Panel 1 is concerned with minimality. It contains possible feature sets for the categories "apple" and "pomegranate." There are more features for "apple" than for "pomegranate," reflecting the fact that "apple" is the more familiar item. This difference will result in "apple" being rated more similar to itself than is "pomegranate," because the more features an item has, the more common features there are when the item is compared to itself. This idea is detailed in the calculations given below each pair, where the contrast model has been used to calculate the similarity between the members of the pair. For purposes of simplicity, here and elsewhere, we will assume that the function f simply assigns a value of 1 to each feature in a set of common or distinctive features.[5]

Panel 2 is concerned with symmetry. It compares the similarity of "pomegranate" to "apple" versus that of "apple" to "pomegranate." As the calculations show, the contrast model is compatible with the fact that "pomegranate" is more similar to "apple" than vice versa as long as parameter b exceeds parameter c.

Panel 3 demonstrates that the contrast model is compatible with violations of the triangle inequality: "lemon" is similar to "orange," and "orange" is similar to "apricot," but "lemon" is not similar to "apricot." As the calculations show, the violation will be pronounced whenever the weight given to common features, a, exceeds that given to either set of distinctive features, b or c, because then similarity will be relatively large for the first two pairs but not for the third.

---

5. These feature sets are derived from the work of Smith et al. (1988), who had 30 subjects list features of 15 different instances of "fruit" (including "apple," "pomegranate," "orange," "lemon," and "apricot").

Table 2.1
Some illustrations of the contrast model.

Apple	Apple	Pomegranate	Pomegranate
red	red	red	red
round	round	round	round
hard	hard		
sweet	sweet		
trees	trees		

$\mathrm{Sim}(A, A) = a(5) - b(0) - c(0)$ $\mathrm{Sim}(P, P) = a(2) - b(0) - c(0)$

Pomegranate	Apple	Apple	Pomegranate
red	red	red	red
round	round	round	round
	hard	hard	
	sweet	sweet	
	trees	trees	

$\mathrm{Sim}(P, A) = a(2) - b(0) - c(3)$ $\mathrm{Sim}(A, P) = a(2) - b(3) - c(0)$

Lemon	Orange	Orange	Apricot	Lemon	Apricot
yellow	orange	orange	red	yellow	red
oval	round	round	round	oval	round
sour	sweet	sweet	sweet	sour	sweet
tree	tree	tree	tree	tree	tree
citrus	citrus	citrus		citrus	
ade	ade	ade		ade	

$\mathrm{Sim}(L, O) = a(3) - b(3) - c(3)$ $\mathrm{Sim}(O, A) = a(3) - b(3) - c(1)$ $\mathrm{Sim}(L, A) = a(1) - b(5) - c(3)$

Apple	Plum	Apple	Fruit
red	red	red	red
round	round	round	round
hard	soft	hard	hard
sweet	sweet	sweet	sweet
trees	trees	trees	

$\mathrm{Sim}(A, P) = a(4) - b(1) - c(1)$ $\mathrm{Sim}(A, F) = a(4) - b(1) - c(0)$

Finally, panel 4 establishes that the contrast model is compatible with the fact that a category can serve as a nearest neighbor to numerous instances. Among "fruit" instances, "plum" is often rated most similar to "apple." But as the calculations show, "fruit" is an even closer neighbor to "apple." The reason is that "fruit" is more abstract than "plum" and hence includes fewer distinctive features.

In sum, the contrast model offers a satisfactory account of the phenomena that plagued the geometric approach, and we will use the model in what follows.

However, we should note that the contrast model does have some limitations. First, it does not tell us what an item's features are. For each domain of inquiry, like that of plant categories, researchers need independent procedures for determining the features of the various items (asking people to list features of items is one such procedure, albeit a rough one).

Second, the contrast model does not offer any theory of the function f that measures the salience of each set of features. Such a theory would have to address issues about the intensity of individual features (for instance, a more saturated color might be assigned a greater salience than a less saturated one), as well as issues about the diagnosticity of features (for instance, a feature that discriminates among relevant objects might be assigned a higher salience than one that does not). The theory would also have to specify how and why people differ in the salience they assign to the same feature in the same context.

Third, although the contrast model tells us *what* is computed—measures of sets of common and distinctive features—it says little about the algorithms used to effect the computation. Thus, the model does not tell us whether the features of two items are compared simultaneously or sequentially, and if the latter, in what order.

As we will see, in applying the contrast model we will have to add auxiliary assumptions to deal with these three limitations.[6]

2.3   Similarity and Categorization

Now that we have some insight into the measurement of similarity, we are in a position to appreciate that similarity underlies some important phenomena in categorization.

6. A more specific (and more remediable) limitation of the contrast model concerns additivity. Most applications of the model assume that the salience assigned to a set of features is an additive function of the individual saliences of the features that constitute the set. In fact, though, Tversky (1977) derived the contrast model from a set of qualitative axioms, and his derivation does not yield additivity of feature saliences. More recently Osherson (1987) has derived the contrast model from a different set of qualitative axioms, and his derivation does guarantee the additivity of feature saliences.

2.3.1   Typicality Effects

People can reliably order the instances of any category with respect to how "typical" or "prototypical" or "representative" they are of the category. Table 2.2 presents typicality ratings for the categories "fruit" and "bird." These ratings were obtained by instructing subjects to rate typicality on a 7-point scale, with 7 corresponding to the highest typicality and 1 to the lowest (Malt and Smith 1984). "Apple" and "peach" are considered typical fruits, "raisin" and "fig" less typical, and "pumpkin" and "olive" atypical. Similar variations are found among the instances of "bird." Ratings like these have been obtained for numerous categories and have been shown to be relatively uncorrelated with the frequency or familiarity of the instances (Mervis, Catlin, and Rosch 1976).

What is most important about these ratings is that they predict how efficiently people can categorize various instances. Consider an experimental task that is frequently used to study categorization. On each trial a subject is given the name of a target category, such as "bird," followed by a test item. The subject must decide as quickly as possible whether the test item names an instance of the target category, such as "robin," or a noninstance, such as "trout." The main data of interest are the decision times for correct categorizations. When the test item in fact names a member of the target category, categorization times decrease with the

Table 2.2
Typicality ratings for 15 instances of "fruit" and "bird" (from Malt and Smith 1984).

Fruit	Rating	Bird	Rating
apple	6.25*	robin	6.89
peach	5.81	bluebird	6.42
pear	5.25	seagull	6.26
grape	5.13	swallow	6.16
strawberry	5.00	falcon	5.74
lemon	4.86	mockingbird	5.47
blueberry	4.56	starling	5.16
watermelon	4.06	owl	5.00
raisin	3.75	vulture	4.84
fig	3.38	sandpiper	4.47
coconut	3.06	chicken	3.95
pomegranate	2.50	flamingo	3.37
avocado	2.38	albatross	3.32
pumpkin	2.31	penguin	2.63
olive	2.25	bat	1.53

*Ratings were made on a 7-point scale, with 7 corresponding to the highest typicality.

typicality of the test item. With "bird" as the target, for example, test items corresponding to "robin" and "swallow" are categorized more quickly (by somewhere between 50 and 100 milliseconds) than those corresponding to "owl" and "vulture," which in turn are categorized more quickly (again by between 50 and 100 milliseconds) than test items corresponding to "flamingo" and "penguin" (see, for example, Smith, Shoben, and Rips 1974).

These results in no way rest on the verbal nature of the paradigm. If the task is modified so that the test items are pictures of particular objects (for instance, a pictured robin or vulture or trout), the results are virtually unchanged. Furthermore, to the extent that there is variation in the accuracy of these categorizations (in either the verbal or the pictorial task), error rates also decrease with the typicality of the test items. These effects are extremely reliable: they have been documented in more than 50 experiments that have used many different variants of the verbal and pictorial categorization tasks (for a partial review, see Smith and Medin 1981).

There is also evidence that categorization depends on typicality in more naturalistic settings. A child developing language acquires the names of typical category members before those of atypical ones. And if children are asked to sort pictured objects into categories, their sortings resemble those of adults more if the objects are typical than if they are atypical (Mervis 1980; Rosch 1978).

2.3.2 Typicality as Similarity

A general interpretation of the above findings is that the typicality of an instance is a measure of its similarity to its category, and categorization amounts to determining that an item is sufficiently similar to the target category. In what follows we will flesh out this interpretation.

If typicality is really similarity, then the contrast model should be able to predict typicality ratings. To test this, we (1) select a domain of instances, (2) estimate the features of the instances and the category (remember, the contrast model does not supply these), (3) apply the contrast model to each instance-category pair, and (4) see whether this estimate of instance-category similarity correlates with the rated typicality of the instance in the category.

The instances we will use as well as their features are taken from a study by Malt and Smith (1984), in which subjects had 90 seconds to list all the features they could think of for each instance. Table 2.3 contains a small subset of the features obtained. In the experiment 30 subjects were each presented 15 instances of "bird"; they collectively produced more than 50 features, each feature being produced by more than one subject. Table 2.3 considers only nine of the instances and six of the features: flies, sings, lays

Table 2.3
Illustrations of how to use listed properties to calculate an instance's similarity to prototype.

Features	Robin	Bluebird	Swallow	Starling	Vulture
Flies	+	+	+	+	+
Sings	+	+	+	+	−
Lays eggs	+	+	+	−	−
Is small	+	+	+	+	−
Nests in trees	+	+	+	+	+
Eats insects	+	+	+	+	−
Similarity to bird	6−0−0=6	6−0−0=6	6−0−0=6	5−.5−0=4.5	2−2−0=0

eggs, is small, nests in trees, and eats insects. The rows of the table list the six features; the columns give the instances in order of decreasing typicality, with the last column representing the category "bird." Each entry in the resulting matrix is a + or a −, where + indicates that at least two subjects listed the feature for that instance and a − indicates that either one or no subjects did. To determine the entries for "bird," a feature was assigned a + only if a majority of the instances had a + for that feature. The category "bird" thus contained the frequent features of the instances.

The contrast model was used to determine the similarity of each instance in table 2.3 to "bird." In making the calculations (given at the bottom of the table), it was assumed that (1) all features are equally salient (that is, f assigns a value of 1 to each feature, which means that the salience of a set of common or distinctive features is simply the number of features it contains), and (2) common features count more than distinctive ones, with features distinct to the category counting more than those distinct to the instance (specifically, $a = 1$, $b = \frac{1}{2}$, $c = \frac{1}{4}$). The contrast model correctly segregates the instances in table 2.3 into three levels of typicality (3 high, 3 medium, and 3 low), though it makes few distinctions among the instances within each level. Finer distinctions can readily be made by assuming that features differ in their salience or by considering more features.

You can verify that had the average similarity of an instance to all other instances been computed (rather than its similarity to "bird"), virtually the identical similarity scores would have been obtained. Hence, the success of the contrast model in predicting typicality does not depend on whether a category is taken to be an abstraction or a set of instances.

Let us now look briefly at how the above account could be extended into a model of categorization that could explain some of the experimental results mentioned earlier. The general ideas are (1) an item will be categorized as an instance of a category if and only if it exceeds some criterial

Table 2.3 (continued)

Sandpiper	Chicken	Flamingo	Penguin	Bird
+	−	−	−	+
+	−	−	−	+
+	+	−	+	+
+	−	−	−	+
−	−	−	−	+
+	−	−	−	+
$5-.5-0=4.5$	$1-2.5-0=-1.5$	$0-3-0=-3$	$1-2.5-0=-1.5$	

level of similarity to the category, and (2) the time needed to determine that an item exceeds this criterial level of similarity is less the more similar the item in fact is to the category. When these two assumptions are joined with the claim that an item's typicality reflects its similarity to its category, it follows that more typical items will be categorized faster.

Fleshing out this model requires making specific assumptions about the algorithms used to implement the contrast model. One possibility is to assume that all features of the instance and category are compared in parallel—with common features incrementing a similarity counter and distinctive features decrementing it—and the outcomes of these feature comparisons become available at different points in time. If an instance is only moderately similar to its category, the process may have to wait for late-arriving feature matches (common features) to reach threshold. In contrast, if an instance is highly similar to its category, the early-arriving feature matches may suffice to pass threshold.

A related approach is expressed in terms of *spreading activation* (a mechanism that figures centrally in memory; see chapter 1). When an item and category are presented, activation from these two sources begins to spread to the features associated with them, with the activation from each source being subdivided among its features. If the two sources of activation intersect at some features (common features), further processing is undertaken to determine that an instance-category relation holds. Because the number of intersecting or common features generally increases with the typicality of an instance to its category, there are more opportunities for an intersection with typical than atypical instances, and hence more opportunities for an early termination of the process (Collins and Loftus 1975). (In this model, features distinct to the category or item slow the process by thinning the activation from each source.)

The above models may suffice for the case where only one category is relevant (as in the experiments described earlier), but often people have to decide which of *n* relevant categories is the correct one (Is this plant a mushroom or a toadstool? Is that car a Chevy or a Ford?). In such cases a categorization model has to consider the relation of an item to the categories that contrast with the correct one. Thus, a categorization decision may consider something like the ratio between the similarity of the instance to the target category versus the similarity of the instance to all contrasting categories (Nosofsky 1986).[7]

2.3.3   Beyond Similarity

The approach we have taken accurately describes categorization in many cases, but some recent experiments demonstrate situations where categorization is based on something other than similarity.

Two studies by Rips (1989) suffice to make the point. In the first study, on each trial a subject was presented a description of an object that mentioned only a value on a single dimension (say, an object's diameter). Then the subject decided which of two categories the object belonged to, where prior work had established that the object was between the subject's average values for the two categories. For example, one item was "an object three inches in diameter," and the associated categories were "pizzas" and "quarters." Although the object was if anything closer to the average diameter of a quarter (indeed, another group of subjects had judged it more similar to a quarter), subjects judged it more likely to be a pizza than a quarter, presumably because there is an official constraint on the size of quarters but not on the size of pizzas. This kind of situation obtained on all trials, as one category always allowed more variability on the relevant dimension than did the other, and subjects consistently chose the high-variability category. These results indicate that categorization decisions consider variability as well as similarity.

A second study by Rips (1989) provides further evidence against similarity-based categorization. Subjects were told about an animal that started out with typical bird properties but suffered an accident that caused many of its properties to resemble those of an insect. Subjects were further told that eventually this animal mated with a normal female of its species, who produced normal young. Subjects rated this creature as more likely to be a

---

7. It is worth pointing out that tasks other than categorization are affected by typicality, including memory and reasoning tasks. As one example, when asked to generate from memory all instances of a category, subjects retrieve instances in order of decreasing typicality (Rosch 1978). Examples of typicality effects on reasoning will be discussed in chapter 3. The general point is that a similarity-to-category computation may be a general component of mental life.

"bird" than an "insect," but more similar to an "insect" than a "bird." Here we have a situation where categorization and similarity go in different directions.

In these studies subjects seem to be reasoning more than categorizing. Rather than restricting themselves to the features of the test item and target categories—for instance, the features of the accident-prone bird and the categories "bird" and "insect"—subjects seem to be bringing to bear other beliefs and knowledge—for instance, "Animals produce offspring of the same kind as themselves." And rather than just comparing features, subjects seem to be constructing arguments—for instance, "This animal accidentally acquired insect properties but it produced normal bird off-spring, so probably it's still a bird." In short, subjects seem to be reasoning inductively. Although it is not yet known which situations lead to reasoning-based categorization and which to similarity-based categorization, it seems plausible that similarity is involved in rapid, automatic decisions, whereas reasoning comes into play in slower, more deliberative decisions.[8]

2.4   Summary and Other Issues

The essential story goes as follows. Categories, at least basic ones, seem to be readily distinguishable from other classes in that they have far greater coding potential and induction potential. Further, categories, at least basic ones, tend to maximize within-category similarity while minimizing between-category similarity. The latter property allows categorization to occur by determining a test item's similarity to known exemplars, or to a summary of the category.

Detailing the categorization process requires specifying a precise means for computing similarity between a pair of items. Both geometric and featural approaches to similarity offer such means, but a number of empirical phenomena (such as asymmetries in similarity judgments) indicate that the featural approach, particularly Tversky's (1977) contrast model, is best for measuring the similarity among categories and their instances. Studies have shown that the similarity of an instance to a category as determined by the contrast model is part of what lies behind the instance's typicality to its category. And an instance's typicality to its category predicts numerous aspects of categorization decisions such as their speed and accuracy. Although the extent of these claims is somewhat compromised by demon-

8. The distinction of interest is phrased here in terms of "similarity versus reasoning" for purposes of exposition. In a more extensive treatment of the issue, similarity itself would be a kind of inductive reasoning, and the distinction of interest would be between similarity and quasi-deductive forms of reasoning (Osherson, Smith, and Shafir 1986).

strations of reasoning-based categorization, our essential story still covers a lot of ground.

In order to keep our focus on similarity, we have had to deemphasize other issues in categorization research. Three such issues deserve at least brief mention.

First, it was noted at a couple of points that a category may be thought of either as an abstract summary or as a set of exemplars. (The similarity proposal was phrased so that it was noncommittal on this issue.) The category "bird," for example, could be mentally represented either by its own set of features or by a set of specific exemplars ("robin," "bluejay," and so on), each with its own set of features. Though at first blush it seems more natural to think of a category as an abstraction, it is apparent that an exemplar representation coupled with the right similarity algorithms can account for much of the data in categorization.

Further, studies on this issue have often found that the ease of learning an instance-category relation is better predicted by the similarity of the instance to the other category exemplars than by the similarity of the instance to a summary representation (see, for example, Estes 1986; Medin and Schaffer 1978). However, other arguments favor an abstract summary. For example, frequently we learn facts about a general class rather than about specific exemplars, such as "All birds lay eggs," and it seems likely that we store such facts as summary information. Given the mixed evidence on this issue, some sort of hybrid position (abstraction-plus-exemplar) may be called for.

Second, we have dealt in this chapter mainly with "simple" categories— roughly those denoted by single words like "apple" and "bird"—and have ignored conjunctive categories—roughly those denoted by more than one word like "dry apple" and "very large bird." Because many conjunctive categories are novel combinations and hence cannot be learned from experience, there must be some procedures for composing conjunctive categories out of simple ones. (This is similar to the composition-of-meaning issue addressed in Larson 1990.)

A number of composition processes have been proposed, particularly for the case where a single modifier is applied to a simple category as in "dry apple." One of these proposals is an extension of the similarity model advanced earlier (Smith et al. 1988). Roughly, the modifier selectively changes those features of the simple category that are mentioned in the modifier (for example, *dry* changes the taste feature of *apple* but not its size feature); then a decision about whether or not an item is an instance of the conjunctive category can be made in exactly the same way as before (by employing the contrast model). Some other models of composition involve reasoning-based categorization (see, for instance, Cohen and Murphy 1984); still other proposals involve applications of *fuzzy set theory*, a generalization of traditional set theory that provides functions for relating membership in conjunctive sets (categories) to membership in simpler ones (see, for instance, Zadeh 1982).

Third, virtually everything in this chapter assumes that natural kind and artifact kind categories do not have definitions and consequently that categorization with such categories involves something other than instantiating a definition. This position has been widely accepted in psychology (see, for example, Smith and Medin 1981). Though some of the best-known arguments for the position come from work in philosophy of mind (for example, Kripke 1972; Putnam 1975; and see chapter 7), there is a gap between the psychological and philosophical work on this problem (see Rey 1983).

Suggestions for Further Reading

For further discussion of the distinguishing characteristics of categories and their dependence on taxonomic level, see Rosch et al. 1976 and Rosch 1978. For a look at other distinctions between categories, particularly those that have to do with kinds, see Schwartz 1979.

On the matter of measuring similarity between instances and categories, perhaps the single most important paper is Tversky 1977. For a discussion of the geometric approach in general, see Shepard 1974.

A psychological perspective on typicality effects and categorization is provided in Smith and Medin 1981. For a philosophical perspective on these same issues, see Rey 1983. Murphy and Medin 1985 offers a summary of the reasoning-based approach to categorization. Finally, for a more advanced treatment of many of the problems considered in this chapter, with a particular emphasis on the similarity-reasoning distinction, see Smith 1989.

Categorization is intimately connected to concepts; indeed, psychologists often assume that a concept is a mental representation of a category. The psychological study of concept development is discussed in chapter 6. An analysis of concepts is also essential for an understanding of language, particularly its development, as words may be construed as names of concepts. Language development is the subject of Pinker 1990. In addition to psychological studies, there is of course a rich tradition of analyses of concepts in philosophy of mind; here, chapter 7 and Schwartz 1977 provide a useful entry point into the recent literature.

Categorization is also related to inductive reasoning. As noted earlier, categorization sometimes involves a kind of inductive reasoning. In other cases, however, inductive reasoning reduces to something like similarity-based categorization, and these cases are discussed in chapter 3.

Research on how we categorize objects has also proven useful for understanding how we categorize people. For recent reviews of work on person categorization, see Cantor and Kihlstrom 1986 and Markus and Zajonc 1985.

Questions

2.1 Use the contrast model to determine the ordering by typicality of the five vegetables given below (the features are given under the name of each instance). Assume that all features are weighted equally and that $a = 1$, $b = \frac{1}{2}$, and $c = \frac{1}{2}$.

Stringbean	Carrot	Cauliflower	Seaweed	Broccoli	Vegetable
green	orange	white	green	green	green
long	long	round	long	long	long
hard	hard	hard	stringy	bushy	hard

2.2 In question 2.1, what changes are there in the ordering of typicality if color is weighted three times more than the other features?

2.3 It was noted in the text that the feature similarity model can be extended to explain categorization with a conjunctive category like "dry apple." Can such a feature model be extended to a conjunction like "fake apple"?

References

Armstrong, S. L., L. R. Gleitman, and H. Gleitman (1983). What some concepts might not be. *Cognition* 13, 263–308.

Cantor, N., and J. Kihlstrom (1986). *Personality and social intelligence.* Englewood Cliffs, NJ: Prentice-Hall.

Cohen, B., and G. L. Murphy (1984). Models of concepts. *Cognitive Science* 8, 27–60.

Collins, A. M., and E. F. Loftus (1975). A spreading-activation theory of semantic processing. *Psychological Review* 82, 407–428.

Estes, W. K. (1986). Array models for category learning. *Cognitive Psychology* 18, 500–549.

Gelman, S. A., and E. Markman (1986). Categories and induction in young children. *Cognition* 23, 183–209.

Gelman, S. A., and A. W. O'Reilly (1988). Children's inductive inferences with superordinate categories: The role of language and category structure. *Child Development* 59, 876–887.

Kripke, S. (1972). Naming and necessity. In D. Davidson and G. Harman, eds., *Semantics of natural language.* Dordrecht, Holland: Reidel.

Krumhansl, C. (1978). Concerning the applicability of geometric models to similarity data: The interrelationship between similarity and spatial density. *Psychological Review* 85, 445–463.

Larson, R. K. (1990). Semantics. In D. N. Osherson and H. Lasnik, eds., *Language: An invitation to cognitive science, volume 1.* Cambridge, MA: MIT Press.

Malt, B. C., and E. E. Smith (1984). Correlated properties in natural categories. *Journal of Verbal Learning and Verbal Behavior* 23, 250–269.

Markus, H., and R. B. Zajonc (1985). The cognitive perspective in social psychology. In G. Lindzey and E. Aronson, eds., *The handbook of social psychology.* New York: Random House.

Medin, D. L. (1983). Structural principles in categorization. In T. Tighe and B. Shepp, eds., *Perception, cognition and development: Interactional analyses.* Hillsdale, NJ: L. Erlbaum Associates.

Medin, D. L., and M. M. Schaffer (1978). A context theory of classification learning. *Psychological Review* 85, 207–238.

Mervis, C. B. (1980). Category structure and the development of categorization. In R. Spiro, B. C. Bruce, and W. F. Brewer, eds., *Theoretical issues in reading comprehension.* Hillsdale, NJ: L. Erlbaum Associates.

Mervis, C. B., J. Catlin, and E. Rosch (1976). Relationships among goodness-of-example, category norms and word frequency. *Bulletin of the Psychonomic Society* 7, 268–284.

Murphy, G. L., and D. L. Medin (1985). The role of theories in conceptual coherence. *Psychological Review* 92, 289–316.

Nosofsky, R. M. (1986). Attention, similarity, and the identification-categorization relationship. *Journal of Experimental Psychology: General* 115, 39–57.

Osherson, D. N. (1987). New axioms for the contrast model of similarity. *Journal of Mathematical Psychology* 31, 93–103.

Osherson, D. N., E. E. Smith, and E. B. Shafir (1986). Some origins of belief. *Cognition* 24, 197–224.

Pinker, S. (1990). Language acquisition. In D. N. Osherson and H. Lasnik, eds., *Language: An invitation to cognitive science, volume 1*. Cambridge, MA: MIT Press.

Putnam, H. (1975). The meaning of 'meaning'. In K. Gunderson, ed., *Language, mind, and knowledge*. Minneapolis, MN: University of Minnesota Press.

Rey, G. (1983). Concepts and stereotypes. *Cognition* 15, 237–262.

Rips, L. J. (1989). Similarity, typicality, and categorization. In S. Voisniadou and A. Ortony, eds., *Similarity, analogy, and thought*. New York: Cambridge University Press.

Rosch, E. (1978). Principles of categorization. In E. Rosch and B. B. Lloyd, eds., *Cognition and categorization*. Hillsdale, NJ: L. Erlbaum Associates.

Rosch, E., C. Mervis, D. Gray, D. Johnson, and P. Boyes-Braehm (1976). Basic objects in natural categories. *Cognitive Psychology* 3, 382–439.

Schwartz, S. P. (1977). *Naming, necessity and natural kinds*. Ithaca, NY: Cornell University Press.

Schwartz, S. P. (1979). Natural kind terms. *Cognition* 7, 301–315.

Shepard, R. N. (1962). The analysis of proximities: Multidimensional scaling with an unknown distance function. I. *Psychometrika* 27, 125–140.

Shepard, R. N. (1974). Representation of structure in similarity data: Problems and prospects. *Psychometrika* 39, 373–421.

Skyrms, B. (1986). *Choice and chance: An introduction to inductive logic*. 3rd ed. Belmont, MA: Wadsworth.

Smith, E. E. (1989). Concepts and induction. In M. I. Posner, ed., *Foundations of cognitive science*. Cambridge, MA: MIT Press.

Smith, E. E., and D. L. Medin (1981). *Categories and concepts*. Cambridge, MA: Harvard University Press.

Smith, E. E., D. N. Osherson, L. J. Rips, and M. Keane (1988). Combining prototypes: A modification model. *Cognitive Science* 12, 485–527.

Smith, E. E., E. J. Shoben, and L. J. Rips (1974). Structure and process in semantic memory: A featural model for semantic decisions. *Psychological Review* 81, 214–241.

Tversky, A. (1977). Features of similarity. *Psychological Review* 84, 327–352.

Tversky, A., and I. Gati (1982). Similarity, separability and the triangular inequality. *Psychological Review* 89, 123–154.

Tversky, A., and J. W. Hutchinson (1986). Nearest neighbor analysis of psychological spaces. *Psychological Review* 93, 3–22.

Zadeh, L. (1982). A note on prototype theory and fuzzy sets. *Cognition* 12, 291–297.

Chapter 3
Judgment
Daniel N. Osherson

Examine statements (1a–c). The first will strike you as almost certainly true, the second as almost certainly false. By contrast, the truth of the third is not so evident, and you may feel an intermediate degree of conviction about it.

(1) a. It will be hotter in Rome than in London at noon on July 4, 1995.

     b. It will be hotter in Oslo than in Athens at noon on July 4, 1995.

     c. It will be hotter in Rome than in Athens at noon on July 4, 1995.

Your reaction to (1a–c) amounts to a judgment about their respective probabilities. It is this kind of judgment that occupies the present chapter.

   The degree of belief that a person invests in a newly encountered statement depends in part on the information (and misinformation) stored in memory. Statement (1c), for example, is likely to be assigned a different probability by a meteorologist than by a stockbroker. To compare the principles of probability attribution employed by different people, we must equate the background beliefs that intervene in probability judgments. This is most easily achieved by posing questions of the following kind, in which all relevant information is stated explicitly:

The Three-Card Problem
Three cards are in a hat. One is red on both sides (the red-red card). One is white on both sides (the white-white card). One is red on one side and white on the other (the red-white card). A single card is drawn randomly and tossed into the air.

a.   What is the probability that the red-red card was drawn?

b.   What is the probability that the drawn card lands with a white side up?

c.   What is the probability that the red-red card was drawn, assuming that the drawn card lands with a red side up?

Think carefully about these questions, and write your answers down.

If you gave the answers one-third to (a), one-half to (b), and one-half to (c), then your judgment corresponds to the majority opinion of college undergraduates, as revealed in classroom demonstrations and published data (see, for example, Bar-Hillel and Falk 1982).[1] In this case it is likely that you will respond with probability one-half to the following question, which is just the contrary of (c):

c'.   What is the probability that the red-red card was *not* drawn, assuming that the drawn card lands with a red side up?

For future reference, table 3.1 summarizes the judgments corresponding to questions (a), (b), (c), and (c').

It is an important albeit elementary fact that there is so much agreement about the three-card problem. It suggests considerable uniformity in the mental processes that underlie probability judgments in different people. Another feature of these judgments will emerge once we consider the relation between probability attributions and our willingness to accept wagers at various odds.

3.1 Wagers

3.1.1 Probability Functions

We will henceforth conceive of a person's probability judgment as embodied in a certain kind of function, to be called a *probability function* or *p-function*.

---

1. Most people reason as follows about (c). The red face showing excludes only the white-white card. This leaves the red-red and red-white cards as the remaining, equiprobable alternatives.

Table 3.1
Probability attributions in the three-card problem.

Statement	Abbreviation	Judged probability
(a) The red-red card was drawn.	RR	1/3
(b) The drawn card lands with a white side up.	W-up	1/2
(c) The red-red card was drawn, assuming that the drawn card lands with a red side up.	RR assuming that R-up	1/2
(c') The red-red card was not drawn, assuming that the drawn card lands with a red side up.	not-RR assuming that R-up	1/2

A p-function maps pairs of statements into probabilities. Specifically, for each pair (S, A) of statements in its domain, a person's p-function maps (S, A) into the probability that the person attributes to S while assuming A. For example, if you think that the probability is .6 that Mudrunner will finish first assuming that it rains the day of the race, then your p-function assigns .6 to the following pair of statements:

(2)   a.   Mudrunner will finish first. ($= S$)

       b.   It rains the day of the race. ($= A$)

For a given individual I we let "P_I" symbolize I's p-function. For explicitness we write

$$P_I(S \text{ assuming that } A)$$

instead of $P_I(S, A)$ or $P_I(S|A)$ (the latter notation is familiar from probability theory).

People often attribute probabilities to statements in the absence of any assumptions at all (or at least, in the absence of any interesting assumptions not shared by everyone else). Suppose that you assign probability .9 to statement (1a) in this unconditional sense. Now the assumption that $1 + 1 = 2$ is really no assumption at all, so you can be expected to assign the same .9 probability to statement (1a) while assuming $1 + 1 = 2$. This equivalence leads us to the following abbreviation. Given a statement S, we write $P_I(S)$ instead of $P_I(S \text{ assuming that } 1 + 1 = 2)$. $P_I(S)$ may thus be construed as the probability (without assumptions) that individual I attributes to statement S.

To illustrate our notation, suppose that your probability judgments about the three-card problem conform to table 3.1. Then

(3)   a. $P_{you}(RR) = \frac{1}{3}$.

    b. $P_{you}(W\text{-up}) = \frac{1}{2}$.

    c'. $P_{you}(not\text{-}RR$ assuming that R-up$) = \frac{1}{2}$.

3.1.2   Fair Bets

A person's p-function helps determine the wagers that person is willing to accept. By a *bet* on a statement S is meant an agreement whereby (1) the bettor is paid a specified sum W of money if S is true and (2) the bettor pays a specified sum L of money if S is false. Such a bet is called *fair* for an individual I just in case $P_I(S) = L/(W + L)$. Intuitively, a bet is fair for I just in case I believes that I would win the bet L out of $W + L$ times if the bet could be played repeatedly; in this case, I would break even in the long run. To illustrate, suppose that I assigns probability $\frac{1}{5}$ to statement (4):

(4)   Brazil wins the World Soccer Championship in 1998.

Then any of the following bets is fair for I:

    I wins \$4 if (4) is true; pays \$1 otherwise.

    I wins \$8 if (4) is true; pays \$2 otherwise.

    Etc.

Next we consider conditional bets. By a *bet* on a statement S *assuming* a statement A is meant an agreement whereby (1) the bettor is paid a specified sum W if both A and S are true, (2) the bettor pays a specified sum L if A is true but S is false, and (3) no money changes hands if A is false. As before, such a bet is called *fair* for an individual I just in case $P_I(S$ assuming that $A) = L/(W + L)$. To illustrate, suppose that I assigns the probability $\frac{3}{5}$ to (2a) assuming that (2b). Then the following bet is fair for I:

    I wins \$2 if it rains the day of the race and Mudrunner finishes first.

    I pays \$3 if it rains the day of the race and Mudrunner does not finish first.

    No payments are made if it does not rain the day of the race.

For small sums of money people are usually willing to accept bets that are fair or favorable for them and reject the others. Indeed, betting arrangements for small sums are a typical means of determining the probabilities that people assign to various statements. From (3) it may be inferred that you would accept the following bets:

(5) Bet (a): Win $4.20 if RR; lose $2.10 otherwise. [Since
      $P_{you}(RR) = \frac{1}{3}$.]

     Bet (b): Win $2.00 if W-up; lose $2.00 otherwise. [Since
      $P_{you}(W\text{-up}) = \frac{1}{2}$.]

     Bet (c): Win $4.00 if R-up and not-RR; lose $4.00 if R-up and RR;
      neither win nor lose if not-R-up. [Since $P_{you}(\text{not-RR}$
      assuming that R-up$) = \frac{1}{2}$.]

3.1.3 Dutch Books

The bets that you accepted at (5) have an interesting property. *No matter what card is drawn in the three-card problem, and no matter how it lands, you are guaranteed to lose money.* To verify this fact, observe that the draw has exactly three possible outcomes:

Possibility 1: Some card other than red-red is drawn, and it lands with a white side up, that is, W-up and not-RR.

Possibility 2: Some card other than red-red is drawn, and it lands with a red side up, that is, R-up and not-RR.

Possibility 3: The red-red card is drawn, and it lands (of course) with a red side up, that is, R-up and RR.

Notice that it is impossible that both RR and not-R-up.

Now if possibility 1 obtains, then you lose bet (a), win bet (b), and neither win nor lose bet (c); overall, you lose $.10. If possibility 2 obtains, then you lose bet (a), lose bet (b), and win bet (c); overall, you lose $.10. If possibility 3 obtains, then you win bet (a), lose bet (b), and lose bet (c); overall you lose $1.80. Thus, you lose no matter what happens.

To recapitulate, your judgment about the three-card problem led you to assign certain probabilities to the statements (a), (b), and (c') of table 3.1. These probability attributions led you to accept as fair the bets (a), (b), (c) of (5). It turns out, however, that the joint outcome of these bets is bound to be unfavorable. In the terminology of probability theory, a *Dutch book* has been made against you.

Most people (including the present author) are lured into Dutch books on first encountering the three-card problem. Let us see how to avoid them in principle, and then analyze the psychological factors that lead us into situations of this kind.

3.2   How to Avoid Dutch Books

Not every p-function is open to a Dutch book. Those immune to such traps can be characterized with the aid of some probability theory. We will begin with a few preliminary concepts.

3.2.1   Logical Truth, Exclusion, and Equivalence

Roughly, a *logical truth* is a statement that is true in every conceivable circumstance. For example:

Either all frogs croak or some frog does not croak.

Two statements are called *logically exclusive* just in case there is no conceivable circumstance in which both are true. For example:

The heaviest poodle weighs more than 60 pounds.

The heaviest poodle weighs less than 40 pounds.

Similarly, two statements are *logically equivalent* just in case they have the same truth-value in every conceivable circumstance. For example:

Not all philosophers are more than six feet tall.

Some philosopher is not more than six feet tall.

We will limit attention here to statements that fall into the domain of whatever p-function is in question (so that we need not consider statements like "Beauty honors truth" to which many people do not attribute probabilities). Moreover, we will make the reasonable assumption that if S_1, S_2 are statements in this restricted sense, then so are

(6)   a.   not S_1,

    b. S_1 or S_2,

    c. S_1 and S_2.

Statement (6c) is known as the *conjunction* of S_1 and S_2.

3.2.2   Bayesian P-Functions

These preliminaries in hand, consider a p-function P such that for all statements S_1, S_2 the following conditions hold:

(7)   a. $P(S_1) \geqslant 0$.

    b.   If S_1 is logically true, then $P(S_1) = 1$.

    c.   If S_1 and S_2 are logically exclusive, then $P(S_1 \text{ or } S_2) = P(S_1) + P(S_2)$.

d.   If $P(S_2) \neq 0$, then $P(S_1 \text{ and } S_2) = P(S_1 \text{ assuming } S_2)P(S_2)$.

Conditions (7a–d) may be paraphrased informally as follows:

a.   No probability is negative.

b.   The probability of a logical truth is 1.

c.   The probability that one of two logically exclusive statements is true equals the sum of their respective probabilities.

d.   The probability of a conjunction of two statements equals the probability of the first assuming the second times the probability of the second.

A p-function that satisfies conditions (7a–d) automatically satisfies a variety of other conditions. In particular, with respect to any statements S_1, S_2, (7a–d) imply (8a–d):

(8)   a. $P(\text{not-}S_1) = 1 - P(S_1)$.

b.   If S_1 and S_2 are logically equivalent, then $P(S_1) = P(S_2)$.

c.   *Bayes's Theorem*
If $P(S_2) \neq 0$, then $P(S_1 \text{ assuming } S_2) =$
$$\frac{P(S_2 \text{ assuming } S_1)P(S_1)}{P(S_2)}.$$

d. $P(S_1 \text{ and } S_2) \leqslant P(S_1)$.

The deduction of (8a–d) from (7a–d) is given in the Appendix.

Conditions (7a–d) are known as *Kolmogorov's axioms*, and they suffice to develop the elementary portion of classical probability theory.[2] Consequence (8c) is so fundamental to applications of this theory that any p-function that satisfies (7a–d) (and hence satisfies (8a–d)) will henceforth be qualified as *Bayesian*.

3.2.3   The Dutch Book Theorem

Bayesian p-functions stand in the following relation to Dutch books:

Dutch Book Theorem
Suppose that individual *I* is willing to accept any bet that is fair for *I* (in the sense defined earlier). Then a Dutch book can be made against *I* if and only if P_I is not Bayesian.

2. Condition (7d) is usually interpreted as the *definition* of the expression "$P(S_1$ assuming $S_2)$." However, in the present context it is more naturally treated as an axiom. It is worth pointing out, as well, that in standard treatments of probability the role played by statements (7a–d) is generally given to events. The two formulations are equivalent, however.

A proof of the Dutch book theorem is given by Skyrms (1986).

Thus, Bayesian judgment is a guarantee against falling for a Dutch book. Conversely, some Dutch book can be contrived against anyone manifesting a non-Bayesian p-function (and willing to accept apparently fair bets). Of course, Bayesian judgment is no guarantee against foolish bets in general. A person may accept an even money wager that Ronald Reagan will finish first in the next Boston Marathon without violating (7a–d). This bet is not a Dutch book.

Now let us return to the three-card problem (which you may wish to reread at this point). It is likely that your p-function yields the following judgments:

(9) $P_{you}(\text{RR}) = \frac{1}{3}$. (This is (a) of table 3.1.)

$P_{you}(\text{R-up}) = \frac{1}{2}$.

$P_{you}(\text{R-up assuming that RR}) = 1$.

Plugging these values into Bayes's theorem (8c), we see that P_{you} is Bayesian only if

(10) $P_{you}(\text{RR assuming that R-up}) = [(1)(\frac{1}{3})]/\frac{1}{2} = \frac{2}{3}$.

Comparing (10) to the judgment you actually made (see (c) of table 3.1), we must conclude that P_{you} is not Bayesian. The Dutch book theorem thus implies that you are open to a Dutch book. And this is what we observed in section 3.1.3.

3.3 Non-Bayesianism or Reasoning Illusions?

The conclusion that a person's p-function is non-Bayesian has such far-reaching consequences that we should not be hasty in drawing it. In particular, answers to the three-card problem seem too slender a basis for global evaluation of a person's probability function. Hence, we will consider the possibility that the responses recorded in table 3.1 result from a reasoning illusion that is atypical of our considered judgment.

3.3.1 Illusions in Other Domains

To see what is at issue, a perceptual analogy might be helpful. Consider the Müller-Lyer illusion of figure 3.1. Although the two horizontal lines are of equal length, the presence of the arrowheads disturbs our perceptual judgment and favors the impression that the top line is longer than the bottom line. Does this illusion imply that the human visual system lacks a mechanism for comparing line lengths? The answer must be no, because in the

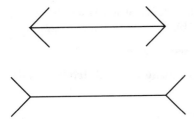

Figure 3.1
The Müller-Lyer illusion.

absence of arrowheads we judge the comparative length of parallel lines with great precision.

In the same way, we may qualify as illusory the impression of nongrammaticality engendered by sentences like (11):

(11)   The horse raced past the barn fell.

(11) is a well-formed English sentence and is perceived as such upon reflection. Its apparent nongrammaticality arises from minor imperfections in human parsing mechanisms. As before, these imperfections ought not blind us to the existence of mental systems that yield, in more favorable circumstances, a correct verdict about the grammaticality of sentences.

There are also estimation illusions, such as the following "anchoring" effect discovered by Tversky and Kahneman (1974). These investigators asked subjects to estimate various quantities stated in percentages. For example, one estimate concerned the percentage of African countries in the United Nations. Prior to each estimate, a number between 0 and 100 was determined by spinning a wheel of fortune in the subject's presence. Subjects were instructed first to indicate whether that number was higher or lower than the value of the quantity to be estimated and then to estimate the quantity by moving upward or downward from the given number. Despite the evident, arbitrary character of these "anchors," they had considerable impact on estimates. For example, the median estimates for the percentage of African countries in the United Nations were 25 and 45 percent for groups that received 10 and 65, respectively, as starting points. This effect of anchoring was not dissipated by offering monetary rewards for accuracy.

A similar phenomenon is reported by Slovic, Fischhoff, and Lichtenstein (1980). They describe a study in which subjects were asked to judge the lethality of various potential causes of death using different, arithmetically equivalent formats. For example, one group of subjects judged the lethality of heart attacks by responding to question (12a), whereas another group responded to the equivalent question (12b).

(12) a. For each 100,000 people afflicted, how many died?

b. For each person who died, how many were afflicted but survived?

To facilitate comparison of the judgments, the answers to (12) were converted into estimates of deaths per 100,000 people afflicted. The average estimates for the two groups were found to be 13,011 and 131, respectively. Thus, a minor change in question wording changed the estimated death rate by a factor of nearly 100. Similar effects arose for other hazards and question formats. (See chapter 4 for a discussion of similar findings.)

Finally, there are illusions of reasoning, in which apparently sound arguments lead to unacceptable conclusions. An example is the notorious "surprise quiz paradox," which seems to establish the following claim:

(13) It is impossible for the instructor of an intelligent class to announce at the beginning of the term that there will be a surprise quiz at some point in the semester and then in fact to administer such a quiz during the term.

Here is the "proof" of (13). Suppose that the class meets 30 times during the term (we will use 30 for concreteness; any other number works as well). It is clear that the instructor cannot administer the quiz at the 30th meeting since in this case it would be no surprise. For, the students (being intelligent) can be expected to reason as follows:

(14) "Here we are at the 30th and last meeting. No surprise quiz has been given to this point, so it must be given today. Let us therefore expect its occurrence."

It is equally clear that the quiz cannot be administered at the 29th meeting either. For here again, its occurrence would be no surprise to intelligent students. This time they would reason as follows:

(15) "Here we are at the 29th and second-to-last meeting. No surprise quiz has been given to this point, so it must be given either today or next meeting. Now it can't be given next meeting (the last), since then it would be no surprise [see (14)]. That leaves only today for it to arise. Let us therefore expect its occurrence."

What about giving the quiz at the 28th meeting? Well, the students (being intelligent) can rely on the reasoning in (14) and (15) to rule out days 30 and 29 for the quiz. This leaves meeting 28 as the only possibility, thereby eliminating any surprise.

By working backward through the class meetings in this way, you can see that there is *no* day on which the instructor can give the quiz without the students expecting it. Statement (13) is thus proved. Right?

3.3.2   The Thesis of Bayesian Competence

Anchoring and format phenomena constitute illusions inasmuch as subjects recognize that such influences on their judgment are regrettable and should be avoided where possible. The surprise quiz paradox is similarly illusory since those caught in its web are persuaded in advance that its proof must be faulty. Returning now to probability judgment, might the three-card problem represent nothing more than a reasoning illusion that masks an underlying Bayesian p-function? The illusion in this case would rest on the indiscernability of the two faces of the red-red card. To see what is at issue, refresh your memory of the three-card problem and then examine the following argument about the probability of "RR assuming that R-up":

> Altogether the three cards have six sides. If the drawn card lands with a red side up, the hidden side can be the white side of the red-white card or *either* side of the red-red card. These are the only possibilities, and they are equally likely. Consequently, the probability in these circumstances of a red underside is 2-out-of-3. Since the drawn card has a red underside if and only if it is red-red, we conclude that the probability of RR assuming that R-up is $\frac{2}{3}$.

Observe that the estimate of $\frac{2}{3}$ matches the calculation given by Bayes's theorem starting from the judgments recorded in (9). Since most people appear to be convinced by the reasoning in the preceding argument, we are tempted to conclude that people's plausibility functions are typically Bayesian after all, despite their answers to tricky questions like the three-card problem (where it is easy to confound the distinct sides of the red-red card). We might thus claim that human judgment is Bayesian at the level of *competence* even if Bayesianism is sometimes violated at the level of *performance.*

Despite its reassuring character, the thesis of Bayesian competence is difficult to reconcile with judgments elicited by other problems, to be examined shortly. More importantly, there appear to be principles of a non-Bayesian nature that provide a systematic description of a wide range of judgmental phenomena. One such principle has been proposed by Kahneman and Tversky (1972, 1973). Its core idea is that probability attributions often rest on judgments of similarity. We will now consider this idea in some detail and then return to the question of Bayesian competence.

3.4   Similarity and Judged Probability

3.4.1   The Similarity Thesis

The principle advanced by Kahneman and Tversky may be formulated as follows:

(16)   *Similarity Thesis*
Let x be an object and let C be a category. To judge the probability that x is a member of C, people often rely on their perception of x's similarity to C (the greater the similarity, the greater the probability).

The similarity thesis most readily applies to categories that manifest typicality structure in the sense discussed in chapter 2. As in that chapter, we will take the contrast model (Tversky 1977) to be the underlying theory of similarity. Recall that the contrast model applies not only to judgments of similarity between objects but also to judgments of similarity between an object and a concept.

It should be noted that Kahneman and Tversky often use the term *representativeness* in place of *similarity*, and their thesis includes several subtleties not expressed by (16) (see Tversky and Kahneman 1982a). Nonetheless, the present version of the similarity thesis has considerable explanatory power, as we will now see.

3.4.2   Nonuse of Prior Odds

To test the similarity thesis, Kahneman and Tversky (1973) presented 85 subjects with the following instructions:

A panel of psychologists have interviewed and administered personality tests to 30 engineers and 70 lawyers, all successful in their respective fields. On the basis of this information, thumbnail descriptions of the 30 engineers and 70 lawyers have been written. You will find on your forms five descriptions, chosen at random from the 100 available descriptions. For each description, please indicate your probability that the person described is an engineer, on a scale from 0 to 100.

The same task has been performed by a panel of experts, who were highly accurate in assigning probabilities to the various descriptions. You will be paid a bonus to the extent that your estimates come close to those of the expert panel.

The subjects who read the foregoing instructions will be called the *low engineer* group. A different group of 86 subjects—the *high engineer* group—were given identical instructions except that the numbers 70 and 30 were reversed: these subjects were told that the set from which the descriptions had been drawn consisted of 70 engineers and 30 lawyers.

Subjects in both groups were presented with the same five descriptions. For example:

(17)   Jack is a 45-year-old man. He is married and has four children. He is generally conservative, careful, and ambitious. He shows no interest in political and social issues and spends most of his free time on his many hobbies, which include home carpentry, sailing, and mathematical puzzles.

The probability that Jack is one of the 30 engineers [or 70 engineers for the high engineer group] in the sample of 100 is ____ percent.

If the subjects manifested Bayesian judgment, how should the responses of the low and high engineer groups differ to question (17)? Let us use the following abbreviations:

ENG: The person whose description was drawn randomly from the sample of 100 is an engineer.

DES: This particular thumbnail description—namely, (17)—happened to be chosen from the 100 descriptions prepared by the panel of psychologists.

Then, question (17) amounts to evaluating the probability of the statement "ENG assuming that DES." By Bayes's theorem, this probability may be calculated as follows:

$$P(\text{ENG assuming that DES}) = \frac{P(\text{DES assuming that ENG})P(\text{ENG})}{P(\text{DES})}.$$

We may assume that subjects in both the low and high engineer groups assigned the same, average value to the term $P(\text{DES assuming that ENG})$; the number of engineers in the sample of 100 does not affect the probability that a given engineer has the characteristics listed in (17). Likewise, the two groups of subjects may be assumed to assign the same value of .01 to $P(\text{DES})$.

Consider next $P(\text{ENG})$, the probability that in advance of any particular information concerning him, Jack is an engineer. The low engineer group would be expected to assign probability .3 to this statement, whereas the high engineer group should assign it probability .7. To verify this expectation, Kahneman and Tversky posed the following problem to all subjects:

(18)   Suppose now that you are given no information whatsoever about an individual chosen at random from the sample.

The probability that this man is one of the 30 engineers [or 70 engineers for the high engineer group] is ____ percent.

As expected, the low and high engineer groups gave the appropriate responses of 30 and 70 percent, respectively.

Putting the three terms together, we see that if the subjects responded in Bayesian fashion, then the respective estimates of P(ENG assuming that DES) by the two groups have the following forms:

$$\frac{P(\text{DES assuming that ENG}) \ .30}{.01} \ ,$$

$$\frac{P(\text{DES assuming that ENG}) \ .70}{.01} \ .$$

The ratio of these answers is .3/.7 or .43. In sum, if the subjects manifested Bayesian reasoning, the answers of the low and high engineer groups should stand in the ratio .43.

In fact, the obtained ratio was very close to 1. That is, the low and high engineer groups offered essentially identical estimates of P(ENG assuming that DES). These results contradict the hypothesis that the subjects' judgment is Bayesian.

The quantity P(ENG) is known as the *prior odds* for the statement "ENG assuming that DES." Kahneman and Tversky's subjects apparently ignored prior odds in their deliberations, even though their responses to (18) show that the prior odds were not far from consciousness.

What prediction does the similarity thesis make regarding Kahneman and Tversky's study? According to the similarity thesis, the judged probability that Jack is an engineer depends on the similarity of Jack to the category "engineer." Let ENG be the feature-set evoked in subjects' minds by the category "engineer," and let JACK be the feature-set evoked by description (17). The contrast model asserts that the similarity of Jack to "engineer" depends exclusively on the weights of the feature-sets ENG ∩ JACK, ENG − JACK, and JACK − ENG (see the discussion in section 2.2.2). The same dependency holds between, on the one hand, the similarity of Jack to "lawyer" and, on the other hand, the feature-sets LAW ∩ JACK, LAW − JACK, and JACK − LAW (where LAW is the feature-set for "lawyer").

Since prior odds do not enter any of these terms, they are identical for both the low and high engineer groups of subjects. Consequently, the similarity thesis predicts—as in fact obtained in the experiment—that subjects in the two groups will give identical estimates of the probability that Jack is an engineer. Moreover, by reflecting on the features likely to be associated with "engineer" and "lawyer," it may be seen that ENG ∩ JACK has more features than LAW ∩ JACK, and that ENG − JACK and JACK − ENG have fewer features than LAW − JACK and JACK − LAW, respectively. Therefore, according to the contrast model, JACK is more similar to "engineer" than to "lawyer," so both groups should respond to question (17) with a high probability. This latter prediction of the similarity thesis is also confirmed by Kahneman and Tversky's data.

What does the similarity thesis predict about the judged probability that Dick, described in (19), is one of the engineers in the sample of 100?

(19)   Dick is a 30-year-old man. He is married with no children. A man of high ability and high motivation, he promises to be quite successful in his field. He is well liked by his colleagues.

Kahneman and Tversky constructed this description so as to be uninformative about Dick's profession. As a consequence, Dick is equally similar to "lawyer" and "'engineer." The similarity thesis thus predicts that both groups will judge the probability that Dick is an engineer to be 50 percent. Such was the experimental result obtained.

3.4.3   The Conjunction Fallacy

Another test of the similarity thesis is provided by the following problem, which Tversky and Kahneman (1983) posed (among others of the same form) to 89 undergraduates at Stanford University and the University of British Columbia:

(20)   Linda is 31 years old, single, outspoken, and very bright. She majored in philosophy. As a student, she was deeply concerned with issues of discrimination and social justice, and also participated in antinuclear demonstrations.

Please rank the following statements by their probability, using 1 for the most probable and 8 for the least probable.

a.   Linda is a teacher in elementary school.

b.   Linda works in a bookstore and takes yoga classes.

c.   Linda is active in the feminist movement.

d.   Linda is a psychiatric social worker.

e.   Linda is a member of the League of Women Voters.

f.   Linda is a bank teller.

g.   Linda is an insurance salesperson.

h.   Linda is a bank teller and is active in the feminist movement.

Eighty-nine percent of the subjects ranked alternative (20h) as more likely than alternative (20f). Such a judgment has the form

$$P(S_1 \text{ and } S_2) > P(S_1),$$

contradicting consequence (8d) of the probability axioms (7). Once again, then, a large majority of subjects manifested non-Bayesian judgment. This time the transition to a Dutch book is remarkably swift; see question 3.1b.

Nonrespect of (8d) is known as the *conjunction fallacy*. It is such a flagrant violation of standard probability theory that one is led to suspect that Tversky and Kahneman's subjects did not understand the problem put to them. In particular, in the context of alternative (h) of problem (20), it seems possible that subjects understood (f) to mean

(f*)   Linda is a bank teller and is *not* active in the feminist movement.

Note that no fallacy is committed by assigning (h) a higher probability than (f*).

To investigate subjects' interpretation of (f), Tversky and Kahneman posed the same problem (20) to 88 new subjects. For half the participants, however, the conjunctive statement (h) was deleted from the alternatives, whereas for the other half the conjuncts (c) and (f) were deleted. Thus, no subject saw alternative (f) of the original problem in the context of alternative (h). The results of this manipulation were consistent with the first study. The first subgroup's probability rank for "Linda is a bank teller" was lower than that of the second group for "Linda is a bank teller and is active in the feminist movement."

In a further control experiment Tversky and Kahneman replaced alternative (f) in problem (20) by

(f')   Linda is a bank teller whether or not she is active in the feminist movement.

Alternative (f') is not open to the unintended interpretation (f*). Only 16 percent of 75 new subjects rated (h) as less likely than (f').

Tversky and Kahneman also investigated the possibility that subjects simply did not notice the relationship between alternatives (f) and (h) in problem (20). One hundred and forty-two additional subjects received problem (20) with all but alternatives (f) and (h) deleted. They were asked simply to check which of the two alternatives was more likely. Eighty-five percent of the subjects committed the conjunction fallacy.

The participants in the foregoing studies had no background in probability or statistics. However, the same fallacy rate was obtained on problem (20) using medical students, graduate students in psychology, and graduate students in education, all of whom had taken one or more courses in statistics. Doctoral students in the decision science program of the Stanford University Graduate School of Business also gave essentially identical results. Finally, Tversky and Kahneman present data on medical judgment showing that internists are prey to the same fallacy in judgments about symptomatology.

The similarity thesis allows us to understand the compelling nature of the conjunction fallacy. Tversky and Kahneman asked another group of undergraduates to rank alternatives (a)–(h) of problem (20) by "the degree to which Linda resembles the typical member of that class." The subjects rated Linda as more similar to a feminist bank teller (alternative (h)) than to a bank teller (alternative (f)). The similarity thesis thus predicts that subjects will assign higher probability to alternative (h) of problem (20) than to alternative (f). That is, the similarity thesis predicts the conjunction fallacy in the present case.

It is worth verifying that the contrast model of similarity is consistent with subjects' judgment that Linda resembles "feminist bank teller" more than "bank teller." To see this, observe that (1) the number of features shared by Linda and the category "feminist bank teller" is greater than the number shared by Linda and "bank teller" and (2) the number of discrepant features is likely smaller in the former case than in the latter.

The enhanced similarity of an object (here, Linda) to a conjunctive category ("feminist bank teller") compared to one of its constituents ("bank teller") is known as the *conjunction effect* (see Smith and Osherson 1984). We can measure the size of the conjunction effect by subtracting the second similarity judgment (suitably quantified) from the first. Likewise, we may measure the size of the conjunction fallacy in a problem like (20) by subtracting the average probability attributed to the bank teller alternative from that attributed to the feminist bank teller alternative. The similarity thesis leads us to expect that the size of the conjunction fallacy is roughly predictable from the size of the conjunction effect, when these two phenomena are compared across problems like (20). This prediction was confirmed in a systematic study by Shafir, Smith, and Osherson (1987).

3.4.4   Random Processes

For a third application of the similarity thesis, consider the following question, due again to Kahneman and Tversky (1972):

> On each round of a game, 20 marbles are distributed at random among five children: Alan, Ben, Carl, Dan, and Ed. Consider the following distributions:
>
> | I | | II | |
> |------|---|------|---|
> | Alan | 4 | Alan | 4 |
> | Ben | 4 | Ben | 4 |
> | Carl | 5 | Carl | 4 |
> | Dan | 4 | Dan | 4 |
> | Ed | 3 | Ed | 4 |
>
> In many rounds of the game, will there be more results of type I or of type II?

A significant majority of subjects judged distribution I to be more frequent than distribution II, whereas in fact the reverse is true.

To deduce this judgment phenomenon from the similarity thesis, we note that most people find distribution I to be a more typical example of the category "randomly generated" than is distribution II (which is too orderly). In light of the close relation between typicality and similarity (see section 2.3.2), we infer that distribution I is more similar to the foregoing category than is distribution II. The similarity thesis thus implies that subjects will view distribution I as more likely than distribution II to be generated randomly. This prediction conforms with Kahneman and Tversky's results.

A parallel analysis underlies subjects' responses to the following problem (Kahneman and Tversky 1972):

> All families of six children in a city were surveyed. In 72 families the *exact order* of births of boys and girls was G B G B B G.

> What is your estimate of the number of families surveyed in which the *exact order* of births was B G B B B B?

In fact, the two sequences are about equally likely. The sequence G B G B B G, however, resembles the random processes involved in sex determination more than does the sequence B G B B B B. Accordingly, a large majority of subjects judged the latter sequence to be less frequent than the former among families of six children.

3.3.5   Predictive Asymmetries

Similarity considerations also help to explain subjects' responses to the following problem:

(21)   Which of the following events is more probable?

   a.   That a girl has blue eyes if her mother has blue eyes.

   b.   That the mother has blue eyes if her daughter has blue eyes.

   c.   The two events are equally probable.

Tversky and Kahneman (1980) posed this question to 165 college students. Fewer than half judged the two events to be equally probable. Sixty-nine subjects judged alternative (a) to be more likely than alternative (b). Twenty-one students made the contrary judgment. On the other hand, a large majority of another group of 91 students affirmed that the probability of blue eyes in successive generations is equal.

These data suggest that the p-functions of a considerable fraction of college students conform to the following conditions (where MBE = the mother has blue eyes and DBE = the daughter has blue eyes):

(22) a. P(DBE assuming that MBE) $>$ P(MBE assuming that DBE).

   b. P(DBE) $=$ P(MBE).

Such p-functions are not Bayesian. Bayes's theorem (8c) yields

(23) P(DBE assuming that MBE) $= \dfrac{P(\text{MBE assuming that DBE})P(\text{DBE})}{P(\text{MBE})}$.

By (22b) the ratio P(DBE)/P(MBE) $= 1$, so (23) implies that P(DBE assuming that MBE) $= P$(MBE assuming that DBE), contradicting (22a). Tversky and Kahneman describe several additional problems of this nature.

The similarity thesis does not directly apply to problem (21). We rely instead on the following variant:

(24) Let x and y be objects, and let C be a category. To judge the probability that x is a member of C assuming that y is a member of C, people often rely on their perception of the similarity of x to y (the greater the similarity, the greater the probability).

To apply (24) to problem (21), recall the discussion of asymmetry in similarity judgment from chapter 2. According to the contrast model (and in accordance with experimental studies), the judged similarity of a less prominent object to a more prominent object is greater than that of the latter to the former. Mothers may well be more prominent psychologically than daughters since mothers are the causes or origins of daughters and not vice versa. The upshot is that daughters resemble mothers more than mothers resemble daughters. As a consequence, (24) predicts that P(DBE assuming that MBE) will be judged to be higher than P(MBE assuming that DBE) by most subjects. Such was the obtained result.

Thus, we have seen that numerous reasoning tasks reveal non-Bayesian judgment on the part of college students and professionals; on the other hand, subjects' responses to these problems conform to the similarity thesis.[3] Now let us return to the question of Bayesian competence.

3.5 The Coexistence Thesis

3.5.1 The Case against Bayesian Competence

We saw in section 3.2 that the only defense against Dutch books (aside from refusing bets you deem fair) is to respect conditions (7a–d) on p-functions. Such p-functions were labeled *Bayesian*. In section 3.3.2 we

---

3. For additional tests of the similarity thesis, see questions 3.4 and 3.5.

articulated the thesis of Bayesian competence, according to which most people's p-functions are fundamentally Bayesian even if this fact is sometimes hidden by reasoning illusions of various kinds.

In section 3.4 we examined findings that suggest that if Bayesian competence exists at all, it lies at a mental level that is often inaccessible to subjects. Moreover, we saw that there exist non-Bayesian principles such as the similarity thesis that provide convincing accounts of several reasoning phenomena. The temptation is thus strong to attribute these operative principles to subjects' competence in place of the inoperative Bayesian principles (7a–d).

Since the thesis of Bayesian competence is difficult to defend, we are led to modify it. Our modified hypothesis is that Bayesian reasoning is one of several potentialities that coexist in competence. On this view, human judgment is expected to conform to Bayesian principles on some occasions and to non-Bayesian principles like the similarity thesis on other occasions. This new hypothesis may be called the *coexistence thesis*. To defend it, we will first underline the diversity of principles that intervene in naive probability judgment and then examine studies that support the coexistence thesis in more direct fashion.

3.5.2   The Multiplicity of Reasoning Principles

Similarity principles are not sufficient to account for all the peculiarities of human judgment. Consider, for example, the following question (due to Tversky and Kahneman 1983):

> In four pages of a novel (about 2,000 words), how many words would you expect to find that have the form $----ing$ (seven-letter words that end with *ing*)? Indicate your best estimate by circling one of the values below:
>
> 0   1–2   3–4   5–7   8–10   11–15   16+

A second version of the question, posed to a different group of subjects, requested estimates for words of the form $-----n-$. Despite the fact that all words of the first form are also words of the second form, the estimates for $----ing$ words were almost three times higher than the estimates for $-----n-$ words. To explain these findings, the relevant mechanism seems to be not similarity but *availability in memory*: in this case the power of different word forms to retrieve relevant examples from subjects' memories (for more discussion, see Tversky and Kahneman 1973).

Yet another reasoning mechanism is responsible for the findings of the following study (Tversky and Kahneman 1983). Subjects were 115 participants in the Second International Congress on Forecasting, held in

Istanbul, Turkey, in July 1982. Half of the subjects evaluated the probability of (25a), whereas the other half evaluated the probability of (25b):

(25) a. A complete suspension of diplomatic relations between the USA and the Soviet Union, sometime in 1983.

b. A Russian invasion of Poland, and a complete suspension of diplomatic relations between the USA and the Soviet Union, sometime in 1983.

Despite the fact that (25a) is included in (25b), the probability estimates for (25b) were more than three times higher than those for (25a). In this case the explanation of subjects' judgments hinges on the concept of "plausible, causal scenario" (for discussion, see Tversky and Kahneman 1980).

The point of these examples is to underline the multiplicity of principles that underlie human judgment. Might not a Bayesian mechanism also lie in place, ready for activation in the right circumstances? In fact, several studies provide evidence in favor of this possibility.

3.5.3   Glimmers of Bayesianism

Bar-Hillel (1982) posed subjects the following problem:

A certain town is served by two hospitals. In the larger hospital about 45 babies are born each day, and in the smaller hospital about 15 babies are born each day. As you know, about 50 percent of all babies are boys. The exact percentage of baby boys, however, varies from day to day. Sometimes it may be higher than 50 percent, sometimes lower.

For a period of 1 year, each hospital recorded the days on which more than 60 percent of the babies born were boys. Which hospital do you think recorded more such days?

In different versions of the problem given to separate groups, the proportion of boys was changed from 60 percent to 70 percent, 80 percent, or 100 percent.

The 60-percent version of the problem was originally devised by Kahneman and Tversky (1972), who discovered that most subjects ignored the overall number of babies born in each hospital and asserted that the two hospitals recorded the same number of days on which more than 60 percent of the babies born were boys. This answer is at variance with the theory of probability, which implies that the larger sample of babies will tend to show less percentage-deviation from 50 percent.

Bar-Hillel's results suggest that—Kahneman and Tversky's original findings notwithstanding—a nascent appreciation of the role of sample size is present in most subjects. For, compared to the 60-percent version of the problem, subjects correctly chose the smaller hospital significantly more often in the 70-, 80-, and 100-percent versions (with a majority of correct responses for the 100-percent version).

For a second example, let us again consider the conjunction fallacy. Tversky and Kahneman (1983) posed the following problem to 260 undergraduates at Stanford University and the University of British Columbia:

(26)   Consider a regular six-sided die with four green faces and two red faces. The die will be rolled 20 times and the sequence of greens (G) and reds (R) will be recorded. You are asked to select one sequence, from a set of three, and you will win $25 if the sequence you chose appears on successive rolls of the die. Please check the sequence of greens and reds on which you prefer to bet.

1.   R G R R R

2.   G R G R R R

3.   G R R R R R

Since option 1 is a subsequence of option 2, the former is strictly more probable than the latter (see the conjunction principle (8d)). Nonetheless, a majority of subjects chose to bet on sequence 2, probably because it is the best example of the category "randomly generated." The same results were obtained in a second experiment in which option 2 was replaced by R G R R R G (which also includes option 1 as a subsequence).

These results, like those discussed in section 3.4.3, indicate insensitivity on the part of college students to the conjunction rule. However, a different conclusion emerges from a follow-up study carried out by Tversky and Kahneman (1983). Eighty-eight new subjects were given problem (26) with the third sequence removed. Instead of selecting a sequence on which to bet, however, they were to indicate which of the following two arguments, if either, they found to be correct:

Argument 1
The first sequence (R G R R R) is more probable than the second (G R G R R R) because the second sequence is the same as the first with an additional G at the beginning. Hence, every time the second sequence occurs, the first sequence must also occur. Consequently, you can win on the first and lose on the second, but you can never win on the second and lose on the first.

Argument 2
The second sequence (G R G R R R) is more probable than the first (R G R R R) because the proportions of R and G in the second

sequence are closer than those of the first sequence to the expected proportions of R and G for a die with four green and two red faces.

A large majority of subjects chose the probabilistically correct argument 1.

Studies by Ajzen (1977), Fischhoff, Slovic, and Lichtenstein (1979), and Tversky and Kahneman (1982b) provide additional evidence of Bayesian reasoning on the part of subjects whose answers to some problems have a decidedly non-Bayesian character.

3.5.4   What Factors Encourage Bayesian Reasoning?

The foregoing studies support the coexistence thesis inasmuch as they suggest the existence of Bayesian reasoning schemes in the competence of subjects who give non-Bayesian responses to other problems. The coexistence hypothesis is incomplete, however, without supplementary theses about the kinds of circumstances that evoke one kind of reasoning rather than another.

To grasp the issue, consider the following study reported by Tversky and Kahneman (1983). Subjects read the description (20) of Linda followed by the crucial alternatives of bank teller and feminist bank teller. They were asked to indicate which of the following two arguments they found more convincing:

Argument 1
Linda is more likely to be a bank teller than she is to be a feminist bank teller, because every feminist bank teller is a bank teller, but some women bank tellers are not feminists, and Linda could be one of them.

Argument 2
Linda is more likely to be a feminist bank teller than she is likely to be a bank teller, because she resembles an active feminist more than she resembles a bank teller.

This study thus parallels the one involving rolls of a die (see (26)). In the former study subjects usually recognized the persuasiveness of the conjunction principle, once made explicit. In contrast, a majority of subjects in the study concerning Linda rejected argument 1, based on the conjunction principle, in favor of the similarity-based argument 2. What factors explain subjects' different responses to these formally parallel problems?

A similar discrepancy between subjects' performance in parallel settings emerges from the following pair of problems (Tversky and Kahneman 1983):

(27) a.   A health survey was conducted in a sample of adult males in British Columbia, of all ages and occupations.

Please give your best estimate of the following values:

What percentage of the men surveyed have had one or more heart attacks?

What percentage of the men surveyed both are over 55 years old and have had one or more heart attacks?

b.   A health survey was conducted in a sample of 100 adult males in British Columbia, of all ages and occupations.

Please give your best estimate of the following values:

How many of the 100 participants have had one or more heart attacks?

How many of the 100 participants both are over 55 years old and have had one or more heart attacks?

Sixty-five percent of the subjects responding to problem (27a) assigned a strictly higher estimate to the second question, thereby committing the conjunction fallacy. In contrast, only 25 percent of the subjects responding to problem (27b) made the same error.

Several hypotheses have been advanced about the factors that lead subjects to Bayesian versus non-Bayesian reasoning. Nisbett et al. (1983), for example, argue that correct, probabilistic reasoning is encouraged by emphasizing the role of chance in producing the events in question and by clarifying the sampling process responsible for the objects or persons actually observed. These factors seem to apply to the two pairs of studies just described, as well as to others reported by Nisbett et al.

A related hypothesis stems from the distinction between *external* and *internal* uncertainty, formulated by Kahneman and Tversky (1982). To see the distinction, note that people are inclined to view the uncertainty of a coin toss as due to external, causal mechanisms whose behavior defies prediction. In contrast, a person's uncertainty about naming the capital of Pakistan reflects internal ignorance. Kahneman and Tversky draw attention to the distinct phenomenologies associated with the two types of uncertainty and suggest that distinct judgmental mechanisms are associated with each. It is tempting to speculate that Bayesian reasoning is more readily triggered by external uncertainty than by its internal counterpart.

Confirmation of hypotheses like those of Nisbett et al. and Kahneman and Tversky would go a long way toward confirming the coexistence thesis.

3.6   The Impossibility of Perfect Bayesianism

3.6.1   Toward a Bayesian Ideal?

The Dutch book theorem embodies a major advantage of Bayesian p-functions. Other advantages stem from the role of probability theory in the physical and social sciences (which are more comprehensible to people with Bayesian intuitions). It is therefore fortunate that human probability judgment is malleable to some degree and that initiation in statistics and probability theory leads most people to a more Bayesian conception of chance. Indeed, several experimental studies point to genuine improvement in probability judgment in the wake of introductory statistics courses. (For a review of this literature, see chapter 9 of Holland et al. 1986.)

Could study and reflection render our probability functions perfectly Bayesian? Is flawless Bayesianism even possible in principle, allowance being made for occasional lapses of memory and errors of a clerical nature? We will see that under mild assumptions the answer to these questions is negative: perfect Bayesianism is a logical impossibility for any computer-simulable agent evaluating the probabilities of statements in a moderately expressive language. This is the content of two theorems presented in the next section. Later we will examine their consequences for human judgment.

3.6.2   Two Theorems

Let P be a given probability function. We will formulate two conditions on P that imply that P is not Bayesian. By the *domain* of P is meant the class of statements to which P assigns probabilities.

Consider an arbitrary program written in BASIC for your home computer. We will call such a program *elementary* if it requests exactly one integer as input from the keyboard. We take the output of an elementary program to be the first number (if there is any) that the program prints after receiving its sole input.

Our first condition asserts that P attributes probabilities to claims about the input-output behavior of elementary programs:

> *Condition 1*
> The domain of P includes all statements of the form
>
>> Elementary program B produces output n when given input m
>> (where n and m are integers).

Our second condition asserts that P's probability attributions arise from processes that are mechanical in nature and thus capable of computer simulation:

Condition 2
P is a computable function.

The following theorem is a corollary of basic results in the theory of computation:[4]

(28)   Let probability function *P* meet conditions 1 and 2. Then *P* is not Bayesian.

Condition 1 might seem a bit strong inasmuch as only a minority of people know how to program BASIC. On the other hand, almost everyone knows how to do sums. For this reason we are led to weaken condition 1 in the following way. An *addition statement* is defined to be any sentence built from the following material: decimal expressions for nonnegative integers; the addition operator, denoted by $+$; the equality relation, denoted by $=$; the logical connectives *and* and *not*; variables $x, y, z, \ldots$ for nonnegative integers; and the quantifier *some nonnegative integer is such that*.... Examples of addition statements are the following:

$3 + 3 = 2.$

Some nonnegative integer x is such that $x + 5 = 8$.

It is not true that some nonnegative integer x is such that $x + x = x$.

We may now replace condition 1 with the following weaker claim:

Condition 1'
The domain of *P* includes all addition statements.

On the other hand, condition 2 seems unnecessarily weak. Let us strengthen it to the following claim:

Condition 2'
A CRAY II computer [reputed to be the fastest currently available] can be programmed in such a way that for every statement *S* in the domain of *P*, the CRAY II computes the value $P(S)$ in less than $1000L$ hours, where L is the number of characters used to write *S* in English.

It turns out that our revised conditions give the same result as before, namely:

---

4. It suffices to observe that any statement of the form exhibited in condition 1 is either logically true or logically false. Hence, by (7b) and (8a), if *P* is Bayesian and meets condition 1, such statements are assigned 1 and 0, respectively. *P* thus cannot meet condition 2, since this would contradict the unsolvability of the halting problem (see Davis and Weyuker 1983).

(29)   Let probability function P meet conditions 1' and 2'. Then P is not Bayesian.

Theorem (29) is a consequence of a result due to Fischer and Rabin (1974).

3.6.3   Judgmental Heuristics

Conditions 1 and 2 are likely to be true of the human probability function (suitably idealized). Regarding condition 1, it may be remarked that programmers often have strong intuitions about programs they write or examine. Regarding condition 2, the assertion that our p-functions are computable amounts to the claim that the neural activity giving rise to our probability judgment is simulable by a computer (of suitable size and design). If we accept the claim that human p-functions conform to the two conditions, it follows from theorem (28) that perfect Bayesianism is not humanly possible. Similar remarks apply to theorem (29). As a consequence, the thesis of Bayesian competence and the coexistence thesis ought to be understood as applying to problems of restricted complexity.

The two theorems do not suffice to explain the non-Bayesian responses of subjects to the problems described in previous sections. Such problems are well within the complexity limits of human calculation, and subjects' performance must be interpreted in light of non-Bayesian strategies. Nonetheless, Bayesian calculations are often likely to be more difficult and time consuming than, for example, similarity assessment.[5] In this sense, the latter kind of calculation represents an imperfect but convenient *heuristic* for reducing the mental cost of reaching a judgment. For judgments of increasing complexity, the use of heuristics becomes inevitable, as revealed by the two theorems. (See also the discussion of heuristics in chapter 5.) A good heuristic, of course, would be easy to apply and would produce few errors. In contrast, we have seen that whatever their ease of application, human heuristics give rise to errors in a significant number of circumstances.

At what point do statements become so complex for the human decision-maker as to require non-Bayesian heuristics? The answer to this question is not yet in sight. Fruitful investigation of the matter would no doubt require contributions from (at least) the study of language, memory, categorization, problem solving, judgment, and computational complexity.

Recourse to heuristics is not typically a conscious choice, as if the Bayesian option were considered and set aside. The result is that subjects

---

5. Note, for example, that simple versions of the contrast model involve little more than counting operations (see chapter 2). Moreover, the similarity calculations of the contrast model can be carried out in largely parallel fashion.

can be led into striking errors of judgment even in the face of decisions important to them, for instance, involving monetary or medical outcomes (for examples drawn from medical practice, see Chapman and Chapman 1971; Eddy 1982). We can therefore see that by analyzing the nature and origins of human judgment, and by evaluating the risks and benefits of heuristic decision strategies, cognitive science renders an important service to us all.

Appendix: Proof of (8a–d)

In what follows, assume that probability function P satisfies (7a–d). Let statements S_1, S_2 be given.

A.1   Proof of (8a)

To prove: $P(\text{not-}S_1) = 1 - P(S_1)$.
Proof: The statement "S_1 or not-S_1" is a logical truth. So by (7b),

(i) $P(S_1 \text{ or not-}S_1) = 1$.

Since S_1 and not-S_1 are logically exclusive, (7c) implies

(ii) $P(S_1 \text{ or not-}S_1) = P(S_1) + P(\text{not-}S_1)$.

From (i) and (ii) we infer

(iii) $P(S_1) + P(\text{not-}S_1) = 1$.

(8a) follows immediately from (iii).

A.2   Proof of (8b)

To prove: If S_1 and S_2 are logically equivalent, then $P(S_1) = P(S_2)$.
Proof: Since S_1 and S_2 are logically equivalent, S_1 and not-S_2 are logically exclusive. So by (7c),

(i) $P(S_1 \text{ or not-}S_2) = P(S_1) + P(\text{not-}S_2)$.

By (8a),

(ii) $P(\text{not-}S_2) = 1 - P(S_2)$.

Equations (i) and (ii) yield

(iii) $P(S_1 \text{ or not-}S_2) = [1 + P(S_1)] - P(S_2)$.

On the other hand, "S_1 or not-S_2" is a logical truth. So by (7b),

(iv) $P(S_1 \text{ or not-}S_2) = 1$.

Equations (iii) and (iv) yield

(v) $1 = [1 + P(S_1)] - P(S_2)$.

Equation (v) implies (8b).

A.3   Proof of (8c)

To prove: If $P(S_2) \neq 0$, then $P(S_1 \text{ assuming that } S_2) = \dfrac{P(S_2 \text{ assuming that } S_1)P(S_1)}{P(S_2)}$.

Proof: Suppose that $P(S_2) \neq 0$. Then by (7d),

(i) $P(S_1 \text{ assuming that } S_2) = \dfrac{P(S_1 \text{ and } S_2)}{P(S_2)}$.

The statements S_1 *and* S_2 and S_2 *and* S_1 are logically equivalent. So (8b) yields

(ii) $P(S_1 \text{ and } S_2) = P(S_2 \text{ and } S_1)$.

By (7d) again,

(iii) $P(S_2 \text{ and } S_1) = P(S_2 \text{ assuming that } S_1)P(S_1)$.

Equations (ii) and (iii) imply

(iv) $P(S_1 \text{ and } S_2) = P(S_2 \text{ assuming that } S_1)P(S_1)$.

Substituting (iv) into (i) yields the desired equation.

A.4   Proof of (8d)

To prove: $P(S_1 \text{ and } S_2) \leqslant P(S_1)$.
Proof: S_1 is logically equivalent to $(S_1 \text{ and } S_2)$ *or* $(S_1 \text{ and not-}S_2)$. So by (8b),

(i) $P(S_1) = P(S_1 \text{ and } S_2) \text{ or } (S_1 \text{ and not-}S_2))$.

On the other hand, the two statements S_1 *and* S_2 and S_1 *and not-*S_2 are logically exclusive. So (i) and (7c) yield

(ii) $P(S_1) = P(S_1 \text{ and } S_2) + P(S_1 \text{ and not-}S_2)$.

By (7a), $P(S_1 \text{ and not-}S_2) \geqslant 0$. Along with (ii), this fact implies

(iii) $P(S_1) \geqslant P(S_1 \text{ and } S_2)$.

Suggestions for Further Reading

There are numerous introductions to statistical inference and probability. Among these, I recommend Wonnacott and Wonnacott 1985. For an exposition of the Dutch book theorem and of alternative philosophical conceptions of chance, there is no better place to start than Skyrms 1986. In a related vein, Fine 1973 provides a survey and critique of alternative foundational approaches to probability theory.

The surprise quiz paradox is discussed in Sainsbury 1988.

A thorough introduction to the theory of computation and algorithmic complexity is provided in Davis and Weyuker 1983. The best point of entry into the growing literature on probability judgment is Kahneman, Slovic, and Tversky 1982. A more recent survey may be found in Holland et al. 1986. Arkes and Hammond 1986 is a collection of readings about the relevance of research on human judgment to social, medical, economic, and political decision making.

An underlying assumption of this chapter has been that degrees of belief can be treated like probabilities and thereby held up to the yardstick of classical probability theory. Reasons have been advanced, however, for thinking that rational belief need not conform to the probability axioms but rather is governed by laws of a different nature. Excellent points of entry into this discussion are Shafer 1976, 1981.

If belief in one statement raises the probability attributed to another statement, we say that the first "confirms" the second. For example, the statement *Mr. Jones finished second in the 1987 New York marathon* confirms the statement *Mr. Jones was born after 1927* but not the statement *Mr. Jones was born on a Tuesday*. Skyrms 1986 provides a philosophical introduction to the theory of confirmation. A psychological approach may be found in Osherson, Smith, and Shafir 1986.

An important subtopic in the theory of confirmation concerns the impact of new data on the probabilities attributed to prior beliefs. One normative viewpoint is presented in chapter 11 of Jeffrey 1983. A different perspective is presented in Harman 1986. For a descriptive, psychological theory, see Klayman and Ha 1987.

The relation between theories of confirmation and successful scientific inquiry is discussed in Osherson and Weinstein 1986, 1989 and Kelly and Glymour 1987.

A limiting case of confirmation is logical implication. For an introduction to this topic, see Jeffrey 1980. The psychology of logical implication is discussed from diverse perspectives in Rips 1983, 1987, Johnson-Laird 1983, Cheng and Holyoak 1985, and Cheng et al. 1986.

Research on human judgment has turned out to be fundamental to understanding various forms of social interaction. Nisbett and Ross 1980 provides an introduction to these issues; see also chapter 7 of Holland et al. 1986.

A history of probability conceptions is available in Hacking 1975. The development of probability notions in children is treated in Piaget and Inhelder 1975; see also chapter 6 of this volume.

Probability judgment is intimately connected to a person's choice of action in risky situations. The psychology of choice occupies chapter 4.

The findings reviewed both here and in chapter 4 raise questions about human rationality (or its absence). Nisbett and Borgida (1975), for example, see "bleak implications for human rationality" in the results of judgment studies. Chapter 7 is devoted to a philosophical discussion of the question of human rationality.

Questions

3.1 a. Jones assigns $\frac{5}{8}$ probability to the statement that either the Red Sox will clinch the American League pennant or the Celtics will win the NBA championship (or both of these events will occur). At the same time Jones assigns $\frac{4}{5}$ probability to the statement that the Red Sox will not clinch the American League pennant, and he assigns $\frac{3}{4}$ probability to the statement that the Celtics will not win the NBA championship. Suppose that Jones is willing to accept any (modest) bet that is fair for him (in the sense of section 3.1.2). Show that Jones is open to a Dutch book.

   b. Suppose that you assign probability $\frac{1}{10}$ to the statement *Linda is a bank teller* and probability $\frac{2}{10}$ to the statement *Linda is a bank teller and is active in the feminist movement*. Suppose furthermore that your p-function conforms to (8a)—in other words, that $P_{you}(\text{not-}S) = 1 - P_{you}(S)$, for all statements S. Show that a Dutch book can be made against you.

3.2 Deduce the following proposition from conditions (7a–d):

   Let statements S_1 and S_2 be given. If $P(S_2) \neq 0$ and $P(S_2) \neq 1$, then $P(S_1) = P(S_1$ assuming that $S_2)P(S_2) + P(S_1$ assuming that not-$S_2)P(\text{not-}S_2)$.

   You may use consequences (8a–d), which have already been proved from (7a–d).

3.3 Casscells, Schoenberger, and Grayboys (1978) presented 60 students and staff members at the Harvard University Medical School with the the following question. (The *prevalence* of a disease is the percentage of the population that has it, and the *false positive rate* of a test for a disease is the probability of a positive outcome in an individual without the disease.)

If a test to detect a disease whose prevalence is $\frac{1}{1000}$ has a false positive rate of 5 percent, what is the chance that a person found to have a positive result actually has the disease, assuming that you know nothing about the person's symptoms or signs?

Almost half of the participants responded with 95 percent. The average answer was 56 percent. The correct response depends on the probability of detecting the disease if present. Assume that the test is perfect in this respect. What is the Bayesian answer to the question?

3.4 Nisbett, Zukier, and Lemley (1981) asked subjects in one group to rate the utility of various items of information about college students for predicting the amount of shock that given students would take if they were in an experiment in which they were asked to tolerate as much shock as possible. Items like "Catholic," "from Detroit," and "3.1 grade point average" were judged to have little or no predictive value in this regard. A second group of subjects was asked to estimate the amount of shock that would be taken by music majors versus engineering majors. Finally, a third group made the same type of prediction with respect to students described either as "Catholic music majors from Detroit with a 3.1 grade point average" or "Catholic engineering majors from Detroit with a 3.1 grade point average."

The results of the study were as follows. Engineering majors were predicted to take much more shock than music majors. On the other hand, Catholic engineering majors from Detroit with a 3.1 grade point average were predicted to take only a little more shock than Catholic music majors from Detroit with a 3.1 grade point average.

Students who accept much shock in the circumstances described above can be termed "shocktakers." We may interpret the results of Nisbett et al.'s study as follows:

Subjects judge the probability that an engineering major is a shocktaker as considerably higher than the probability that a music major is a shocktaker.

Subjects judge the probability that a Catholic engineering major from Detroit with a 3.1 grade point average is a shocktaker as only slightly higher than the probability that a Catholic music major from Detroit with a 3.1 grade point average is a shocktaker.

In sum, the addition of irrelevant attributes seems to "dilute" the impact of the relevant differences in major. How can this dilution effect be explained in terms of the similarity thesis and the contrast model?

3.5 Shafir, Smith, and Osherson (1987) report experiments indicating that a majority of college students assign a higher probability to statement (i) than to statement (ii):

(i)   Every single bank teller in Concord, Massachusetts, is conservative.

(ii)   Every single feminist bank teller in Concord, Massachusetts, is conservative.

Compare this finding to the data reported in section 3.4.3 and attempt to explain it in light of the similarity thesis.

3.6 The following problem is due to Nisbett et al. (1983):

Harold is the coach for a high school football team. One of his jobs is selecting new members for the varsity team. He says the following of his experience: "Every year we add 10–20 younger boys to the team on the basis of their performance at the tryout practice. Usually the staff and I are extremely excited about the potential of two or three of these kids—one who throws several brilliant passes or another who kicks several field goals from a remarkable distance. Unfortunately, most of these kids turn out to be only somewhat better than the rest." Why do you suppose that the coach usually has to revise downward his opinion of players that he originally thought were brilliant?

Formulate your answer as concisely as possible and compare it (when you have the opportunity) with the opinion of a statistician. (Otherwise, see Nisbett et al. 1983 or Kahneman and Tversky 1973.)

References

Ajzen, I. (1977). Intuitive theories of events and the effects of base-rate information on prediction. *Journal of Personality and Social Psychology* 35, 303–314.

Arkes, H., and K. Hammond (1986). *Judgment and decision making*. Cambridge: Cambridge University Press.

Bar-Hillel, M. (1982). Studies of representativeness. In Kahneman, Slovic, and Tversky 1982.

Bar-Hillel, M., and R. Falk (1982). Some teasers concerning conditional probabilities. *Cognition* 11, 109–122.

Casscells, W., A. Schoenberger, and T. Grayboys (1978). Interpretation by physicians of clinical laboratory results. *New England Journal of Medicine* 299, 999–1000.

Chapman, L., and J. Chapman (1971). Test results are what you think they are. *Psychology Today*, November, 18–22, 106–110.

Cheng, P., and K. Holyoak (1985). Pragmatic reasoning schemas. *Cognitive Psychology* 17, 391–416.

Cheng, P., K. Holyoak, R. Nisbett, and L. Oliver (1986). Pragmatic versus syntactic approaches to training deductive reasoning. *Cognitive Psychology* 18, 293–328.

Davis, M., and E. Weyuker (1983). *Computability, complexity, and languages*. New York: Academic Press.

Eddy, D. M. (1982). Probabilistic reasoning in clinical medicine: Problems and opportunities. In Kahneman, Slovic, and Tversky 1982.

Fine, T. (1973). *Theories of probability*. New York: Academic Press.

Fischer, M. J., and M. O. Rabin (1974). Super exponential complexity of Presburger's arithmetic. *SIAM-AMS Proceedings* 7, 27–41.

Fischhoff, B., P. Slovic, and S. Lichtenstein (1979). Subjective sensitivity analysis. *Organizational Behavior and Human Performance* 23, 339–359.

Hacking, I. (1975). *The emergence of probability*. Cambridge: Cambridge University Press.

Harman, G. (1986). *Change in view*. Cambridge, MA: MIT Press.

Holland, J. H., K. J. Holyoak, R. E. Nisbett, and P. R. Thagard (1986). *Induction: Processes of inference, learning, and discovery*. Cambridge, MA: MIT Press.

Jeffrey, R. (1980). *Formal logic: Its scope and limits*. 3rd ed. New York: McGraw-Hill.

Jeffrey, R. (1983). *The logic of decision*. 2nd ed. Chicago: University of Chicago Press.

Johnson-Laird, P. (1983). *Mental models*. Cambridge, MA: Harvard University Press.

Kahneman, D., P. Slovic, and A. Tversky, eds. (1982). *Judgment under uncertainty: Heuristics and biases*. Cambridge: Cambridge University Press.

Kahneman, D., and A. Tversky (1972). Subjective probability: A judgment of representativeness. *Cognitive Psychology* 3, 430–454.

Kahneman, D., and A. Tversky (1973). On the psychology of prediction. *Psychological Review* 80, 237–251.

Kahneman, D., and A. Tversky (1982). Variants of uncertainty. *Cognition* 11, 143–158.

Kelly, K., and C. Glymour (1987). On convergence to the truth and nothing but the truth. Ms., Carnegie-Mellon University.

Klayman, J., and Y.-W. Ha (1987). Confirmation, disconfirmation, and information in hypothesis testing. *Psychological Review* 94, 211–228.

Nisbett, R., and E. Borgida (1975). Attribution and the psychology of prediction. *Journal of Personality and Social Psychology* 32, 932–943.

Nisbett, R., D. Krantz, C. Jepson, and Z. Kunda (1983). The use of statistical heuristics in everyday inductive reasoning. *Psychological Review* 90, 339–363.

Nisbett, R., and L. Ross (1980). *Human inference: Strategies and shortcomings of social judgment.* Englewood Cliffs, NJ: Prentice-Hall.

Nisbett, R., H. Zukier, and R. Lemley (1981). The dilution effect: Nondiagnostic information weakens the implications of diagnostic information. *Cognitive Psychology* 13, 248–277.

Osherson, D., E. Smith, and E. Shafir (1986). Some origins of belief. *Cognition* 24, 197–224.

Osherson, D., and S. Weinstein (1986). Identification in the limit of first order structures. *Journal of Philosophical Logic* 15, 55–81.

Osherson, D., and S. Weinstein (1989). Paradigms of truth detection. *Journal of Philosophical Logic* 18, 1–42.

Piaget, J., and B. Inhelder (1975). *The origin of the idea of chance in children.* New York: Norton.

Rips, L. (1983). Cognitive processes in propositional reasoning. *Psychological Review* 90, 38–71.

Rips, L. (1987). Mental muddles. In M. Brand and R. Harnish, eds., *The representation of knowledge and belief.* Tucson, AZ: University of Arizona Press.

Sainsbury, R. M. (1988). *Paradoxes.* Cambridge: Cambridge University Press.

Shafer, G. (1976). *A mathematical theory of evidence.* Princeton, NJ: Princeton University Press.

Shafer, G. (1981). Jeffrey's rule of conditioning. *Philosophy of Science* 48, 337–362.

Shafir, E., E. Smith, and D. Osherson (1987). Typicality and reasoning fallacies. Ms., MIT.

Skyrms, B. (1986). *Choice and chance: An introduction to inductive logic.* 3rd ed. Belmont, MA: Wadsworth.

Slovic, P., B. Fischhoff, and S. Lichtenstein (1980). Fact versus fears: Understanding perceived risk. In R. Schwing and W. A. Albers, eds., *Societal risk assessment: How safe is safe enough?* New York: Plenum.

Smith, E., and D. Osherson (1984). Conceptual combination with prototype concepts. *Cognitive Science* 8, 337–361.

Tversky, A. (1977). Features of similarity. *Psychological Review* 84, 327–352.

Tversky, A., and D. Kahneman (1973). Availability: A heuristic for judging frequency and probability. *Cognitive Psychology* 5, 207–232.

Tversky, A., and D. Kahneman (1974). Judgment under uncertainty: Heuristics and biases. *Science* 185, 1124–1131.

Tversky, A., and D. Kahneman (1980). Causal schemes in judgments under uncertainty. In M. Fishbein, ed., *Progress in social psychology.* Hillsdale, NJ: L. Erlbaum Associates.

Tversky, A., and D. Kahneman (1982a). Judgments of and by representativeness. In Kahneman, Slovic, and Tversky 1982.

Tversky, A., and D. Kahneman (1982b). Evidential impact of base rates. In Kahneman, Slovic, and Tversky 1982.

Tversky, A., and D. Kahneman (1983). Extensional versus intuitive reasoning: The conjunction fallacy in probability judgment. *Psychological Review* 90, 292–315.

Wonnacott, R., and T. Wonnacott (1985). *Introductory statistics.* 4th ed. New York: Wiley.

Chapter 4
Choice
Paul Slovic

I cannot, for want of sufficient premises, advise you what to determine, but if you please I will tell you how.... My way is to divide half a sheet of paper by a line into two columns; writing over the one Pro, *and over the other* Con. *Then, during three or four days' consideration, I put down under the different heads short hints of the different motives, that at different times occur to me* for *or* against *the measure. When I have thus got them all together in one view, I endeavor to estimate the respective weights ... [to] find at length where the balance lies.... And, though the weight of reasons cannot be taken with the precision of algebraic quantities, yet, when each is thus considered, separately and comparatively, and the whole matter lies before me, I think I can judge better, and am less liable to make a rash step; and in fact I have found great advantage for this kind of equation, in what may be called* moral *or* prudential algebra.

Benjamin Franklin, 1772
(cited in Bigelow 1887)

Choice (also known as decision making) is the essence of intelligent, purposeful behavior. Although decision making has been studied for centuries by philosophers, mathematicians, economists, and statisticians, it has a relatively short history within psychology. The first extensive review of the theory of decision making was published in the *Psychological Bulletin* by Edwards (1954). This paper introduced psychologists to the "exceedingly elaborate, mathematical and voluminous" (p. 380) economic literature on choice and reviewed the handful of relevant experimental studies then in existence.

Edwards's review was followed by a rapid proliferation of theories of choice and decision making, along with carefully controlled experiments designed to test these theories. This work followed two parallel streams. One of these streams, the theory of riskless choice, had its origins in the notions of utility maximization put forth by Jeremy Bentham and James Mill. The first formal economic theories based on these notions assumed that decision makers are (1) completely informed about the possible courses of action and their consequences, (2) infinitely sensitive to differences in alternatives, and (3) rational in the sense that they can rank order the possible choices and make decisions so as to maximize some subjective measure of value or welfare—usually designated by the term *utility*.

The second stream, the theory of risky choice, deals with decisions made in the face of uncertainty about the events that will determine the outcomes of one's actions. Maximization also plays a key role in these theories, but the quantity to be maximized becomes, due to the uncertainty involved, *expected utility*. Tests of the theory that individuals behave so as to maximize expected utility have been the topic of hundreds of experiments, most of which studied reactions to well-defined manipulations of simple gambles as their basic research paradigm.

Between 1955 and 1960 another development was taking place that was to have a profound influence on the study of decision making. This was the work of Simon (1956), who sharply criticized the notion of maximization as used in expected utility theory. Simon argued that actual decision-making behavior is better described in terms of *bounded rationality*. A boundedly rational decision maker attempts to attain some satisfactory, though not necessarily maximal, level of achievement, a goal that was labeled *satisficing*. Simon's conceptualization highlighted the role of perception, cognition, and learning in decision making and directed researchers to examine the psychological processes by which decision problems are represented and information is used in action selection. (See chapter 5 for further discussion.)

In recent years the information-processing view has dominated the empirical study of decision making. Both streams of research, on risky and riskless choice, have been merged in a torrent of studies aimed at understanding the mental operations associated with judgment and decision making. The result has been a far more complicated portrayal of decision making than that provided by the utility maximization theory. It is now generally recognized that, although utility maximization can predict the *outcomes* of some decision-making processes, it provides only limited insight into the *processes* by which decisions are made. This does not necessarily mean that utility maximization is not a valid principle for prescribing how decisions *should* be made. Indeed, as we will see, utility theory still forms the basis for the analysis of many applied decision problems.

In sum, the theoretical status of the field of decision making is now undergoing a period of reexamination and criticism. Nevertheless, a coherent body of empirical findings exists and is beginning to be applied toward the solution of important practical problems faced by individuals, organizations, and societies in the world outside the laboratory. Some paths leading to this state of affairs are described in this chapter.

4.1 Decision Theory: A Model for Rational Choice

Decision theory provides a model, based on the maximization of expected utility, that serves as a "rational" basis for making decisions (for discussions of rationality in judgment, see chapters 3 and 7). It is rational in the sense that it attempts to prescribe a course of action that is consistent with the decision maker's goals and expectations and maximizes the decision maker's expected satisfaction.

In this model, decisions made in the face of risk are typically represented by a payoff matrix in which the rows correspond to alternative acts the decision makers can select and the columns correspond to possible states of nature. In the cells of the payoff matrix are consequences contingent on the joint occurrence of a decision and a state of nature, and a "payoff" representing the subjective value or "utility" of each consequence. A simple illustration for a traveler is given in table 4.1. An analogous pictorial representation takes the form of a decision tree (see figure 4.1). Trees

Table 4.1
Matrix form of a simple decision problem.

		State of nature	
Alternative act		Sun (E_1)	Rain (E_2)
A_1	Carry umbrella	(+1) Stay dry carrying umbrella	(+1) Stay dry carrying umbrella
A_2	Leave umbrella	(+2) Dry and unburdened	(0) Wet and unburdened

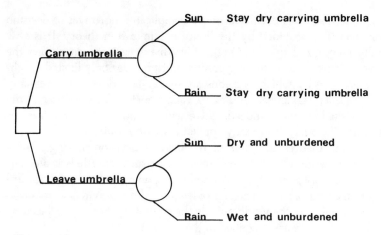

Figure 4.1
Decision tree for the traveler. The tree should be read from left to right. Decision points are indicated by squares. Points of uncertainty, and their associated probabilities, are indicated by circles.

have the advantage of being better able to represent complex problems involving sequences of decisions over time.

Since it is impossible to make a decision that will turn out best in every eventuality, decision theorists view choice alternatives as gambles and try to choose according to the "best bet." In 1738 Bernoulli defined the notion of best bet as one that maximizes the quantity

$$EU(A) = \sum_{i=1}^{n} P(E_i)U(X_i),$$

where $EU(A)$ represents the expected utility of a course of action, A, that has consequences $X_1, X_2, \ldots, X_n$ depending on events $E_1, E_2, \ldots, E_n$; $P(E_1)$ represents the probability of the ith outcome of that action; and $U(X_i)$ represents the utility of that outcome. If we assume that the values in parentheses in the cells of table 4.1 represent the traveler's utilities for the various consequences and if the probability of sun and rain are taken to be 0.6 and 0.4, respectively, we can compute the expected utility for carrying the umbrella (A_1) or leaving it behind (A_2) as follows:

$$EU(A_1) = 0.6(+1) + 0.4(+1) = 1.0$$

$$EU(A_2) = 0.6(+2) + 0.4(0) = 1.2.$$

In this situation, leaving the umbrella would be the recommended act because it has greater expected utility than taking the umbrella along.

The same form of analysis can be applied to computing the expected utility of much more complex and consequential decisions. In their excellent primer on decision analysis Behn and Vaupel (1982) apply the decision tree shown in figure 4.2 to the choice dilemmas faced by a woman who may be a carrier for hemophilia. The woman faces four sequential decisions. She has to decide whether to take a carrier test. She has to decide whether to become pregnant. If she does become pregnant, she has to decide whether to take the amniocentesis test and then whether to have an abortion or give birth. Her later decisions will be influenced by the results of her earlier decisions. Her problem is complicated by the clash of conflicting consequences. She wants a child but feels that giving birth to a hemophiliac son would have great costs for herself, her family, the child, and society. She would prefer not to take the painful, somewhat dangerous, and costly amniocentesis test, which is the only way to learn whether the fetus is male or female (hemophilia is passed from the mother to her male offspring). She would prefer not to have an abortion, and she knows that, if she aborts a male fetus, the chances (in most situations) are 50 percent that the fetus would have been a normal child; however, the fetus might be a hemophiliac and she would prefer not to give birth to a hemophiliac. The deepest ethical dilemmas in this problem stem from these conflicting values concerning parenthood, abortion, and the pain and other costs of hemophilia, and from the weight given to the interests and preferences of the woman, her husband, the child, and society. Using this tree diagram as an aid, a skilled decision counselor may be able to help the woman and her husband think through this difficult choice.

A major advance in decision theory came when von Neumann and Morgenstern (1947) developed a formal theoretical justification for the criterion of maximizing expected utility. They showed that, if an individual's preferences satisfied certain basic axioms of rational behavior, then that individual's decisions could be described as the maximization of expected utility. Savage (1954) later generalized the theory to allow the $P(E_i)$ values to represent subjective or personal probabilities, defined in terms of people's beliefs about the likelihoods of events.

Maximization of expected utility commands respect as a guideline for wise behavior because it follows directly from axiomatic principles that presumably would be accepted by any rational person. One such principle, that of *transitivity*, asserts that, if a person prefers outcome A to outcome B and outcome B to outcome C, then that person should prefer outcome A to outcome C. Any individual who is deliberately and systematically intransitive can be turned into a "money pump." Let us assume that Harry prefers A to B, B to C, and C to A. You can say to him, "I'll give you C. Now, for a penny, I'll take back C and give you B." Since he prefers B to C, he accepts. Next you offer to replace B with A for another penny and again he accepts. You complete the cycle by offering to replace A by C for

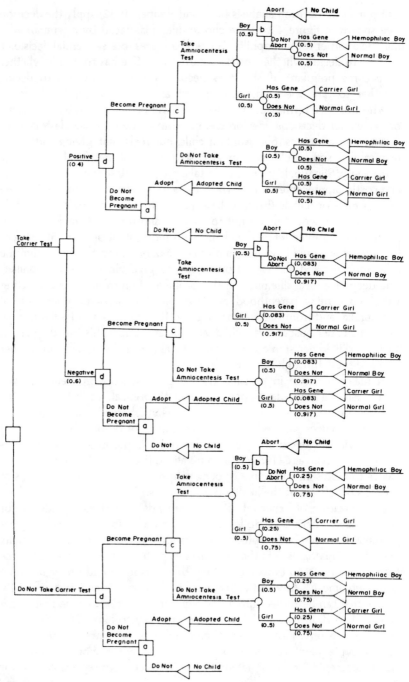

Figure 4.2
Decision tree for a woman who may be a carrier for hemophilia. From Behn and Vaupel 1982.

another penny; Harry accepts and is three cents poorer, back where he started, and ready for another round.

A second important tenet of rationality, known as the *extended sure-thing principle*, states that, if an outcome X_i is the same for two risky actions, then one should disregard the value of X_i in choosing between the two options. Another way to state this principle is that outcomes that are not affected by one's choice should not influence one's decision.

These two principles, combined with several others of technical importance, imply a rather powerful conclusion: subjective values or utilities exist for each possible outcome such that act X is preferred to act Y if and only if the expected utility of X exceeds the expected utility of Y.

Following the development of this axiomatic justification, expected utility maximization has achieved great stature as the cornerstone of approaches designed to help people make optimal decisions. The applied field of *decision analysis* assumes that rational decision makers will wish to follow the basic axioms and thus will select actions that are logically consistent with their basic preferences for outcomes (utilities) and their beliefs about the probabilities of the events on which those outcomes depend. Given this assumption, the practical problem becomes one of enumerating the choice options and critical outcomes within the framework of decision trees and measuring the various utilities and probabilities so that expected utility can be calculated for each choice option.

To see how decision analysis applies to expected utility maximization, consider the problem of a physician attempting to help a patient with cancer of the larynx (voice box) choose between surgery and radiation therapy (McNeil, Weichselbaum, and Pauker 1981). Surgery produces longer life expectancy but carries with it the loss of normal speech (some communication is possible through esophageal speech or the use of mechanical aids). Radiation therapy creates nausea and hair loss but entails little risk of long-term side effects (for those who survive the cancer). Speech remains normal. The physician/analyst needs to elicit two utility curves from the patient. One curve represents the patient's preferences for surviving varying numbers of years with normal speech. The second represents the patient's preferences for surviving varying numbers of years with artificial speech, as a consequence of surgery. The utilities for these curves are obtained by asking the patient to equate hypothetical situations offering periods of guaranteed survival with gambles offering a .5 chance of death within a few months (considered zero years of survival) and a .5 chance of survival for a specified period. Other questions ask the patient to indicate how many years of survival with artificial speech would be equivalent in utility to a specified period of survival with normal speech. Figure 4.3 describes this sequential process of developing the utility curves for normal and artificial speech.

To determine the optimal therapy, the analyst calculates the expected utility (EU) for surgery and for radiation therapy according to the formula

$$EU = \sum_i U_i P_i,$$

where U represents the utility of living up to age i with or without normal speech (depending upon which alternative is being evaluated) and P_i indicates the probability of living up to age i. The utilities are determined from the right-hand panel of figure 4.3. The probabilities are obtained from survival data for patients treated by surgery or radiation. The treatment with the higher expected utility is then recommended to the patient.

Besides its applications to medical problems, decision analysis has been applied to such complex and diverse problems as deciding whether or not to seed hurricanes, selecting experiments for space missions, and choosing whether to build a nuclear or a coal-burning power plant. For further details about the theory and practice of decision analysis, see Raiffa 1968 and von Winterfeldt and Edwards 1986.

4.2   Cognitive Processes in Decision Making

Whereas the normative study of decision making attempts to determine what choices a person *should* make, descriptive studies examine the nature of unaided decisions. The first hypothesis that was tested was, not surprisingly, that people actually do choose in ways that maximize their expected utility. Early studies measured subjective probabilities and utilities for simple gambles and used these values with moderate success to predict people's choices among these gambles (Davidson, Suppes, and Siegel 1957; Mosteller and Nogee 1951; Tversky 1967a,b). However, other studies tested the descriptive validity of the utility axioms and observed numerous violations of transitivity, the sure-thing principle, and other basic principles of the rational model (Allais 1953; Coombs and Huang 1976; Ellsberg 1961; Kahneman and Tversky 1979; MacCrimmon and Larsson 1976; Slovic and Tversky 1974; Tversky 1969). Consider, for example, the paradox put forth by Allais (1953) that contrasts the hypothetical decision situations shown in table 4.2, each involving a pair of gambles (with payoffs expressed in units of one million dollars). Most people prefer gamble 1 to gamble 2, presumably because the small probability of missing the chance of a lifetime to become rich seems very unattractive. At the same time most people also prefer gamble 4 to gamble 3, presumably because the large difference between the payoffs dominates the small difference between the chances of winning. However, this seemingly innocent pair of preferences is incompatible with utility theory. The first preference implies that

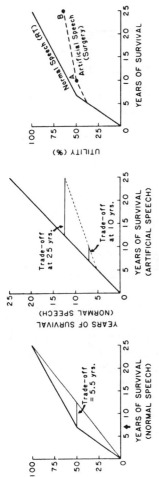

The left panel is a plot of utility or preference for various lengths of survival with normal speech. The light diagonal line represents the utility for a person who values a year of life in the short term and a year in the long term as equivalent. The bold line represents that of a person who places greater value on short-term years. When faced with a choice between a 50:50 risk of dying in the next few weeks in order to have a chance of a full life expectancy of 25 years, on the one hand, and a shorter guaranteed intermediate survival, on the other, such a person would choose the latter. In other words, the patient would be willing to "trade off" a portion of the life expectancy to avoid the risk of the gamble. The person in question considers a 50:50 gamble between 0 and 25 years of survival (average, 12.5) equivalent to seven years of certain survival (lower arrow). Thus, 5.5 years would be traded off to avoid the gamble. Since the average utility of the gamble is (0 per cent + 100 per cent)/2, we can plot a point corresponding to seven years and 50 per cent utility.

The center panel summarizes a quality comparison between artificial speech (horizontal axis) and normal speech (vertical axis). The bold line summarizes the relation for a person for whom the two states are equivalent. The broken line summarizes that relation for a person for whom artificial speech would constitute an important loss of quality of life. Such people would usually trade off some period of survival to maintain normal speech. The patient described here considers 10 years of survival with artificial speech to be equivalent to only seven years of survival with normal speech, and 25 years of survival with artificial speech to be equivalent to 12.5 years with normal speech.

The right panel combines the time and quality preferences derived in the left and center panels to create utility curves for comparing survivals with artificial and normal speech. Point A reflects the trade-off made at 10 years, and Point B that at 25 years. In other words, the utility of 10 years of survival with artificial speech equals that of seven years with normal speech. RT denotes radiotherapy. For survivals below five years, this person would not be willing to trade off any years to maintain normal speech.

Figure 4.3
Construction of utility curves for survival with normal speech and with artificial speech. From McNeil, Weichselbaum, and Pauker 1981.

Table 4.2
Decision paradox presented by Allais (1953).

Situation 1. Choose between

Gamble 1:	$\frac{1}{2}$ with probability 1
Gamble 2:	$2\frac{1}{2}$ with probability .10
	$\frac{1}{2}$ with probability .89
	0 with probability .01

Situation 2. Choose between

Gamble 3:	$\frac{1}{2}$ with probability .11
	0 with probability .89
Gamble 4:	$2\frac{1}{2}$ with probability .10
	0 with probability .90

$$.11u(\tfrac{1}{2}) > .10u(2\tfrac{1}{2}) + .01u(0),$$

whereas the second preference implies the opposite:

$$.10u(2\tfrac{1}{2}) + .01u(0) > .11u(\tfrac{1}{2}).$$

Savage (1954) offered an illuminating introspective analysis of Allais's example, illustrating how it violates the extended sure-thing principle (common outcomes should be disregarded) of utility theory. He admitted that he intuitively preferred gamble 1 to gamble 2 and gamble 4 to gamble 3. Then he adopted another way of looking at the problem: the gambles can be operationalized by a lottery with 100 numbered tickets, one of which is drawn at random to determine the outcome according to the payoff matrix presented in figure 4.4. If one of the tickets numbered 12 to 100 is drawn, it does not matter, in either situation, which gamble is chosen. Hence, one should consider only the possibility that one of the tickets numbered 1 to 11 is drawn, in which case the two choice situations are identical. Limiting our attention to tickets 1 to 11, the problem in both situations is whether a $10 : 1$ chance of winning $2\frac{1}{2}$ million dollars is preferred to the certainty of winning $\frac{1}{2}$ million dollars. If one prefers gamble 1 to gamble 2, then, by the sure-thing principle, one should also prefer gamble 3 to gamble 4.

Another well-known violation of the extended sure-thing principle occurs in the following problem, created by Ellsberg (1961):

Imagine an urn known to contain 90 balls. Thirty of the balls are red, the remaining 60 are black and yellow in unknown proportion. One ball is to be drawn at random from the urn. Consider acts 1 and 2 and their associated payoffs, displayed in table 4.3. If you bet on red, act 1, you will win $100 if a red ball is drawn and nothing if a black or yellow ball is drawn. If you bet on black, act 2, you will win $100 if a black ball is drawn and nothing if a red or yellow ball is drawn.

Ticket number

		1	2-11	12-100
Situation 1	Gamble 1	$\frac{1}{2}$	$\frac{1}{2}$	$\frac{1}{2}$
	Gamble 2	0	$2\frac{1}{2}$	$\frac{1}{2}$
Situation 2	Gamble 3	$\frac{1}{2}$	$\frac{1}{2}$	0
	Gamble 4	0	$2\frac{1}{2}$	0

Figure 4.4
Matrix representation of Allais's problem. From Slovic and Tversky 1974.

Now consider acts 3 and 4 in table 4.3, under the same circumstances.

In this problem the extended sure-thing principle implies that one must choose either acts 1 and 3 or acts 2 and 4 in the two situations. Most people select acts 1 and 4, thus violating the principle. Presumably, they prefer to bet on payoffs whose probabilities are known precisely rather than on payoffs with ambiguous probabilities.

Transitivity of preferences is another key principle of expected utility theory, because it is necessary for the existence of any stable utility function. Tversky (1969) demonstrated violations of transitivity in a situation in which gambles varied in probability and payoff as shown in table 4.4. The gambles were constructed so that adjacent gambles had small differences in probability, which subjects tended to ignore when making choices. However, for comparisons between gambles lying far apart in the chain, the cumulative difference in probability of winning (or expected value) dominated the decision. Thus, subjects preferred a to b, b to c, c to d, d to e, but e to a, thereby violating transitivity. Tversky's subjects did not realize their preferences were intransitive and some even denied this possibility emphatically.

Some decision theorists have interpreted these and other violations as indicating that utility theory is neither normatively nor descriptively valid. Others have defended the logical soundness of the axioms and argued that the fact that people violate them indicates the need for help from decision analysis (Raiffa 1968; Savage 1954; Tversky and Kahneman 1986).

As it became apparent that people's choices were not strictly consistent with utility maximization, the experimental study of decision making be-

Table 4.3
Actions and expected payoffs in the problem posed by Ellsberg (1961).

| | 30 | 60 | |
	Red	Black	Yellow
Act 1: Bet on red	$100	$0	$0
Act 2: Bet on black	$0	$100	$0
Act 3: Bet on red or yellow	$100	$0	$100
Act 4: Bet on black or yellow	$0	$100	$100

Table 4.4
Gambles used as stimuli by Tversky (1969). Reprinted by permission of the author.

Gamble	Probability of winning	Payoff	Expected value
a	7/24	5.00	1.46
b	8/24	4.75	1.58
c	9/24	4.50	1.69
d	10/24	4.25	1.77
e	11/24	4.00	1.83

gan to focus on information processing. Cognitive psychology, with its emphasis on internal processes, mental limitations, and the ways in which the processing of information is shaped by these limitations, has come to have a profound influence on experimental research.

4.2.1   Confronting Human Limitations: Bounded Rationality

The traditional view of human beings' higher mental processes assumes that we are, in Shakespeare's words, "noble in reason, infinite in faculties." A twentieth-century expression of this esteem was provided by a well-known economist who asserted, "We are so built that what seems reasonable to us is likely to be confirmed by experience or we could not live in the world at all" (Knight 1921, 227).

Research in cognitive psychology has painted a much more modest picture of human capabilities. In his influential study of classification and coding, Miller (1956) demonstrated the limitations of people's ability to attend to and process sensory signals. Similarly, Bruner, Goodnow, and Austin (1956) observed that subjects in concept formation tasks were experiencing a condition of cognitive strain, which they attempted to reduce by employing simplification strategies. About the same time, the classical view of behavioral adequacy in decision making was being challenged on psychological grounds. A leading critic of utility maximization was Simon (1959), who observed,

> The classical theory is a theory of a man choosing among fixed and known alternatives, to each of which is attached known consequences. But when perception and cognition intervene between the decision-maker and his objective environment, this model no longer proves adequate. We need a description of the choice process that recognizes that alternatives are not given but must be sought; and a description that takes into account the arduous task of determining what consequences will follow on each alternative. (p. 272)

As an alternative to the maximization hypothesis, Simon introduced the notion of *bounded rationality*, which asserts that cognitive limitations force decision makers to construct simplified models of their problems. Simon argued that the decision maker behaves rationally with respect to this simplified model. To predict decisions, we must understand how this simplified model is constructed through processes of perception, thinking, and learning.

According to Simon, the key to simplification was the replacement of the maximization goal by the *satisficing* principle: outcomes are first classified as "satisfactory" or "unsatisfactory" with respect to each of the relevant attributes; the first alternative that satisfies this level of aspiration for each attribute is selected. In choosing an apartment, for example, a student may select the first one that is satisfactory with regard to cost, distance from school, and size. What is considered as satisfactory on each of these criteria may change with time and experience as one's aspiration level increases or decreases (see chapter 5).

Satisficing is simpler than utility maximization in several important respects. It bypasses the problems of evaluating the overall utility of each outcome or of comparing diverse attributes. It does not call for detailed exploration of all the available alternatives, and it requires only a very limited computational capacity.

During the past twenty years the skeleton theory of bounded rationality has been fleshed out. As noted in chapter 3, we have learned much about human cognitive limitations and their implications for decision making. Numerous studies have shown that people (including experts) have great difficulty in judging probabilities, making predictions, and otherwise attempting to cope with uncertainty (Kahneman, Slovic, and Tversky 1982). Detailed studies of information processing in choice have substantiated many of the general concepts and specific hypotheses proposed by Simon. Information-processing studies have provided evidence not only for satisficing but indeed for a wide variety of cognitive mechanisms for making decisions (see, for example, Bettman 1979; Lopes 1982; Johnson and Payne 1985; Payne 1982; Payne, Laughhunn, and Crum 1980, 1981; Slovic, Lichtenstein, and Fischhoff 1988; Svenson 1979; Montgomery and Svenson 1989).

4.2.2   Framing and Response-Mode Effects

Choice processes have been studied in ways too numerous to review here. Let us look at just one of them, an idiosyncratic line of research that seems to have important implications for descriptive and normative theory and for the practice of decision analysis. This series of studies has examined the consistency of preferences in light of changes in the ways that the choice problem is described or the preference is expressed.

If stable preferences exist within an individual, and if these preferences are accurately measured, then they should be invariant across equivalent versions of the same choice problem and across equivalent ways of measuring preference within the same problem.

A sizable body of research shows that such invariance does not exist. Preferences seem remarkably sensitive to the way in which a choice problem is described or "framed" and the mode of response by which the preference is expressed.

Framing Effects

The important work of Kahneman and Tversky (1979; Tversky and Kahneman 1981) has demonstrated the strong effects of framing on choice behavior. Much as a visual scene can be viewed from different vantage points (and look quite different from each), the same decision problem can be subject to alternative frames and evoke different preferences in each. The effect of framing decision outcomes in terms of either gains or losses is shown by the following pairs of problems, given by Tversky and Kahneman (1981) to separate groups of subjects:

Problem 1
Imagine that the U.S. is preparing for the outbreak of an unusual Asian disease, which is expected to kill 600 people. Two alternative programs to combat the disease have been proposed. Assume that the exact scientific estimates of the consequences of the programs are as follows:

If Program A is adopted, 200 people will be saved.

If Program B is adopted, there is 1/3 probability that 600 people will be saved, and 2/3 probability that no people will be saved.

Which of the two programs would you favor?

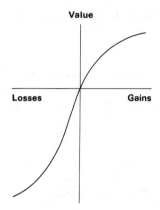

Figure 4.5
A typical value function. From Kahneman and Tversky 1979.

Problem 2
(Same cover story as problem 1.)

If Program C is adopted, 400 people will die.

If Program D is adopted, there is 1/3 probability that nobody will die, and 2/3 probability that 600 people will die.

Which of the two programs would you favor?

Although the two problems are formally identical, the preferences they evoke tend to be quite different. In a study of college students, 72 percent chose program A over program B, whereas 78 percent (of a different group) chose program D over program C. Kahneman and Tversky explain this reversal of preference through reference to a value function representing the psychological perception of gains and losses relative to some psychologically neutral reference point (see figure 4.5). As the figure indicates, the value function is steeper for losses than for gains, meaning that a given change in status hurts more as a loss than it pleases as a gain. Another important feature is that the value function is concave above the reference point and convex below it, meaning, for example, that the subjective difference between gaining (or losing) $10 and $20 is greater than the difference between gaining (or losing) $110 and $120. The "save lives" frame of problem 1 induces a reference point of 600 lives lost, whereas the "people will die" wording of problem 2 induces a reference point of no lives lost. Thus, the outcomes of problem 1 fall on the concave gain region of the value function and the outcomes of problem 2 fall on the convex loss region, which leads to the different choice responses.

Another example of framing effects comes from the following problems posed by Kahneman and Tversky (1982):

Problem 1
Imagine that, in addition to whatever else you have, you have been given a cash gift of $200. You are now asked to choose between (A) a sure gain of $50 and (B) a 25 percent chance of winning $200 and a 75 percent chance of winning nothing.

Problem 2
Imagine that, in addition to whatever else you have, you have been given a cash gift of $400. You are now asked to choose between (C) a sure loss of $150, and (D) a 75 percent chance of losing $200 and a 25 percent chance of losing nothing.

Most people choose A over B and D over C. Yet the options presented in the two problems are identical with respect to their final outcomes. There is no valid reason to prefer the gamble in one version and the sure outcome in the other. Choosing the sure gain in the first problem yields a total gain of $200 plus $50, or $250. Choosing the sure loss in the second version yields the same result through the deduction of $150 from $400. The choice of the gamble in either problem yields a 75 percent chance of winning $200 and a 25 percent chance of winning $400. If the respondents to these problems took a comprehensive view of the consequences, as is assumed by theories of rational choice, they would combine the cash gift with the available options and evaluate the composite outcome. Instead they ignore the gift and evaluate the first problem as a choice between gains and the second as a choice between losses. The reversal of preferences is induced by the two different frames given these problems.

Numerous other framing effects have been demonstrated (see, for example, Hershey and Schoemaker 1980; Schoemaker and Kunreuther 1979; Slovic, Fischhoff, and Lichtenstein 1982; Thaler 1985). As Tversky and Kahneman have pointed out, these effects are important because they are sizable (often inducing complete reversals of preference), because they violate the rational model of choice (utility theory), and because they determine the pleasure or pain, satisfaction or dissatisfaction associated with experiencing the outcomes of one's choices.

Response-Mode Effects

The way in which individuals express their preferences in a decision problem is an important aspect of framing. Although people are sometimes free to choose their manner of responding, more often some external source defines the problem as one of judgment (evaluating options individually) or choice (selecting one from two or more options). Utility theory presumes an equivalence between judgment and choice on the grounds that every option has a value or utility that determines its attractiveness in both contexts. However, research has demonstrated that the information-processing mechanisms used in making choices are often quite different from the mechanisms employed in judging single options. As a result, choices and evaluative judgments of the same options often differ to a considerable extent.

An early demonstration of response-mode effects used simple gambles as stimuli (for instance, .3 chance to win $16 and .7 chance to lose $4). Slovic and Lichtenstein (1968) found that ratings of a gamble's attractiveness and choices between pairs of gambles were influenced primarily by the *probabilities* of winning and losing, whereas buying and selling prices (for instance, "What's the most you would pay for a chance to play this gamble?" or "What's the least amount for which you would sell a ticket to play it?") were primarily determined by the *dollar amounts* that could be won or lost.

Lichtenstein and Slovic (1971) built upon this result. They hypothesized that, if people process information differently when making choices and setting prices, it should be possible to construct pairs of gambles such that the same individual would choose one member of the pair but set a higher price on the other. They demonstrated this predicted effect in several studies, including one conducted on the floor of the Four Queens Casino in Las Vegas (Lichtenstein and Slovic 1973). A typical pair of gambles in that study consisted of

Bet A: 11/12 chance to win 12 chips

1/12 chance to lose 24 chips

Bet B: 2/12 chance to win 79 chips

10/12 chance to lose 5 chips,

where each chip was worth 25 cents. Each subject first made a simple choice, A or B. Later the subject indicated a minimum selling price for each bet ("What's the least amount for which you would sell a ticket to play it?"). For this pair of gambles, bets A and B were chosen about equally often, across subjects. However, bet B received a higher selling price about 88 percent of the time. Of the subjects who chose bet A, 87 percent gave a higher selling price to bet B. This is no minor inconsistency. Lichtenstein and Slovic (1971) showed that subjects who persisted in this pattern of preferences could be turned into "money pumps," continuously giving money to the experimenters without ever playing the gambles.

These response-mode induced reversals of preference have been replicated in numerous other studies of risky choice (reviewed in Slovic and

Lichtenstein 1983). Of particular interest is a replication of the original Lichtenstein and Slovic studies performed by two economists, Grether and Plott (1979). Grether and Plott were concerned about reversals because they imply that preferences are not stable and consistent as utility theory demands. They conducted a series of experiments "to discredit the psychologists' works as applied to economics" (p. 623). Their design was based on thirteen criticisms or explanations that would eliminate the preference-reversal phenomenon, or render it irrelevant to economic theory. One explanatory factor was that the original experimenters were psychologists, which might have led the subjects to behave peculiarly. To eliminate reversals, they introduced numerous manipulations such as using special incentive systems to heighten motivation, controlling for the effects of previous wins or losses, and having economists conduct the study. To their surprise, preference reversals remained much in evidence despite their vigorous attempts to eradicate them. More recently Tversky, Sattath, and Slovic (1988) have demonstrated that preference reversals resulting from response-mode effects are not limited to gambles but are systematically present across a wide range of choice problems.

What accounts for the strong response-mode effects that have been observed in so many different studies? Several explanatory concepts have been proposed. Two of these, justification and compatibility, will be discussed below.

4.2.3   Justification and Choice

One reason that choices may differ systematically from judgments of individual options is that choice may invoke qualitative reasoning of a form very different from the mechanisms used in making single judgments. One hypothesis is that much of the deliberation prior to choice consists of constructing a concise, coherent reason or set of reasons that justifies the selection of one option over the others (for instance, "I prefer this gamble because it has a much better chance of winning" or "I prefer that gamble because I desperately need $20 and that is the only option that gives me a chance to get that amount").

Tversky (1972) provided evidence in support of an "elimination by aspects" model of choice, which gives justification processes a key role. According to this model, options are viewed as sets of aspects; that is, a car has a model type, a price, a certain level of gasoline consumption, and so forth. At each stage in the choice process, one aspect is selected, with probability proportional to its importance. The options that are not adequate for each selected aspect are eliminated from the set of options considered at the following stage. For example, one might start by eliminating all vehicles that are not compact four-door sedans. Within this class

Table 4.5
Example of paired options used in the study conducted by Slovic (1975).

	Cash	Coupon book worth
Gift package A	$10	——
Gift package B	$20	$18

of vehicles the next attribute considered might be price—all cars costing more than, say, $9,000 might then be eliminated. The next attribute could be fuel economy, with a requirement that the vehicle get 20 or more miles per gallon in city driving. This process could continue until only one vehicle remained or until the small set of alternatives could be evaluated according to some other rule. Tversky argued that elimination by aspects is an appealing process because it is easy both to apply and to justify. It permits a choice to be resolved in a clear-cut fashion without reliance on relative weights, trade-off functions, or other numerical computations and eases demands on the decision maker's limited capacity for intuitive calculation.

The importance of justification processes can also be seen in a study of difficult choices conducted by Slovic (1975). Each of two options was defined by two dimensions differing in importance. To maximize the difficulty of choice, the paired options were designed to have equal worth by making the option that was superior on the more important dimension be so inferior on the lesser dimension that its advantage was canceled. For example, one pair of options involved gift packages with two components, cash and a coupon book offering miscellaneous products and services with a stated monetary value. The subject was shown two such gift packages with one component missing, as in table 4.5. The subject supplied a value for the missing component such that the two options would be equally attractive. After equating various pairs of options, subjects made choices from among the equated pairs. Contrary to expectation, decisions regarding these equally attractive alternatives were not made randomly. Instead, subjects consistently selected the option that was superior on the more important dimension. Slovic hypothesized that this result occurred because reliance on the more important dimension makes a better justification ("I chose this gift package because it provided more cash") than random selection ("They looked about equally attractive, so I flipped a coin"). Tversky, Sattath, and Slovic (1988) showed that the findings by Slovic (1975) stemmed from a general tendency for the more important dimension to be weighted more heavily in choice than in the mode where the subject makes the two options match in value. They attributed the difference between choice and matching both to justification processes and to compatibility effects (see next section).

Justification processes appear to explain the finding by Huber, Payne, and Puto (1982) that the tendency to choose A over B is increased by adding a third option, A', that is inferior to A in all respects (but is not inferior to B). It appears that the presence of A' in the choice set provides an alternative that A is clearly superior to, thereby increasing A's justifiability, even in comparison with B.

Tyszka (1981) and Montgomery (1983) have also advocated theories based on the concept of justification. Montgomery proposed a model that describes the decision process as a search for a dominance structure, whereby decision makers restructure decision problems until they find a perspective that shows a (relatively) conflict-free way to make a choice. This search may involve bolstering or deemphasizing the importance of certain attributes or collapsing two or more attributes into a more comprehensive one.

4.2.4   Compatibility and Choice

Another general mechanism that might underlie response-mode effects is the compatibility principle (Tversky, Sattath, and Slovic 1988). According to this principle, the weight of any input component of a stimulus is enhanced by its compatibility with the output (response). The rationale for this principle is that noncompatibility between input and output requires additional mental transformations, which increase effort and error and reduce impact (Fitts and Seeger 1953; Wickens 1984). Thus, one explanation of why a gamble's payoffs are weighted more heavily in the pricing response mode than in choice is that, being expressed in monetary terms, payoffs are more compatible with prices than with choices.

Demonstration of compatibility effects comes from a study by Slovic, Griffin, and Tversky (in press). The subjects were asked to predict the judgments of an admissions committee of a small, selective college regarding several applicants. For each applicant the subjects received two items of information: a rank on verbal SAT score and the presence or absence of strong extracurricular activities. The subjects were told that the admissions committee ranks all 500 applicants and accepts about the top fourth. Half of the subjects predicted the rank assigned to each applicant, whereas the other half predicted whether each application was accepted or rejected.

The compatibility principle implies that the numerical data (rank SAT) will weigh more heavily in the numerical prediction task, whereas the categorical data (the presence or absence of extracurricular activities) will be relatively more important in the categorical prediction of acceptance or rejection. The results confirmed the hypothesis. For each pair of applicants, in which neither one was better on both items of information, the percentage of responses that favored the applicant with the higher SAT score was

Table 4.6
Example of information given to subjects in study conducted by Slovic and MacPhillamy (1974).

	Student A	Student B
Need for Achievement	——	474
English Skills	470	566
Quantitative Ability	674	——

recorded. Summing across all pairs, this value was 61.4 percent in the numerical prediction task and 44.6 percent in the categorical prediction task. The difference between the groups is highly significant. Evidently, the numerical data had more impact in the numerical task, whereas the categorical data had more impact in the categorical task, consistent with the compatibility principle.

Compatibility may also explain the results of a study by Slovic and MacPhillamy (1974), in which subjects were asked to predict, on the basis of test scores, which of two students, A or B, would get the higher grade-point average in college. One test was common (that is, scores were available for both students); the others were not. In the example shown in table 4.6 the common test is English Skills. The other information was unique: Quantitative Ability for student A and Need for Achievement for student B.

A comparison based on the common dimension involves a simple evaluation of the difference between two scores on the same test, whereas a comparison based on the unique dimensions requires a more complicated evaluation of the relative importance of two different tests. The compatibility principle predicts that the common dimension will be weighted more heavily than the unique dimension because its implications for choice are more directly apparent. This is precisely the result that was observed. In a postexperimental interview most subjects indicated that they did not intend to give more weight to the common dimension and were unaware of doing so.

4.2.5   Labile Values

In considering the influence of behavioral research on choice theories, March (1978) argued that the same limited cognitive capacity that makes it hard for us to predict the future consequences of our acts also makes it hard for us to ascertain our future preferences among those consequences. "Human beings have unstable, inconsistent, incompletely evoked, and imprecise goals at least in part because human abilities limit preference orderliness" (p. 598). March drew upon a rich and diverse array of observations to argue that, contrary to normative theory, preferences are neither absolute, stable, consistent, precise, nor unaffected by the choices they are presumed to control. The framing and response-mode effects described above represent a few pertinent examples of this disorderliness.

Even when cognitive capacity is not strained, preferences may be labile because we do not really know what we want or how we will experience certain outcomes. When considering simple, familiar decision consequences, one's preferences may be well articulated. But the most interesting and important decisions in our lives tend to have novel, unfamiliar, and complex outcomes. In such circumstances our values may be incoherent, not sufficiently thought through (Fischhoff, Slovic, and Lichtenstein 1980). When we think about societal risks, for example, we may have contradictory values (for example, a strong aversion to catastrophic losses of life, but an awareness that we are no more moved by a plane crash with 500 fatalities than one with 300). We may occupy different roles in life (parents, workers, children), each of which produces clear-cut but inconsistent values. We may vacillate between incompatible but strongly held positions (for instance, freedom of speech is inviolate, but it should be denied authoritarian movements). We may not even know how to begin thinking about some issues (for instance, the appropriate trade-offs between the outcomes of surgery for cancer versus the very different outcomes from radiation therapy). We may underestimate our ability to adapt to extremely good or extremely bad circumstances such as winning a lottery or losing a limb (Brickman, Coates, and Janoff-Bulman 1978; Cameron et al. 1973). Our views may change so much over time (say, as we near the hour of decision or the time for experiencing the consequences) that we become disoriented as to what we really think.

At times it seems as though there are rival selves within the same individual, each vying for legitimacy. Schelling (1982) pointed to people who set alarm clocks but do not respond to them, and people who want to quit smoking but cannot. A striking empirical demonstration of multiple selves is provided by Christensen-Szalanski (1984), who recorded the changes in attitudes of pregnant women toward anesthesia before, during, and after labor. The women preferred to avoid using anesthesia during childbirth when asked one month prior to labor and during early labor. During active labor, their preferences shifted suddenly toward using anesthesia. Their preferences shifted back toward avoiding anesthesia when they were asked again one month after childbirth.

Fischhoff, Slovic, and Lichtenstein (1980) noted the problems that labile preferences pose for the measurement of values. Although some practitioners have been sensitive to the possibility that complex elicitation methods may induce errors of assessment (for example, Bursztajn and Hamm 1982; Edwards 1977; Llewellyn-Thomas et al. 1982; von Winterfeldt 1975), most applications of decision analysis assume that people know their own values and that the methods are unbiased channels for translating subjective feelings into analytically usable expressions. Fischhoff, Slovic, and Lichtenstein argued that the strong effects of framing and information-processing considerations, acting upon inchoate preferences, can make elicitation procedures major forces in shaping the expression of values. In such cases the method becomes the message. As shown above, subtle aspects of how problems are posed, questions are phrased, and responses are elicited can have a substantial effect on people's expressed preferences.

4.3   Managing Preferences

There are two potential reactions to the problems posed by labile values, one conservative and one radical. The conservative (decision-theoretic) response assumes that true expressions of value are possible and attempts to clarify them through education (to reduce the uncertainty surrounding preferences) and the use of sophisticated elicitation techniques (to reduce biases). Consider, for example, the problem described earlier in which a physician/analyst attempts to help a patient with cancer of the larynx choose between surgery and radiation therapy. The conservative approach attempts to assess utility functions for varying lengths of survival with and without normal speech—as was illustrated in figure 4.3. The difficulty that patients have in forecasting how they would adapt to artificial speech or radiation therapy means that some education would have to take place prior to the value-assessment procedure. That education might include contact with other patients who did and did not choose surgery. How did these people react to the consequences of their decision? Did they correctly anticipate what it would be like to live without normal speech? Would they make the same decision again? After the education is completed, multiple assessment techniques would be employed to ensure that the patient's utility functions are faithfully captured.

The radical reaction to lability is to abandon the decision-analytic approach on the grounds that it seeks to determine utility functions that do not exist and, as a result, has false pretensions about being able to identify the optimal decision. In the example of laryngeal cancer, decision analysis could produce utility functions that do not truly represent the patient's concerns, leading to recommendations of actions that are not in the patient's best interests. Furthermore, the analytical process itself might raise the patient's anxiety about doing the right thing and increase the chances that the patient would later regret the decision. One possible alternative approach begins with the same educational effort but then asks directly, "Which option do you prefer?" Patient and physician would then sift and weigh alternative reasons (or justifications), trying to develop a rationale for action. A strong rationale might buffer the patient from postdecision regret and make it easier to accept the consequences of the decision. If the patient is an intuitive decision theorist, this process could involve utility functions and maximization rules. However, quite different justifications could be equally legitimate if they have been thoughtfully derived.

Both education and the creation of justifications are forms of deliberate preference management. We manage our preferences in many ways. Aware, to some extent, of our multiple selves and changing tastes, we do such things as join Christmas clubs that bind us to our current preferences (Thaler and Shefrin 1981), much as Ulysses forced his crew to tie him to the mast so that he might withstand the lure of the Sirens.

Deeper understanding of framing effects, which used car salespeople have had for a long time and psychologists are beginning to acquire, could help us manage our preferences more effectively (Thaler 1985). Suppose, for example, that a person with $5,500 in a bank account misplaces a $100 bill. Rather than isolating and dwelling on this painful loss, assimilating it into one's total account may ease the sting by exploiting the perception that $5,500 is not that different from $5,600. Because neither perspective on the loss is inherently the "right" one, the choice between them could be a strategic decision, dependent upon the circumstances. If it is important to ensure that the mistake does not recur, then it might be best to isolate the loss, so as to maximize its impact. If the loss could not have been prevented, or if its impact has been traumatic, then one might well assimilate it, thus reducing the distress it is causing.

The concept of preference management reflects the deep interplay between descriptive phenomena and normative principles. Experimental study of decision processes appears to be forging a new conception of preference, one that may require serious restructuring of normative theories and approaches toward improving decision making.

Suggestions for Further Reading

Decision analysis is examined in detail in Behn and Vaupel 1982 and von Winterfeldt and Edwards 1986. Both are comprehensive and well written. The latter covers technical issues in greater detail as well as the interface between cognitive psychology and decision analysis.

Methods used to study choice processes and the detailed findings obtained with these methods are explored in Bettman 1979, Lopes 1982, Johnson and Payne 1985, Payne 1982, Payne, Laughhunn, and Crum 1980, 1981, van Raiij 1983, and Svenson 1979.

methods are explored in Bettman 1979, Lopes 1982, Johnson and Payne 1985, Montgomery and Svenson 1989, Payne 1982, Payne, Laughhunn, and Crum 1980, 1981, van Raiij 1983, and Svenson 1979.

Comprehensive overviews of psychological studies of decision making are presented in Abelson and Levi 1985 and Slovic, Lichtenstein, and Fischhoff 1988. An excellent set of papers contrasting psychological analyses of choice with economic analyses is presented in Hogarth and Reder 1986.

Questions

4.1 Think of a difficult choice that you have faced in the past or may face in the future. Try to draw a decision tree for this choice, along the lines of the trees in figure 4.1 or figure 4.2. Does this tree seem to clarify your thinking about the problem? What information do you need about critical events and critical outcomes?

4.2 Consider the same choice problem you selected for question 4.1. List the possible actions. Then list the arguments for and against each action, in the style of Benjamin Franklin's letter, quoted at the beginning of the chapter. Does this approach seem natural? Helpful? Compelling?

4.3 What do you think are some of the practical implications of knowing about framing and response-mode effects? How might a clever salesperson employ framing to influence a potential buyer's perception of the cost of a new car?

4.4 The value function shown in figure 4.5 raises some interesting possibilities for combining outcomes in ways that maximize their total subjective value and presumably maximize the pleasure (or minimize the pain) felt by experiencing these events. Thaler and Johnson (1986) call this *hedonic framing*. Two principles of hedonic framing are (1) segregate gains and (2) integrate losses. They pose a problem similar to the following:

> Mr. A was given tickets to two lotteries involving the World Series. He won $50 in one lottery and $20 in the other. Mr. B was given a ticket to a single, larger World Series lottery. He won $75. Who was happier? How might the value function influence the experience of multiple outcomes in this and other situations?

References

Abelson, R. P., and A. Levi (1985). Decision making and decision theory. In G. Lindzey and E. Aronson, eds., *The handbook of social psychology*, vol. 1. 3rd ed. New York: Random House.

Allais, M. (1953). Le comportement de l'homme rationnel devant le risque: Critique des postulats et axiomes de l'école américaine. *Econometrica* 21, 503–546.

Behn, R. D., and J. W. Vaupel (1982). *Quick analysis for busy decision makers*. New York: Basic Books.

Bettman, J. R. (1979). *An information processing theory of consumer choice*. Reading, MA: Addison-Wesley.

Bigelow, J., ed. (1887). *The complete works of Benjamin Franklin*, vol. 4. New York: Putnam.

Brickman, P., D. Coates, and R. Janoff-Bulman (1978). Lottery winners and accident victims: Is happiness relative? *Journal of Personality and Social Psychology* 36, 917–927.

Bruner, J. S., J. J. Goodnow, and G. A. Austin (1956). *A study of thinking*. New York: Wiley.

Bursztajn, H., and R. M. Hamm (1982). The clinical utility of utility assessment. *Medical Decision Making* 2, 161–165.

Cameron, P., G. D. Titus, J. Kostin, and M. Kostin (1973). The life satisfaction of nonnormal persons. *Journal of Counseling and Clinical Psychology* 41, 207–214.

Christensen-Szalanski, J. J. J. (1984). Discount functions and the measurement of patients' values: Women's decisions during childbirth. *Medical Decision Making* 4, 47–58.

Coombs, C. H., and L. C. Huang (1976). Tests of the betweenness property of expected utility. *Journal of Mathematical Psychology* 13, 323–337.

Davidson, D., P. Suppes, and S. Siegel (1957). *Decision making: An experimental approach*. Stanford, CA: Stanford University Press.

Edwards, W. (1954). The theory of decision making. *Psychological Bulletin* 51, 380–417.

Edwards, W. (1977). How to use multiattribute utility measurement for social decision making. *IEEE Transactions on Systems, Man, and Cybernetics*, SMC-7, 326–340.

Ellsberg, D. (1961). Risk, ambiguity, and the Savage axioms. *Quarterly Journal of Economics* 75, 643–669.

Fischhoff, B., P. Slovic, and S. Lichtenstein (1980). Knowing what you want: Measuring labile values. In T. Wallsten, ed., *Cognitive processes in choice and decision behavior.* Hillsdale, NJ: L. Erlbaum Associates.

Fitts, P. M., and C. M. Seeger (1953). S-R compatibility: Spatial characteristics of stimulus and response codes. *Journal of Experimental Psychology* 46, 199–210.

Grether, D. M., and C. R. Plott (1979). Economic theory of choice and the preference reversal phenomenon. *American Economic Review* 69, 623–638.

Hershey, J. C., and P. J. H. Schoemaker (1980). Risk taking and problem context in the domain of losses: An expected utility analysis. *Journal of Risk and Insurance* 47, 111–132.

Hogarth, R. M., and M. W. Reder, eds. (1986). The behavioral foundations of economic theory. *The Journal of Business* 82 (no. 4, pt. 2).

Huber, J., J. W. Payne, and C. Puto (1982). Adding asymmetrically dominated alternatives: Violations of regularity and the similarity hypothesis. *Journal of Consumer Research* 9, 90–98.

Johnson, E. J., and J. W. Payne (1985). Effort and accuracy in choice. *Management Science* 31, 395–414.

Kahneman, D., P. Slovic, and A. Tversky, eds. (1982). *Judgment under uncertainty: Heuristics and biases.* New York: Cambridge University Press.

Kahneman, D., and A. Tversky (1979). Prospect theory. *Econometrica* 47, 263–292.

Kahneman, D., and A. Tversky (1982). The psychology of preference. *Scientific American* 246 (January), 160–173.

Knight, F. H. (1921). *Risk, uncertainty, and profit.* Boston: Houghton-Mifflin.

Lichtenstein, S., and P. Slovic (1971). Reversals of preference between bids and choices in gambling decisions. *Journal of Experimental Psychology* 89, 46–55.

Lichtenstein, S., and P. Slovic (1973). Response-induced reversals of preference in gambling: An extended replication in Las Vegas. *Journal of Experimental Psychology* 101, 16–20.

Llewellyn-Thomas, M., H. J. Sutherland, R. Tibshirani, A. Ciampi, J. E. Till, and N. F. Boyd (1982). The measurement of patients' values in medicine. *Medical Decision Making* 2, 449–462.

Lopes, L. L. (1982). *Toward a procedural theory of judgment.* (Report WHIPP 17.) Madison, WI: Department of Psychology, Wisconsin Human Information Processing Program.

MacCrimmon, K. R., and S. Larsson (1976). Utility theory: Axioms versus "paradoxes." In M. Allais and O. Hagen, eds., *Rational decisions under uncertainty.* Special volume of *Theory and Decisions.*

McNeil, B. J., R. Weichselbaum, and S. G. Pauker (1981). Speech and survival: Tradeoffs between quality and quantity of life in laryngeal cancer. *The New England Journal of Medicine* 305, 982–987.

March, J. G. (1978). Bounded rationality, ambiguity, and the engineering of choice. *The Bell Journal of Economics* 9, 587–608.

Miller, G. A. (1956). The magical number seven, plus or minus two: Some limits on our capacity for processing information. *Psychological Review* 63, 81–97.

Montgomery, H. (1983). Decision rules and the search for a dominance structure: Towards a process model of decision making. In P. Humphreys, O. Svenson, and A. Vari, eds., *Analyzing and aiding decision processes.* Amsterdam: North Holland.

Montgomery, H., and O. Svenson, eds. (1989). *Process and structure in human decision making.* New York: Wiley.

Mosteller, F., and P. Nogee (1951). An experimental measurement of utility. *Journal of Political Economics* 59, 371–404.

Payne, J. W. (1982). Contingent decision behavior. *Psychological Bulletin* 92, 382–401.

Payne, J. W., D. J. Laughhunn, and R. Crum (1980). Translation of gambles and aspiration level effects in risky choice behavior. *Management Science* 26, 1039–1060.

Payne, J. W., D. J. Laughhunn, and R. Crum (1981). Further tests of aspiration level effects in risky choice behavior. *Management Science* 27, 953–958.

Raiffa, H. (1968). *Decision analysis.* Reading, MA: Addison-Wesley.

Savage, L. J. (1954). *The foundation of statistics.* New York: Wiley.

Schelling, T. C. (1982). Identifying that authentic self. Paper presented at the meeting of the Working Group on Rationality, Paris.

Schoemaker, P. J. H., and H. C. Kunreuther (1979). An experimental study of insurance decisions. *Journal of Risk and Insurance* 46, 603–618.

Simon, H. A. (1956). Rational choice and the structure of the environment. *Psychological Review* 63, 129–138.

Simon, H. A. (1959). Theories of decision making in economics and behavioral science. *American Economic Review* 49, 253–283.

Slovic, P. (1975). Choice between equally valued alternatives. *Journal of Experimental Psychology: Human Perception and Performance* 1, 280–287.

Slovic, P., B. Fischhoff, and S. Lichtenstein (1982). Response mode, framing, and information-processing effects in risk assessment. In R. M. Hogarth, ed., *New directions for methodology of social and behavioral science: Question framing and response consistency.* San Francisco: Jossey-Bass.

Slovic, P., D. Griffin, and A. Tversky (in press). Compatibility effects in judgment and choice. In R. M. Hogarth, ed., *Insights in decision making: Theory and applications.* Chicago: University of Chicago Press.

Slovic, P., and S. Lichtenstein (1968). The relative importance of probabilities and payoffs in risk-taking. *Journal of Experimental Psychology Monograph Supplement* 78 (3, pt. 2), 1–18.

Slovic, P., and S. Lichtenstein (1983). Preference reversals: A broader perspective. *American Economic Review* 73, 596–605.

Slovic, P., S. Lichtenstein, and B. Fischhoff (1988). Decision making. In R. C. Atkinson, R. J. Herrnstein, G. Lindzey, and R. D. Luce, eds., *Stevens' handbook of experimental psychology.* 2nd ed. New York: Wiley.

Slovic, P., and D. J. MacPhillamy (1974). Dimensional commensurability and cue utilization in comparative judgment. *Organizational Behavior and Human Performance* 11, 172–194.

Slovic, P., and A. Tversky (1974). Who accepts Savage's axiom? *Behavioral Science* 19, 368–373.

Svenson, O. (1979). Process descriptions of decision making. *Organizational Behavior and Human Performance* 23, 86–112.

Thaler, R. H. (1985). Mental accounting and consumer choice. *Marketing Science* 4, 199–214.

Thaler, R. H., and E. J. Johnson (1986). Hedonic framing and the break-even effect. Ms., Graduate School of Management, Cornell University, Ithaca, NY.

Thaler, R. H., and H. M. Shefrin (1981). An economic theory of self control. *Journal of Political Economy* 89, 392–406.

Tversky, A. (1967a). Additivity, utility and subjective probability. *Journal of Mathematical Psychology* 4, 175–202.

Tversky, A. (1967b). Utility theory and additivity analysis of risky choices. *Journal of Experimental Psychology* 75, 27–36.

Tversky, A. (1969). Intransitivity of preferences. *Psychological Review* 76, 31–48.

Tversky, A. (1972). Elimination by aspects: A theory of choice. *Psychological Review* 79, 281–299.

Tversky, A., and D. Kahneman (1974). Judgment under uncertainty: Heuristics and biases. *Science* 185, 1124–1131.

Tversky, A., and D. Kahneman (1981). The framing of decisions and the psychology of choice. *Science* 211, 453–458.

Tversky, A., and D. Kahneman (1986). Rational choice and the framing of decisions. *Journal of Business* 59, 5251–5278.

Tversky, A., S. Sattath, and P. Slovic (1988). Contingent weighting in judgment and choice. *Psychological Review* 95, 371–384.

Tyszka, T. (1981). Simple decision strategies vs. multi-attribute utility theory approach to complex decision problems. *Praxiology Yearbook* 2.

van Raiij, W. F. (1983). Techniques of process tracing for decision making. In L. Sjöberg, T. Tyszka, and J. Wise, eds., *Human decision making.* Bodafors, Sweden: Doxa.

von Neumann, J., and O. Morgenstern (1947). *Theory of games and economic behavior.* Princeton, NJ. Princeton University Press.

von Winterfeldt, D. (1975). *An overview, integration and evaluation of utility theory for decision analysis.* (SSRI Technical Research Report 75–9.) Los Angeles: University of Southern California.

von Winterfeldt, D., and W. Edwards (1986). *Decision analysis and behavioral research.* New York: Cambridge University Press.

Wickens, C. D. (1984). *Engineering psychology and human performance.* Columbus, OH: Merrill.

Chapter 5

Problem Solving

Keith J. Holyoak

The ability to solve problems is one of the most important manifestations of human thinking. The range of problems people encounter is enormous: planning a dinner party, tracking deer, diagnosing a disease, winning a game of chess, solving mathematical equations, managing a business. This radical diversity of problem domains contrasts with the relative specificity of many human cognitive activities, such as vision, language, basic motor skills, and memory activation, which have a relatively direct biological basis and which all normal individuals accomplish with substantially uniform proficiency. In the course of normal development we all learn, for example, to speak a native language; but without specialized experience we will never acquire any competence in deer tracking or chess playing.

On the other hand, all normal people do acquire considerable competence in solving at least some of the particular types of problems they habitually encounter in everyday life. We might therefore suspect that problem solving depends on general cognitive abilities that can potentially be applied to an essentially unlimited range of domains. We will see, in fact, that such diverse cognitive abilities as perception, language, sequencing of actions, memory, categorization, judgment, and choice all play important roles in human problem solving.

The ability to solve problems is clearly a crucial component of intelligence. Furthermore, the phenomena of problem solving present many intriguing puzzles that must be accounted for by a successful theory of problem solving. For example, consider the differences between the best computer programs for playing chess and the performance of the very best human players. Before selecting its next move, such a chess-playing program is likely to assess billions of alternative possible continuations of the game. In contrast, the human grand master may consider a mere dozen alternatives—and then proceed to select a better move than the program did. What mechanisms allow the best move to so readily "come to mind" for the grand master? And what kind of learning processes allow this sort of expertise to be acquired from problem-solving experience? These and other questions about human problem solving will be the focus of this chapter.

In order to understand the nature of human problem solving, it is useful to first consider the nature of problems. We can often learn a great deal about how problems are solved by considering how they *could* be solved. That is, a *task analysis* of problems can provide information about constraints that the nature of the problem imposes on the nature of the problem solver. We will also see that task analysis suggests that problem solving is intimately connected with *learning*. An intelligent problem solver uses the results of solution attempts to acquire new knowledge that will help solve similar problems more readily in the future.

We will begin by characterizing the nature of problem solving and the fundamental theoretical issues the topic raises for cognitive science. The most influential theoretical treatment of human problem solving, that of Newell and Simon (1972), will be used to frame some of these issues. In addition, we will briefly consider the implications of neuropsychological evidence regarding the basic components of problem-solving skill. We will then examine in more detail one of the major concerns of recent research, the acquisition of expertise in particular problem-solving domains, such as chess or physics. Finally, we will examine some alternatives to Newell and Simon's perspective, emphasizing aspects of problem solving that seem to involve parallel and unconscious information processing.

5.1   The Nature of Problem Solving

5.1.1   Problem Solving as Search

A problem arises when we have a *goal*—a state of affairs that we want to achieve—and it is not immediately apparent how the goal can be attained. Some valuable clues to the nature of problem solving can be found in the everyday metaphors we use to talk about it (Lakoff and

Turner 1989). It is conventional to think of abstract states such as goals as metaphorical spatial locations, and event sequences as metaphorical paths leading from one state to another. This spatial conception permeates descriptions of problem solving. We speak of "searching for a way to reach a goal," "getting around roadblocks" encountered along the way, finding a "shortcut" solution, "getting lost" in the middle of a solution, "hitting a deadend" and being forced to "backtrack," "approaching the problem from a different angle," and so on.

This conception of problem solving as search in a metaphorical space, which underlies our commonsense understanding, has been elaborated to provide a rigorous theoretical framework for the analysis of problem solving. Although some of the theoretical ideas can be traced back to Gestalt psychologists such as Duncker (1945), the modern formulation of a general theory of problem solving as search is due to Newell and Simon (1972). In their problem-space formulation, the representation of a problem consists of four kinds of elements: a description of the *initial state* at which problem solving begins; a description of the *goal state* to be reached; a set of *operators*, or actions that can be taken, which serve to alter the current state of the problem; and *path constraints* that impose additional conditions on a successful path to solution, beyond simply reaching the goal (for instance, a constraint of finding the solution using the fewest possible steps).

The *problem space* consists of the set of all states that can potentially be reached by applying the available operators. A *solution* is a sequence of operators that can transform the initial state into the goal state in accord with the path constraints. A problem-solving *method* is a procedure for finding a solution. Problem solving is thus viewed as search: methods are used to find a solution path among all the possible paths emanating from the initial state and goal state. Figure 5.1 provides a graphical illustration of a search space. Each circle represents a possible state of affairs, and the arrows represent possible transitions from one state to another that can be effected by applying operators. A sequence of arrows leading from the initial state to the goal state constitutes a solution path.

The problem-space analysis immediately yields a mathematical result with brutal implications for the feasibility of solving problems. If at each step in the search any of F operators might be applied, and a solution requires applying a sequence of D steps (that is, D is the "depth" of the search), then the number of alternative operator sequences is F^D. As F and D get even modestly large, F^D becomes enormous. A typical game of chess, for example, might involve a total of 60 moves, with an average of 30 alternative legal moves available at each step along the way. The number of alternative paths would thus be 30^{60}, a number so astronomical

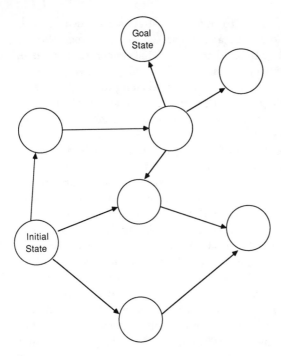

Figure 5.1
A graphical illustration of a search space for a problem.

that not even the fastest computer can play chess by exploring every possible move sequence. The fact that the size of the search space increases exponentially with the depth of the search is termed *combinatorial explosion*, a property that makes many problems impossible to solve by exhaustive search of all possible paths.

Humans, with their limited short-term memories, are actually far less capable of "brute-force" search than are computers. For example, human chess players are unable to "look ahead" more than three or four moves. Yet a human grand master can play superlative chess, better than any computer program yet devised. How can this be? The answer is that humans use problem-solving methods that perform *heuristic search*—rather than attempting the impossible task of examining all possible operator sequences, people consider only a small number of alternatives that seem most likely to yield a solution. Intelligent problem solving, in fact, consists largely of the use of methods for heuristic search. Some heuristic search methods are very general and can be applied to virtually any problem; others are much more specific and depend on detailed knowledge of a particular problem domain. As we will see, the development of expertise is largely the acquisition of knowledge that restricts the need for extensive search.

The efficacy of heuristic search depends in part on the nature of the problem to be solved. A major distinction is whether the *best possible* solution is required, or whether any reasonable solution that achieves the goal will suffice. Heuristic methods are seldom much use in solving "best solution" problems. An example is the notorious "traveling salesman" problem. This problem involves taking the locations of a number of cities (say, ten) and trying to find the shortest possible route that passes through each of the cities exactly once. Due to combinatorial explosion, this problem has an enormous search space of possible routes once the number of cities grows at all large. No one has found a method other than "brute-force" search of all possible routes that guarantees finding the shortest route. However, if the goal is simply to find a route that is reasonably short by some criterion, heuristic search methods may be useful. Human problem solvers are particularly good at what Simon (1981) calls *satisficing*: finding reasonably good but not necessarily optimal solutions.

5.1.2   Heuristic Search: Means-Ends Analysis

Search for a problem solution can proceed in either of two directions: forward from the initial state to the goal state, or backward from the goal state to the initial state. Forward search involves applying operators to the current state to generate a new state; backward search involves finding operators that could produce the current state. In general, it is most efficient to search in whichever direction requires fewest choices at each decision point. For example, if there is only way to reach the goal state, it may be easiest to work backward from the goal.

Newell and Simon (1972) suggested a small number of general heuristic search methods. One of the most important of these, *means-ends analysis*, involves a mixture of forward and backward search. The key idea underlying means-ends analysis is that search is guided by detection of differences between the current state and the goal state. Specifically, means-ends analysis involves the following steps:

1. Compare the current state to the goal state and identify differences between the two. If there are none, the problem is solved; otherwise, proceed.
2. Select an operator that would reduce one of the differences.
3. If the operator can be applied, do so; if not, set a new *subgoal* of reaching a state at which the operator could be applied. Means-ends analysis is then applied to this new subgoal until the operator can be applied or the attempt to use it is abandoned.
4. Return to step 1.

Suppose, for example, that you have the goal of trying to paint your living room. The obvious difference between the current state and the goal state is that the room is unpainted. The operator "apply paint" could reduce this difference. However, to apply this operator you need to have paint and a brush. If these are lacking, you now set the subgoal of getting paint and brush. These could be found at a hardware store. So you set the subgoal of getting to a hardware store. And so on, until the conditions for applying the operator are met, and you can finally reduce the difference in the original problem.

Means-ends analysis illustrates several important points about intelligent heuristic search. First, it is explicitly guided by knowledge of the goal. Second, an initial goal can lead to subsequent subgoals that effectively decompose the problem into smaller parts. Third, methods can be applied *recursively*; that is, in the course of applying a method to achieve a goal, the entire method may be applied to achieve a subgoal. Thus, in step 3 of means-ends analysis, the method may be reapplied to the subgoal of reaching a state in which a desirable operator is applicable. (Recursion is also an important property of human language; see Lasnik 1990.)

5.1.3   Planning and Problem Decomposition

The idea that the process of problem solving is a kind of search suggests a separation between the initial *planning* of a solution and its actual *execution*. It is usually advantageous to perform at least a partial search by "looking ahead" for a solution before actually applying any operators. The obvious advantage of planning is that by anticipating the consequences of possible actions, one can avoid the unfortunate consequences of making overt errors.

The importance of planning varies with the extent to which error recovery is possible. Rich (1983) distinguishes three types of erroneous solution attempts, which she terms *ignorable, recoverable,* and *irrecoverable.* An ignorable solution attempt, as the term implies, can simply be set aside and another attempt made. For example, if you try to unlock a door with the wrong key, you can simply try another key. The initial error need have no consequences beyond a little wasted time. In contrast, a recoverable solution attempt requires some explicit "undoing" to get back to the state prior to the error. For example, if you find you have made an error in solving a crossword puzzle, you will need to erase the erroneous entry and any other entries that depended on it. Finally, an irrecoverable solution attempt simply cannot be undone. If you are playing chess, for example, you are not allowed to "take back" a regrettable move. Nor can a general who commences a surprise attack on the enemy later restore the prior state of affairs. In chess and war as in golf, the problem solver must "play it as it lays."

To the extent that errors are irreversible, or reversible only with diffi-culty, or simply unduly time-consuming, planning is especially important. By imagining the consequences of actions prior to an overt solution at-tempt, one can identify dead ends without actually executing actions. In addition, planning provides information that can be used to monitor and learn from an overt solution attempt. By explicitly anticipating the consequences of applying operators, the problem solver generates expecta-tions that can be compared to what actually happens when the operators are applied. If the actual effects of operators differ from their expected effects, this may trigger revision of the plan as well as revision of beliefs about what will happen in similar future applications of the relevant opera-tors. Problem solving thus provides valuable information that can guide learning (Holland et al. 1986).

Planning often is combined with a process of *problem decomposition*, in which an overall problem is broken into parts, such that each part can be achieved separately. Suppose, for example, that you need to select a slate of officers to run a club. Rather than trying to select people to fill the entire slate at once, it makes more sense to decompose this goal into several subgoals: selecting a president, a treasurer, and so on. Each of these subgoals defines a problem that can be attacked independently. Finding a solution to each subgoal will require fewer steps than solving the overall compound goal. Because search increases exponentially with the number of steps, solving all the subgoals, each of which requires a relatively small number of steps, is likely to require far less total search than would have been needed to solve the entire problem at once.

Unfortunately, realistic problems are seldom perfectly decomposable into parts that can be solved completely independently. In our example, choices of officers for the various positions interact in various ways. For example, the same person cannot be both president and treasurer, and the various officers need to get along with each other—Sally might make a fine president and Joe a good treasurer, but if they dislike each other they would make a poor combination. But despite this lack of complete independence, total search may be minimized by first making some tenta-tive decisions about each subgoal and then later working on integrating the components into a workable overall plan. That is, the problem solver can take advantage of the fact that some problems are *partially decomposable* (Simon 1981). This can best be done if foresight is used to form a coherent overall plan before actually beginning an overt solution attempt. Thus, before actually proposing a slate of officers, we could check for compatibil-ity of the tentative list of choices and make corrections where needed. The general strategy is to first try to solve each subgoal independently, but to note constraints on how the individual decisions interact, and then to check that these constraints are satisfied before finalizing the overall solution attempt. Planning is thus particularly important in effectively reducing search for partially decomposable problems.

5.1.4 Production-System Models of Problem Solving

Newell and Simon's problem-space analysis is highly abstract and is potentially compatible with a variety of specific representations and algorithms. In practice, however, their approach has been closely tied to a particular type of formal model, the *production system* (Newell 1973). The central component of a production system is a set of *production rules* (also termed *condition-action rules*). A typical production rule might be

IF you have a paint roller

and you have paint
and you have a surface ready to paint
and the surface is large
and your goal is to paint the surface

THEN roll the paint onto the surface

and expect the surface to be painted.

This rule represents the knowledge required for appropriate application of a problem-solving operator. The "then" portion of the rule specifies the action to be taken and the expected state change it will bring about; the "if" portion consists of a set of clauses describing when the operator could and should be invoked. Note that the clauses in the condition of this rule are of two types. The first four describe *preconditions* that must be met before the operator can be applied—you need a roller before you can roll. The fifth clause specifies a *goal* for which the operator is useful—if you want to paint, consider using a roller. The goal restriction helps to limit search, because it means this rule will only be considered when the relevant goal has arisen.

A typical production system operates by cycling through the following steps:

1. The conditions of rules are matched against the currently active portion of memory (for instance, the representation of the current problem state) to identify those rules with conditions that are fully satisfied.
2. If more than one rule is matched, procedures for *conflict resolution* select one of the matched rules.
3. The selected rule is *fired*; that is, its action is taken.
4. Return to step 1.

Production-system models of problem solving have been extremely influential in the development of modern cognitive science. Within artificial intelligence such models have been used to develop *expert systems* that help perform such tasks as medical diagnosis and mineral exploration. In cognitive psychology Anderson's ACT* model (1983) is predicated on the claim that human cognition is fundamentally a production system. Alternative models of this general form have many important differences; nonetheless, rule-based systems have provided a common theoretical language that fosters communication among researchers in several of the disciplines that make up cognitive science. Their successful applications have also spread the influence of Newell and Simon's approach to problem solving and to cognition in general.

Production-system models have several virtues. First, they provide a direct method of instantiating knowledge about how to traverse a problem space by applying operators. Second, the knowledge is clearly procedural. Although our example rule looks very linguistic, rules differ from simple descriptions in that they act as instructions for appropriate action. Third, the knowledge is encoded in a highly modular fashion. It is relatively easy to add new rules to the system without unduly disrupting the operation of the older rules. Production systems are therefore capable of modeling learning from problem-solving experience (Anderson 1983; Rosenbloom and Newell 1986).

5.1.5   The Brain and Problem Solving

Our discussion so far has focused on analyses of problem solving based on task analyses and computational considerations, rather than on evidence regarding the way problem solving is actually performed by the brain. As is the case for other major cognitive activities, however, it is valuable to consider the implications of neuropsychological evidence in characterizing the basic components of human problem solving. We can attempt to understand the functional decomposition of problem-solving skills in terms of the functions of relatively localized brain areas, as has been done for language and vision.

This is not an easy task. Localization of functions must be inferred either from lesion experiments with animals, which obviously differ radically from humans in their cognitive abilities, or from clinical studies of brain-damaged individuals, who seldom have injuries confined to a single clear anatomical region. These general limitations of available neuropsychological evidence are compounded in the case of problem solving. Given its integrative nature, problem-solving ability is likely to be impaired to some degree whenever any major cognitive function, such as memory or language, is disturbed. It is therefore especially difficult to identify brain areas that are selectively implicated in problem solving or planning per se.

Nonetheless, there is some evidence that implicates the *frontal lobes* of the cerebral cortex as an area of special importance in problem solving (Stuss and Benson 1986). This large area at the front of the cortex appears to play a role in a broad range of cognitive and emotional responses. However, careful clinical observations and a few experimental studies have revealed some interesting selectivity in the deficits that result from damage to this area. Part of the selectivity concerns what is *not* seriously affected. People with frontal lesions typically are not intellectually impaired as measured by traditional IQ tests. In some cases they are able to function reasonably well in professions in which they were experienced prior to incurring the injury. Nonetheless, some major decrements in cognitive abilities can be identified. A major source of difficulty is novelty: frontal-lobe patients may be able to perform well-learned tasks using old information, yet have great difficulty solving new types of problems. As the great Russian psychologist A. R. Luria put it, "When intellectual operations demand the creation of a program of action and a choice between several equally probable alternatives, the intellectual activity of patients with a marked 'frontal syndrome' is profoundly disturbed" (1969, 749).

Based on an extensive review of the literature on the effects of frontal lesions, Stuss and Benson (1986, 222) suggested six broad classes of deficits: deficit in the ordering or handling of sequential behaviors; impairment in establishing or changing a set; impairment in maintaining a set, particularly in the presence of interference; decreased ability to monitor personal behavior; dissociation of knowledge from the direction of response; and altered attitudes.

Each of these classes of deficits is linked to problem solving. The ability to plan and execute sequences of actions is, of course, essential. Establishing, changing, and maintaining a "set" requires the ability to selectively attend and respond to goal-relevant information. On a categorization task, for example, frontal-lobe patients are likely to repeat errors despite corrective feedback and be unable to shift from one basis of classification to another. For example, a person who has learned to sort a set of objects by color will have great difficulty sorting by shape instead. Patients have difficulty monitoring their own behavior; they may behave in socially unacceptable ways even though they appear to understand that their behavior is wrong. Similarly, they have trouble translating verbal instructions into appropriate actions. A patient may be told to return to work, may express a desire to return to work, and yet fail to do so. Finally, "altered attitudes" are apparent in failure to set goals or care about the future: the person appears to lack "drive" or "motivation."

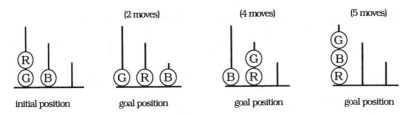

Figure 5.2
The "Tower of London" puzzle. The three goal states represent three levels of difficulty, given the initial state. From Shallice 1982.

Shallice (1982) conducted a study that specifically examined the manner in which frontal-lobe patients approach novel problems requiring planning and organized sequential action. He tested patients with various forms of brain damage, as well as control subjects, on their ability to solve various versions of the "Tower of London" puzzle (see figure 5.2). This puzzle consists of three differently colored beads and three pegs of different lengths. The experimenter places the beads in a starting configuration, and the subject must then move them into a new configuration defined by the experimenter, in a minimum number of moves. The number of moves required to achieve the goal defines the level of difficulty.

Although all of the groups of brain-damaged subjects were impaired in their performance relative to the control subjects, those with damage to the left frontal lobe showed the greatest decrement, particularly for the more difficult versions of the puzzle. The nature of the errors made by the frontal-lobe subjects indicated that they had difficulty in planning; they could not establish an appropriate order of subgoals. The deficit was not due to a general limitation of short-term memory, as variations in the patients' performance on a digit-span test could not account for the differences in problem-solving success. (A subsequent experiment suggesting limits on the above finding is described by Shallice (1988).)

Stuss and Benson (1986) argue that the frontal lobes are crucial in *executive control* of cognition. The frontal-lobe syndrome in large part appears to involve a loss in ability to control cognitive processes: the ability to select and maintain goals, to plan sequential activities, to anticipate the consequences of actions, to monitor the effects of actions, and to revise plans on the basis of feedback. These neuropsychological observations have several implications for theories of problem solving and planning, most of which are consistent with other evidence obtained with normal subjects. The crucial importance of selective attention and of the ability to organize sequential action would be expected on the basis of task analysis. The fact that the deficits are primarily observed when the patient faces novel problems suggests that expertise leads to a reduction in the requirements for executive control. The gap between verbal knowledge and action is consistent with the claim that developing skill in solving new problems involves a process of *proceduralization*: translating verbal knowledge into procedures, perhaps encoded as production rules (Anderson 1983). It appears that proceduralization is impaired by frontal-lobe damage.

The motivational component of the syndrome emphasizes the significance of an aspect of problem solving that is often neglected in computational approaches to problem solving. Unless the organism cares about the future, there is no clear basis for establishing or maintaining goals; and without goals, problem solving simply disintegrates.

5.1.6   What Must a Theory of Problem Solving Explain?

Our survey of the nature of problem solving has raised a number of issues that an adequate theory must explain: namely, how goals are formed; how heuristic methods develop; how problems can be decomposed; and how planning is conducted. In addition, a theory must explain how learning takes place during problem solving, and how knowledge acquired in one problem situation is transferred to another.

Many of these issues are related to one of the central questions that has been addressed by research on problem solving: how does a novice problem solver become an expert? We will now consider some of the relevant evidence.

5.2   The Development of Expertise

What makes expert problem solvers better than novices? Clearly, experts in a domain have had more training and practice than have novices, but what exactly is it that experts have learned? Have they learned how to reason better in general, or perhaps to become more skilled in applying heuristic search methods, such as means-ends analysis? Let us look at two domains in which a considerable amount of research has examined differences in the problem-solving methods of experts and novices: playing chess and solving textbook physics problems.

5.2.1   Expertise in Chess

The pioneering work on expertise in chess playing was reported by De Groot (1965). In order to determine what makes a master chess player better than a weaker player, De Groot had some of the best chess players in the world "think out loud" as they selected chess moves. By analyzing these problem-solving *protocols*—transcripts of what the players said as they reached a decision—De Groot was able to observe some distinct differences in the ways in which masters and novices selected moves.

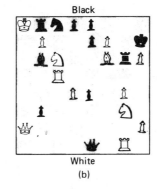

Figure 5.3
Examples of chess configurations: (a) real middle game; (b) random counterpart. From Chase and Simon 1973.

His results did not support any of the obvious hypotheses about the masters' having superior general reasoning ability or greater proficiency in means-ends analysis. Nor was it the case that the masters performed more extensive search through the vast space of alternative possible moves. In fact, if anything the masters considered fewer alternative moves than did the weaker players. However, the master players spent their time considering relatively good moves, whereas the weaker players spent more time exploring bad moves. It appeared that the masters were able to exploit knowledge that led them very quickly to consider the best moves possible, without extensive search.

The most striking difference between the two classes of players was observed in a test of their perceptual and memory abilities. Chase and Simon (1973) extended De Groot's results. In the test the player saw a chess position, drawn from the middle portion of an actual chess game, which was presented for just 5 seconds. An example board position is depicted in figure 5.3a. After the board was removed, the player was asked to reconstruct it from memory. In Chase and Simon's experiment the subject was either an expert master player (M), a very good class A player (A), or a beginning player (B). The number of pieces correctly recalled over seven trials by each player is depicted in figure 5.4a. The results showed that the greater the expertise of the player, the more accurately the board was recalled.

One might suppose that this result indicates that master chess players have particularly good memories. However, this is not generally the case. To assess this possibility, Chase and Simon also performed the test using random board positions such as the one illustrated in figure 5.3b. As the

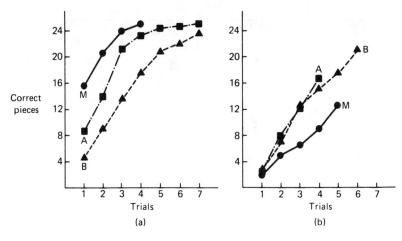

Figure 5.4
Number of pieces recalled correctly by master (M), class A player (A), and beginner (B) over trials: (a) for actual board positions; (b) for random board positions. From Chase and Simon 1973.

results shown in figure 5.4b indicate, the master player's advantage was entirely eliminated in this condition.

On the basis of these and other related findings, Chase and Simon argued that master players have learned to recognize large meaningful perceptual units corresponding to board configurations that tend to recur in real chess games. These units are stored as unitary *chunks* in long-term memory. Such chunks can be used to encode quickly and accurately the configuration of a novel but realistic board. They are useless, however, in encoding random positions, in which meaningful patterns are unlikely to occur. Chunks also serve as the conditions of production rules that suggest good moves. These rules would have the form, "IF Pattern *P* is present on the board, THEN consider Move *M*." Such specific rules would direct the master player quite directly to the relatively small number of alternative moves that are serious candidates, without having to search through large numbers of highly implausible possibilities. It seems likely that the development of specialized rules that are cued by perceptual units contributes to the acquisition of expertise in many domains other than playing board games.

5.2.2   Expertise in Physics

The conclusions derived from studies of chess have been confirmed and extended by work on expert-novice differences in solving physics problems. A study by Chi, Feltovich, and Glaser (1981) provided especially

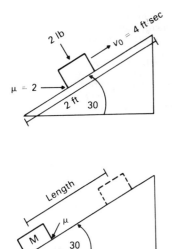

Novice 1: "These deal
with blocks on an
incline plane."
Novice 2: "Inclined plane
problems, coefficient
of friction."
Novice 3: "Blocks on
inclined planes with
angles."

Figure 5.5
Diagrams of two problems categorized together by novices, and samples of explanations
given. From Chi, Feltovich, and Glaser 1981.

interesting results. These investigators asked experts and novices to sort
physics problems into clusters on the basis of similarity. Novices tended
to base their sortings on relatively superficial features of the problem
statements. For example, figure 5.5 depicts the diagrams for two problems
that were often grouped together by novices. A glance at the diagrams
associated with each problem indicates that they look very similar;
the novices explained that both are "inclined planes" problems. In fact,
although both of these problems involve inclined planes, very different
procedures are required to solve them. By contrast, figure 5.6 shows two
problem diagrams that experts classified as belonging together. These look
very different; however, the experts explained that both problems can be
solved by the law of "conservation of energy."

In general, the work of Chi, Feltovich, and Glaser (1981) and others
indicates that experts have learned *schemas* for identifying important categories of problems. These problem schemas are based on features relevant
to the selection of solution procedures. Problem schemas in physics are
based on more abstract features than those included in the perceptual
chunks available to the chess master; but like perceptual chunks, abstract
problem schemas function to vastly reduce the amount of search required
to find appropriate solutions. In general, expertise in problem solving
is in large part the result of the development of sophisticated mental
representations for categorizing problems in the domain. (For a more

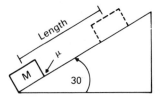

Expert 1: "Conservation of energy."
Expert 2. "Work-energy theorem:
They are all straightforward
problems.
Expert 3: "These can be done from
energy considerations. Either
you should know the principle
of conservation of energy, or
work is lost somewhere."

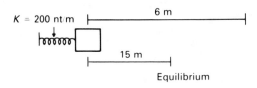

Equilibrium

Figure 5.6
Diagrams of two problems categorized together by experts, and samples of explanations given. From Chi, Feltovich, and Glaser 1981.

detailed discussion of expert-novice differences, see Chi, Glaser, and Rees 1982.)

5.2.3 How Does Expertise Develop?

Research comparing the performance of expert and novice problem solvers tells us a great deal about how to characterize the differences in the knowledge used by people at different skill levels; however, it tells us less about how an initially unskilled problem solver can eventually become an expert. A number of theoretical efforts have, however, attempted to describe learning mechanisms that might allow some combination of direct problem-solving experience, instruction, and exposure to solved examples— the obvious types of environmental inputs available to the learner—to produce increased expertise. (See also the discussion of knowledge reorganization in chapter 6.)

Most models of learning have assumed a production-system representation for procedural knowledge; accordingly, learning is mainly treated as the acquisition of new production rules. The general idea is that by inspecting the results of a solution attempt, learning mechanisms can encode important regularities into new rules. This "inspection" process need not necessarily be conscious. For example, Larkin (1981) has developed a computer simulation that can learn to solve physics problems more efficiently. The program starts by using means-ends analysis to find unknown quantities by using equations. For example, to find the value of acceleration, a, it might use the equation $V_f = V_i + at$ (final velocity equals initial velocity plus acceleration times time). The learning mechanism could then form a new production rule that checks to see whether V_i, V_f, and t are known (the condition), and if so asserts that a can be found (the action). This new rule will then eliminate the need to apply means-ends analysis to solve future problems with this form. The result of this learning mechanism is a shift from a novice strategy of working backward from the goal, using means-ends analysis and subgoaling, to a more expert strategy of working forward from the givens to the unknown goal quantity. Protocol studies with human experts and novices in physics have found evidence for such a shift from backward to forward search (Larkin et al. 1980).

It is far from clear, however, that this type of change in strategy is simply the result of forming new rules based on solutions initially found by means-ends analysis. In fact, Sweller, Mawer, and Ward (1983) found that use of a means-ends strategy can actually impair acquisition of expertise in solving mathematics problems. They argue that means-ends analysis focuses attention on the specific features of the problem situation required to reach the stated goal, reducing the degree to which other important aspects of problem structure are learned. Sweller, Mawer, and Ward found that a forward-search strategy developed more rapidly when learners were encouraged to explore the problem statements more broadly, simply calculating as many variables as possible. They suggested that less directed exploration of the problems facilitated acquisition of useful problem schemas.

In addition to acquiring new rules and schemas, expertise may be improved by combining old rules in more efficient ways. For example, if two rules apply one after another, it may be possible to construct a single rule that combines the effects of both. This process is termed *composition* (Anderson 1983; Lewis 1978). As noted earlier, Anderson (1983, 1987) also stresses the role of a process of *proceduralization*, which uses very general productions for following verbal instructions to construct more specific productions to execute a solution procedure.

Finally, learning mechanisms can also make use of solved examples that are provided to illustrate solution procedures. As we will see, examples can sometimes be retrieved and used to solve subsequent problems by analogy. In addition, learners can use examples when they are first presented to actively construct useful rules and schemas. Chi et al. (1989) have found that good and poor learners use solved examples of physics problems in radically different ways. Good learners generate inferences that serve to explain *why* the examples can be solved in the illustrated manner, whereas poor learners encode them in a much more passive manner (for instance, they fail to ask questions while studying the examples). The development of expertise clearly depends not only on the nature of environmental inputs provided to problem solvers but also on the learning skills they bring to the task.

5.3   Restructuring and Parallelism in Problem Solving

5.3.1   Ill-defined Problems

The search metaphor for problem solving, as elaborated into formal models by Newell and Simon and others, has clearly been extremely useful in understanding human problem solving. However, neither the metaphor nor the models derived from it capture the full richness of the mental processes that underlie problem-solving skill. The search perspective seems most appropriate when the problem solver has a clear goal, understands the initial state and constraints, and knows exactly what operators might be useful. Given an appropriate method, finding a solution is then indeed a search through a well-defined space of possibilities; if a solution path exists, it will be found by patiently "grinding it out."

Many of the most difficult problems that beset us, however, have a very different quality. If your goal is to write a brilliant novel, from what initial state are you starting? How would you recognize that your goal was achieved? As another example, what operators are applicable in trying to resolve the conflict between Israel and the Palestinians? Or in developing a theory of superconductivity? Reitman (1964) observed that many problems, such as these, are *ill defined* in that the representations of one or more of the basic components—the goal, initial state, operators, and constraints—are seriously incomplete. Ill-defined problems are usually hard, and not simply because the search space is large. Indeed, many ill-defined problems seem difficult, not because we are swamped by the task of searching through an enormous number of alternative possibilities, but because we have trouble thinking of even one idea worth pursuing. Consider, for example, the "radiation problem" used by Duncker (1945) in his studies of problem solving:

> Suppose you are a doctor faced with a patient who has a malignant tumor in his stomach. To operate on the patient is impossible, but unless the tumor is destroyed, the patient will die. A kind of ray, at a sufficiently high intensity, can destroy the tumor. Unfortunately, at this intensity the healthy tissue that the rays pass through on the way to the tumor will also be destroyed. At lower intensities the rays are harmless to healthy tissue but will not affect the tumor, either. How can the rays be used to destroy the tumor without injuring the healthy tissue?

Although most people who try to solve this problem can think of some sort of suggestion of dubious practicality (for instance, send high-intensity rays down the esophagus), very few suggest the idea of irradiating the tumor from multiple directions simultaneously with low-intensity rays, focusing the rays so that the tumor receives a higher dosage than does the surrounding healthy tissue. Yet most people will agree that this is a rather good solution to the problem, once it is pointed out to them. To actually discover the solution, however, usually requires more than dogged search, since the operator "create multiple ray sources" is unlikely to even be considered.

5.3.2   Restructuring, Insight, and Analogies

To understand how ill-defined problems can be solved, it is useful again to look at everyday language. We speak of "looking at the problem in a new light," having the solution "just pop out," and realizing the answer was "staring me in the face all along." These metaphors suggest that a solution may not always be reached by a gradual serial search process; rather, it may be achieved suddenly as the result of "seeing" the problem differently. The notion that problem solving shares certain important properties with perception was a major theme of the Gestalt psychologists such as Duncker (1945) and Maier (1930), who proposed that solutions sometimes require insight based on a *restructuring* of the problem representation. People do not always simply establish a representation of a problem and then perform search; rather, they sometimes change their representations in major ways. It is interesting that although Newell and Simon's treatment of search and means-ends analysis was foreshadowed by Duncker's ideas, the Gestalt emphasis on the importance of restructuring was largely lost in their formulation (see Newell 1985).

Until recently there was very little experimental evidence supporting the notion that some problems are solved by restructuring and sudden insight. Recently, however, work by Metcalfe (1986a,b; Metcalfe and Wiebe 1987) has established several criteria that distinguish the process of solving "insight" problems from the process of solving "routine" problems. Her experiments compared people's performance in predicting their own ability to solve algebra problems (routine) versus a variety of insight problems, such as the following:

> A landscape gardener is given instructions to plant four special trees so that each one is exactly the same distance from each of the others. How could the trees be arranged?[1]

One major distinction involved subjects' ability to predict whether they would eventually be able to solve the problem, for those problems they

1. The gardener could build a hill, plant one tree at the top, and plant three others in an equilateral triangle around the base of the hill. Assuming the hill is built to the appropriate height, the four trees will form a tetrahedron in which each of the four corners is equidistant from every other corner.

could not solve immediately. For algebra problems, subjects' "feelings of knowing" accurately predicted their eventual success; that is, people were able to tell which algebra problems they would be able to solve if they tried, and which would prove intractable. In contrast, subjects were completely unable to predict which insight problems they would be able to solve (Metcalfe 1986b).

A second major distinction was apparent in a measure of subjects' changes in expectations during the course of problem solving. Metcalfe and Wiebe (1987) had subjects rate how "warm" they felt as they worked on each problem: that is, how close they believed they were to finding a solution. If people were using means-ends analysis, or any heuristic-search method involving a comparison of the current state and the goal state, they should be able to report getting "warmer" as they approached the goal (since they would know that the difference between the current state and the goal was being progressively reduced). On the other hand, if a solution was discovered on the basis of a rapid restructuring of the problem, the problem solver would not be able to report increased warmth prior to the insight.

Figure 5.7 depicts the striking difference that emerged between the patterns of warmth ratings obtained for insight and for algebra problems. Each of the histograms in the figure shows the distribution of subjects' warmth ratings at a particular time prior to achieving a solution. A rating of 1 indicates least warmth (feeling nowhere close to a solution), whereas a rating of 7 indicates maximal warmth (the problem seems virtually solved). The histograms in each column are ordered in time from bottom to top, from 60 seconds prior to the solution to the time a solution was actually found. For the algebra problems (right-hand column), the ratings shift gradually to the right of the histogram as the time of solution approaches, indicating that subjects accurately reported getting warmer and warmer as they neared a solution. For the insight problems (left-hand column), the results are utterly different. The ratings do not shift as the time of solution approaches. Rather, most subjects rate themselves as "cold" until they suddenly solve the problem, at which point their rating jumps from maximally cold to maximally warm.

Metcalfe's results thus provide empirical evidence that insight is a real psychological phenomenon. For a problem that requires insight, people are unable to assess how likely they are to solve it, either in advance of working on the problem or as they actually are working on it. If they eventually succeed in finding a solution, they are genuinely surprised.

Although restructuring and insight do play a role in problem solving, we are far from a full understanding of the mechanisms involved. In some cases restructuring may be triggered by finding an *analogy* between the target problem at hand and some other situation (the *source* analogue) from a very

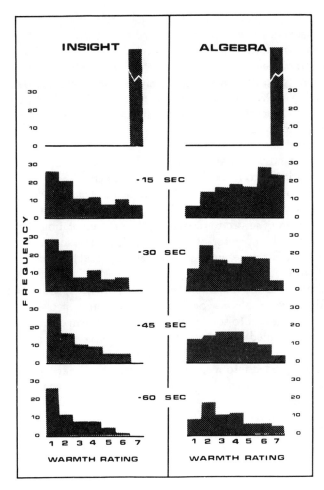

Figure 5.7
Frequency histograms of warmth ratings for correctly solved insight and algebra problems. The panels, from bottom to top, give the ratings 60, 45, 30, and 15 seconds before solution. As shown in the top panel, a 7 rating was always given at the time of solution. From Metcalfe and Wiebe 1987.

different domain. For example, Gick and Holyoak (1980, 1983) performed a series of experiments in which subjects first read a story about a general who wished to conquer a fortress located in the middle of a country. Many roads radiated out from the fortress, but these were mined so that although small groups of men could pass over them safely, any large group would detonate the mines. Yet the general needed to get his entire army to the fortress to capture it. He accomplished this by dividing his men into small groups, dispatching each to the head of a different road, and having all the groups converge simultaneously on the fortress.

Does this story remind you of any of the problems we have discussed? It is, of course, an analogue to Duncker's radiation problem. When college students were asked to use the fortress problem to help solve the radiation problem, most of them came up with the idea of using converging low-intensity rays. The analogy served to restructure their representation of the target problem so that the operator of creating multiple ray sources was constructed and used. (Of course, analogies may also be used to help solve problems that do not require restructuring.)

How can a useful analogy be found? It is often difficult; Gick and Holyoak found that many subjects would fail to notice on their own that the fortress story was relevant to solving the radiation problem even when the analogues were presented in immediate succession. Accessing a source analogue from a different domain than the target is yet more difficult when the source has been encoded into memory in a different context (Spencer and Weisberg 1986). In the absence of guidance from a teacher, analogical access requires that features of the target problem must serve as retrieval cues, which will activate other related situations by a process of spreading activation (see chapter 1). The greater the similarity of the two analogues, the more likely the source will be retrieved (Holyoak and Koh 1987).

5.3.3   Parallel Constraint Satisfaction

One of the hallmarks of Newell and Simon's approach to problem solving is an emphasis on the serial nature of the solution process. A problem is typically decomposed into subproblems; then each subgoal is solved, one by one. For any particular subgoal, alternative operators are tried sequentially in the search for a solution path. Parallel processing is certainly not entirely excluded; in particular, the process of matching the current problem state against the conditions of production rules is typically assumed to be performed in parallel. Nonetheless, the serial aspects of the solution process are theoretically most central.

The notion of restructuring, in contrast, suggests that parallel (and largely unconscious) information processing may have a major impact on problem solving. The role of spreading activation in the retrieval of potential source analogues is one example of how parallel access to information stored in long-term memory may redirect conscious problem solving. It is also possible that the way in which active information is used to construct a solution may sometimes involve parallel integration of knowledge rather than strictly sequential processing. Indeed, this is the intuition that appears to have led the Gestalt psychologists to claim that problem solving was similar to perception. The following quotation from Maier (1930, 116) illustrates this connection (as well as the notorious vagueness that left Gestalt theories of problem solving in ill repute):

> First one has one or no gestalt, then suddenly a new or different gestalt is formed out of the old elements. The sudden appearance of the new gestalt, that is, the solution, is the process of reasoning. How and why it comes is not explained. It is like perception: certain elements which one minute are one unity suddenly become an altogether different unity.

One of the major advances of modern cognitive science has been to build much more explicit models of how parallel processes are used in perception; consequently, we can now begin to delve more deeply into what it might mean for problem solving to have the perceptionlike quality that a unified interpretation of an input typically emerges from parallel integration of information at an unconscious level. A key idea is the concept of *parallel constraint satisfaction*, which was illustrated in the work of Marr and Poggio (1976) on vision, applied to analogical reasoning by Hofstadter (1984), and described in more general terms by Rumelhart et al. (1986) (see also chapter 1 of the epilogue).

The idea of finding a solution that satisfies the constraints of the problem is, of course, by now familiar. For example, in section 5.1.3 we looked at the problem of selecting a slate of officers, in which it is necessary to consider interactions between the decisions about each position (for instance, the person selected as president must get along with the treasurer). We saw that the overall problem of choosing a slate can be decomposed into the subproblems of filling each position. These subproblems can be solved separately, with a subsequent check to make sure no interactive constraints are violated. This form of constraint satisfaction is not inherently parallel.

Sometimes, however, the interactive constraints are so pervasive that it is not feasible to solve each subgoal separately and only then check that all constraints are satisfied. In addition, satisfying a constraint is not always an all-or-nothing matter. For example, a possible president-treasurer pair may be compatible to some degree; if each person is individually an excellent choice for the position, the pair may be satisfactory despite some degree of interpersonal tension. When the solution of each subgoal depends in a

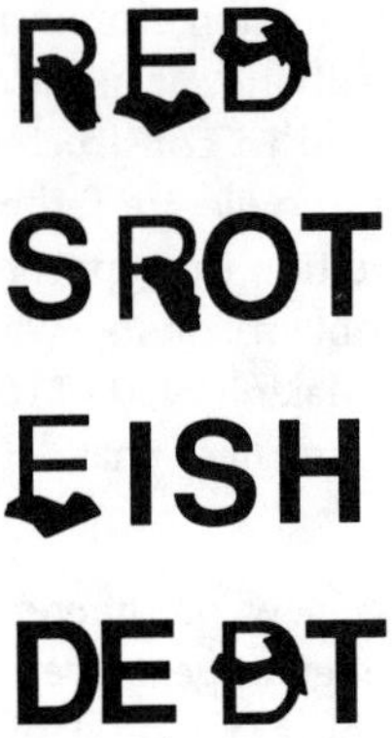

REB

SROT

EISH

DE BT

Figure 5.8
The top word has a clear interpretation even though each of its constituent letters is ambiguous, as illustrated by the three lower words. From McClelland, Rumelhart, and Hinton 1986.

major way on the solution of other subgoals, and the best solution requires trade-offs between competing constraints, it is most efficient to solve all the subgoals incrementally in parallel, allowing information about the results accruing in each subproblem to affect the emerging decisions about the other subproblems. The problem can still be decomposed, but the solution process is interactive.

Figure 5.8 depicts a striking perceptual example of when parallel constraint satisfaction is important. If our problem is to recognize a word, search can be sharply reduced if the problem is decomposed into the subproblems of recognizing each constituent letter. But as figure 5.8 illustrates, the subgoals of identifying the individual letters cannot always be solved independently. You probably recognize the top word in the figure as RED, even though each of the letters is partially obscured. In fact, as the other three words in the figure show, each letter in RED is ambiguous: the R could be a P, the E could be an F, and the D could be a B. Clearly, our interpretation of each individual letter is affected by the interpretations we give the others. Each subgoal of identifying a letter is influenced not only by the constraints provided by the visual input at that position but also by the constraints imposed by the surrounding letters. The solution process is highly interactive, with information about possible letters at each position being integrated to form the optimal "gestalt."

At first glance, the recognition of RED in figure 5.8 seems to create a paradoxical "chicken and egg" problem: you need to identify the letters to recognize the word, but you need to identify the word to recognize the letters. This recognition problem can, however, be solved by parallel

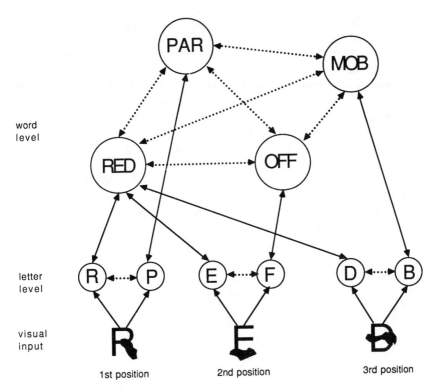

Figure 5.9
An illustration of a network of knowledge that could allow recognition of the top word in figure 5.8 by parallel constraint satisfaction.

constraint satisfaction. Figure 5.9 provides a highly simplified illustration of how the process might operate for this example, based on the interactive activation model of word perception proposed by McClelland and Rumelhart (1981). The reader's knowledge consists of the direct visual input, and information in long-term memory about the letters and words of English. Letters and words are represented by nodes, with connecting arrows that capture the interactions among them. The solid arrows represent positive support. For example, the solid arrow connecting the nodes for "R in first position" and "RED" means that if the first letter is R, then the word may be RED (and vice versa). The broken arrows represent negative counterevidence. Thus, if the first letter is R, then it can't be P, and vice versa.

This network of knowledge can be used to recognize the word at the top of figure 5.8 by parallel constraint satisfaction. The process begins with the visual inputs at each letter position providing support for the letters consistent with the input (for instance, the first letter looks like either R or

P). As letter nodes gather support, they pass support to the words with which they are consistent. Thus, the "R" node supports "RED" (and many other words beginning with R that are not illustrated in the figure), the "P" node supports "PAR," and so on. In addition to this bottom-up processing, the system also produces top-down effects because the links between letter and word nodes are bidirectional. As some word nodes begin to receive support, they in turn pass support to the nodes representing their constituent letters. Nodes that gather support tend to suppress their competitors ("R" tends to disconfirm "P," and vice versa). The winning interpretation is based on a set of nodes that are mutually supportive ("R" in first position, "E" in second position, "D" in third position, and "RED"). This set will effectively cooperate to suppress their partially supported competitors. Thus, because "RED" is the only word node that is supported by the visual input at all three positions, it becomes the best-supported word node. And in the process, each of the letters that supports "RED" becomes the dominant letter interpretation.

Higher-level problem solving, of course, is not simply perception. Is there any reason, beyond Gestalt intuitions, to suppose that parallel constraint satisfaction also plays a role in the kinds of restructuring we discussed earlier? In fact there is. One clear possibility arises in the process of solving a target problem by analogy, as discussed earlier. For example, how could a person make use of the fortress problem to help solve the radiation problem? Clearly, part of the person's task will be to find the best *mapping*, or set of correspondences, between the elements of the source and target. That is, the person must realize that the general's goal of capturing the fortress corresponds to the doctor's goal of destroying the tumor and that the army's ability to do the capturing is like the rays' capacity to destroy. How can this mapping be established? The problem of finding the best overall mapping can be decomposed into the subproblems of finding the best mapping for each of the constituent elements (just as the problem of word recognition can be decomposed into the subproblems of identifying the constituent letters). But as in the perceptual example in figure 5.8, the subgoals of mapping elements cannot be accomplished in isolation. Why, for example, should we map the fortress onto the tumor, rather than, say, onto the rays? After all, neither pair is highly similar in meaning.

Holyoak and Thagard (1989) have proposed a model of how analogical mappings can be constructed by parallel constraint satisfaction. The basic idea is simple, as illustrated in figure 5.10. The nodes in this figure represent some possible mappings between elements of the radiation and fortress problems, and the arrows represent positive and negative relations between possible decisions, just as in figure 5.9. Of course, the basis for supporting and disconfirming relations is very different for analogy than it is for word recognition. One major constraint on analogical mappings

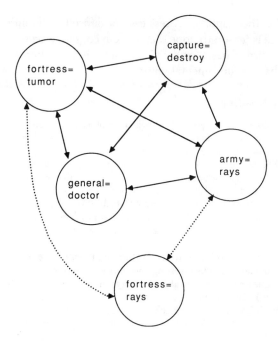

Figure 5.10
A simplified constraint-satisfaction network for finding an analogical mapping between elements of the "fortress" and "radiation" problems.

is that each pair of mapped elements in the source and target should play consistent roles. Holyoak and Thagard term this constraint *structural consistency* (see also Falkenhainer, Forbus, and Gentner 1986). Suppose, for example, that "capturing" maps onto "destroying." If the analogy is structurally consistent, then the capturer in the fortress problem would have to map onto the destroyer in the radiation problem ("army = rays"), and the object of capturing would map onto the object of destruction ("fortress = tumor"). In fact, as illustrated in figure 5.10, the intuitively correct mappings between elements in the two problems form a mutually consistent set and hence support each other.

A closely related constraint on mapping is that the mapping should be *one to one*: if an element of one analogue maps onto a particular element in the other analogue, it probably doesn't also map onto a different element. Thus, the mapping "fortress = tumor" contradicts "fortress = rays" (as does "army = rays"). The structurally consistent mappings thus not only support each other but tend to discredit alternative mappings as well.

Holyoak and Thagard found that a constraint-satisfaction model of analogical mapping provided a good account of a wide range of data regarding when people find the mapping process easy or difficult. Although many hurdles remain, there is reason to hope that work in cognitive science is beginning to establish a firmer basis for the Gestalt intuition that human perception and thinking have a fundamental unity.

Suggestions for Further Reading

A number of books can be explored for more detailed discussions of aspects of problem solving. Newell and Simon 1972 is a classic, but difficult. Rich 1983 is a good introduction to artificial intelligence that provides extensive discussion of Newell and Simon's approach to problem solving. The most highly developed production-system model of cognition is presented in Anderson 1983; this book includes chapters on learning in the context of problem solving. Klahr, Langley, and Neches 1987 is a collection of papers on learning within production systems, and Michalski, Carbonell, and Mitchell 1983, 1986 are two volumes of papers on machine learning, several of which involve problem solving. A thorough treatment of the analysis of verbal protocols as a method of studying problem solving is provided in Ericsson and Simon 1984.

A detailed survey of frontal-lobe functions is provided in Stuss and Benson 1986. Polya 1957 and Wickelgren 1974 discuss useful problem-solving heuristics in an informal manner. A discussion of relations among learning, categorization, analogy, and problem solving is contained in Holland et al. 1986. The Gestalt notion of restructuring is articulated in Duncker 1945. There are many books on creative thinking; Perkins 1981 is engaging to read. The papers cited in section 5.3.3 provide the best available treatments of parallel constraint satisfaction.

Questions

5.1 Can you think of any way in which means-ends analysis might lead a problem solver away from the goal in some situations?

5.2 How does problem decomposition reduce the size of the search space?

5.3 Does research on expertise provide any useful suggestions about how best to teach novices?

5.4 What defines an "insight" problem?

5.5 What qualities make a problem suitable for solution by parallel constraint satisfaction?

5.6 A robot in an office can perform a small number of actions: it can PUSH an object, PICK-UP an object, CARRY an object, PUT-DOWN an object, or WALK by itself. It can PICK-UP an object only if that object has nothing else on it and if its own arm is empty. It can PUSH an object even if that object has something else on it.

   a. Write a production rule appropriate for using the operator PICK-UP. Include relevant preconditions and a goal.

   b. Suppose the robot is in room B and a table with a typewriter on it is in room A. The robot is instructed to move the table into room B. List the subgoals that would be established by means-ends analysis in the course of solving this problem, using the fewest possible number of operators.

5.7 A problem can be solved in five steps. At each step any one of ten operators can be applied. How many possible paths are there in the search space?

5.8 For each of the following problems, state whether a failed solution attempt is ignorable, recoverable, or irrecoverable: (i) cutting a board into three pieces of equal length; (ii) finding a path through a maze; (iii) catching a fly ball in a baseball game; (iv) guessing the password on a computer account.

References

Anderson, J. R. (1983). *The architecture of cognition.* Cambridge, MA: Harvard University Press.

Anderson, J. R. (1987). Skill acquisition: Compilation of weak-method problem solutions. *Psychological Review* 94, 192–210.

Chase, W. G., and H. A. Simon (1973). The mind's eye in chess. In W. G. Chase, ed., *Visual information processing.* New York: Academic Press.

Chi, M. T. H., M. Bassok, M. Lewis, P. Reimann, and R. Glaser (1989). Self-explanations: How students study and use examples in learning to solve problems. *Cognitive Science* 13, 145–182.

Chi, M. T. H., P. J. Feltovich, and R. Glaser (1981). Categorization and representation of physics problems by experts and novices. *Cognitive Science* 5, 121–152.

Chi, M. T. H., R. Glaser, and E. Rees (1982). Expertise in problem solving. In R. J. Sternberg, ed., *Advances in the psychology of human intelligence,* vol. 1. Hillsdale, NJ: L. Erlbaum Associates.

De Groot, A. D. (1965). *Thought and choice in chess.* The Hague: Mouton.

Duncker, K. (1945). On problem solving. *Psychological Monographs* 58 (Whole No. 270).

Ericsson, K. A., and H. A. Simon (1984). *Protocol analysis: Verbal reports as data.* Cambridge, MA: MIT Press.

Falkenhainer, B., K. D. Forbus, and D. Gentner (1986). The structure-mapping engine. In *Proceedings of the Meeting of the American Association for Artificial Intelligence.* Los Altos, CA: Kaufmann.

Gick, M. L., and K. J. Holyoak (1980). Analogical problem solving. *Cognitive Psychology* 12, 306–355.

Gick, M. L., and K. J. Holyoak (1983). Schema induction and analogical transfer. *Cognitive Psychology* 15, 1–38.

Hofstadter, D. R. (1984). The Copycat project: An experiment in nondeterministic and creative analogies. A. I. Laboratory Memo 755, MIT, Cambridge, MA.

Holland, J. H., K. J. Holyoak, R. E. Nisbett, and P. R. Thagard (1986). *Induction: Processes of inference, learning, and discovery.* Cambridge, MA: MIT Press.

Holyoak, K. J., and P. Thagard (1989). Analogical mapping by constraint satisfaction. *Cognitive Science* 13, 295–355.

Holyoak, K. J., and P. Thagard (1989). Analogical mapping by constraint satisfaction. *Cognitive Science.*

Klahr, D., P. Langley, and R. Neches, eds. (1987). *Production system models of learning and development.* Cambridge, MA: MIT Press.

Lakoff, G., and M. Turner (1989). *More than cool reason: The power of poetic metaphor.* Chicago: University of Chicago Press.

Larkin, J. H. (1981). Enriching formal knowledge: A model for learning to solve textbook physics problems. In J. R. Anderson, ed., *Cognitive skills and their acquisition.* Hillsdale, NJ: L. Erlbaum Associates.

Larkin, J. H., J. McDermott, D. P. Simon, and H. A. Simon (1980). Expert and novice performance in solving physics problems. *Science* 208, 1335–1342.

Lasnik, H. (1990). Syntax. In D. N. Osherson and H. Lasnik, eds., *Language: An invitation to cognitive science, volume 1.* Cambridge, MA: MIT Press.

Lewis, C. H. (1978). Production system models of practice effects. Doctoral dissertation, University of Michigan, Ann Arbor.

Luria, A. R. (1969). Frontal lobe syndromes. In P. J. Vinken and G. W. Bruyn, eds., *Handbook of clinical neurology,* vol. 2. Amsterdam: North Holland.

McClelland, J. L., and D. E. Rumelhart (1981). An interactive activation model of context effects in letter perception: Part 1. An account of basic findings. *Psychological Review* 88, 375–407.

McClelland, J. L., D. E. Rumelhart, and G. E. Hinton (1986). The appeal of parallel distributed processing. In D. E. Rumelhart, J. L. McClelland, and the PDP Research Group, *Parallel distributed processing: Explorations in the microstructure of cognition*. Vol. 1: *Foundations*. Cambridge, MA: MIT Press.

Maier, N. R. F. (1930). Reasoning in humans. I. On direction. *Journal of Comparative Psychology* 10, 115–143.

Marr, D., and T. Poggio (1976). Cooperative computation of stereo disparity. *Science* 194, 283–287.

Metcalfe, J. (1986a). Feeling of knowing in memory and problem solving. *Journal of Experimental Psychology: Learning, Memory, and Cognition* 12, 288–294.

Metcalfe, J. (1986b). Premonitions of insight predict impending error. *Journal of Experimental Psychology: Learning, Memory, and Cognition* 12, 623–634.

Metcalfe, J., and D. Wiebe (1987). Intuition in insight and noninsight problem solving. *Memory and Cognition* 15, 238–246.

Michalski, R., J. G. Carbonell, and T. M. Mitchell, eds. (1983). *Machine learning: An artificial intelligence approach*. Palo Alto, CA: Tioga Press.

Michalski, R., J. G. Carbonell, and T. M. Mitchell, eds. (1986). *Machine learning: An artificial intelligence approach*, vol. 2. Los Altos, CA: Kaufmann.

Newell, A. (1973). Production systems: Models of control structures. In W. G. Chase, ed., *Visual information processing*. New York: Academic Press.

Newell, A. (1985). Duncker on thinking: An inquiry into progress in cognition. In S. Koch and D. Leary, eds., *A century of psychology as science*. New York: McGraw-Hill.

Newell, A., and H. A. Simon (1972). *Human problem solving*. Englewood Cliffs, NJ: Prentice-Hall.

Perkins, D. N. (1981). *The mind's best work*. Cambridge, MA: Harvard University Press.

Polya, G. (1957). *How to solve it*. Garden City, NY: Doubleday/Anchor.

Reitman, W. (1964). Heuristic decision procedures, open constraints, and the structure of ill-defined problems. In W. Shelley and G. L. Bryan, eds., *Human judgments and optimality*. New York: Wiley.

Rich, E. (1983). *Artificial intelligence*. New York: McGraw-Hill.

Rosenbloom, P. S., and A. Newell (1986). The chunking of goal hierarchies: A generalized model of practice. In Michalski, Carbonell, and Mitchell 1986.

Rumelhart, D. E., P. Smolensky, J. L. McClelland, and G. E. Hinton (1986). Schemata and sequential thought processes in PDP models. In J. L. McClelland, D. E. Rumelhart, and the PDP Research Group, *Parallel distributed processing: Explorations in the microstructure of cognition*. Vol. 2: *Psychological and biological models*. Cambridge, MA: MIT Press.

Shallice, T. (1982). Specific impairment of planning. In D. E. Broadbent and L. Weiskrantz, eds., *The neuropsychology of cognitive function*. London: The Royal Society.

Shallice, T. (1988). *From neuropsychology to mental structure*. Cambridge: Cambridge University Press.

Simon, H. A. (1981). *The sciences of the artificial*. 2nd ed. Cambridge, MA: MIT Press.

Spencer, R. M., and R. W. Weisberg (1986). Is analogy sufficient to facilitate transfer during problem solving? *Memory and Cognition* 14, 442–449.

Stuss, D. T., and D. F. Benson (1986). *The frontal lobes*. New York: Raven Press.

Sweller, J., R. F. Mawer, and M. R. Ward (1983). Development of expertise in mathematical problem solving. *Journal of Experimental Psychology: General* 112, 639–661.

Wickelgren, W. A. (1974). *How to solve problems*. San Francisco: W. H. Freeman.

Chapter 6

Cognitive Development

Susan Carey

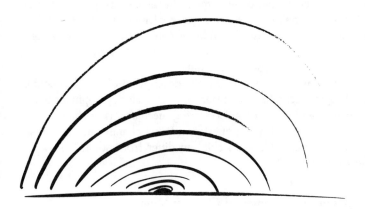

Many chapters in this volume characterize the richness of human knowledge. Conceptual structures of many types support our understanding of the world, our powers of inference, and our problem-solving skills. Accounting for the *acquisition* of these structures is the goal of the field of cognitive development. Its major twentieth century figure is Jean Piaget, a Swiss biologist and psychologist who published his first scientific paper at the age of 11 and who did not slow down until his death at 84, some fifty books and hundreds of papers later. Piaget dubbed his field of inquiry *genetic epistemology* (that is, genesis of knowledge) and sought to understand the growth of knowledge in the history of ideas as well as in the individual. This chapter will focus on the acquisition of knowledge by individuals, both as children and as adults.

6.1 The Components of a Theory of Cognitive Development

Because a theory of cognitive development is a theory of change, a first step is to discover what kinds of changes there are. For any case of knowledge acquisition we focus on, we must characterize the initial state (that is, the starting point for the target developmental change), describe the changes that occur, and specify the mechanisms producing change. These are the components of an account of knowledge acquisition at all levels of development—whether we are trying to account for the changes underlying an adult's becoming an expert at chess, an adult's learning quantum mechanics, or a child's attaining an understanding of the social and physical world. However, there is one important difference between knowledge acquisition in adulthood and knowledge acquisition in childhood. As far as we know, genetically programmed changes in brain structure are completed by late adolescence. Thus, maturational mechanisms play no role in adult cognitive development. In the case of the child, it is possible that maturationally driven changes contribute to the course of cognitive development; it is also possible, of course, that many developmental changes in childhood are entirely accounted for by the same kinds of learning mechanisms that operate in adults.

In this chapter we will concentrate on the description of developmental change. Providing an accurate description of cognitive development is far from a trivial matter and is prior to discovering mechanisms of change. We will want answers to the following questions: What changes in the course of cognitive development? How do children differ from adults? How do novices differ from experts?

6.2   The Locus of Developmental Change: Memory

When we study children of different ages carrying out any particular task, we normally see behavioral changes. Usually (though not always) children improve as they get older. For example, suppose you show subjects a series of photographs of faces and then ask them to pick out the faces they have just seen from other photographs included as distractors. Two-year-olds succeed on this task if you limit the number of faces for them to encode to just *one* before you ask them to pick that one from a pair. In contrast, adults can perform at a 90 percent success rate with initial set sizes of 30 or even more, depending upon how similar the distractors are to the targets. Such dramatic developmental improvement is the rule in studies of cognitive development. But what changes in the child's cognitive apparatus underlie this change in performance? Is there developmental improvement in pattern recognition, generally? Is there developmental improvement in memory, generally? Do 2-year-olds know less about how faces differ from each other, so they are less able to pick out what is distinctive about a newly seen face? These are very different possibilities (and there are many more, of course); each could be contributing to the observed developmental differences between 2-year-olds and adults. As we will see, locating the sources of developmental change is a difficult matter.

6.2.1   Memory Span

A very robust finding is that digit memory span increases markedly between age 4 and adulthood; in fact, it more than doubles. That is, adults can repeat strings of seven randomly ordered digits (plus or minus a few) after an experimenter reads them; 4-year-olds can repeat only about three. But what causes this behavioral improvement? One possibility is that the behavioral change reflects a change in immediate memory capacity per se; that is, memory span itself is increasing. With increasing age there are more "slots" in short-term memory. If this is correct, we would be locating the change at a relatively abstract level, at what is called a *domain-general* level, because the change would affect memory for material from any content area or domain. And indeed, memory span for letters, for words (under many conditions), and for many other kinds of materials doubles between age 4 and adulthood, which is consistent with the claim that memory capacity itself is changing.

There is another possibility, however. Four-year-olds, after all, know much less about digits, letters, and words than do adults. Furthermore, adults surely exploit their knowledge of numbers and letters when encoding lists of such items in short-term memory. For example, if the list you are to remember begins 7, 4, 1, you might notice that these count down by 3s; another part of a list might be part of your telephone number. If you notice such relations on encoding, retrieval will be enhanced (see chapter 1). Perhaps the difference between 4-year-olds and adults lies in the knowledge available to organize the input. On this view, 4-year-olds do not have an information-processing limit on memory, do not have a shorter memory span than do adults. They are simply less efficient at putting some materials into short-term memory, because of their relatively impoverished knowledge of those materials. On this account, the developmental change in question is located at what is called a *domain-specific* level, in the particular knowledge of the materials to be remembered.

To see that more slots and more knowledge are really quite different possibilities, ask yourself two questions. First, can you think of an experimental test that would decide between the two? If data can be brought to bear on deciding the issue, they are clearly different accounts. Second, think about the mechanisms of change that would underlie development in each case. It is difficult to imagine any but a maturational mechanism underlying an increase in the number of slots of short-term memory; alternatively, learning mechanisms clearly underlie acquiring knowledge of numbers and the alphabet. That is, we learn about numbers and the alphabet in the course of such experiences as learning to read and studying arithmetic.

Data can indeed be brought to bear on deciding between these two possibilities. If materials could be found about which 4-year-olds and adults have equal knowledge, the two positions make different predictions. If the domain-general account is correct, then no matter what the material, the 4-year-olds' memory span for it should be less. Alternatively, if the domain-specific account is correct, then memory span for materials on which adults and children are truly matched for knowledge should be the same. Chi (1976) reviewed the data on age differences in memory span and found two cases for which the equal knowledge condition was met: nonsense figures that are meaningless to both adults and children, and high-frequency concrete nouns (like *table, cat*) that are equally familiar to both adults and children. In both cases the ratio of adult's memory span to 4-year-old's memory span fell from the usual 2 : 1 to 1.3 : 1. Equating knowledge of the materials almost erased the developmental difference in memory span.

6.2.2 Speed of the Central Processor

In sum, it appears that in spite of the robust finding of developmental differences in digit span, letter span, and memory spans for hosts of other materials, *memory span* itself does not change with development, at least after age 4. In this case the most abstract, domain-general level is not the locus of the developmental change. This does not mean, of course, that no domain-general changes occur in the information processor. Kail (1986) has argued for a maturationally driven increase in the speed of the central processor. Many researchers have noted that children are slower than adults at just about any task on which they are compared. This observation permits two competing explanations. (Before you read on, ask yourself what the two competing explanations are.)

Domain-specific
Novices at any skill are slower than experts. Even among adults, novice carpenters, for example, work more slowly than expert carpenters. One consequence of practicing a skill is becoming faster at its execution (Anderson 1981). The relative slowness of children could just reflect their being universal novices; relative to adults, children are novices in every domain. Developmental differences in speed may simply reflect domain-specific expertise, resulting from more practice at every skill.

Domain-general
With maturation, the central processor carries out its operations faster.

Kail presents two arguments that there is a domain-general component to age-related increases in speed at cognitive tasks, resulting from increased speed of the central processor. The first argument rests on techniques from information-processing psychology that allow us to decompose the total reaction time to execute some task into components. For example, suppose your task is to state whether *a* and *A* depict the same letter, albeit in different typographical cases. This task requires visual processing, leading to mental representations of the visual displays. Central processes then match these visual representations to stored mental representations and thus recognize them as lowercase and uppercase *a*'s, respectively. Further central processes note that these are versions of the same letter and plan the response "Same." Finally, motor processes execute the response. All of these processes take time, and contribute to the total time needed to carry out the task. Techniques exist that allow us to estimate the times for some of the purely central processes (Sternberg 1969). Kail compared the developmental courses (between ages 8 and 16) of speed of execution of two very different central processes (deciding whether two letters in different cases match or not, and mentally rotating a stimulus). He found identical exponential growth functions for the two types of processes. That is, speed at carrying out each of these two central processes increased exponentially, and the exponential rate was the same for both.

Kail's second argument relies on cases where child experts are compared with adult novices; children are still slower. The study he cites (Roth 1983) compared child chess experts with adult chess novices. The children had studied chess for thousands of hours and played thousands of games, could compete successfully with adult masters, and yet were slower on a variety of tasks that required making judgments about chess positions. These data are suggestive of a maturationally driven change in the speed of the central processor.

6.2.3   Metamemorial Development

A distinction must be drawn between two ways in which cognitive development may proceed at a domain-general level. First, the underlying information-processing device may change in various ways that have an impact on all computations using that device. Increases in memory span and increases in the speed of the central processor are examples of domain-general changes of this type. Second, knowledge itself varies in its abstractness. Some knowledge, such as mathematical knowledge, has implications for learning and reasoning in many other content domains. Therefore, acquisition of such knowledge would constitute a kind of domain-general developmental change. When seeking to locate the sources of developmental changes, we must consider the possibility of domain-general changes of both sorts.

Consider metamemorial knowledge (knowledge about memory). There is no doubt that young children lack explicit knowledge of many aspects of memory; for instance, they are unrealistic about how much they can remember, and they do not realize that some things might be easier to remember than others. Because they have a relatively impoverished conception of what is involved in memorizing something, they are unable to appreciate the need for mnemonic strategies, and they are unable to devise appropriate ones. For example, suppose someone asks you to re-member the following list and tells you that you may repeat it back in any order you like: *table, dog, spoon, chair, cat, fork, lamp, bird, knife, rug, pig, plate.* Even if you heard this list only once, it would be fairly easy for you to recall all the items. This is so even though there are 12 of them, thus exceeding your memory span of 7 ± 2. You would notice the obvious structure in this list and organize your memory into the categories of "furniture," "dining implements," and "animals." Further, you would rehearse aspects of the list as you heard additional items. Young children do neither: they do not rehearse, and they do not cluster items in free recall. Indeed, they do not spontaneously use any of a wide range of mnemonic devices that could help them succeed in any given memory task (see Flavell 1985; Kail 1979). There is marked improvement in the use of mnemonic strategies between the ages of 5 and 10. If 5- or 6-year-olds are taught to use a particular mnemonic device such as rehearsal, they can do it, and their performance on memory tasks improves as a result of using it (again supporting the claim that the differences between children and adults on short-term memory tasks is not memory capacity as such). However, they do not spontaneously use this strategy unless specifically instructed to, even after they have been taught it.

Such metamemorial knowledge is relatively domain-general; it applies to remembering any kind of material. The mechanisms by which it is acquired are most likely learning mechanisms. Knowledge about memory is part of a rich body of concepts concerning the human mind, knowledge, and the acquisition and use of knowledge. Throughout childhood the theory of mind is being elaborated; metamemorial development reflects and depends upon this elaboration.

6.3   The Locus of Developmental Change: Reasoning and Thinking

The problem of separating the contributions of relatively domain-specific and relatively domain-general developmental changes is ubiquitous. It arises when we try to understand more complex cognitive development, as well as when we try to understand relatively simple cognitive achievements such as memory for lists. Following Piaget, most students of cognitive development have sought the best characterization of how children at various ages think differently from each other and from adults. Piaget believed that there are four major stages of cognitive development: *sensori-motor* (birth to age 2, during which time the child is not capable of symbolic representations), *preoperational* (age 2 to 6, during which time the child is egocentric, unable to distinguish appearance from reality, and incapable of certain types of logical inferences), *concrete operational* (age 6 to 12, during which time the child becomes capable of the logic of classification and linear orderings), and *formal operational* (age 12 and beyond, during which time the child becomes capable of formal, deductive, logical reasoning). The age estimates are rough; different children reach the cognitive milestones at different ages.

According to Piaget's stage theory, the reasoning anomalies exhibited by children at a certain age (say, age 5) in *all* content areas are due to characteristics of these children's cognitive stage. Similarly, the successes of older children (say, 8-year-olds) on the same tasks are made possible by their having reached the next stage. Thus, Piaget's theory locates developmental change at the domain-general level of description.

6.3.1   Preoperational and Concrete Operational Thought

For purposes of illustration, let us concentrate on the most well studied of Piaget's stage transitions: the transition between preoperational thought and concrete operational thought. A discussion of Piaget's long intellectual history, even with respect to his views of this one transition, is beyond the scope of this chapter. In the course of his career he tried many different formulations of how the thinking of preschool children differs from that of late elementary school children. As he developed each new formulation, he did not abandon his earlier views; rather, he sought an understanding of how the different formulations were related to each other. To understand Piaget's theory, it is necessary to know something about the kinds of domain-general changes he posited. Some of his hypotheses are listed in table 6.1. It is also necessary to know what kinds of changes, at the behavioral level, the stage changes are meant to account for.

Piaget presented hundreds of phenomena that (he claimed) diagnose the fundamental differences between the thought processes of the young child (say, age 4) and those of the older child (say, age 10). To get a flavor of how Piaget's theory worked, let us look at a small sampling of these phenomena and consider how each exemplified one or more of the hypothesized domain-general changes listed in table 6.1. Most of these phenomena have been replicated literally thousands of times. The issue in evaluating Piaget's stage theory is not whether the phenomena he discovered are real and replicable; if one does the experiment as Piaget did, one finds what he found. As our first example, let us take the most famous finding: young children apparently do not realize that basic quantities such as weight, quantity of matter, and volume are conserved over changes in shape. Many thousands of children have been tested on the

Table 6.1
Piagetian proposals for the difference between preoperational and concrete operational children.

Preoperational children	Concrete operational children
Can focus on only one dimension of a task at a time	Can coordinate two dimensions
Cannot represent linear orders or make transitive inferences over linear orderings	Can represent linear orders and make transitive inferences
Cannot represent classes or the inclusion relation among classes	Can represent classes and the class-inclusion relation
Are egocentric; cannot consider others' points of view	Can adopt others' viewpoints
Have no notion of physical causality	Grasp physical causality
Cannot distinguish appearance from reality	Grasp the appearance-reality distinction

basic procedure. First they are asked to make two balls that contain equal amounts of playdough. Then they watch while one of the balls is flattened into a pancake, and they are asked whether both the remaining ball and the pancake still contain the same amount of playdough, whether they still weigh the same amount, and whether they still would displace the same amount of water. The universal finding is that young children (say, 5-year-olds) maintain that the quantity of playdough, the weight, and the volume have changed, whereas older children (say, 10-year-olds) unhesitatingly reply that quantity, weight, and volume are conserved, that the two blobs of playdough look different but are really the same, and that one is wider, but it's also flatter.

It does seem that in answering these questions about weight, amount of matter, and volume, the young child fails to distinguish appearance from reality, where the older child succeeds; it does seem that the younger child focuses on just one dimension where the older child succeeds in coordinating two. Thus, Piaget's theory accounts for the responses of the nonconserving child in terms of domain-general limitations such as those listed in table 6.1. Nonconservation is only one in a wide range of Piagetian phenomena, supposedly reflecting the preschool child's characteristic modes of thought. To get a feeling for the variety of phenomena, consider the following (Piaget's explanation for each phenomenon given in parentheses):

1. *Seriation.* Shown a series of sticks, arranged in order of length, and then asked to reproduce this series, young children cannot do so. They make two groups (the short sticks and the long sticks), or else they alternate short-long, short-long, short-long. The problem is solved by

age 7 or 8. (Preoperational children's responses reflect their inability to construct linear orderings and to coordinate two dimensions—that is, to see one stick as simultaneously larger than a second stick and smaller than a third.)

2. *Transitivity.*   If young children are taught that a particular red ball is heavier than an orange ball, and that the orange ball is heavier than a yellow ball, they can draw no conclusion about the relative weights of the red and yellow balls. This problem is solved by age 8 or so. (Preoperational children's responses reflect their inability to construct and make transitive inferences over linear orderings.)

3. *Communications game.*   Children are seated on opposite sides of a barrier, so that they can see only the objects on their own side. The experimenter indicates an object on one child's side of the barrier (say, a small black cube) and that child's task is to describe it so that the other child can pick the corresponding object from his side. A typical interchange between 5-year-olds is

Child 1:   It's this one.

Child 2 (pointing at random):   This one?

Child 1:   Yes.

This problem is solved by age 9 or 10. (The young child's performance reflects the egocentricity of preoperational children.)

4. *Mountain problem.*   The child is looking at a model of a mountain with different objects on its sides (for example, a ski jump, a house, a road, and a tree). She is asked to draw it as it appears to her, and also to draw it as it appears to the experimenter. Five-year-old children draw the same picture each time: namely, a picture from their own point of view. This problem is solved by age 8 or 9. (Another reflection of the preoperational child's egocentricity.)

5. *Childhood animism.*   Young children maintain that the sun, the wind, clouds, cars, fires, and even rocks rolling down hills are alive. By age 10, life is attributed only to animals and plants. (Reflects the preoperational child's inability to understand mechanical causality.)

6. *Gender constancy.*   Young children maintain that a girl can be changed into a boy by cutting her hair and inducing her to wear different clothes and play with different toys. By age 7 or 8, children conserve gender over this type of superficial transformation. (Another reflection of the preoperational child's inability to distinguish appearance from reality.)

7. *Class inclusion.*   Children are shown 8 flowers, 5 daisies, and 3 roses. Asked to count the flowers, the daisies, and the roses, they do so correctly. Asked which there are more of—daisies or flowers—young children answer, "More daisies." Children succeed on this task by age 8 or so. (The

young children's failure reflects their inability to construct class-inclusion hierarchies and their inability to coordinate two dimensions of a task at once—that is, to see the daisies as both daisies and flowers at the same time.)

This is a very small sampling of the questions to which 4- to 6-year-olds give surprisingly nonadult answers. Piaget's program was to bring order to this bewildering catalogue of differences between preschool children, on the one hand, and 10-year-olds, on the other. As the list indicates, in some cases the behavior of the preoperational child transparently reflects what Piaget took to be the underlying domain-general deficiencies (for instance, young children's behavior on the mountain task reflects egocentricity). In other cases the relation between the child's behavior and the stage characterization is not so clear. Childhood animism, for example, was taken to reflect the child's lack of a concept of physical causality. According to this view, the only causal schema young children have is intentional causation. But they see the wind, clouds, the sun, moving cars, and so forth, as causal agents, since they clearly affect other objects. Therefore, children invest them with beliefs, desires, and finally life.

Piaget's vision was an extremely powerful one. He sought to characterize the *systematic* differences between the young child and the older child—and just a few systematic differences at that (differences like those in table 6.1). This short list supposedly captures how 4-year-olds differ from 10-year-olds in a way that enables us to understand the 4-year-old's limitations in reasoning about morality, spatial perspective, physical quantities, games of marbles, friendship, numbers, geometry, and so forth—indeed, about any particular subject. If Piaget were right, then the problem of explaining cognitive development would be simplified. If we could explain the developmental changes that characterize each stage-shift, we would then understand the hundreds of changes in thinking and reasoning about specific problems.

As in the memory example, the mechanisms we would consider to underlie a stage-shift would depend on the nature of the shift. In some of Piaget's writings it seemed that he was positing changes in the child's actual representational capacity. If children literally cannot represent linear orders, or class inclusion, then it is difficult to see how they could learn to do so; some maturational mechanism would be implicated in such a change. In other writings it seemed that Piaget was positing metaconceptual development: the child becomes aware of knowledge, of inference, and of learning. Metaconceptual understanding is one important aspect of children's knowledge of people, part of their theory of mind, and thus is learned like any other knowledge. Piagetian stage-shifts, like domain-general changes in memory capacity, could be of two types: (1) changes in the fundamental representational capacity of the underlying information processor, or (2) changes due to knowledge acquisition, albeit very abstract knowledge.

6.3.2   Challenges to the Existence of Preoperational Thought

Research on cognitive development has challenged Piaget's stage theory, calling into question the degree to which most of the developmental differences he observed should be located at the domain-general level of abstraction. The criticism has been particularly vigorous when Piaget's claim is interpreted as a claim about the child's representational capacity. The challenges take two forms. First, by simplifying Piaget's tasks, or by studying different tasks that require the capacity in question, researchers have demonstrated that preschool children have many of the representational or computational capacities Piaget thought they lacked. Second, researchers have provided alternative explanations for the Piagetian phenomena that had previously been taken as evidence that young children lacked the capacity in question.

Linear Orderings and Transitivity

To take an oversimplified example from this research: The claims that young children cannot construct linear orderings or make transitive inferences over linear orderings were supported by their behavior on tasks involving seriation and transitivity of length, weight, and so forth. Consider the transitivity problem, wherein 4-year-olds who know that a green stick is longer than a yellow stick, and that the yellow stick is longer than a red stick, cannot deduce that the green stick must be longer than the red stick. It may be the case that the 4-year-old simply cannot remember the premises. Indeed, Bryant and Trabasso (1971) showed that given enough drill with the premises, 3- and 4-year-old children could construct five- or six-item series. They could impose a linear ordering on the following series: the yellow stick is longer than the orange stick; the orange stick is longer than the black stick; the black stick is longer than the red stick; the red stick is longer than the white stick; and the white stick is longer than the green stick. They could do this even though they never saw the lengths, and even though they were presented the pairwise terms of information in random orders. To do so, they needed to be drilled on the pairwise comparisons hundreds of times, over different sessions. However, once they had learned all the pairs, they could easily draw the relevant transitive inferences. In the present example, this requires inferring the relative lengths of the orange stick and the red stick, which the 3- and 4-year-olds could do.

Bryant and Trabasso deny Piaget's claim that the preschool child lacks a fundamental representational capacity (namely, the capacity to represent ordered series). This is not to say, however, that there is no development with regard to transitive inferences. No doubt there is important meta-conceptual development. The preschool child can represent the relation "shorter than," can construct a linear series by concatenating pairs that stand in this relation, and can derive some inferences from this representation. But this does not mean that the child is *explicitly aware* of the notion of transitivity. For example, it is unlikely that the preschool child could be taught to explicitly distinguish relations that are transitive (like "shorter than") from relations that are not (like "is in love with"). This is because the preschool child's metalinguistic and metaconceptual knowledge is so limited: preschool children have difficulty focusing on language, as opposed to the world described by language. They can reason about sticks, but not about words like *stick*. Until they have a clear, explicit conception of language, per se, they will find it difficult to focus on argument structure, per se.

Bryant and Trabasso's work exemplifies both components of the denial of Piagetian claims: a positive demonstration that young children have the representational capacity in question (preschool children clearly can represent linear orderings and make deductive inferences over them) and a diagnosis of their problem with the standard Piagetian task (in this case memory limitations). There is more to the story, however: we must explain the extreme memory limitations of preschool children. Why do they need so many trials in order to learn the series? One source of young children's memory limitation is lack of metaconceptual knowledge. Their lack of an explicit analysis of memory demands, plus their lack of explicit knowledge of the logical properties of relations such as "shorter than," most probably keeps them from coming up with efficient strategies for memorizing the experimental series.

Our conclusions concerning developmental differences in the capacity to represent linear orderings parallel our conclusions concerning developmental differences in memory capacity. It appears that there are no domain-general changes in information-processing capacity in either case. In this sense, development does not proceed at a domain-general level. Memory span does not grow with age; children do not *become* capable of representing linear orderings. Also, in both cases there is one sense in which developmental changes *are* captured at a domain-general level: acquisition of abstract metaconceptual knowledge plays a role in the developmental differences in performance on both memory tasks and inference tasks.

Egocentricity

Consider the case of preschool children's egocentricity—their apparent inability to conceive of other people's points of view. Until age 6 or 7 children give egocentric responses on the mountain problem and in the communications game. Nonegocentric responses become dominant between the ages of 8 and 10. These are just a few of the many tasks Piaget studied in which a shift from egocentric to nonegocentric responses occurs around age 7. The consistency in age across a large number of tasks is one source of support for Piaget's stage theory. This consistency supports the claim that around age 7 the child first becomes capable of nonegocentric thinking.

It turns out that this consistency was illusory. There are now many indications that preschool children are not egocentric across the board and that they acquire nonegocentric abilities at various ages. For example, Flavell has studied young children's understanding of the conditions under which other people can see what they see. The "egocentric" response would be to assume that other people's perceptual experience is the same as one's own. A very simple task is to ask a child to show his mother a photograph. Even a 2-year-old turns the photo toward his mother, so that she can see it and he cannot. Using many such simple tasks, Flavell has shown that 2-year-olds realize that in order for someone else to see something, that person must have a direct line of sight to it (no barrier), must have his eyes open, and must be looking at it. Children do not assume that others can see what they can see. Flavell calls the 2-year-old's ability *level 1 perspective taking* (Flavell et al. 1981).

However, 2- and 3-year-old children systematically fail at a wide range of related tasks, those requiring what Flavell calls *level 2 perspective taking*. In level 1 tasks children must simply decide whether someone else sees what they see. In level 2 tasks both participants are seeing the same thing, but for various reasons the two have different mental representations of it. Until age 4 the child cannot coordinate two different mental representations of the same thing. For example, imagine the experimenter and the child seated opposite each other, looking at a picture of a turtle that is lying flat on the table, oriented so that it appears right side up to the experimenter. Children up to the age of 4 will say (correctly) that the turtle appears upside down to them and will maintain (incorrectly) that the turtle appears upside down to the experimenter as well (Flavell et al. 1981). Similarly, suppose an experimenter shows you a tiny portion of a line drawing, as in figure 6.1a, and asks you what the line drawing depicts. You answer that you do not know. The experimenter shows you that the drawing is of an elephant (figure 6.1b) and then once again covers up all but the portion in figure 6.1a. The experimenter next brings in another person and tells you that this person has never seen the drawing before. The question is, Does this new person, who sees what is on figure 6.1a, know what the line drawing depicts? As long as some part of the drawing is visible, 3-year-olds maintain that the new person knows it is an elephant, can see that it is an elephant (Taylor 1985). If the drawing is completely

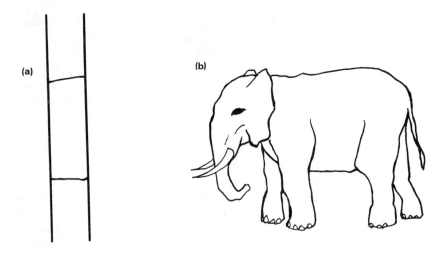

Figure 6.1
(a) View of elephant's side; front and back of elephant are occluded by two pieces of paper.
(b) View of whole elephant.

covered, this becomes a level 1 perspective-taking task, and the 3-year-old succeeds.

So far we have seen that even 2-year-olds are not egocentric when level 1 perspective taking is at issue and that the transition from egocentric responses to nonegocentric responses on level 2 perspective-taking tasks occurs around age 4. Let us look at one more example of a task on which a shift from egocentric to nonegocentric responses occurs well before the putative stage-shift from preoperational to concrete operational thought. Suppose a child and an experimenter are setting up a party for some dollhouse dolls who want to drink some apple juice. They find a dollhouse table, dollhouse chairs, and dolls. "Now what do we need?" the experimenter asks. "Some glasses," the child answers, and so the experimenter brings out a shot glass—a little glass to a child or adult, but a big glass to a dollhouse doll. The experimenter then asks the child whether this is a big glass or a little glass. Young children take their own point of view and respond that it is a little glass. If then asked, "That's right, for you it is a little glass; what about the dolls? For the dolls, is it a big glass or a little glass?," young children respond impatiently, "A little glass," still taking their own point of view. Just as Piaget predicted, young children make the egocentric response. Slightly older children spontaneously take the dolls' point of view at the first question, answering that it is a big glass, but have difficulty when asked whether it is big or little for themselves. Some take the dolls' point of view for both questions. However, in this case the switch from the egocentric to the nonegocentric response occurs when children are around 2 years and 9 months old, not at age 7 as Piaget's stage theory would predict. By age 4 all children can switch back and forth with ease, coordinating the two frames of reference (Carey, unpublished data).

Two conclusions about the young child's egocentricity follow from such observations. First, children do make egocentric errors. A common developmental pattern is that younger children fail at some task through failing to appreciate the other person's perspective, whereas older children succeed. However, Piaget's characterization of preschool children as *generally* egocentric is false. Preschool children have no domain-general inability to appreciate that other people have points of view that differ from their own. Some egocentric errors have been corrected by age 2, others by age 3, others by age 4, and so on, whereas others are not corrected until age 8 or 10. Even adults are often egocentric in certain respects.

If the problem is not egocentricity per se, what is it? The point that is hard to grasp is that there is *no single* problem. Bigness, for example, is an inherently relative concept; something is big or small relative to some standard. Young children have difficulty in any task that offers a choice of frames of reference, but not all such tasks involve egocentric errors. For example, suppose you show a young child two tiny shoes, one for a newborn infant and one for a toddler. Both are small, but one is smaller than the other. If you indicate the toddler's shoe and ask, "Is this a small shoe?," a child under the age of 5 will answer, "No, the big shoe," meaning the bigger of the two shoes. Here the child takes the other shoe as the standard of comparison, rather than a mentally represented standard-sized shoe. Children can use such a standard (if there is no infant shoe present); the problem arises when they must shift from one frame of reference to another. This is also the problem in the apple juice case—not egocentricity, but sensitivity to subtle cues telling the child what frame of reference is relevant to the judgment in question.

Different problems underlie children's failure at tasks requiring level 2 perspective taking. These require that children focus on the representation rather than on the thing represented. They can reason about whether the experimenter sees something or not but apparently cannot reason about how that thing looks to the experimenter. Thus, the appropriate context for understanding level 2 perspective-taking errors seems to be the child's knowledge of mental representations. Characterizing the problem precisely is a subtle matter, but it seems clear that its locus is not a domain-general limitation leading to egocentric judgments in all content areas.

6.3.3 Consequences of Abandoning Piagetian Stage Theory for Studies of Cognitive Development

It now seems unlikely that the grand simplifying description of universal developmental stages that Piaget proposed is correct—especially if the stages are interpreted as reflecting domain-general changes in the representational or computational capacity of the information processor. It seems that cognitive development is mainly the result of acquiring knowledge in particular content domains. In the rest of the chapter we will leave Piagetian stage theory and consider what kinds of questions arise when we try to understand domain-specific knowledge acquisition.

If cognitive development is to be undersood in terms of domain-specific knowledge acquisition, we must decide what domains of knowledge we should study. We could study how children learn the alphabet, or the days of the week, but somehow these seem like relatively trivial domains, and the answer (rote memorization) seems already clear. We want to study knowledge that seems to pose interesting conceptual problems for the child or that seems to have broad implications for the child's conceptual functioning. These criteria would be met by many domains of knowledge, including the domain of metaconceptual knowledge. Metaconceptual knowledge has now played two related roles in our story. We have seen that with respect to both memory development and reasoning, one sense in which the locus of development is domain-general is well supported by the data: the sense that acquisition of metaconceptual knowledge influences the child's performance on tasks. Additionally, some egocentric responses reflect the child's impoverished conceptions of mental representations; these conceptions are one aspect of metaconceptual knowledge. Indeed, metaconceptual knowledge has broad implications for the child's functioning outside the laboratory as well. What children understand about their own and others' minds is crucial to their making sense of why people do what they do. Adults understand their own and other people's behavior in terms of intentional causality, in terms of the beliefs and the desires of the actors. If asked why Jennie opened the cookie jar, an acceptable answer is that she was hungry, or that she wanted a cookie, and that she thought there were cookies in the jar. When do children have such a theory? What is its origin? How are we to explain children's failures—in other words, in what ways does their theory differ from adults'? How does the theory of mind evolve?

6.4   The Preschool Child's Theory of Mind

As indicated earlier, for any target developmental change, we must characterize the initial state and the changes that occur. For this example, we will take the failures of 3- and 4-year-olds as our target, so we will want to understand where 2- to young 3-year-olds begin. Two- and 3-year-olds have some aspects of the adult theory of mind. They solve level 1 perspective-taking tasks, which shows they understand quite a bit about the perceptual experiences of others. They have mastered many words for talking about beliefs and desires (*want, need, think, know, remember, hope,* and so on), and they seem to use them to mean what adults do (Shatz, Wellman, and Silber 1983). They know that dreams, ideas, and mental pictures are different from real objects. That is, they know that they can rotate a mental picture just by thinking about it, but they cannot do so to a real object; they know that others see and can touch a real cookie but cannot see or touch the child's idea of a cookie (Wellman and Estes 1986). Thus, by age 3 they have concepts of mental representations, and they grasp some fundamental differences between mental representations and reality. However, 3-year-olds fail startlingly on a series of tasks designed to diagnose whether they understand want-belief causation. They seem to be unable to attribute *false* beliefs to others.

A few studies demonstrate the 3-year-old's difficulties with false beliefs. In one, a child (Johnny) is shown a matchbox and asked what is inside it; reasonably, he answers, "Matches." The box is opened and M&Ms are revealed, a salient event. Johnny is allowed to eat a few and the box is closed. A new child (Amy) enters, who has not seen the box before. Johnny is asked what Amy will think is in the matchbox. "M&Ms," he answers (Perner, Leekam, and Wimmer 1987). Indeed, when Johnny is asked what he thought was in the box when he first saw it, before it was opened, he answers, "M&Ms" (Gopnik and Astington 1988). Apparently he cannot even report his own previous false belief.

In a closely related task reported by Wimmer and Perner (1983), a young child watches two puppets eating cookies from a cupboard. Cookie Monster is getting more than his share and Big Bird is upset. Cookie Monster leaves; Big Bird explains he will hide the cookies under the bed, and then does so. Cookie Monster returns, and the child is asked whether Cookie Monster knows where the cookies are. The child gives the nonegocentric answer, "No" (nonegocentric because the child knows where the cookies are; the child does not assume that because she knows where they are, Cookie Monster knows where they are). When asked where Cookie Monster thinks the cookies are, however, or where Cookie Monster will look, the child answers, "Under the bed" (where they are, rather than where Cookie Monster last saw them).

Both of these false-belief tasks are solved by age 4. The task for researchers in cognitive development is to understand the conceptual difficulty the 3-year-old is having. Piaget would have said, "Egocentricity," but we have seen that this notion has no explanatory force; 3-year-olds are nonegocentric in many of their judgments, so we cannot explain these failures by appeals to the preschool child's egocentricity. We do know that there is no simple artifact underlying the child's performance. Many, many different versions of the task have been tried. For example, in the puppet version, children are asked whether Cookie Monster saw the cookies being moved—they all answer correctly. Children are told why the cookies are being moved. These stories are like Punch and Judy shows; children love them and pay close attention. Yet they still fail to draw the inference that Cookie Monster will look in the cupboard for the cookies.

Cognitive developmentalists are now carrying out studies to decide among different possible characterizations of the 3-year-old's conceptual difficulty. The false-belief paradigm has some of the characteristics of level 2 perspective-taking tasks. The child must keep straight two different representations of the same event (it looks like two lines to her, but I know it's an elephant; he thinks it's in the cupboard, but I know it's under the bed). There may be development in the child's ability to focus on representations, themselves, as opposed to the ability to focus on the world directly. This would locate these phenomena in the domain of understanding the nature of representations in general, not just mental representations. Alternatively, the false-belief phenomena may reflect an incomplete view of how mental representations are formed; the child may think that mental representations are faithful copies of the world and may fail to take into account the temporal-spatial contexts in which knowledge states are formed. This would locate the false-belief phenomenon in the context of the child's understanding of epistemology, in the context of the child's understanding of belief fixation.

We see, then, that even when we focus on domain-specific knowledge acquisition, characterizing the child's conceptual difficulties is a delicate and complex task.

6.5   The Concept of a Person: What Is Innate?

As we push the program of understanding knowledge acquisition backward in development, the characterization of the initial state becomes the characterization of the inborn knowledge that gets the human conceptual system off the ground. This leads us into the debate between scholars who believe that humans are born with complex, rich knowledge structures (rationalists) and those who believe that humans are endowed at birth only with relatively impoverished sensorimotor reflexes (empiricists). The same question arises with respect to language acquisition and the genesis of visual knowledge—indeed, with respect to all areas of cognition. Note that the disagreement is over *what* is innate, not over whether *something* is innate.

As we have seen, by age 2 the child has constructed a rich concept of people, including views about others' perceptual and mental experiences. The knowledge of the 2- and 3-year-old is then the initial state for the conceptual readjustment that occurs around age 4. We must understand the child's failure in the false-belief paradigm in terms of that initial state, and we must characterize the change in the child's theory of mind that allows the 4-year-old to succeed. But what of the origin of the 2-year-old's knowledge? What knowledge does the young infant bring to the task of learning about people? Many observations of infants at the end of the first year of life suggest that they have already constructed a rich conception of people. For example, 7-month-olds seem to interpret a change in where their mother is looking as an indication that something interesting is happening in the new place; at least, they themselves look where their mother is now looking, even if it means turning around (Scaife and Bruner 1975). Children just a few months older engage in what is called *social referencing*. If they are placed in a situation they don't know how to react to (say, a new room with a stranger), they will look to their mother and interpret her emotional expression as an indication of safety or danger (Campos and Stenberg 1981). These observations show that infants conceive of other people as sources of relevant information that can guide their own choices, and perhaps even that they conceive of other people as communicative partners.

It has even been suggested that 3-month-olds think of other people as potential communicative partners. Their animated response (smile, excitement) to faces differs from their response to various inanimate objects. Babies of this age become upset when a person stands in front of them, perfectly still, whereas they are not upset when an object is placed in front of them and remains perfectly still (Tronick et al. 1978). Another study showed that babies of this age are sensitive to the contingency of a person's response to them. A videotape situation can be set up so that a mother can interact with her baby, but the mother's image is presented to the baby on a video monitor. The baby reacts normally in this situation. After a while, the baby is played a videotape of this mother's previous interaction—so the stimulus is still his mother, moving, talking, cooing, and so on, but her actions are no longer tuned to his. Babies cease looking, turn away, and often cry (Murray and Trevarthen 1985).

Such observations can be interpreted in many ways. One is that babies attempt to communicate with other people and understand that other people attempt to communicate with them. Or—to mention just one other possible interpretation—perhaps babies are sensitive to any kind of contingent response to their own actions and so are upset when some kind of contingent responding ceases. Thus, Murray and Trevarthen's observation may have nothing to do with babies' particular expectations of people as communicative partners. Experiments could resolve this issue. For example, consider a rattle, moving and making noises contingent on the baby's action. Would the same response patterns be observed? If so, the "sensitivity to contingent response" hypothesis would be supported. Suppose this is so. That is, suppose that 3-month-olds do not yet have particular expectations of people as social partners, but that part of their innate endowment is to be sensitive to contingent reactions. This sensitivity would help them build up knowledge of people, for people are the main source of contingent reactions.

All of the data are not in. It may be that babies are endowed with some innate knowledge of people. If they are not, we must then provide an account of the innate knowledge they do have that allows them to learn so efficiently so fast. This is part of the program for understanding conceptual development in any particular domain of knowledge, along with providing an account of subsequent change.

6.6   Knowledge Reorganization

One of the hallmarks of phenomena such as the child's failures on the false-belief task, or on conservation of weight tasks, is that it is very difficult to teach the child to succeed. Piaget's stage theory predicts that training attempts should meet with no success, since according to the stage theory, the child's failures reflect the lack of some underlying computational capacity. Only when the child has moved into the next stage should training be possible. Theories of cognitive development that locate most developmental change at the domain-specific level must also be able to account for the extreme difficulty in moving children beyond their misconceptions. Such theories deal with this problem by noting that knowledge acquisition is not the mere accumulation of new facts. In many important cases knowledge is restructured in the course of acquisition. Knowledge restructuring is difficult to achieve—whether by children, adults, or even mature scientists.

You can get a feeling for what is involved in knowledge restructuring, and for what it is like to be a child in a conservation task, by considering the following conservation problem. Imagine a glass tube like the one in figure 6.2a, held in place by a clamp C and fitted with a disk D that is free to move up or down. The disk can be supported as in figure 6.2b. Now imagine that you pour a cup of water in the tube; as a result, a certain weight W is required to support the water and hold the disk at location L (figure 6.2b). Next consider the apparatus in figure 6.2c, which is identical except that the glass tube has an odd shape; at the bottom its diameter is the same as the diameter of the tube in figure 6.2a, but it narrows shortly above location L', which corresponds to L in figure 6.2b. The question is this: if we pour a cup of water in this tube, does the weight W' required to

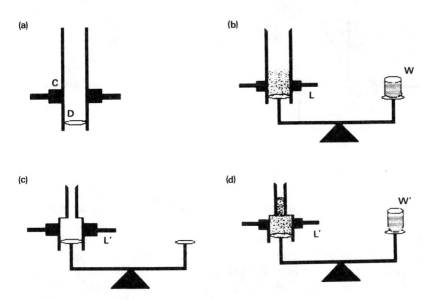

Figure 6.2
(a) Tube supported by clamps (C), movable disk (D) free to slide within it. (b) Tube with one cup of water in it, disk supported at level L by weight W. (c) New configuration of tube. (d) Tube with one cup of water in it, disk supported at level L' by weight W'.

support the water and hold the disk at location L' (figure 6.2d) equal W, or is it greater than W or less than W? Before you read on, figure out how you would answer this question.

Most nonphysicists reason that the weights would be the same: W' would equal W. This is because the weight of water is not influenced by the shape of the container. Even 8-year-olds, who succeed on conservation of weight tasks, know that. However, this answer is incorrect. The correct answer is that W' will be greater than W. How much greater depends upon how high the column of water in the narrow tube is, and thus it depends upon the narrowness of the upper portion of the tube.

It is difficult to explain this answer fully without going into the relevant part of physics, but the following remarks will give a flavor for the explanation. Two physical magnitudes are relevant to this problem: force and pressure. Weight is a force, the value of which depends upon mass and gravity. The weights of the two quantities of water are indeed the same in the two apparatuses. But the pressures exerted on the disks by the water are not, and the function of the weights, W and W', is to exert enough pressure to hold the disks in place. The nonphysicist's misconception is due to thinking of the weights as providing a measure of the weight of the water and the disk, rather than as exerting pressure.

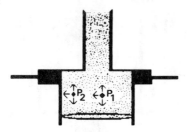

Figure 6.3
Pressure on two points in the water in the apparatus of figure 6.2d.

To understand intuitively why the pressure depends upon the total height of the tube, recall that if you dive into a lake and swim down, the pressure on your ears increases. Divers must learn to clear their ears to avoid popping an eardrum. At 13 feet or so, you have submitted your body to 1 atmosphere of additional pressure (1 atmosphere is the pressure at sea level due to the air above); at 26 feet, 2 atmospheres; and so on. This is as true in a swimming pool as in Lake Michigan. All that matters is the column of water above you; the total mass of water around you does not matter. Even if there were a tube of water, just the right diameter for you to fit into, 13 feet of water above you would lead to an increase in the pressure on your body of 1 atmosphere.

Now consider again the odd-shaped tube. At any depth in the water the pressure is at equilibrium; otherwise, currents would be set up. Thus, the pressure exerted in all directions at point P_1 is the same as the pressure exerted at point P_2, even though only P_1 is under the tall column of water (figure 6.3). This means that the total pressure on the disk is a joint function of the highest column of water and the cross section of the disk, making the total pressure on the disk much greater in the odd-shaped tube.

Another way of understanding this phenomenon intuitively is to imagine the tube to be made of slightly flexible rubber. If you were to squeeze the rubber at a point above L', so as to constrict the top part of the tube, you would need to exert quite some pressure to raise the water level. This would exert pressure downward as well as sideways and would be reflected in a greater W' needed to keep the disk in place.

Though such demonstrations might help a nonphysicist to begin to see why W' would be greater than W, they do not suffice to explain this issue fully. It would be easy to devise another related problem for which the nonphysicist's intuitions would again be shaky. This is because nonphysicists do not know the interrelations among physical variables such as *force, pressure, weight,* and *mass.* Therefore, they do not know which physical variables are relevant to which aspects of the description of the physical world. This formulation even understates the nonphysicists' problem: their conceptual systems do not even represent *pressure* and *force* as two distinct physical magnitudes. Rather, their intuitive theories of the world conflate these, along with *energy*, into a single, undifferentiated notion of causal power. Forces, energies, and pressures cause objects to move, or keep them in place. Nonphysicists make no consistent distinctions among these quite different physical magnitudes. Of course, then, they cannot represent the precise relations among them.

As students learn physics, they master the distinctions among these and other physical magnitudes, and they learn the laws that relate them. They become able to solve a host of real-world problems, at both a quantitative and a qualitative level. But because these physical magnitudes are interrelated in complex ways, this learning takes time. People cannot understand what forces are unless they see how they differ from pressure and energy. They cannot understand weight without understanding mass and force, and they cannot understand mass without understanding something about matter. As students learn physics, they learn a new conceptual structure, which is articulated in terms of concepts that differ from those of their intuitive theories of the world, and which relates entities in the world in ways that are new to them. This is part of what is meant by the claim that knowledge is "restructured" in the course of acquisition. Often, simple training experiences cannot erase a misconception because that misconception is related to many other misconceptions. That is why it takes several years to master the physics needed to really understand the problem of figure 6.2.

The example in figure 6.2 serves to reinforce the points made earlier about Piaget's theory of preoperational thought. Many college-educated, sophisticated adults fail to answer the question about W and W' correctly. (As in Piagetian conservation studies, the subject is not given credit for a correct answer unless the answer can be justified in a way that shows that the reasoning leading to it is correct.) Yet college-aged subjects have surely reached the "stage" of concrete operational thought. Adults surely grasp the distinction between appearance and reality and can coordinate two dimensions of a task at once; yet they cannot generate an answer to this question. The reason, of course, is that they lack relevant domain-specific knowledge—in this case, knowledge of physics. This is also true in the case of 6-year-olds faced with problems involving conservation of quantity, weight, and volume. The child's intuitive physics does not yet distinguish various physical magnitudes: *volume, weight* or *weight, density*. To make these distinctions, children must restructure their understanding of physical objects and construct a new way of thinking about matter (Piaget and Inhelder 1974; Smith, Carey, and Wiser 1985). The scope of the knowledge reorganization required is comparable to what adults must undergo to understand the problem in figure 6.2; and this is why simple training studies in conservation experiments with children fail.

In the search for the correct description of what changes during cognitive development, many open questions remain. One concerns the relative contribution of domain-general and domain-specific changes. I have argued here that the latter make a larger contribution to the differences observed between children and adults than do the former. A second question concerns the type of domain-general changes that occur: (1) changes in the speed or representational power of the mind or (2) acquisition of abstract knowledge with wide application across particular content areas. I have argued here that domain-general changes of the former type play almost no role in the description of cognitive development, at least after age 4. Also still needed is a precise description of the restructuring that occurs in the course of complex knowledge acquisition.

Two considerations led to this chapter's concentration on the description of developmental change. First, characterizing what changes occur in the course of cognitive development is an extremely difficult task, one that is the source of most of the controversy in the field. Second, once we have a clear understanding of the actual changes that occur, we will be in a better position to search for the maturational and learning mechanisms subserving them.

Suggestions for Further Reading

To learn more about Piaget's theory, you might want to sample the writings of Piaget himself. A good source is Gruber and Voneche 1977, which consists of selections from all of Piaget's writings, along with excellent introductory material and commentary.

For an extended analytic evaluation of Piaget's theory, see Gelman and Baillargeon 1983. For an elaboration of the argument sketched in this chapter, see Carey 1985a.

Mathematics is a fundamental domain of human knowledge. Our understanding of numbers contributes to our capacity for the social exchanges of commerce and for constructing a scientific understanding of the world. Gelman and Gallistel 1978 provides an excellent account of the 2- to 4-year-old's understanding of numbers and discusses the nature of the reorganization that takes place in children's conception of numbers when they reach the age of 5 or 6.

The study of cognitive development and the study of the adult cognitive system interact in two ways. First, any theory of human concepts must be able to account for their acquisition, so that theories of concept acquisition constrain theories of concepts. Second, when we actually look at children engaged in particular tasks, they frequently behave in nonadult ways. Often insights from the study of the adult cognitive system provide explanations for these failures. Markman 1989 offers an elegant case study of both sides of the interaction between students of cognitive development and students of adult cognitive processes. Markman's topic is the nature of human concepts themselves, as discussed in chapter 2.

Historians of science, cognitive scientists, science educators, and students of cognitive development in children all agree that knowledge is reorganized in the course of development. Carey 1985b discusses several attempts to characterize the nature of knowledge reorganizations and presents a case study of the acquisition and reorganization of biological knowledge. Keil 1989 presents a different view of the young child's conceptions of animals and living things and emphasizes the importance of understanding human concepts in the context of the theories in which they are embedded.

Many psychologists, including Piaget, have built on the analogy between scientific theories and intuitive theories. An excellent place to begin exploring this analogy is Karmiloff-Smith and Inhelder 1974/75. Karmiloff-Smith and Inhelder studied young children's attempts at balancing blocks, together with their theories of the conditions needed for blocks to balance. Their paper illustrates several respects in which intuitive theories, even those held by young children, function like scientists' explicitly held theories.

Questions

6.1 Attempts at educating children out of their misconceptions often fail. The literature is littered with failed training studies. Think about what Piaget's interpretations of these failures would have been. What other explanation for the failure of education might be offered?

6.2 Students of developmental psychology and of the history of science agree that knowledge is "restructured" in the course of acquisition. What could be meant by "restructuring" in such claims?

References

Anderson, J. R. (1981). *Cognitive skills and their acquisition*. Hillsdale, NJ: L. Erlbaum Associates.

Bryant, P. E., and T. Trabasso (1971). Transitive inferences and memory in young children. *Nature* 232, 456–458.

Campos, J. J., and C. Stenberg (1981). Perception, appraisal, and emotion: The onset of social referencing. In M. Lewis and L. Rosenblum, eds., *Infant social cognition: Empirical and theoretical considerations*. Hillsdale, NJ: L. Erlbaum Associates.

Carey, S. (1985a). Are children fundamentally different thinkers and learners from adults? In S. F. Chipman, J. W. Segal, and R. Glaser, eds., *Thinking and learning skills*, vol. 2. Hillsdale, NJ: L. Erlbaum Associates.

Carey, S. (1985b). *Conceptual change in childhood*. Cambridge, MA: MIT Press.

Chi, M. (1976). Short-term memory limitations in children: Capacity or processing deficits? *Memory and Cognition* 4, 559–572.

Flavell, J. H. (1985). *Cognitive development*. 2nd ed. Englewood Cliffs, NJ: Prentice-Hall.

Flavell, J. H., B. Abrahams, K. Croft, and E. R. Flavell (1981). Young children's knowledge about visual perception: Further evidence for the Level 1–Level 2 distinction. *Developmental Psychology* 17, 99–103.

Gelman, R., and R. Baillargeon (1983). A review of some Piagetian concepts. In J. H. Flavell and E. M. Markman, eds., *Handbook of child psychology*, vol. 3. 4th ed. New York: Wiley.

Gelman, R., and C. R. Gallistel (1978). *The child's understanding of number*. Cambridge, MA: Harvard University Press.

Gopnik, A., and J. W. Astington (1988). Children's understanding of representational change and its relation to the understanding of false belief and the appearance-reality distinction. *Child Development* 59, 26–37.

Gruber, H. E., and J. J. Voneche (1977). *The essential Piaget*. New York: Basic Books.

Kail, R. (1979). *The development of memory in children*. San Francisco: W. H. Freeman.

Kail, R. (1986). Sources of age differences in speed of processing. *Child Development* 57, 969–987.

Karmiloff-Smith, A., and B. Inhelder (1974/75). If you want to go ahead, get a theory. *Cognition 3*, 195–212.

Keil, F. (1989). *Concepts, kinds, and cognitive development*. Cambridge, MA: MIT Press.

Markman, E. (1989). *Categorization and naming in children: Problems in induction*. Cambridge, MA: MIT Press.

Murray, L., and C. Trevarthen (1985). Emotional regulation of interactions between two-month-olds and their mothers. In T. M. Field and N. Fox, eds., *Social perception in infants*. Norwood, NJ: Ablex.

Perner, J., J. R. Leekam, and H. Wimmer (1987). Three-year-olds' difficulty with false belief: The case for a conceptual deficit. *British Journal of Developmental Psychology 5*, 125–137.

Piaget, J., and B. Inhelder (1974). *The child's construction of quantities*. London: Routledge and Kegan Paul.

Roth, C. (1983). Factors affecting developmental change in speed of processing. *Journal of Experimental Child Psychology 35*, 509–528.

Scaife, M., and J. Bruner (1975). The capacity for joint visual attention in the infant. *Nature 253*, 265–266.

Shatz, M., H. M. Wellman, and S. Silber (1983). The acquisition of mental verbs: A systematic investigation of the first reference to mental state. *Cognition 14*, 301–321.

Smith, C., S. Carey, and M. Wiser (1985). On differentiation: A case study of the development of size, weight, and density. *Cognition 21*, 177–237.

Sternberg, S. (1969). The discovery of processing stages: Extensions of Donders' method. In W. G. Koster, ed., *Attention and performance 2*. Amsterdam: North Holland.

Taylor, M. (1985). The development of children's ability to distinguish what they know from what they see. Doctoral dissertation, Stanford University, Stanford, CA.

Tronick, E. Z., H. Als, L. Adamson, S. Wise, and T. B. Brazelton (1978). The infant's response to entrapment between contradictory messages in face-to-face interaction. *Journal of the American Academy of Child Psychiatry 17*, 1–13.

Wellman, H. M., and D. Estes (1986). Early understanding of entities: A reexamination of childhood realism. *Child Development 57*, 910–923.

Wimmer, H., and J. Perner (1983). Beliefs about beliefs: Representation and constraining function of wrong beliefs in young children's understanding of deception. *Cognition 13*, 103–128.

Chapter 7

Rationality

Stephen P. Stich

Contemporary cognitive science is a rapidly growing, intellectually cosmo-
politan domain in which disciplines with different methodologies and different traditions find themselves confronting overlapping questions. When
things go well, insights and theories from one discipline can make significant contributions to projects that began in another discipline. When things
go less smoothly, the methods or findings of one research program can
become targets for attack from across disciplinary boundaries. Both of
these phenomena are to be found when authors from the various fields that
contribute to cognitive science take up the topic of rationality. In this area,
empirical, conceptual, normative, and practical issues are woven together in
ways that are still far from clear.

This chapter begins by sketching some very disturbing empirical
findings—findings that have led some investigators to conclude that normal adult human subjects often do a singularly bad job at the business of
reasoning, even when they are calm, clearheaded, and under no pressure to

Parts of this chapter are adapted from Stich 1985 and Stich 1988. Thanks are due to Warren
Dow for editorial assistance and for sound advice on matters substantive and stylistic.

perform quickly. If this is right, it threatens to have bleak implications for all sorts of social institutions and practices (think of juries and public referenda, for example) that presuppose that the average citizen is generally pretty rational. To the extent that people's reasoning can be improved, this research also promises to have important implications for education.

The experimental studies exploring the foibles and shortcomings of human reasoning have no shortage of critics, however. Prominent among them are certain philosophers who maintain that the pessimistic interpretation of various experimental findings is conceptually incoherent. When we analyze just what it is for a reasoning strategy to be normatively appropriate, these critics argue, it emerges that the sort of widespread irrationality that has allegedly been uncovered is in fact a logical or conceptual impossibility. In section 7.2 we will take a critical look at two prominent arguments aimed at establishing that pervasive irrationality could not be experimentally demonstrated. The first of these maintains that rationality is a precondition for mental representation. Assessing that argument will require some exploration of how we go about determining what a mental state represents.

As the discussion unfolds, the issue of what distinguishes good reasoning from bad will become increasingly urgent. In section 7.3 we will look at one of the central methods that philosophers have used in attempting to answer this question: the method of conceptual analysis. But here it will be the philosophers who are on the spot, for that method seems to presuppose a very traditional account of concepts that may have been undermined by recent empirical work. Moreover, even if the method of conceptual analysis is compatible with empirical studies of conceptual structure, it is far from clear that this method can tell us what we really want to know about reasoning and the cognitive processes that underlie it. As we will see, there is reason to doubt that conceptual analysis is capable of producing defensible criteria for the goodness or badness of a pattern of reasoning, and thus there is reason to doubt that it can provide much assistance in deciding which cognitive processes we should try to get people to acquire. At the end of section 7.3 we will take a brief look at some of the alternatives that are available if conceptual analysis is not up to the task of separating good reasoning from bad.

7.1 The Experimental Exploration of Human Reasoning: Some Examples

In chapters 3 and 4 we have already come across some striking illustrations of the sort of cognitive processes that many investigators would classify as normatively substandard. For example, many people assign probabilities in such a way that a Dutch book can be made against them. Moreover, subjects sometimes ignore prior odds when estimating probabilities, and they can easily be tempted to commit the "conjunction fallacy" in which the probability of a conjunction like

> Linda is a bank teller and is active in the feminist movement.

is judged to be higher than the probability of one of its own conjuncts,

> Linda is a bank teller.

People also often make very different choices between logically identical sets of options, depending on how those options are described or "framed." For example, against the background assumption that if we do nothing 600 people will die, most people choose a program that will save 200 people for sure rather than a program with a $\frac{1}{3}$ probability of saving all 600 and a $\frac{2}{3}$ probability of saving no one. However, if the first program is described as one in which 400 people will die for sure, and the second is described as one in which there is a $\frac{1}{3}$ probability that no one will die and a $\frac{2}{3}$ probability that 600 people will die, most people favor the second program.

7.1.1 Belief Perseverance

Reasoning is the process by which a person's store of beliefs is modified and updated as the result of new information or new insight about the relations among existing beliefs. Reasoning also has a role to play in the generation of new wants and desires. Thus, for example, a person who wants to travel in France and who learns that American tourists must now have visas to enter France may come to want a visa. In the philosophical literature this process by which wants (or desires) and beliefs lead to the formation of new wants is sometimes called "practical reasoning" to contrast it with the "theoretical reasoning" in which beliefs give rise to other beliefs. Often in theoretical reasoning the belief updating will involve both the addition of new beliefs and the removal of old ones. So, for example, if I were to tell you that a mutual friend named Mary who lived in Boston has moved to California, your cognitive system might well add the belief that Mary lives in California and remove the belief that she lives in Boston. Now let's suppose that my report is the only evidence you have for believing that Mary lives in California. It seems plausible that if this evidence is completely undermined, and if your cognitive system is rational, then it should remove the belief that Mary lives in California and restore the belief that she lives in Boston. If, for example, you became convinced that I had lied to you, or that I was myself misinformed, it would seem very odd if you nonetheless continued to believe that Mary lives in California. However, in a disturbing series of experiments Ross and his colleagues have shown that sometimes this is exactly what subjects do. (See Ross, Lepper, and Hubbard 1975; Ross and Anderson 1982. For a good introduction to this literature, see chapter 8 of Nisbett and Ross 1980.)

In one such experiment subjects were presented with the task of distinguishing between authentic and inauthentic suicide notes. Some of the notes, they were told, had been found by the police, whereas others were written by students as an exercise. As the subjects worked on the task, they were provided with false feedback indicating that overall they were performing close to the average level, or (for another group of subjects) much above the average level, or (for a third group of subjects) much below the average level. Following this, each subject was "debriefed," and the predetermined nature of the feedback was clearly explained. The subjects not only were told that their feedback had been false but also were shown the experimenter's instruction sheet assigning them to a particular group and specifying the details of the feedback that they had been given. Subsequent to this, and allegedly for quite a different reason, subjects were asked to fill out a questionnaire on which they were asked to estimate their actual performance at the suicide note task they had completed, to predict how well they would do on related tasks, and to rate their ability at suicide note discrimination and similar tasks. The striking finding was that even after debriefing, subjects who had initially been assigned to the success group continued to rate their performance and abilities far more favorably than did subjects in the average group. Subjects initially assigned to the failure group showed the opposite pattern of results. Additional experiments suggest that these results reflect a robust phenomenon that manifests itself in many variations on the experimental theme, including some conducted outside the laboratory setting. The phenomenon has been labeled *belief perseverance*.

It is worth noting that one of Ross's motives for investigating belief perseverance was a very practical concern about experiments with human subjects. In experimental psychology it is not uncommon to dupe subjects into having potentially harmful beliefs (like the belief that they have latent suicidal tendencies) and then to explain the deception at the end of the experiment. Ross was troubled by the possibility that subjects would retain beliefs they had been duped into holding, even though it seems irrational for them to do so since they no longer believe the evidence on which the potentially harmful beliefs are based. The results obtained by Ross and others indicate that this kind of prima facie irrational pattern of cognition is something we may have to reckon with not only in the laboratory but in everyday life as well.

7.1.2 Pseudodiagnosticity

Suppose you are interested in the effectiveness of a new drug in treating a certain disease, and you have evidence that 79 percent of patients suffering from the disease who have taken the drug recover completely within a month. What would you conclude about the efficacy of the drug? Do you think it is likely to be effective, that it is not likely to be effective, or that you don't have enough evidence to form a judgment? Take a moment and think about it. If you are like most people, you will have inferred that it *is* likely to be effective. But perhaps you should think again. Though I told you that 79 percent of patients who took the drug recovered, I did not tell you anything about the spontaneous recovery rate among patients who did not take the drug. And without that information you are not in a very good position to conclude anything at all. For suppose the spontaneous recovery rate is also 79 percent. In that case the best hypothesis is that the drug is useless. Or suppose that the spontaneous recovery rate is higher than 79 percent—in fact, suppose it is as high as 98 percent. In that case the best hypothesis would be that the drug actually impedes recovery. The need for this sort of control is one of the first lessons students are taught about experimental design in the biological and social sciences. Without special instruction, however, most people seem quite unaware of how important such information is, and quite prepared to ignore it even when it is readily available.

Just how reluctant people are to seek out diagnostically relevant information is illustrated in an experiment by Doherty et al. (1979). These investigators set subjects the task of determining whether a certain archaeological find had come from Coral Island or from Shell Island. The find was a clay pot, and the subjects were given a list of the pot's characteristics:

Smooth clay (not rough)

Curved handles (not straight)

and so on for a number of other binary characteristics. The subjects were then given a booklet from which they could get some data about the kinds of pots that had been produced on the two islands. The data were arrayed as shown in table 7.1, with each pair of percentages covered by an opaque sticker as indicated. On one page of the booklet there were a total of 12 stickers, and in order to get the data they needed, subjects were permitted to peel off any 6 of them. The most useful or "diagnostic" information would be gleaned only if subjects removed both stickers in a given row, and therefore the optimal strategy would be to select three row-pairs. However, only 11 of 121 subjects removed three pairs; 9 removed two pairs, and 30 removed one pair. The remaining 71 subjects (59 percent)

Table 7.1
Sample of data given subjects in the experiment by Doherty et al. (1979).

	Coral Island	Shell Island
Curved handles	21%	87%
Straight handles	79%	13%
Smooth clay	19%	91%
Rough clay	81%	9%

removed no pairs at all! Thus, the majority of subjects formed their belief about which island the clay pot had come from on the basis of "pseudo-diagnostic" information. Though it was readily available, they chose not to seek out the information that would be of most use to them.

There might be some temptation to suppose that results like these are artifacts of the rather artificial experimental format. However, as Nisbett and Ross (1980) point out, the logic exhibited by these experimental subjects

> is suspiciously similar to the logic shown by poorly educated lay-people in discussing a proposition such as "does God answer prayers?" "Yes," such a person may say, "because many times I've asked God for something and He's given it to me." (p. 92)

7.1.3   The Selection Task

One of the most extensively investigated examples of prima facie failure in reasoning is the "selection task" first studied by Wason and Johnson-Laird (Wason 1968a, b, 1977; Wason and Johnson-Laird 1970; Johnson-Laird and Wason 1970). In a typical selection task experiment subjects are presented with four cards like those in figure 7.1. Half of each card is masked. Subjects are then given the following instructions:

> Your job is to determine which of the hidden parts of these cards you need to see in order to answer the following question decisively:
>
> FOR THESE CARDS IS IT TRUE THAT IF THERE IS A CIRCLE ON THE LEFT THERE IS A CIRCLE ON THE RIGHT?
>
> You have only one opportunity to make this decision; you must not assume that you can inspect the cards one at a time. Name those cards which it is absolutely essential to see.

If you've not seen this problem before, think about it and write down your answer.

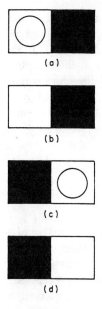

Figure 7.1
The selection task.

Wason and Johnson-Laird found that most subjects correctly reply that they must see card (a). However, many subjects also conclude that they must see card (c). And this is a mistake. To see why it is a mistake, imagine that the mask on (c) is removed. Either there will be a circle under the mask or there won't be. If there is a circle there, then, since there is also a circle on the right, it is true that IF THERE IS A CIRCLE ON THE LEFT THERE IS A CIRCLE ON THE RIGHT. But if there is no circle under the mask on (c), then it does not matter what is on the right. So there was no need to remove the mask on (c), since no matter what was concealed, the capitalized conditional could not have been false. Wason and Johnson-Laird also found that many subjects fail to realize that the mask on (d) must be removed. To see why this is necessary, imagine that the mask is removed and reveals a circle. In that case it is not true that IF THERE IS A CIRCLE ON THE LEFT THERE IS A CIRCLE ON THE RIGHT. And you could not have known this unless you had removed the mask.

In the years since Wason and Johnson-Laird's first studies of the selection task many further studies have looked at related tasks that vary from this one along a number of dimensions. Some of those studies have indicated that subjects do a much better job on structurally analogous problems if the subject matter of the problem is more realistic, or more familiar to them, or if it can be fit into one or another preexisting schema for reasoning. These results have provided a rich data base for theorists trying to understand the cognitive mechanisms underlying this sort of reasoning (Griggs and Cox 1982; Rips 1983; Cheng and Holyoak 1985; and chapter 9 of Holland et al. 1986). For our purposes in this chapter, however, the most important finding in the selection task literature is that in many cases subjects do very poorly on a task that is quite trivial from a logician's point of view. This suggests that the cognitive mechanisms being exploited in these tasks cannot make fluent use of elementary logical principles.

7.2   Is Irrationality Possible? Two Arguments for a Negative Answer

The experiments discussed in the previous section are just the tiny tip of a very large iceberg. During the last two decades there have been hundreds of studies exploring ways in which the reasoning strategies that subjects exploit depart from one or another widely accepted normative precept (see chapter 3). (Some of the most interesting of these studies are collected in Kahneman, Slovic, and Tversky 1982. For an excellent review of the literature, see Nisbett and Ross 1980.) On the basis of this growing body of literature, many people have been tempted to conclude that Aristotle and the long tradition that followed him were just wrong in thinking that Man is a rational animal. These studies, it is claimed, demonstrate that ordinary people are quite *irrational* in their everyday reasoning and that this irrationality should be taken into account in designing political and social institutions. (Among those who have seen bleak implications in this research are Nisbett and Borgida (1975) and Stich (1985). For some attempts to take account of cognitive shortcomings in the design of social systems, see Dawes 1971, 1979 and Suppes 1982.) Not all cognitive scientists have been persuaded by this pessimistic interpretation, however. Indeed, some theorists have argued that the pessimistic interpretation is itself incoherent. In this section we will look at a pair of influential arguments for this view. The first argument turns on the nature of mental representation, or *intentionality* as philosophers call it. The second focuses on the analysis of rationality itself. Part of what makes these arguments important is that each raises deep foundational questions about the basic conceptual apparatus used in cognitive science.

7.2.1   The First Argument: Mental Representation Presupposes Rationality

Philosophers and psychologists have long been puzzled by a very curious feature of beliefs, a feature shared with desires and with certain other representational (or *intentional*) psychological states. Unlike many other sorts of psychological states, beliefs are *about* things; they have propositional *content*; they *represent* the world, or some aspect of the world, as being in a certain way. The standard locutions for attributing beliefs to people employ an embedded *content sentence* that expresses the content of the belief. Some of the properties of the content sentence—most conspicuously its truth or falsity—are shared by the belief it is used to attribute. So, for example, we might attribute a pair of beliefs to Andrea by saying

(1)   Andrea believes that kangaroos are carnivores.

and

(2)   Andrea believes that Los Angeles is east of Reno.

The content sentences in (1) and (2) are "kangaroos are carnivores" and "Los Angeles is east of Reno," the first of which is false while the second, surprisingly, is true. Correspondingly, the belief attributed by (1) is false and the belief attributed by (2) is true.

Now what is puzzling in all this is how it is possible for a psychological state to represent the world as being a certain way. In virtue of what is one of Andrea's beliefs about the eating habits of kangaroos, while another is about the location of Los Angeles and Reno? These questions seem all the more perplexing if we suppose that mental states like those being attributed to Andrea are ultimately to be identified with states of the brain. For then we must say how a pattern of neural activity in Andrea's brain could possibly be about Reno or kangaroos. A general answer to this question would be a theory about the nature of mental representation.

Quite a number of such theories are to be found in the cognitive science literature, and the disputes among their advocates are very lively, to say the least. (Two good surveys of this area are Fodor 1985 and Haugeland 1984.) However, one point is widely conceded by theorists with very different perspectives on the problem of mental representation—namely, that any system of mental representation must exhibit some degree of rationality. To see why this is so, let us first adopt the simplifying assumption that under ordinary circumstances people will assert or assent to a sentence when and only when they believe it. Now, following Quine (1960), let us imagine that we are trying to figure out the beliefs of a native informant whose language is entirely unknown to us. If our informant asserts *Ga bu xiong* whenever an elephant ambles into view, and will not assent to that sentence when there is no elephant nearby, we will have good reason to think that the content of the belief he is expressing when he says *Ga bu xiong* has something to do with there being an elephant in the vicinity. If, on the other hand, our informant does not assent to *Ga bu xiong* when there is an elephant in full view, but does assert it when an airplane flies overhead, this would be a good reason to doubt that the belief he is expressing has anything to do with elephants. Why is this? Why should we not think that *Ga bu xiong* expresses the belief that there is an elephant in the vicinity, even in the case where our informant never has that belief in the presence of an elephant and always acquires it when a plane flies overhead? The beginning of the answer is that if our informant really did form his beliefs in this way, he would be astoundingly irrational. And, as Quine notes, the fact that our hypothesis about the content of our informant's beliefs leads us to attribute wildly irrational patterns of cognitive activity to him is generally an overwhelming reason to conclude that our hypothesis is mistaken. But why is this? Why does the attribution of flagrant irrationality impugn our hypotheses about the content of the informant's beliefs? An answer that has seemed plausible to many is that some degree of rationality is built into the concepts of content and mental representation. Part of what it is to be the belief *that p*—part of what it is to *have that content*—is to interact reasonably rationally with perception and with other mental states.

Since the point is of considerable importance, we would do well to consider a second example, this one focusing on the interactions among beliefs. Once again, imagine that we are trying to determine the beliefs of a native informant. This time let us suppose that we've made a fair amount of progress with relatively simply beliefs. We've determined that when the informant says *Ga bu xiong*, he is expressing the belief that there is an elephant nearby, when he says *Pon bu themp*, he is expressing the belief that it is raining, and so on for lots of other native sentences that we can abbreviate S_1, S_2, S_3, and so on. We now notice that there are devices in our informant's language that form compound sentences from two simpler ones, and we want to determine the content of the beliefs that our informant expresses with these compound sentences. Let's suppose that the word *nehtfi* is one such compounding device and that our informant uses it to make sentences like S_1 *nehtfi* S_2. (Need a mnemonic? Try spelling *nehtfi* backward.) Suppose further that we notice certain patterns in our informant's assents and dissents. If at a given time our informant assents to S_1 *nehtfi* S_2 but not to either S_1 or S_2 by itself, and if at some later time (perhaps in light of new evidence) he changes his mind and assents to S_1, he will also typically assent to S_2. By contrast, if he changes his mind and comes to assent to S_2 (when he had previously assented to S_1 *nehtfi* S_2 but not to either S_1 or S_2), this does not typically lead to his changing his mind about S_1. If we read the arrow as 'leads to', then the pattern of cognitive activity just described can be summarized as follows:

Believing   *Believing*

S_1

and $\longrightarrow$ S_2

S_1 nehtfi S_2

S_2

and $\times$ S_1

S_1 nehtfi S_2

This pattern would be rational if the belief expressed by S_1 *nehtfi* S_1 is a conditional belief—the belief that if S_1 then S_2. Thus, that pattern supports the hypothesis that the conditional does indeed capture the content of the belief. But now let us make a rather different set of assumptions. Suppose that it is often the case that our informant assents to S_1 *nehtfi* S_2 and to S_1 but does not assent to S_2, and that if he acquires the belief S_2 when he already believes S_1 *nehtfi* S_2, this generally leads him to believe S_1. This pattern of cognitive activity might be represented as follows:

Believing   *Believing*

S_1

and $\times$ S_2

S_1 nehtfi S_2

S_2

and $\longrightarrow$ S_1

S_1 nehtfi S_2

It would count overwhelmingly against the hypothesis that the belief expressed by S_1 *nehtfi* S_2 is the conditional belief, if S_1 then S_2, since on that hypothesis our informant's cognitive processes would be strikingly irrational.

What we have just seen is that there seems to be a strong link between content or mental representation, on the one hand, and rationality on the other. If a belief does not interact with other beliefs and with perceptual evidence in ways that would be tolerably rational for the belief that p, then that belief cannot have p as its content; it cannot *be* the belief *that p*. But how rational is "tolerably rational"? Or, to put the question another way, how much *ir*rationality is enough to undermine a given hypothesis about the content of a belief? One leading theorist, D. C. Dennett, has urged that only *perfect* rationality will do. "When a person falls short of perfect rationality," Dennett maintains, "... there is no coherent intentional description" of the person's mental states (Dennett 1978, 20). If Dennett is right, then clearly there must be something wrong with the pessimistic interpretation of the empirical studies recounted earlier, since no experiment could possibly demonstrate that people systematically invoke irrational strategies of reasoning. To see this, assume that a subject does reason irrationally. Then if Dennett is right, the subject's mental states "have no coherent intentional description," which is another way of saying that they are not representational, or that they have no content. But since reasoning is a process of generating and modifying beliefs and other representational states, a subject whose mental states are not representational cannot reason at all. And obviously a subject who cannot reason at all cannot reason irrationally. Thus, Dennett's insistence that perfect rationality is a prerequisite for content leads to a reductio ad absurdum of the pessimistic claim that people often reason irrationally.

Dennett is perhaps a bit extreme in claiming that mental representation requires perfect rationality. However, as Cherniak (1986) has noted, Dennett is heir to a long philosophical tradition that holds that in order to count as a cognitive agent with contentful mental states, an organism must approximate a highly idealized standard of rationality. Cherniak also develops a series of arguments aimed at showing that this tradition is seriously mistaken. If it were the case that mental representation required a close approximation to idealized rationality, then, Cherniak maintains, no creatures that are even remotely like us could ever have mental representations.

In a particularly striking argument for this conclusion, Cherniak focuses on the cognitive resources that would be necessary to maintain even elementary logical consistency in our beliefs. One way to check for simple "truth-functional" consistency is to use the familiar truth-table method. But this apparently simple task would overwhelm computational devices that are vastly more powerful than a human brain. Consider, for example, a computer that is so fast that it can check a line in a truth-table in the time it takes a light ray to traverse the diameter of a proton. And suppose this computer "was permitted to run for twenty billion years, the estimated time from the 'big-bang' dawn of the universe to the present. A belief system containing only 138 logically independent propositions would overwhelm the time resources of this supermachine" (Cherniak 1986, 93). It is obvious that our own belief systems contain many more than 138 logically independent propositions, and equally obvious that our brains are nowhere nearly as fast or as durable as the supermachine Cherniak imagines. Thus, it is quite preposterous to suppose that brains like ours could use the truth-table technique to maintain consistency even among relatively small belief sets containing just a few hundred logically independent propositions. Moreover, as Cherniak notes, analogous problems beset all other techniques for maintaining elementary logical consistency. Nor is this sort of problem limited to deductive consistency. In chapter 3 we saw that it is impossible for cognitive systems like ours to have perfectly Bayesian probability functions. Thus, in both deductive and probabilistic reasoning, there will be no way to avoid using computationally tractable *heuristic strategies* that will sometimes yield the wrong answer.

The moral Cherniak would have us draw is that Dennett and the tradition to which he is heir are wrong to think that mental representation requires anything even close to perfect rationality. But, as we saw earlier, mental representation does seem to be undermined by really flagrant irrationality. Thus, Cherniak concludes, mental representation presupposes only "minimal rationality"—a standard that requires that some inconsistencies are sometimes eliminated. It is no easy project to specify the minimal rationality condition in detail. However, if it is granted that mental representation does not require anything like Dennett's standard of perfect rationality, then the first argument purporting to show that widespread irrationality is impossible collapses.

7.2.2   The Second Argument: Rationality Is Inferential Competence

A second argument for the impossibility of irrationality has been suggested by a number of authors and is developed in a particularly sophisticated way by Cohen (1979, 1981, 1982). Cohen's argument combines a pair of ideas drawn from quite different domains. One of them, the idea of an underlying *competence*, has played a large role in modern linguistics (see Chomsky 1965). Theories that invoke the notion of competence attempt to explain actual behavior (or *performance*) in a given domain by appealing to the interaction of a number of underlying mental systems. One of these systems, the one that is identified with the subject's competence in the relevant domain, stores a rich body of information or knowledge about the structure of the domain. The other systems are brought into play when this knowledge is used to accomplish some cognitive task. In the case of language, for example, the judgments speakers actually make about various grammatical properties and relations of sentences count as part of their linguistic performance. To explain this performance, it is hypothesized that speakers have a mentally represented grammar—a complex system of rules that specifies the grammatical properties and relations of sentences in the speaker's language. In making judgments about sentences, the internalized grammar interacts with the attention system, the motivation system, a short-term memory buffer, and other cognitive systems. On certain occasions one or more of these other systems may be responsible for the speaker's reporting a judgment that does not reflect the information encoded in the grammar. For example, the sentence the speaker is being asked to judge may be so long or contain so many levels of embedding that it overtaxes the resources of the short-term memory buffer. On another occasion the speaker's attention may be distracted from the task at hand. These cases are called *performance errors* as a way of indicating that the judgments the speakers are reporting do not correctly reflect their own underlying grammatical competence. A common method for attempting to uncover a subject's underlying competence in a given domain is to construct an idealized theory aimed at predicting most instances of actual performance, excluding those that are plausibly attributable to performance errors of one sort or another.

The other idea that plays a central role in Cohen's argument is the notion of *reflective equilibrium*, which has been widely discussed as a method of validating normative principles both in logic and in ethics. (The classic source in logic is Goodman 1965; in ethics it is Rawls 1971. Good discussions are to be found in Daniels 1979, 1980a, b.) The inputs to the method of reflective equilibrium are "intuitions," which Cohen characterizes as "immediate and untutored inclinations ... to judge that" something is the case. In ethics the relevant intuitions are judgments about which actions are right and which are wrong. In the normative theory of reasoning they are judgments about which specific inferences are acceptable and which are not. According to Cohen, a normative theory of reasoning is simply an idealized theory built on the data of these intuitions. The theory must be built so as to capture the bulk of the data in the simplest way possible. Thus, a completed normative theory will consist of an interlocking set of normative principles of reasoning that should entail most of the intuitions in our data base. Since the normative theory is an idealized theory, it need not aim at capturing all the relevant intuitions of all normal adults. A few scattered exceptions—intuitions that are not entailed by the theory—can be tolerated in the same spirit that we tolerate exceptions to the predictions of the ideal gas laws. A normative theory that succeeds in capturing the majority of our intuitions about the rightness or wrongness of specific inferences in the simplest way possible will be said to have passed the reflective equilibrium test.

Cohen stresses that although intuitions or judgments are the data for a normative theory of reasoning, the normative theories themselves are not theories about intuitions, any more than physics is a theory about observed meter readings, or ethics a theory about intuitions of moral rightness or wrongness. Rather, the normative theory of reasoning is about *good reasoning* or about how one ought to go about the business of cognition. But, Cohen observes, although a normative theory of reasoning is not a theory about people's judgments concerning good and bad reasoning, it is perfectly possible to construct an empirical theory that is concerned with the cognitive system underlying the intuitive judgments that provide the data for the corresponding normative theory. This empirical theory will be a psychological theory, not a logical ... one. It will describe a competence that human beings have—an ability uniformly operative under normal conditions and often under others, to form intuitive judgments about particular instances of ... deducibility or nondeducibility, probability or improbability. This theory will be just as idealized as the normative theory. (Cohen 1981, 321)

Cohen's argument for the inevitable rationality of normal human subjects turns on the special relationship between these two theories—the normative and the psychological theories of reasoning. The essential point is that the empirical theory of human reasoning (that is, the psychological theory that aims to describe the cognitive system underlying intuitive judgments) exploits the same data as the normative theory of reasoning, and exploits them in the same way. In both cases the theorist will construct the simplest and most powerful set of principles that accounts for the bulk of the data. Thus, once a normative theory is at hand, the empirical theory of reasoning competence will be free for the asking, since it will be *identical* with the normative theory of reasoning! Though the empirical theory of reasoning competence "is a contribution to the psychology of cognition," Cohen writes,

it is a by-product of the logical or philosophical analysis of norms rather than something that experimentally oriented psychologists need to devote effort to constructing. It is not only all the theory of competence that is needed in its area. It is also all that is possible, since a different competence, if it actually existed, would just generate evidence that called for a revision of the corresponding normative theory.

In other words, where you accept that a normative theory has to be based ultimately on the data of human intuition, you are committed to the acceptance of human rationality as a matter of fact in that area, in the sense that it must be correct to ascribe to normal human beings a cognitive competence—however often faulted in performance—that corresponds point by point with the normative theory. (Cohen 1981, 321)

It is important to realize that Cohen's view, in contrast with Dennett's, does not entail that people never reason badly. Cohen readily acknowledges that people make inferential errors of many sorts under many circumstances. But he insists that these errors are performance errors, reflecting nothing about the reasoner's underlying, normatively unimpeachable competence. The account Cohen would give of inferential errors is analogous to the account a linguist might give about the errors people make in producing or judging sentences in their own language. Though we sometimes utter sentences that are ungrammatical in our own dialect, this is no reflection on the internalized grammatical rules that constitute our linguistic competence. These rules cannot generate strings that are ungrammatical in our dialect, because to be grammatical in our dialect just is to be generated by the rules we have internalized. However, as noted earlier, our utilization of these rules is subject to a whole host of potential misadventures that may lead us to utter ungrammatical sentences: slips of the tongue, failures of memory, lapses of attention, and many more. It is certainly possible to study these failures and thereby to learn something about the way the mind exploits its underlying competence. But though such studies might reveal interesting defects in performance, they could not reveal defects in competence. Analogously, Cohen tells us, we may expect all sorts of defects in inferential performance, due to inattention, memory limitations, and the like. Study of these failings may indicate something interesting about the way we exploit our underlying inferential competence. But such a study could no more indicate a defective inferential competence than a study of grammatical errors could reveal that the speaker's linguistic competence is defective. For just as what is grammatical is determined by internalized linguistic rules, so too what is rational is determined by internalized inferential rules.

If Cohen is right, those who see bleak implications in the empirical studies of human reasoning will have to reconsider. For, although Cohen grants that people sometimes do a bad job of reasoning, he insists that their errors are performance errors. The tacitly known rules that guide inferential practice are normatively beyond reproach, though sometimes other factors intervene and prevent our tacit knowledge from manifesting itself in actual performance. Cohen concedes that there is room for improvement in people's actual inferential performance. But if we want to help people do a better job of reasoning, we need not worry about teaching them new principles or getting them to abandon old ones. We need only help them make better use of the tacit knowledge they already have. This sanguine view can be sustained, however, only if Cohen is right about the assessment of normative theories of reasoning. If capturing intuitions, or passing the reflective equilibrium test, does not guarantee that a normative theory of reasoning is a good one, then Cohen's argument will come unglued. So let us ask what reason there might be to accept Cohen's account.

Why should we think that a normative theory that passes the reflective equilibrium test must be correct, and that the inferential rules that constitute the theory must be rational? Though Cohen does not tackle this question head on, there is an important philosophical tradition—one that can be traced all the way back to Plato—that tries to address such issues by appeal to the analysis of concepts. A basic assumption underlying this approach is that the concepts we use in ordinary day-to-day thought, and the words we use to express them, have definitions that specify necessary and sufficient conditions for the application of the concept. When we ask whether a given term (like *cat* or *rational* or *justice*) applies in a specific case, we are asking whether the case in question falls within the category carved out by the definition. In order to settle the question, we must first discover the definition of the concept and then determine whether or not the necessary and sufficient conditions we have discovered apply to the case at hand. Think of Plato's dialogues, in which Socrates and his acquaintances struggle to discover the definition of philosophically important terms like *justice*, *piety*, and *love*. Hypothetical counterexamples play a central role in the process. The rationale for using these hypothetical cases is easy to see. For if a proposed definition really gives necessary and sufficient conditions for the application of a concept, then it should be impossible to imagine cases where the concept applies and the conditions do not, or vice versa. So if we can imagine such a case, then we know that the proposed definition is mistaken.

Now let's see how all of this applies to Cohen's argument. Cohen claims that passing the reflective equilibrium test guarantees rationality, and we have asked what grounds he has for this claim. A natural reply for a philosopher working within the tradition of conceptual analysis would be that passing the reflective equilibrium test is necessary and sufficient for rationality because this is the definition of *rationality*. If this is the case, then it should be impossible to imagine situations in which we would not classify a set of inferential rules as rational even though we know that they have passed the reflective equilibrium test. Unfortunately for Cohen's view, it seems all too easy to imagine such situations. Recall that for Cohen, the intuitions that serve as input to the reflective equilibrium test are the very same ones that we would use to build a psychological theory of reasoning competence for the subject—they are in fact the intuitions offered by the subject. Now imagine that we find a subject whose intuitions sanction the conjunction fallacy, the gambler's fallacy, the neglect of base rates, or one of the other troubling patterns of reasoning described earlier. Plainly there is no a priori reason to suppose that there could not be a subject for whom one or more of these patterns of reasoning is in reflective equilibrium. And if there were such a subject, Cohen's account of rationality requires that we classify this subject's inferences as rational. But surely this is wrong. It would be quite absurd to classify these dubious patterns of inference as rational simply because they accord with the subject's inferential competence and thus pass the reflective equilibrium test. The fact that we are not prepared to classify such inferences as rational is a good indication that the analysis of rationality in terms of reflective equilibrium is mistaken.

We can gain some further insight into what has gone wrong in Cohen's argument by taking a closer look at his analogy between grammaticality and rationality. As we have seen, many linguists assume that grammaticality is determined by the linguistic rules a speaker has internalized. Of course, we expect that different speakers will have internalized different linguistic rules. The linguistic competence of an Englishman will differ markedly from the linguistic competence of a Frenchman, and even among English speakers there will be important differences between the rules internalized by a black man from rural Georgia and those internalized by a white woman from London. Since linguistics is a purely descriptive science, and grammaticality is a purely descriptive concept, it doesn't make any sense to ask which internalized rules are best. The Londoner's linguistic competence is neither better nor worse than the Georgian's or the Frenchman's; they are just different. However, rationality is a normative notion, not a purely descriptive one. If different people have different internalized rules of reasoning, it is clearly in order to ask which is better. On Cohen's account of the normative assessment of reasoning, the mere fact that a person has internalized a set of inferential rules establishes that the rules are rational. But this seems flatly incompatible with our concept of rationality. If Cohen's analysis of rationality is inadequate, then his argument that people's underlying reasoning competence must be rational cannot be defended.

7.3   The Strategy of Conceptual Analysis and Other Approaches to the Evaluation of Reasoning

Cohen offers us an account of what it is for a pattern of inference to be rational, and we have just seen that this account will not do. That leaves us with an embarrassing problem. Although our central concern in this chapter has been the evaluation of various patterns of reasoning, it now appears that we are less than clear about what we have been asking, since we have no account of what it is for one pattern of reasoning to be better than another. One strategy for addressing this problem would be to remain within the tradition of conceptual analysis and try to do a better job of analyzing the concept of rationality that is embedded in our ordinary thought and language. Since Cohen's analysis has been found wanting, perhaps the way to proceed is to seek another, more sophisticated set of conditions that will give us a more tenable analysis of rationality.

This idea has been explored by a number of authors, including Stich and Nisbett (1980), who proposed a variation on the reflective equilibrium idea that exploits the intuitions of experts rather than ordinary folk. However, none of the alternative analyses of rationality that have been suggested has gained wide acceptance, and most of them quickly fall victim to the sort of counterexamples that scuttled Cohen's analysis. It is generally all too easy to imagine circumstances in which a set of inferential rules that we would not categorize as rational satisfies the conditions of a proposed analysis, or circumstances in which a set of rules that we would categorize as rational fails to satisfy the conditions (Conee and Feldman 1983; Stich 1988).

Confronted with these difficulties, some philosophers have begun to think that in seeking an account of what distinguishes good reasoning from bad, the strategy of conceptual analysis may not be the right one to pursue. Worries about the strategy fall under two headings. One concern is that the ordinary concept of rationality may not have the sort of definition that philosophers since Plato have sought. Another concern is that, even if we could find a Platonic definition of rationality, it would still not tell us what we want to know.

The first concern has its roots in the work of the philosopher Ludwig Wittgenstein (1953), who argued that many ordinary concepts just do not admit of an analysis into necessary and sufficient conditions. In recent years cognitive psychologists inspired by Wittgenstein have collected data that suggest that the underlying structure of many ordinary concepts is not a set of necessary and sufficient conditions but rather a set of prototypes or feature clusters, and that in applying a concept we assess the similarity of the case at hand to the prototype or feature cluster that anchors the category. (Some of this work is reviewed in chapter 2; for further discussion, see Smith and Medin 1981 and Rey 1983.) Most of the empirical work on the mental representation of concepts has focused on kind terms like *robin, bird,* and *animal,* and to date there have been no studies specifically aimed at the structure of normative concepts like rationality. But it can no longer simply be taken for granted that normative concepts have the sort of Platonic definitions that are presupposed by the strategy of conceptual analysis. If they do not, then all attempts to specify necessary and sufficient conditions for rationality are doomed to failure.

Even if we assume that the concept of rationality has a Platonic definition, however, it is far from clear that the strategy of conceptual analysis can tell us what we really want to know about the acceptability or unacceptability of various patterns of reasoning. To see this, it is useful to begin by asking why we want a normative evaluation of reasoning. Historically, the project of evaluating inferential strategies was often motivated by the observation that different people seem to reason in significantly different ways and thus reach quite different conclusions even when they share most of their data. If it is possible for different people to go about the business of reasoning in different ways, then it is natural to wonder which way is best. And if it is possible to modify the way we ourselves reason, then the project of evaluating reasoning takes on a certain practical urgency. Why should we continue reasoning the way we do if there are better alternatives available?

The analytic strategy proposes to evaluate patterns of reasoning by analyzing the concept of rationality embedded in everyday thought and language and determining which patterns fall within the category picked out by that concept. But even if the project can be carried out, there is something very curious about this way of proceeding. For just as it is possible for other people to *reason* in ways quite different from the way we do, so too it is possible for other people to *evaluate reasoning* in ways quite different from the way we do. Indeed, there is some fragmentary evidence that people in other cultures do evaluate reasoning differently (Hallen and Sodipo 1986). The analytic strategy gives us no reason to think that the concept of rationality and other concepts of cognitive evaluation prevailing in our everyday thought are preferable to the alternatives that might prevail instead. And in the absence of any reason to think that locally prevailing evaluative notions are superior to potential alternatives, it is hard to see why we should care whether the reasoning strategies we use are sanctioned by our own current evaluative concepts.

To put the point more vividly, imagine that you have located some exotic culture that exploits patterns of reasoning very different from your own, and that the notions of inferential evaluation embedded in the language of that culture also differ from yours. Suppose further that the patterns of reasoning exploited by the people of that culture accord quite well with *their* concepts of inferential evaluation, while the patterns of reasoning that you exploit accord quite well with *ours*. Would any of this be of any help at all in deciding which patterns of reasoning you should use? Without some reason to think that one set of evaluative concepts is preferable to the other, it seems clear that the answer is no.

But now, once again, we find ourselves confronting the embarrassing problem with which this section began. If conceptual analysis will not help us to decide which patterns of reasoning we should try to use, how can we make that decision? The best that can be said at this point is that the question is very hard, and all the answers that have been proposed are very controversial. An idea that some theorists have found promising is to look upon patterns of reasoning as cognitive tools or strategies, and to evaluate them as we would evaluate other tools or strategies. Typically, when we evaluate a set of alternative strategies, we want to know which one is best suited to the attainment of our goals. Philosophers sometimes use the term *consequentialist* for this sort of evaluation, because the assessment of a strategy is determined by the probability that the strategy will have the desired consequences. The consequentialist approach is compatible with various different sets of goals, and there are lively debates about which goals to focus on in evaluating patterns of reasoning (Stich, forthcoming). Perhaps the most intuitively plausible suggestion is that *truth* is the appropriate goal in the evaluation of reasoning, and that one pattern of reasoning is better than another if it is more likely to produce true beliefs. Goldman (1986) develops detailed evaluations of various patterns of reasoning along these lines. Another suggestion, which can be traced to pragmatist philosophers like William James, is that reasoning strategies should be evaluated by their success in leading to useful technologies and useful predictions. Some philosophers have argued that these two lines of consequentialist evaluation are bound to converge, since it is only by leading to true beliefs that a pattern of reasoning could foster useful technologies (Rescher 1977). Others have been more skeptical about the link between truth and practical utility (Devitt 1984; Stich, forthcoming). However, the details of this debate fall largely outside the boundaries of cognitive science and are generally pursued by theorists in contemporary metaphysics or epistemology.

Consequentialist accounts of good reasoning have often been viewed with skepticism because it is widely thought that they must inevitably be viciously circular. In order to find out whether a given strategy of reasoning is likely to lead to the desired consequences, it is argued, we must do some research, and this inevitably involves making use of one or another strategy of reasoning. In using these strategies of reasoning to certify a strategy of reasoning, we are begging the question. Though many philosophers have been convinced that this argument undermines the consequentialist approach, Goldman (1986, chap. 5) has offered some impressive reasons to think that this is a mistake. His most persuasive point is that the putative circularity is by no means a special problem for consequentialism. *Any* plausible account of the property or properties that distinguish good reasoning strategies from bad ones will require that we do some reasoning to determine whether a given strategy has those properties. Thus, consequentialism runs no greater danger of circularity than do other accounts.

Another worry that some theorists have raised about consequentialism is that it can lead to relativism. This concern is easiest to see for the pragmatic version of consequentialism, which maintains that one strategy of reasoning is better than another if it is more likely to lead to useful predictions and technologies. It will sometimes (perhaps often) be the case that the likelihood that a given strategy will lead to useful predictions or technologies will depend, in fairly complex ways, on the circumstances in which the strategy is operating. Thus, it may sometimes turn out that one strategy of reasoning is pragmatically superior in one set of circumstances, while another strategy is pragmatically superior in a different set of circumstances. Ultimately, this may lead the pragmatic consequentialist to the relativistic conclusion that different strategies of reasoning may be best for different circumstances or cultures. Some philosophers have thought that this sort of relativism would be a disastrous result; others do not find it at all ominous. (For some discussion, see Stich, forthcoming, chap. 6.) It will be a useful exercise to think through your own reactions to relativism in the assessment of inferential strategies.

Suggestions for Further Reading

As is often the case in areas of great scientific and philosophical ferment, our study of rationality has left us with more questions than answers. Our central question has concerned the rationality or irrationality of ordinary men and women: How good a job do people do at the business of reasoning? The empirical evidence relevant to this question is set out in Nisbett and Ross 1980; some more recent findings are discussed in Holland et al. 1986. Kahneman, Slovic, and Tversky 1982 is the best and most comprehensive anthology of original studies. Another useful anthology that includes historical, philosophical, and empirical essays is Tweney, Doherty, and Mynatt 1981. The philosophical debates over how the concept of good reasoning is best understood are explored in detail in Goldman 1986 and, from a rather different perspective, in Stich, forthcoming.

The best discussion of the relation between rationality and mental representation is Cherniak 1986. A good anthology of essays on this theme, and on the issue of relativism, is Hollis and Lukes 1982. Cohen 1981 includes a substantial number of commentaries by other authors, many of whom are critical of Cohen's controversial argument.

Questions

7.1 In 1962 Thomas Kuhn wrote a fascinating and revolutionary book that many readers interpreted as an attack on the rationality of scientific reasoning. The debate Kuhn began has been taken up by other historians of science as well as by sociologists of science, philosophers, and psychologists who study scientific reasoning. How might the empirical findings and philosophical arguments set out in this chapter be brought to bear on the dispute over the rationality of science? If you get intrigued by this question, you might want to read Kuhn 1962 as well as some of the essays in Gutting 1980 and in Tweney, Doherty, and Mynatt 1981.

7.2 In section 7.2.1 we saw that some degree of rationality seems to be required for any system of mental representation. But we left the general question of the nature of mental representation untouched. What sort of account can be given of the way in which a state of someone's brain can represent events that may have occurred at considerable spatial or temporal distance from that brain? What sort of account can be given of the mental representation of events that never occurred at all? Fodor 1985, 1987 and Haugeland 1984 will give you a good start on this one.

References

Cheng, P., and K. Holyoak (1985). Pragmatic reasoning schemas. *Cognitive Psychology* 17, 391–416.

Cherniak, C. (1986). *Minimal rationality*. Cambridge, MA: MIT Press.

Chomsky, N. (1965). *Aspects of the theory of syntax*. Cambridge, MA: MIT Press.

Cohen, J. (1979). On the psychology of prediction: Whose is the fallacy? *Cognition* 7, 385–407.

Cohen, J. (1981). Can human irrationality be experimentally demonstrated? *Behavioral and Brain Sciences* 4, 317–370.

Cohen, J. (1982). Are people programmed to commit fallacies? Further thoughts about the interpretation of experimental data on probability judgment. *Journal for the Theory of Social Behavior* 12, 251–274.

Conee, E., and R. Feldman (1983). Stich and Nisbett on justifying inference rules. *Philosophy of Science* 50, 326–331.

Daniels, N. (1979). Wide reflective equilibrium and theory acceptance in ethics. *Journal of Philosophy* 76, 256–282.

Daniels, N. (1980a). Reflective equilibrium and archimedian points. *Canadian Journal of Philosophy* 10, 83–103.

Daniels, N. (1980b). On some methods of ethics and linguistics. *Philosophical Studies* 37, 21–36.

Dawes, R. (1971). A case study of graduate admissions: Application of three principles of human decision making. *American Psychologist* 26, 180–188.

Dawes, R. (1979). The robust beauty of improper linear models in decision making. *American Psychologist* 34, 571–582.

Dennett, D. (1978). *Brainstorms*. Cambridge, MA: MIT Press.

Devitt, M. (1984). *Realism and truth*. Oxford: Basil Blackwell.

Doherty, M., C. Mynatt, R. Tweney, and M. Schiavo (1979). Pseudo-diagnosticity. *Acta Psychologica* 43, 11–21.

Fodor, J. (1985). Fodor's guide to mental representation. *Mind* 94, 76–100.

Fodor, J. (1987). *Psychosemantics: The role of meaning in the philosophy of mind*. Cambridge, MA: MIT Press.

Goldman, A. (1986). *Epistemology and cognition*. Cambridge, MA: Harvard University Press.

Goodman, N. (1965). *Fact, fiction and forecast*. Indianapolis, IN: Bobbs-Merrill.

Griggs, R., and J. Cox (1982). The elusive thematic materials effect in Wason's selection task. *British Journal of Psychology* 73, 407–420.

Gutting, G., ed. (1980). *Paradigms and revolutions*. Notre Dame, IN: University of Notre Dame Press.

Hallen, B., and J. Sodipo (1986). *Knowledge, belief and witchcraft*. London: Ethnographica.

Haugeland, J. (1984). The intentionality all-stars. Ms., University of Pittsburgh, Pittsburgh, PA.

Holland, J. H., K. J. Holyoak, R. E. Nisbett, and P. R. Thagard (1986). *Induction: Processes of inference, learning, and discovery*. Cambridge, MA: MIT Press.

Hollis, M., and S. Lukes, eds. (1982). *Rationality and relativism*. Cambridge, MA: MIT Press.

Johnson-Laird, P., and P. Wason (1970). A theoretical analysis of insight into a reasoning task, and Postscript–1977. In Johnson-Laird and Wason 1977.

Johnson-Laird, P., and P. Wason, eds. (1977). *Thinking*. Cambridge: Cambridge University Press.

Kahneman, D., P. Slovic, and A. Tversky, eds. (1982). *Judgment under uncertainty: Heuristics and biases*. Cambridge: Cambridge University Press.

Kuhn, T. (1962). *The structure of scientific revolutions*. Chicago: University of Chicago Press.

Nisbett, R., and E. Borgida (1975). Attribution and the psychology of prediction. *Journal of Personality and Social Psychology* 32, 932–943.

Nisbett, R., and L. Ross (1980). *Human inference: Strategies and shortcomings of social judgment*. Englewood Cliffs, NJ: Prentice-Hall.

Quine, W. (1960). *Word and object*. Cambridge, MA: MIT Press.

Rawls, J. (1971). *A theory of justice*. Cambridge, MA: Harvard University Press.

Rescher, N. (1977). *Methodological pragmatism*. Oxford: Basil Blackwell.

Rey, G. (1983). Concepts and stereotypes. *Cognition* 15, 237–262.

Rips, L. (1983). Cognitive processes in propositional reasoning. *Psychological Review* 90, 38–71.

Ross, L., and C. Anderson (1982). Shortcomings in the attribution process: On the origins and maintenance of erroneous social assessments. In Kahneman, Slovic, and Tversky 1982.

Ross, L., M. Lepper, and M. Hubbard (1975). Perseverance in self perception and social perception: Biased attributional processes in the debriefing paradigm. *Journal of Personality and Social Psychology* 32, 880–892.

Smith, E., and D. Medin (1981). *Categories and concepts.* Cambridge, MA: Harvard University Press.

Stich, S. (1985). Could man be an irrational animal? *Synthese* 64, 115–135.

Stich, S. (1988). Reflective equilibrium, analytic epistemology and the problem of cognitive diversity. *Synthese* 74, 391–413.

Stich, S. (forthcoming). *The fragmentation of reason.* Cambridge, MA: MIT Press.

Stich, S., and R. Nisbett (1980). Justification and the psychology of human reasoning. *Philosophy of Science* 47, 188–202.

Suppes, P. (1982). Rational allocation of resources to scientific research. In L. J. Cohen, ed., *Logic, methodology and philosophy of science.* Amsterdam: North Holland.

Tweney, R., M. Doherty, and C. Mynatt (1981). *On scientific thinking.* New York: Columbia University Press.

Wason, P. (1968a). Reasoning about a rule. *Quarterly Journal of Experimental Psychology* 20, 273–281.

Wason, P. (1968b). "On the failure to eliminate hypotheses ..."—A second look. In Wason and Johnson-Laird 1968.

Wason, P. (1977). Self-contradiction. In Johnson-Laird and Wason 1977.

Wason, P., and P. Johnson-Laird, eds. (1968). *Thinking and reasoning.* Harmondsworth, England: Penguin.

Wason, P., and P. Johnson-Laird (1970). A conflict between selecting and evaluating information in an inferential task. *British Journal of Psychology* 61, 509–515.

Wittgenstein, L. (1953). *Philosophical investigations.* New York: Macmillan.

Epilogue

Chapter 1

Cognitive Activity in Artificial Neural Networks

Paul M. Churchland

In the space of only thirty years artificial intelligence (AI) has developed into one of the largest and most vigorous research programs in human history. In the same period, and for many of the same reasons, the research program of cognitive psychology has largely reclaimed the discipline of psychology from its behaviorist past. We may dispute how successful these interwoven research programs have been, but there will be little dispute over one feature shared by both, namely, their almost complete dissociation from the neurosciences. More specifically, neither program has been either inspired by or much affected by our developing understanding of the microstructure of the empirical brain and of the operations of its elements.

This dissociation did not represent an oversight. Principled reasons were offered for the substantial irrelevance of neuroscience to a general theory

Most of the material in this chapter is drawn from a larger paper entitled "On the Nature of Theories: A Neurocomputational Approach" (Churchland 1989a), which is reprinted in *A Neurocomputational Perspective: The Nature of Mind and the Structure of Science* (Churchland 1989b). My thanks to the editors for permission to use some of that earlier material here. For many useful discussions, thanks also to Terry Sejnowski, Patricia Churchland, David Zipser, Dave Rumelhart, Francis Crick, Stephen Stich, and Philip Kitcher.

of cognitive activity. The "multiple realization argument" urged that cognitive activity could surely be realized, at least in principle, in a considerable variety of quite different physical systems—for example, in electronic, optical, mechanical, chemical, and biological systems—with further room for variation within each. Accordingly, the physical details of any one such system cannot be essential to understanding the general phenomenon that could be displayed by all. The pattern of activity that constitutes cognition must therefore be sought at a more abstract level than the level of neurons and their interactions. Facts at that low level can bear at most on the question of how to engineer only one of many possible implementations of the abstract processes in question. If, however, it is cognition itself that is our concern, rather than its idiosyncratic implementation, then far better for us to address the abstract processes directly, with high-level cognitive theory, and with high-level simulations in general-purpose computers.

This rationale has served to justify a long-standing disinterest in the neurosciences, both within AI and within cognitive psychology. And it has served to protect, from any sustained contradiction, the "symbol-manipulation by structure-sensitive rules" conception of what cognitive activity really consists in. In my view, this has been most unfortunate. The three guiding convictions of this chapter are that the rationale just outlined is importantly flawed, that the symbol/rule paradigm may well comprehend only a vanishingly small percentage of cognitive activity, and that even an elementary understanding of the microstructure of the brain funds a fertile and quite different conception of what cognitive activity really consists in. The aim of this chapter will be to illustrate these counterclaims, most especially the third. So let us begin with the physical structure and the basic activities of certain brainlike systems.

1.1 Elementary Brainlike Networks

The functional atoms of the brain are cells called *neurons* (figure 1.1). These have a natural or default level of activation that can, however, be modulated up or down by external influences. From each neuron there extends a long, thin output fiber called an *axon*, which typically branches at the far end so as to make a large number of *synaptic connections* with either the central cell body or the bushy *dendrites* of other neurons. Each neuron thus receives inputs from a great many other neurons, which inputs tend to excite (or to inhibit, depending on the type of synaptic connection) its normal or default level of activation. The level of activation induced is a function of the *number* of connections, of their size or *weight*, of their *polarity* (stimulatory or inhibitory), and of the *strength* of the incoming signals. Furthermore, each neuron is constantly emitting an output signal along its own axon, a

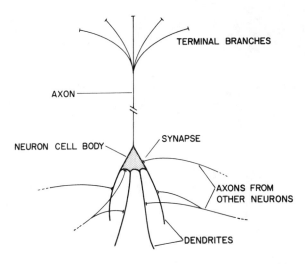

TERMINAL BRANCHES

AXON

SYNAPSE

NEURON CELL BODY

AXONS FROM
OTHER NEURONS

DENDRITES

Figure 1.1
A schematic neuron.

signal whose strength is a direct function of the overall level of activation in the originating cell body. That signal is a train of pulses or *spikes*, as they are called, which are propagated swiftly along the axon. A typical cell can emit spikes along its axon at anything between 0 and perhaps 200 hertz. Neurons, if you like, are humming to one another, in basso notes of varying frequency.

The networks to be explored attempt to simulate natural neurons with artificial units of the kind depicted in figure 1.2. These units admit of various levels of activation, which we will assume to vary between 0 and 1. Each unit receives input signals from other units via "synaptic" connections of various weights and polarities. These are represented in the diagram as small end-plates of various sizes. For simplicity's sake, we dispense with dendritic trees: the axonal end branches from other units all make connections directly to the "cell body" of the receiving unit. The total modulating effect E impacting on that unit is just the sum of the contributions made by each of the connections. The contribution of a single connection is just the product of its weight w_i times the strength s_i of the signal arriving at that connection. Let me emphasize that if for some reason the connection weights were to change over time, then the unit would receive a quite different level of overall excitation or inhibition in response to the very same configuration of input signals.

Let us turn now to the output side of things. As a function of the total input E, the unit modulates its activity level and emits an output signal of a certain strength s_o along its "axonal" output fiber. But s_o is not a direct or *linear* function of E. Rather, it is an S-shaped function as in figure 1.3. The

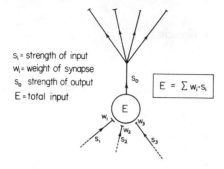

s_i = strength of input
w_i = weight of synapse
s_o strength of output
E = total input

$$E = \sum w_i \cdot s_i$$

Figure 1.2
A neuronlike processing unit.

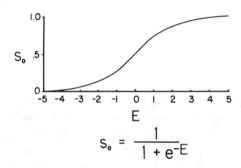

$$S_o = \frac{1}{1 + e^{-E}}$$

Figure 1.3
The sigmoid axonal output function.

reasons for this small wrinkle will emerge later. I mention it here because its inclusion completes the story of the elementary units. Of their intrinsic properties, there is nothing left to tell. They are very simple indeed.

It remains to arrange the elementary units into networks. In the brain, neurons frequently constitute a population all of which send their axons to the site of a second population of neurons, where each arriving axon divides into terminal end branches in order to make many different synaptic connections within the target population. Axons from this second population can then project to a third, and so on. This basic and fairly obvious pattern is the inspiration for the arrangement of figure 1.4.

The units in the bottom or *input layer* of the network may be thought of as "sensory" units, since the level of activation in each is directly determined by aspects of the environment (or perhaps by the experimenter, in the process of simulating some environmental input). The activation level of a given input unit is designed to be a response to a specific aspect or dimension of the overall input stimulus that strikes the bottom layer. The

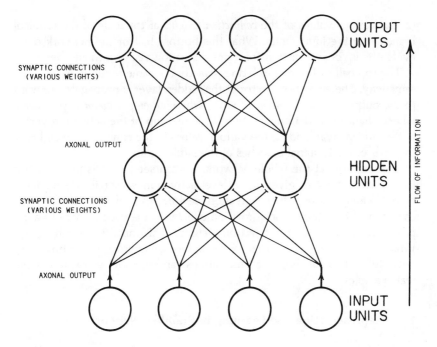

OUTPUT
UNITS

SYNAPTIC CONNECTIONS
(VARIOUS WEIGHTS)

AXONAL OUTPUT

HIDDEN
UNITS

SYNAPTIC CONNECTIONS
(VARIOUS WEIGHTS)

AXONAL OUTPUT

INPUT
UNITS

FLOW OF INFORMATION

Figure 1.4
A simple network.

assembled set of simultaneous activation levels in all of the input units is
the network's *representation* of the input stimulus. We may refer to that
configuration of stimulation levels as the *input vector*, since it is just an
ordered set of numbers or magnitudes. (For our purposes, a vector just *is*
an ordered set of magnitudes.) For example, a given stimulus might produce the vector $\langle .5, .3, .9, .2 \rangle$.

These input activation levels are then propagated upward, via the output
signal in each unit's axon, to the middle layer of the network, to what are
called the *hidden units*. As can be seen in figure 1.4, any unit in the input
layer makes a synaptic connection of some weight or other with every unit
at this intermediate layer. Each hidden unit is thus the target of several
inputs, one for each cell at the input layer. The resulting activation level of
a given hidden unit is essentially just the sum of all of the influences
reaching it from the cells in the lower layer.

The result of this upward propagation of the input vector is a set of
activation levels across the three units in the hidden layer, called the *hidden
unit activation vector*. The values of that three-element vector are strictly
determined by (1) the makeup of the *input vector* at the input layer, and

(2) the various values of the *connection weights* at the ends of the terminal branches of the input units. What this bottom half of the network does, evidently, is convert or transform one activation vector into another.

The top half of the network does exactly the same thing, in exactly the same way. The activation vector at the hidden layer is propagated upward to the output (topmost) layer of units, where an *output vector* is produced, whose character is determined by (1) the makeup of the activation vector at the hidden layer, and (2) the various values of the connection weights at the ends of the terminal branches of the hidden units.

Looking now at the whole network, we can see that it is just a device for transforming any given input-level activation vector into a uniquely corresponding output-level activation vector. And what determines the character of the global transformation effected is the peculiar set of values possessed by the many connection weights. This much is easy to grasp. What is not so easy to grasp, prior to exploring examples, is just how very powerful and useful those transformations can be. So let us explore some real examples.

1.2   Representation and Learning in Brainlike Networks

A great many of the environmental features to which humans respond are difficult to define or characterize in terms of their purely physical properties. Even something as mundane as the vowel sound $\bar{a}$, as in *rain*, resists such characterization, for the range of acoustic variation among acceptable and recognizable instances of $\bar{a}$ is enormous. A female child at 2 years and a basso male at 50 will produce quite different sorts of atmospheric excitations in pronouncing this vowel, but each sound will be easily recognized as an $\bar{a}$ by other members of the same linguistic culture.

This is not to suggest that the matter is utterly intractable from a physical point of view, for an examination of the acoustic power spectrum of voiced vowels begins to reveal some of the similarities that unite $\bar{a}$'s. And yet the analysis continues to resist a simple list of necessary and sufficient physical conditions on being an $\bar{a}$. Instead, being an $\bar{a}$ seems to be a matter of being *close enough* to a *typical* $\bar{a}$ sound along a *sufficient* number of distinct *dimensions of relevance*, where each notion in italics remains difficult to characterize in a nonarbitrary way. Moreover, some of those dimensions are highly contextual. A sound type that would not normally be counted or recognized as an $\bar{a}$ when voiced in isolation may be unproblematically counted as such if it regularly occurs, in someone's modestly accented speech, in all of the phonetic places that would normally be occupied by $\bar{a}$'s. Evidently, what makes something an $\bar{a}$ is in part a matter of the entire linguistic surround. In this way do we very quickly ascend to the abstract and holistic level, for even the simplest of culturally embedded properties.

What holds for phonemes holds also for a great many other important features recognizable by human beings: colors, faces, flowers, trees, animals, voices, smells, feelings, songs, words, meanings, and even metaphorical meanings. At the outset, the categories and resources of physics, and even neuroscience, look puny and impotent in the face of such subtlety.

And yet it is purely physical systems that recognize such intricacies. Short of appealing to magic, or of simply refusing to confront the problem at all, we must assume that some configuration of purely physical elements is capable of grasping and manipulating these features, and by means of purely physical principles. Surprisingly, networks of the kind described in the preceding section have many of the properties needed to address precisely this problem. Let me explain.

Suppose we are submarine engineers confronted with the problem of designing a sonar system that will distinguish between the sonar echoes returned from explosive mines, such as might lie on the bottom of sensitive waterways during wartime, and the sonar echoes returned from rocks of comparable sizes that dot the same underwater landscapes. The difficulty is twofold: echoes from both objects sound indistinguishable to the casual ear, and echoes from each type show wide variation in sonic character, since both rocks and mines come in various sizes, shapes, and orientations relative to the probing sonar pulse.

Enter the network of figure 1.5. This one has 13 units at the input layer, since we need to code a fairly complex stimulus. A given sonar echo is run through a frequency analyzer and is sampled for its relative energy levels at 13 frequencies. These 13 values, expressed as fractions of 1, are then entered as activation levels in the respective units of the input layer, as indicated in figure 1.5. From here they are propagated through the network, being transformed as they go, as explained earlier. The result is a pair of activation levels in the two units at the output layer. We need only two units here, for we want the network eventually to produce an output activation vector at or near $\langle 1, 0 \rangle$ when a mine echo is entered as input, and an output activation vector at or near $\langle 0, 1 \rangle$ when a rock echo is entered as input. In a word, we want it to *distinguish* mines from rocks.

It would of course be a miracle if the network made the desired discrimination immediately, since the connection weights that determine its transformational activity are initially set at random values. At the beginning of this experiment, then, the output vectors are sure to disappoint us. But we proceed to *teach* the network by means of the following procedure.

We procure a large set of recorded samples of various (genuine) mine echoes, from mines of various sizes and orientations, and a comparable set of genuine rock echoes, keeping careful track of which is which. We then

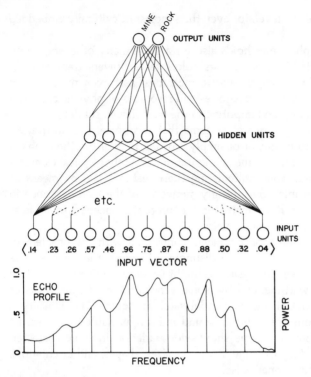

Figure 1.5
Perceptual recognition with a large network.

feed these echoes into the network, one by one, and observe the output vector produced in each case. What interests us in each case is the amount by which the actual output vector *differs* from what would have been the "correct" vector, given the identity of the specific echo that produced it. The details of that error, for each element of the output vector, are then fed into a special rule that computes a set of small changes in the values of the various synaptic weights in the system. The idea is to identify those weights most responsible for the error and then to nudge their values in a direction that would at least reduce the amount by which the output vector is in error. The slightly modified system is then fed another echo, and the entire procedure is repeated.

This provides the network with a "teacher." The process is called "training up the network," and it is standardly executed by an auxiliary computer programmed to feed samples from the training set into the network, monitor its responses, and adjust the weights according to the special rule after each trial. Under the pressure of such repeated corrections, the behavior of the network slowly converges on the behavior we desire.

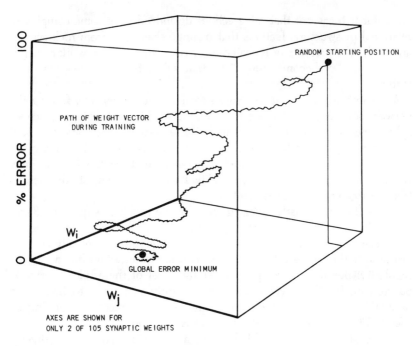

Figure 1.6
Learning: gradient descent in weight/error space.

That is to say, after several thousand presentations of recorded echoes and subsequent adjustments, the network starts to give the right answer close to 90 percent of the time. When fed a mine echo, it generally gives something close to a $\langle 1, 0 \rangle$ output. And when fed a rock echo, it generally gives something close to a $\langle 0, 1 \rangle$.

A useful way to think of this is captured in figure 1.6. Think of an abstract space of many dimensions, one for each weight in the network (105 in this case) plus one dimension for representing the overall error of the output vector on any given trial. Any point in that space represents a unique configuration of weights, plus the performance error that that configuration produces. What the learning rule does is steadily nudge that configuration away from erroneous positions and toward positions that are less erroneous. The system inches its way down an "error gradient" toward a global error minimum. Once there, it responds reliably to the relevant kinds of echoes. It even responds well to echoes that are "similar" to mine echoes, by giving output vectors that are closer to $\langle 1, 0 \rangle$ than to $\langle 0, 1 \rangle$.

There was no guarantee the network would succeed in learning to discriminate the two kinds of echoes, because there was no guarantee that rock echoes and mine echoes would differ in any systematic or detectable way. But it turns out that mine echoes do indeed have some complex of relational or structural features that distinguishes them from rock echoes, and under the pressure of repeated error corrections the network manages to lock onto, or become "tuned" to, that subtle but distinctive weave of features.

We can test whether it has truly succeeded in this by now feeding the network some mine and rock echoes not included in the training set, echoes it has never encountered before. In fact, the network does almost as well classifying the new echoes as it does with the samples in its training set. The "knowledge" it has acquired generalizes quite successfully to new cases. (This example is a highly simplified account of some striking results from Gorman and Sejnowski 1988.)

All of this is modestly amazing, because the problem is quite a difficult one, at least as difficult as learning to discriminate the phoneme $\bar{a}$. Human sonar operators, during a long tour of submarine duty, eventually learn to distinguish the two kinds of echoes with some uncertain but nontrivial regularity. But they never perform at the level of the artificial network. Spurred on by this success, work is currently underway to train up a network to distinguish the various phonemes characteristic of English speech (Zipser and Elman 1987). The idea is to produce a speech-recognition system that will not be troubled by the acoustic idiosyncrasies of diverse speakers, as existing speech-recognition systems are.

The success of the mine/rock network is further intriguing because the "knowledge" the network has acquired, concerning the distinctive character of mine echoes, consists of nothing more than a carefully orchestrated set of connection weights. And it is finally intriguing because there exists a learning algorithm—the rule for adjusting the weights as a function of the error displayed in the output vector—that will eventually produce the required set of weights, given sufficient examples on which to train the network (Rumelhart, Hinton, and Williams 1986a).

How can a set of connection weights possibly embody knowledge of the desired distinction? Think of it in the following way. Each of the 13 input units represents one aspect or dimension of the incoming stimulus. Collectively, they give a simultaneous profile of the input echo along 13 distinct dimensions. Now perhaps there is only one profile that is roughly characteristic of mine echoes; or perhaps there are many different profiles, united by a common relational feature (for instance, that the activation value of unit 6 is always three times the value of unit 12); or perhaps there is a disjunctive set of such relational features; and so forth. In each case it is possible to rig the weights so that the system will respond in a typical fashion, at the output layer, to all and only the relevant profiles.

The units at the hidden layer are very important in this. If we consider the abstract space whose seven axes represent the possible activation levels

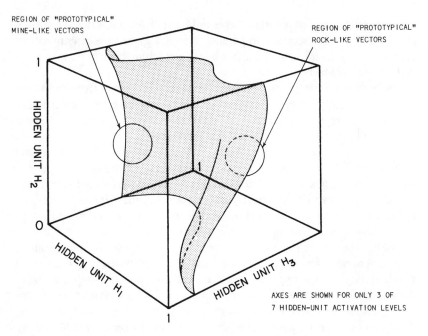

REGION OF "PROTOTYPICAL"
MINE-LIKE VECTORS

REGION OF "PROTOTYPICAL"
ROCK-LIKE VECTORS

1

HIDDEN UNIT H₂

0

HIDDEN UNIT H₁

HIDDEN UNIT H₃

AXES ARE SHOWN FOR ONLY 3 OF
7 HIDDEN-UNIT ACTIVATION LEVELS

1

Figure 1.7
Learned partition on hidden-unit activation-vector space.

of each of the seven hidden units, then what the system is searching for
during the training period is a set of weights that *partitions* this space so
that any mine input produces an activation vector across the hidden units
that falls somewhere within one large subvolume of this abstract space,
whereas any rock input produces a vector that falls somewhere into the
complement of that subvolume (figure 1.7). The job of the top half of
the network is then the relatively easy one of distinguishing these two
subvolumes into which the abstract space has been divided.

Vectors near the center of (or along a certain path in) the mine-vector
subvolume represent *prototypical* mine echoes, and these will produce an
output vector very close to the desired $\langle 1, 0 \rangle$. Vectors nearer to the
surface (strictly speaking, the hypersurface) that partitions the abstract
space represent atypical or problematic mine echoes, and these produce
more ambiguous output vectors such as $\langle .6, .4 \rangle$. The network's discrimina-
tive responses are thus graded responses: the system is sensitive to *similarities* along all of the relevant dimensions, and especially to rough conjunctions of these subordinate similarities.

So we have a system that learns to discriminate hard-to-define perceptual features and to be sensitive to similarities of a comparably diffuse but
highly relevant character. And once the network is trained up, the recog-

nitional task for any given input takes only a split second, since the system processes the input stimulus in parallel. It finally gives us a discriminatory system that performs something like a living creature, both in its speed and in its overall character.

This network is only one instance of a general technique that works well in a large variety of cases. Networks can be constructed with a larger number of units at the output layer, so as to be able to express not just a few, but a large number of distinct discriminations.

One network, aptly called *NETtalk* by its authors (Rosenberg and Sejnowski 1987), takes vector codings for seven-letter segments of printed words as inputs and gives vector codings for phonemes as outputs. These output vectors can be fed directly into a sound synthesizer as they occur, to produce audible sounds. This network learns to transform printed words into audible speech. Though it involves no understanding of the words that it "reads," the network's feat is still very impressive, because at the outset it is given no rules whatever concerning the phonetic significance of standard English spelling. It begins its training period by producing a stream of unintelligible babble in response to text entered as input. But in the course of many thousands of word presentations, and under the steady pressure of the weight-nudging algorithm, the set of weights slowly meanders its way to a configuration that reduces the measured error close to zero. After such training it produces as output, given arbitrary English text as input, perfectly intelligible speech with only rare and minor errors.

This case is significant for a number of reasons. First, the trained network makes a large number of discriminations (79, in fact), not just a binary one. Second, it contains no explicit representation of any *rules*, however much it might seem to be following a set of rules. Third, it has mastered an input/output transformation that is notoriously irregular, and it must be sensitive to lexical context in order to do so. (Specifically, the phoneme it assigns to the center or focal letter of its seven-letter input is in large part a function of the identity of the three letters on either side.) And fourth, it portrays some aspects of a "sensori*motor*" skill, rather than a purely sensory skill: it is producing highly complex behavior.

NETtalk has some limitations, of course. Pronunciations that depend on specifically semantic or grammatical distinctions will generally elude its grasp (unless they happen to be reflected in some way in the corpus of its training words, as occasionally they are), since NETtalk knows neither meanings nor syntax. But such dependencies affect only a very small percentage of the transformations appropriate to any text, and they are in any case to be expected. To overcome them completely would require a network that actually understands the text being read. And even then mistakes would occur, for even humans occasionally misread words as a result of grammatical or semantic confusion. What is arresting about NETtalk is just how very much of the complex and irregular business of text-based pronunciation can be mastered by a simple network with only a few hundred neuronlike units.

Another rather large network, by Lehky and Sejnowski (1988a,b), addresses problems in vision. It takes codings for smoothly varying gray-scale pictures as input, and after training it yields as output surprisingly accurate codings for the curvatures and orientations of the physical surfaces portrayed in the pictures. It solves a form of the very difficult "shape from shading" problem long familiar to theorists in the field of vision. (See Yuille and Ullman 1990.) This network is of special interest because a subsequent examination of the "receptive fields" of the trained hidden units shows them to have acquired some of the same response properties as are displayed by cells in the visual cortex of mature animals. Specifically, they show a maximum sensitivity to spots, edges, and bars in specific orientations. This finding echoes the seminal work of Hubel and Wiesel (1962), in which cells in feline visual cortex were discovered to have receptive fields of this same character. Results of this kind are very important, for if we are to take these artificial networks as models for how the brain works, then they must display realistic behavior not just at the macro level but also at the micro level.

This result is of interest for another reason. Despite a hidden unit's maximum response to such things as sharp edges, or oriented bars, or high-contrast spots, it must be remembered that in fact the network has never been shown any of these things. They lie outside its experience entirely. The network has seen nothing but smoothly varying gray-scale pictures of smoothly curved surfaces. The impulse to regard such hidden units as being "edge detectors" or "bar detectors" should therefore be suppressed. What feature in the environment happens to cause the maximum response in a given unit may have nothing to do with the coding strategies actually employed by the network. This example underscores the importance of looking at the activity across an entire population of units: it is the patterns of distributed activation that carry the coding burden.

Enough examples. You have seen something of what networks of this kind can do, and of how they do it. In both respects they contrast sharply with the kinds of representational and processing strategies that philosophers of science, inductive logicians, cognitive psychologists, and AI workers have traditionally ascribed to human beings (namely, sentencelike representations manipulated by formal rules). You can also see why this theoretical and experimental approach has captured the interest of those who seek to understand how the microarchitecture of the biological brain produces the phenomena displayed in human and animal cognition. Let us now explore the functional properties of these networks in more detail and see how they bear on some of the traditional issues in epistemology and cognitive theory.

1.3   Some Functional Properties of Brainlike Networks

The networks described in the previous section are descended from a device called the *Perceptron* (Rosenblatt 1959), which was essentially just a two-layer as opposed to a three-layer network. Devices of this configuration could and did learn to discriminate a considerable variety of input patterns. Unfortunately, having the input layer connected directly to the output layer imposes very severe limitations on the range of possible transformations a network can perform (Minsky and Papert 1969), and interest in Perceptron-like devices was soon eclipsed by the much faster-moving developments in standard "program-writing" AI, which exploited the high-speed general-purpose digital machines that were then starting to become widely available. Throughout the 1970s research in artificial "neural nets" was an underground program by comparison.

It has emerged from the shadows for a number of reasons. One important factor is just the troubled doldrums into which mainstream or program-writing AI has fallen. The failures of mainstream AI—unrealistic learning, poor performance in complex perceptual and motor tasks, weak handling of analogies, and snaillike cognitive performance despite the use of very large and fast machines—suggest that we need to rethink the style of representation and computation we have been ascribing to cognitive creatures.

Other reasons for the resurgence of interest in networks are more positive. The introduction of additional layers of intervening or "hidden" units produced a dramatic increase in the range of possible transformations that the network could effect. As Sejnowski, Kienker, and Hinton (1986) describe it,

> ... only the first-order statistics of the input pattern can be captured by direct connections between input and output units. The role of the hidden units is to capture higher-order statistical relationships and this can be accomplished if significant underlying features can be found that have strong, regular relationships with the patterns on the visible units. The hard part of learning is to find the set of weights which turn the hidden units into useful feature detectors.

Equally important is the S-shaped, nonlinear response profile (figure 1.3) now assigned to every unit in the network. So long as this response profile remains linear, any network will be limited to computing purely linear transformations. (A transformation $f(x)$ is linear just in case $f(n \cdot x) =$

$n \cdot f(x)$ and $f(x + y) = f(x) + f(y)$.) But a nonlinear response profile for each unit brings the entire range of possible nonlinear transformations within reach of three-layer networks, a dramatic expansion of their computational potential. Now there are *no* transformations that lie beyond the computational power of a large enough and suitably weighted network.

A third factor was the articulation, by Rumelhart, Hinton, and Williams, of the *generalized delta rule* (a generalization, to three-layer networks, of Rosenblatt's original teaching rule for adjusting the weights of the Perceptron), and the empirical discovery that this new rule very rarely got permanently stuck in inefficient "local minima" on its way toward finding the best possible configuration of connection weights for a given network and a given problem. This was a major breakthrough, not so much because "learning by the back propagation of error," as it has come to be called, was just like human learning, but because it provided us with an efficient technology for quickly training up various networks on various problems, so that we could then study their properties and explore their potential.

The way the generalized delta rule works can be made fairly intuitive given the idea of an abstract weight space as represented in figure 1.6. Consider any output vector produced by a network with a specific configuration of weights, a configuration represented by a specific position in weight space. Suppose that this output vector is in error by various degrees in various of its elements. Consider now a single synapse at the output layer, and consider the effect on the output vector that a small positive or negative change in its weight would have had. Since the output vector is a determinate function of system's weights (assuming we hold the input vector fixed), we can calculate which of these possible changes, if either, would have made the greater improvement in output vector. The relevant change is made accordingly. (For more detail, see Rumelhart, Hinton, and Williams 1986b.)

If a similar calculation is performed over every synapse in the network, and the change in its weight is then made accordingly, the resulting shift in the position of the system's overall point in weight space amounts to a small slide *down* the steepest face of the local "error surface." Note that there is no guarantee that this incremental shift moves the system directly toward the global position of zero error (that is why perfection cannot be achieved in a single jump). On the contrary, the descending path to a global error minimum may be highly circuitous. Nor is there any guarantee that the system must eventually reach such a global minimum. On the contrary, the downward path from a given starting point may well lead to a merely local minimum, from which only a large change in the system's weights will afford escape, a change beyond the reach of the delta rule. But in fact this happens relatively rarely, for it turns out that the more dimensions (synapses) a system has, the smaller the probability of there being an intersecting local minimum in *every one* of the available dimensions. The global point is usually able to slide down some narrow cleft in the local topography. Empirically, then, the back-propagation algorithm is surprisingly effective at driving the system to the global error minimum, at least where we can identify that global minimum reliably.

The advantage this algorithm provides is easily appreciated. The possible combinations of weights in a network increase exponentially with the size of the network. Assuming conservatively that each weight admits of only 10 possible values, the number of distinct positions in "weight space" (that is, the number of possible weight configurations) for the simple rock/mine network of figure 1.5 is already 10^{105}! This space is far too large to explore efficiently without something like the generalized delta rule and the back propagation of error to do it for us. But with the delta rule, administered by an auxiliary computer, researchers have shown that networks of the simple kind described here are capable of learning some quite extraordinary skills and of displaying some highly intriguing properties. Let us now explore these further.

An important exploratory technique in cognitive and behavioral neuroscience is to record, with an implanted microelectrode, the electrical activity of a single neuron during cognition or behavior in the intact animal. This is relatively easy to do (in cats, for example), and it does give us tantalizing bits of information about the cognitive significance of neural activity (recall the results of Hubel and Wiesel mentioned earlier). Single-cell recordings give us only isolated bits of information, however, and what we would really like to monitor are the *patterns* of simultaneous neural activation across large numbers of cells in the same subsystem. Unfortunately, effective techniques for simultaneous recording from large numbers of adjacent cells are still in their infancy. The task is extremely difficult.

By contrast, this task is extremely easy with the artificial networks we have been looking at. If the network is real hardware, its units are far more accessible than the fragile and microscopic units of a living brain. And if the network is merely being simulated within a standard computer (as is usually the case), one can write the program so that the activation levels of any unit, or set of units, can be read out on command. Accordingly, once a network has been successfully trained up on some skill or other, one can then examine the collective behavior of its units during the exercise of that skill.

We have already seen the results of one such analysis in the rock/mine network. Once the weights have reached their optimum configuration, the activation vectors (that is, the patterns of activation) at the hidden layer fall into two disjoint classes: the vector space is partitioned in two, as depicted schematically in figure 1.7. But a mere binary discrimination is an atypically simple case. The reader NETtalk, for example, partitions its hidden-unit vector space into fully 79 subspaces. The reason is simple. For each of the 26 letters in the alphabet, there is at least one phoneme assigned to it, and for many letters there are several phonemes that might be signified, depending on the lexical context. As it happens, there are 79 distinct letter-to-phoneme associations to be learned if one is to master the pronunciation of English spelling, and in the successfully trained network a distinct hidden-unit activation vector occurs when each of these 79 possible transformations is effected.

In the case of the rock/mine network, we noted a similarity metric within each of its two hidden-unit subspaces. In the case of NETtalk, we also find a similarity metric, this time across the 79 functional hidden-unit vectors. (A *functional vector* is a vector that corresponds to one of the 79 desired letter-to-phoneme transformations in the trained network.) Rosenberg and Sejnowski did a *cluster analysis* of these vectors in the trained network. Roughly, their procedure was as follows. They asked, for every functional vector in that space, what other such vector is closest to it? The answers yielded about 30 vector pairs. They then constructed a secondary vector for each such pair, by averaging the two original vectors, and asked, for every such secondary vector, what other secondary vector (or so far unpaired primary vector) is closest to it? This produced a smaller set of secondary-vector pairs, on which the averaging procedure was repeated to produce a set of tertiary vectors. These were then paired in turn, and so forth. This procedure produces a hierarchy of groupings among the original transformations, and it comes to an end with a grand division of the 79 original vectors into two disjoint classes.

As it happens, that deepest and most fundamental division within the hidden-unit vector space corresponds to the division between the consonants and the vowels! Looking farther into this hierarchy—into the consonant branch, for example—we find that there are subdivisions into the principal consonant types, and that within these branches there are further subdivisions into the most similar consonants. All of this is depicted in the tree diagram of figure 1.8. What the network has managed to recover, from its training set of several thousand English words, is the highly irregular phonological significance of standard English spelling, plus the hierarchical organization of the phonetic structure of English speech.

Here we have a clear illustration of two things at once. The first lesson is the capacity of an activation-vector space to embody a rich and well-structured hierarchy of categories, complete with a similarity metric embracing everything within it. And the second lesson is the capacity of such networks to embody representations of factors and patterns that are only partially or implicitly reflected in the corpus of inputs. The rock/mine network provides another example of this, in that the final partition made on its hidden-unit vector space corresponds in fact to the objective

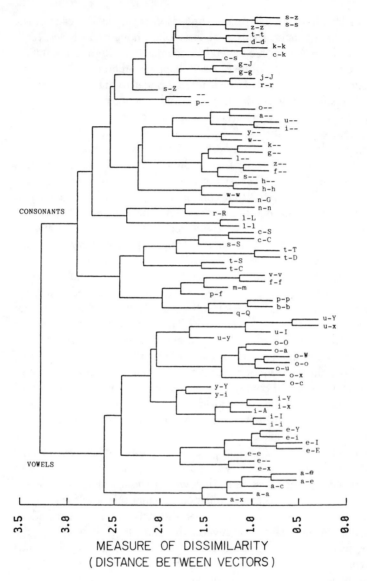

MEASURE OF DISSIMILARITY
(DISTANCE BETWEEN VECTORS)

Figure 1.8
Hierarchy of partitions on hidden-unit vector space (after Rosenberg and Sejnowski 1987).

distinction between sonar targets made of metal and sonar targets made of nonmetal. That is the true uniformity that lies behind the apparently chaotic variety displayed in the inputs.

It is briefly tempting to suggest that NETtalk has the concept of a "hard *c*," for example, and that the rock/mine network has the concept of "metal." But this won't really do, since the vector-space representations at issue do not play a conceptual or computational role remotely rich enough to merit their assimilation to specifically human concepts. Nevertheless, it is plain that both networks have contrived a system of internal representations that truly corresponds to important distinctions and structures in the outside world, structures that are not explicitly represented in the corpus of their sensory input. The value of those representations is that they and only they allow the networks to "make sense" of their variegated and often noisy input corpus, in the sense that they and only they allow the network to respond to those inputs in a fashion that systematically reduces the error messages to a trickle. These, of course, are the functions typically ascribed to *theories*.

What we are confronting here is a possible conception of "knowledge" or "understanding" that owes nothing to the symbolic and sentential categories of current common sense and of traditional approaches in AI. (See chapter 3 of the epilogue.) An individual's overall theory-of-the-world, we might venture, is not a large collection or a long list of stored symbolic items. Rather, it is a specific point in that individual's synaptic weight space. It is a configuration of connection weights, a configuration that partitions the system's activation-vector space(s) into useful divisions and subdivisions relative to the inputs typically fed the system. *Useful* here means 'tends to minimize the error messages'.

A possible objection points to the fact that differently weighted systems can produce the same, or at least roughly the same, partitions on their activation-vector spaces. Accordingly, we might try to abstract from the idiosyncratic details of a system's connection weights and identify its global theory directly with the set of partitions they produce within its activation-vector space. This would allow for differently weighted systems to have the same theory.

There is some virtue in this suggestion, but also some vice. Although differently weighted systems can embody the same partitions and thus display the same output performance on any given input, they will still *learn* quite differently in the face of a protracted sequence of new and problematic inputs. This is because the learning algorithm that drives the system to new points in weight space does not care about the relatively global partitions that have been made in activation space. All it cares about are the individual weights and how they relate to apprehended error. The laws of cognitive evolution, therefore, do not operate primarily at the level of the partitions, at least on the view being explored here. Rather, they operate at the level of the weights. Accordingly, if we want our "unit of cognition" to figure in the *laws* of cognitive development, the point in weight space seems the wiser choice of unit. We need only concede that different global theories can occasionally produce identical short-term behavior.

The level of the partitions certainly corresponds more closely to the "conceptual" level, as understood in commonsense and traditional theory, but the point is that this seems not to be the most important dynamical level, even when explicated in neurocomputational terms. Knowing a creature's vector-space partitions may suffice for the accurate short-term prediction of its behavior, but that knowledge is inadequate to predict or explain the evolution of those partitions over the course of time and cruel experience. If we are to explain the phenomenon of *conceptual change*, therefore, we need to unearth a level of subconceptual combinatorial elements within which different concepts can be articulated, evaluated, and then modified according to their performance. The connection weights provide a level that meets all of these conditions.

This general view of how knowledge is embodied and accessed in the brain has some further appealing features. If we assume that the brains of the higher animals work in something like the fashion outlined, then we can explain a number of puzzling features of human and animal cognition. For one thing, the speed-of-relevant-access problem simply disappears. A network the size of a human brain—with 10^{11} neurons, 10^3 connections on each, 10^{14} total connections, and at least 10 distinct layers of "hidden" units—can be expected, in the course of growing up, to partition its internal vector spaces into many billions of functionally relevant subdivisions, each responsive to a broad but proprietary range of highly complex stimuli. When the network receives a stimulus that falls into one of these classes, the network produces the appropriate activation vector in a matter of only tens or hundreds of milliseconds, because that is all the time it takes for the parallel-coded stimulus to make its way through only two or three or ten layers of the massively parallel network to the functionally relevant layer that drives the appropriate behavioral response. Since information is stored, not in a long list that must somehow be searched, but rather in the myriad connection weights that configure the network, relevant aspects of the creature's total information are automatically accessed by the coded stimuli themselves.

A third advantage of this model is its explanation of the functional persistence of brains in the face of minor damage, disease, and the normal but steady loss of its cells with age. Human cognition degrades fairly gracefully as the physical plant deteriorates, in sharp contrast to the behavior of typical computers, which have a very low fault tolerance. The explanation of this persistence lies in the massively parallel character of the computations the brain performs, and in the very tiny contribution that each synapse or each cell makes to the overall computation. In a large network of 100,000 units, the loss or misbehavior of a single cell will not even be detectable. And in the more dramatic case of widespread cell loss, so long as the losses are more or less randomly distributed throughout the network, the gross character of the network's activity will remain unchanged: what happens is that the *quality* of its computations will be progressively degraded.

A fourth noteworthy feature of networks with this general architecture is the truly vast range of possible conceptual configurations from which they may choose. Consider the following numbers. With a total of roughly 10^{11} neurons with an average of at least 10^3 connections each, the human brain has something like 10^{14} weights to play with. Supposing, conservatively, that each weight will admit of only 10 possible values, the total number of distinct possible configurations of synaptic weights (= distinct possible positions in weight space) is 10 for the first weight, times 10 for the second weight, times 10 for the third weight, and so on, for a total of $10^{10^{14}}$, or $10^{100,000,000,000,000}$!! This is the total number of just barely distinguishable conceptual frameworks employable by humans, given the cognitive resources we currently command. To put this number into some remotely adequate perspective, recall that the total number of elementary particles in the entire universe is only about about 10^{87}. (For an exploration of some of the consequences of such conceptual plasticity, see Churchland 1979, 1988.)

1.4   How Faithfully Do These Networks Depict the Brain?

The functional properties so far observed in these model networks are an encouraging reward for the structural assumptions that went into them. But just how accurate are these models, as depictions of the brain's microstructure? A wholly appropriate answer here is uncertain, for we continue to be uncertain about what features of the brain's microstructure are and are not functionally relevant, and we are therefore uncertain about what is and is not a "legitimate" simplifying assumption in the models we make. Even so, it is plain that the models are inaccurate in a variety of respects, and it is the point of the present section to summarize and evaluate these failings. Let us begin by underscoring the basic respects in which the models appear to be correct.

It is true that real nervous systems display, as their principal organizing feature, layers or populations of neurons that project their axons en masse to some distinct layer or population of neurons, where each arriving axon

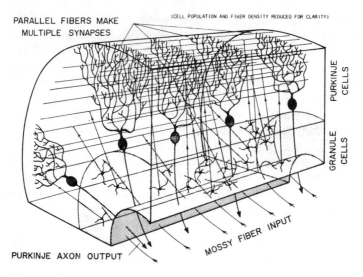

PARALLEL FIBERS MAKE
MULTIPLE SYNAPSES

(CELL POPULATION AND FIBER DENSITY REDUCED FOR CLARITY)

PURKINJE CELLS

GRANULE CELLS

MOSSY FIBER INPUT

PURKINJE AXON OUTPUT

Figure 1.9
Schematic section: cerebellum.

divides into multiple branches whose end bulbs make synaptic connections of various weights onto many cells at the target location. This description captures all of the sensory modalities and their primary relations to the brain; it captures the character of the various areas of the central brain stem; and it captures the structure of the cerebral cortex, which in humans contains at least six distinct layers of neurons, where each layer is the source and/or the target of an orderly projection of axons to and/or from elsewhere.

It captures the character of the cerebellum as well (figure 1.9), a structure discussed in Churchland 1986 in connection with the problem of motor control. In that paper I described the cerebellum as having the structure of a very large "matrix multiplier," as schematized in figure 1.10. Following Pellionisz and Llinas 1982, I ascribed to this neural matrix the function of performing sophisticated transformations on incoming activation vectors. This is in fact the same function performed between any two layers of the three-layered networks described earlier, and the two cases are distinct only in the superficial details of their wiring diagrams. A three-layered network of the kind discussed earlier is equivalent to a pair of neural matrices connected in series, as is illustrated in figure 1.11. The only substantive difference is that in figure 1.11a the end branches synapse directly onto the receiving cell body itself, whereas in figure 1.11b they synapse onto some dendritic filaments extending out from the receiving cell body. The actual connectivity within the two networks is identical. The

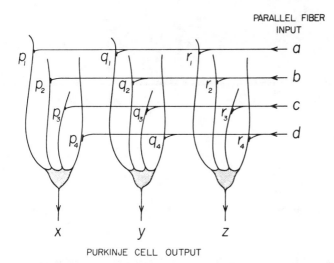

PARALLEL FIBER
INPUT

PURKINJE CELL OUTPUT

Figure 1.10
Neural matrix.

cerebellum and the motor end of natural systems, accordingly, seem further instances of the gross pattern at issue.

But the details present all manner of difficulties. To begin with small ones, note that in real brains an arriving axon makes synaptic contact with only a relatively small percentage of the thousands or millions of cells in its target population, not with every last one of them as in the models. This is not a serious difficulty, since model networks with comparably pared connections still manage to learn the required transformations quite well, though perhaps not so well as a fully connected network.

More seriously, so far as is known, real axons have terminal end bulbs that are uniformly inhibitory, or uniformly excitatory, depending on the type of neuron. We seem not to find a mixture of both kinds of connections radiating from the same neuron, nor do we find connections changing their sign during learning, as is the case in the models. Moreover, that mixture of positive and negative influences is essential to successful function in the models: the same input cell must be capable of inhibiting some cells down the line at the same time that it is busy exciting others. Further, cell populations in the brain typically show extensive "horizontal" cell-to-cell connections *within* a given layer. In the models there are none at all (see, for example, figure 1.4). Their connections join cells only to cells in distinct layers.

These last two difficulties might conceivably serve to cancel each other. One way in which an excitatory end bulb might serve to inhibit a cell in

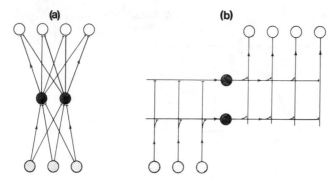

Figure 1.11
The equivalence of nets and matrices. (a) A 3-2-4 associative net. (b) A coupled pair of matrices (3 × 2 and 2 × 4).

its target population is first to make an excitatory connection onto one of the many small *interneurons* typically scattered throughout the target population of main neurons, which interneuron has made an inhibitory synaptic connection onto the target main neuron. Exciting the *inhibitory* interneuron would then have the effect of inhibiting the main neuron, as desired. And such a system would display a large number of short "horizontal" intralayer connections, as is observed. This is just a suggestion, however, since it is far from clear that the elements mentioned are predominantly connected in the manner required.

More seriously still, there are several major problems with the idea that networks in the brain learn by means of the learning algorithm so effective in the models: the procedure of back-propagating apprehended errors according to the generalized delta rule. That procedure requires two things: (1) a computation of the partial correction needed for each unit in the output layer, and via these a computation of a partial correction for each unit in the earlier layers, and (2) a method of causally conveying these correction messages back through the network to the sites of the relevant synaptic connections in such a fashion that each weight gets nudged up or down accordingly. In a computer simulation of the networks at issue (which is currently the standard technique for exploring their properties), both the computation and the subsequent weight adjustments are easily done: the computation is done outside the network by the host computer, which has direct access to and control over every element of the network being simulated. But in the self-contained biological brain, we have to find some real source of adjustment signals, and some real pathways to convey them back to the relevant units. Unfortunately, the empirical brain displays little that answers to exactly these requirements.

Not that it contains nothing along these lines: the primary ascending pathways already described are typically matched by reciprocal or "descending" pathways of comparable density. These allow higher layers to have an influence on affairs at lower layers. Yet the influence appears to be on the activity levels of the lower cells themselves, rather than on the myriad synaptic connections whose weights need adjusting during learning. There may be indirect effects on the synapses, of course, but it is far from clear that the brain's wiring diagram answers to the demands of the back-propagation algorithm.

The case is a little more promising in the cerebellum (figure 1.9), which contains a second major input system in the aptly named *climbing fibers* (not shown in the diagram for reasons of clarity). These fibers envelop each of the large Purkinje cells from below in the same fashion that a climbing ivy envelops a giant oak, with its filamentary tendrils reaching well up into the bushy dendritic tree of the Purkinje cell, which tree is the locus of all of the synaptic connections made by the incoming parallel fibers. The climbing fibers are thus at least roughly positioned to do the job that the back-propagation algorithm requires of them, and they are distributed one to each Purkinje cell, as consistent delivery of the error message requires. Equally, they might serve some other quite different learning algorithm, as advocated by Pellionisz and Llinas (1985). Unfortunately, there is as yet no compelling reason to believe that the modification of the weights of the parallel-fiber-to-Purkinje-dendrite synapses is even within the causal power of the climbing fibers. Nor is there any clear reason to see either the climbing fibers in the cerebellum, or the descending pathways elsewhere in the brain, as the bearers of any appropriately computed error-correction messages appropriate to needed synaptic change.

On the hardware side, therefore, the situation does not support the idea that the specific back-propagation procedure of Rumelhart, Hinton, and Williams is the brain's central mechanism for learning. (Neither, it should be mentioned, did they claim that it is.) And it is implausible on some functional grounds as well. First, in the process of learning a recognition task, living brains typically show a progressive reduction in the reaction time required for the recognitional output response. With the delta rule, however, learning involves a progressive reduction in error, but reaction times are constant throughout. A second difficulty with the delta rule is as follows. A necessary element in its calculated apportionment of error is a representation of what would have been the correct vector in the output layer. That is why back propagation is said to involve a global "teacher," an information source that always knows the correct answers and can therefore provide a perfect measure of output error. Real creatures generally lack any such perfect information. They must struggle along in the absence of any sure compass toward the truth, and their synaptic adjustments must be based on much poorer information.

And yet their brains learn. Which means that somehow the configuration of their synaptic weights must undergo change, change steered in some way by error or related dissatisfaction, change that carves a path toward a regime of decreased error. Knowing this much, and knowing something about the microstructure and microdynamics of the brain, we can explore the space of possible learning procedures with some idea of what features to look for. If the generalized delta rule is not the brain's procedure, as it seems not to be, there remain other possible strategies for back-propagating sundry error measures, strategies that may find more detailed reflection in the brain. If these prove unrealizable, there are other procedures that do not require the organized distribution of any global error measures at all; they depend primarily on local constraints (Hinton and Sejnowski 1986; Hopfield and Tank 1985; Barto 1985; Bear, Cooper, and Ebner 1987).

One of these is worthy of mention, since something along these lines does appear to be displayed in biological brains. *Hebbian* learning (so called after D. O. Hebb, who first proposed the mechanism) is a process of weight adjustment that exploits the temporal coincidence, on either side of a given synaptic junction, of a strong signal in the incoming axon and a high level of excitation in the receiving cell. When such conjunctions occur, Hebb proposed, some physical or chemical change is induced in the synapse, a change that increases its "weight." Of course, high activation in the receiving cell is typically caused by excitatory stimulation from many other incoming axons, and so the important temporal coincidence here is really between high activation among certain of the incoming axons. Those whose high activation coincides with the activation of many others have their subsequent influence on the cell increased. Crudely, those who vote with winners become winners.

A Hebbian weight-adjusting procedure can indeed produce learning in artificial networks (Linsker 1986), although it does not seem to be as general in its effectiveness as is back propagation. On the other hand, it has a major functional advantage over back propagation. The latter has scaling problems, in that the process of calculating and distributing the relevant adjustments expands geometrically with the number of units in the network. But Hebbian adjustments are locally driven; they are independent of one another and of the overall size of the network. A large network will thus learn just as quickly as a small one. Indeed, a large network may even show a slight advantage over a smaller, since the temporal coincidence of incoming stimulations at a given cell will be better and better defined with increasing numbers of incoming axons.

We may also postulate "anti-Hebbian" processes, as a means of reducing synaptic weights instead of increasing them. And we need to explore various possible flavors of each. We still have very little understanding of the functional properties of these alternative learning strategies. Nor are we at all sure that Hebbian learning, as described above, is really how the brain typically adjusts its weights. A good deal of activity-sensitive synaptic modification does seem to occur in the brain, but whether its profile is specifically Hebbian is not yet established. Nor should we expect the brain to confine itself to only one learning strategy, for even at the behavioral level we can discern distinct types of learning. In sum, the problem of what mechanisms actually produce synaptic change during learning is an unsolved problem. But the functional success of the generalized delta rule assures us that the problem is solvable in principle, and other more plausible procedures are currently under active exploration.

Though the matter of how real neural networks generate the right configuration of weights remains obscure, the matter of how they perform their various cognitive tasks once configured is a good deal clearer. If even small artificial networks can perform the sophisticated cognitive tasks illustrated earlier in this chapter, there is no mystery that real networks should do the same or better. What the brain displays in the way of hardware is not radically different from what the models contain, and the differences invite exploration rather than disappointment. The brain is of course very much larger and denser than the models so far constructed. It has many layers rather than just two or three. It boasts perhaps a hundred distinct and highly specialized cell types, rather than just one. It is not a single n-layer network but rather a large committee of distinct but parallel networks, interacting in sundry ways. It plainly commands many spaces of stunning complexity, and many skills in consequence. It stands as a glowing invitation to make our humble models yet more and more realistic, in hopes of unlocking the many secrets remaining.

The multiple realization argument discussed at the beginning of the chapter proceeds from what is surely a true premise: cognition can be realized in systems of widely different physical constitution. But it does not follow that no fundamental insights into the general nature of cognition are likely to be found by examining the microstructure and microactivity of biological brains. On the contrary, such examination reveals a system that uses high-dimensional vector coding for its inputs and that processes information by performing high-speed vector-to-vector transformations by means of a massively parallel architecture. Such systems display characteristics of operation and strategies of information storage that are strikingly different from those artificial systems or postulated strategies inspired by the rule-governed-symbol-manipulation paradigm. A network's spontaneous organization of its activation vector space into a hierarchy of content-addressable and similarity-sensitive concepts is an especially novel and arresting feature. If we have learned this much by seeking inspiration from the empirical brain, we may yet learn more.

Whether cognitive systems of this massively parallel type will prove capable of recreating the full range of cognitive phenomena, including linguistic behavior and other overtly "symbolic" types of behavior, is yet an open question. Here is an area where one places one's research bets and takes one's chances. My own guess is that they will. But that is not important. What is important is that in neural network research we now have an unusually fertile and successful research program to complement and to compete with the more traditional approaches to cognitive science. So long as the relevant alternatives are available to everybody, the future will take care of itself.

Suggestions for Further Reading

For an accessible introduction to the history and current state of the several neurosciences, see P. S. Churchland 1986. For a comprehensive and penetrating introduction to the theory and techniques of parallel distributed processing, see Rumelhart, Hinton, and Williams 1986b. A spirited and strongly critical analysis of the claims of the parallel distributed processing or connectionist approach to cognition has recently been provided by Fodor and Pylyshyn 1988. An exploration of some of the philosophical consequences of this new cognitive paradigm appears in P. M. Churchland (1989b).

Questions

At this stage of inquiry, we confront two broad competing conceptions of the basic nature of cognitive activity: roughly, the paradigm of combinatorial symbols manipulated by structure-sensitive rules versus the paradigm of high-dimensional vector-coding and vector-to-vector transformations. Two questions suggest themselves:

1.1 Does the background requirement of coherence with evolutionary theory in biology provide any presumption in favor of either paradigm? Why or why not?

1.2 Are these two paradigms genuinely competing *alternatives*? Might one be a *subcase* of the other? Or might they be addressing distinct *levels* of explanation?

References

Barto, A. G. (1985). Learning by statistical cooperation of self-interested neuron-like computing elements. *Human Neurobiology* 4, 229–256.

Bear, M. F., L. N. Cooper, and F. F. Ebner (1987). A physiological basis for a theory of synapse modification. *Science* 237, no. 4810.

Churchland, P. M. (1979). *Scientific realism and the plasticity of mind*. Cambridge: Cambridge University Press.

Churchland, P. M. (1986). Some reductive strategies in cognitive neurobiology. *Mind* 95, no. 379, 279–309.

Churchland, P. M. (1988). Perceptual plasticity and theoretical neutrality: A reply to Jerry Fodor. *Philosophy of Science* 55, 167–187.

Churchland, P. M. (1989a). On the nature of theories: A neurocomputational approach. In C. W. Savage, ed., *Scientific theories*. (Minnesota Studies in the Philosophy of Science 14.) Minneapolis, MN: University of Minnesota Press.

Churchland, P. M. (1989b). *A neurocomputational perspective: The nature of mind and the structure of science*. Cambridge, MA: MIT Press.

Churchland, P. S. (1986). *Neurophilosophy: Toward a unified science of the mind-brain*. Cambridge, MA: MIT Press.

Fodor, J. A., and Z. W. Pylyshyn (1988). Connectionism and cognitive architecture: A critical analysis. *Cognition* 28, 3–71.

Gorman, R. P., and T. J. Sejnowski (1988). Learned classification of sonar targets using a massively-parallel network. *IEEE transactions: Acoustics, speech, and signal processing* (forthcoming).

Hinton, G. E., and T. J. Sejnowski (1986). Learning and relearning in Boltzmann machines. In D. E. Rumelhart, J. L. McClelland, and the PDP Research Group, *Parallel distributed processing: Explorations in the microstructure of cognition*. Vol. 1: *Foundations*. Cambridge, MA: MIT Press.

Hopfield, J. J., and D. Tank (1985). "Neural" computation of decisions in optimization problems. *Biological Cybernetics* 52, 141–152.

Hubel, D. H., and T. N. Wiesel (1962). Receptive fields, binocular interactions, and functional architecture in the cat's visual cortex. *Journal of Physiology* 160, 106–154.

Lehky, S., and T. J. Sejnowski (1988a). Computing shape from shading with a neural network model. In E. Schwartz, ed., *Computational neuroscience*. Cambridge, MA: MIT Press.

Lehky, S. R., and T. J. Sejnowski (1988b). Network model of shape-from-shading: Neural function arises from both receptive and projective fields. *Nature* 333 (June 2), 452–454.

Linsker, R. (1986). From basic network principles to neural architecture: Emergence of orientation columns. *Proceedings of the National Academy of Sciences, USA* 83, 8779–8783.

Minsky, M., and S. Papert (1969). *Perceptrons*. Cambridge, MA: MIT Press.

Pellionisz, A., and R. Llinas (1982). Space-time representation in the brain: The cerebellum as a predictive space-time metric tensor. *Neuroscience* 7, 2949–2970.

Pellionisz, A., and R. Llinas (1985). Tensor network theory of the metaorganization of functional geometries in the central nervous system. *Neuroscience* 16, 245–274.

Rosenberg, C. R., and T. J. Sejnowski (1987). Parallel networks that learn to pronounce English text. *Complex Systems* 1, 145–168.

Rosenblatt, F. (1959). *Principles of neurodynamics*. New York: Spartan Books.

Rumelhart, D. E., G. E. Hinton, and R. J. Williams (1986a). Learning representations by back-propagating errors. *Nature* 323 (October 9), 533–536.

Rumelhart, D. E., G. E. Hinton, and R. J. Williams (1986b). Learning internal representations by error propagation. In D. E. Rumelhart, J. L. McClelland, and the PDP Research Group, *Parallel distributed processing: Explorations in the microstructure of cognition*. Vol. 1: *Foundations*. Cambridge, MA: MIT Press.

Sejnowski, T. J., P. K. Kienker, and G. E. Hinton (1986). Learning symmetry groups with hidden units: Beyond the Perceptron. *Physica D* 22D, 260–275.

Yuille, A. L., and S. Ullman (1990). Computational theories of low-level vision. In D. N. Osherson, S. M. Kosslyn, and J. M. Hollerbach, eds., *Visual cognition and action: An invitation to cognitive science, volume 2*. Cambridge, MA: MIT Press.

Zipser, D., and J. D. Elman (1987). Learning the hidden structure of speech. *Journal of the Acoustical Society of America* 83, 1615–1626.

Chapter 2

The Evolution of Cognition

R. C. Lewontin

If it were our purpose in this chapter to say what is actually known about the evolution of human cognition, we could stop at the end of this sentence. That is not to say that a great deal has not been *written* on the subject. Indeed, whole books have been devoted to discussions of the evolution of human cognition and its social manifestations (for example, Lumsden and Wilson 1981), but these works are nothing more than a mixture of pure speculation and inventive stories. Some of these speculations and stories might even be true, but we do not know, nor is it clear, as we will discuss in this chapter, how we would go about finding out. Despite the fact that there is a vast and highly developed mathematical theory of evolutionary processes in general, despite the abundance of knowledge about living and fossil primates, despite the intimate knowledge that we have of our own species' physiology, morphology, psychology, and social organization, we know essentially nothing about the evolution of our cognitive capabilities and there is a strong possibility that we will never know much about it. It is the purpose of this chapter to explain why we are in such a position of ignorance. We need to understand how we go about investigating the evolution of a trait or a complex of traits, and how we try to explain the presence or absence of some feature in a particular species. With that understanding we will see why human cognition is such a difficult case.

2.1   Traits in Evolution

It is important to understand at the outset that it is not traits but organisms that evolve. There are then two related issues about traits in evolution: How have particular traits come into existence and changed during the evolution of some group of organisms? How has the trait influenced the organism in its total evolution? That is, particular traits must be understood as both the objects and subjects of the evolutionary process, as both the consequence of a process of historical organic change and a cause of change. So, for human height, we may well want to know how the human species has grown taller and shorter during its evolution and how and why height became differentiated among different human populations, say, Pygmies and Watusi. But equally, we need to understand how being the size we are, rather than, say, the size of a Green Monkey, has influenced our evolution. One thing is sure: Were we only monkey-sized, you would not now be reading this book, because the development of human technological culture required that we be able to break rocks, to mine, to maintain and control fires, activities that are possible only to creatures large enough to develop considerable kinetic energy with tools. Ants may be terribly clever and terribly strong for their size, but they can never smelt iron. So, the evolutionary questions about cognition are questions of evolution *of* cognition and evolution *through* cognition.

2.2   History, Form, and Function

Evolutionary biology since Darwin, and even before, has consisted of three partly contradictory strains. If, as now seems certain, all complex organisms stem from a single ancestral line in the remote past, then all organisms of which we have a record are related to each other and we can trace a path from one to another through their most recent common ancestors. But by the very nature of genetic inheritance, we expect related organisms to carry similar genes, derived from their common ancestors. The more distant in time those common ancestors are, the more likely that mutation in the genes will have occurred, so that distant relatives are less likely to have identical genes than close relatives. In general, then, for purely historical reasons we expect the degree of similarity of two organisms to reflect their degree of ancestral relationships, which is itself simply an expression of how long ago the organisms shared a common ancestor.

2.2.1   Evolutionary Description

One strain in evolutionary reconstruction emphasizes this historical process of random divergence from a common form as the essential feature of evolution. The question is, Who is related to whom, and how closely? And the answer is provided by similarity of form. In this view, evolution is a *descriptive* science, and its rhetoric is in the paratactic form of chronicles, like the "begats" of the Book of Genesis. Just as "Mahalal lived sixty and five years and begat Jared and Mahalel lived after Jared eight hundred and thirty years and begat sons and daughters," so a human paleontologist might say that *Australopithecus africanus* lived between 1.2 and 4 million years ago, had a cranial capacity of 450 cubic centimeters, and was an ancestor of *Homo habilis*, a form that lived between 1.5 and 2 million years ago, had a cranial capacity of about 750 cubic centimeters, and was an ancestor of modern *Homo sapiens*. Unfortunately, as we will see, it is far from clear that *Australopithecus africanus* really "begat" *Homo habilis* or that *Homo habilis* was our direct ancestor. This particular chronicle is only one of many that can be unfolded from the fossil record. Indeed, *Australopithecus africanus* may have begot many "sons and daughters," any or none of which may have been our ancestor.

The descriptive task includes not only the drawing of patterns of relationship and the history of changes in observed characteristics of living and dead forms but also the drawing of inferences about *unobservable* characteristics of ancestral forms. It is not sufficient for the purposes of reconstructing the cognitive evolution of human beings to describe changes in cranial capacity, the length and pattern of other bones, and the fossil material found in association with the fossil remains of prehumans. We need to reconstruct from those materials the likely patterns of locomotion, manual dexterity, food gathering, communal activities—all those actions that we associate with and are prerequisite to various kinds of cognitive functions. Can we infer erect posture and bipedal locomotion from the skeleton? If so, were the hands used to carry and manipulate objects, freeing the mouth for better things? Was the cranial capacity large enough, and were the frontal and temporal lobes of the brain sufficiently developed that we may suppose a linguistic capability? Are there the broken bones of prey, are there tools, art, fire? These are all part of the evidence about supposed cognitive functions of our ancestors and relatives, some bits more compelling than others, but all related only inferentially to cognition. Any notion of what we mean by human cognition must regard the drawings of bison on the walls of the Lascaux caves by our Upper Paleolithic ancestors around 14,000 years ago as cognitive activity of a very advanced nature, but it is much more problematic to infer cognitive activity of earlier forms from, say, their brain size.

2.2.2   Functional Changes

In contrast to the purely historical relations between organisms, there are similarities and differences that arise for functional reasons. We associate with Darwin the theory of evolution by natural selection, the theory that the shapes and activities of organisms are a consequence of the differential survival and reproduction of different types.

To the extent that some changes in organisms are reproduced whereas others are rejected by natural selection, the historical similarity between species becomes distorted and fails to reveal purely ancestral relations. Thus, quite unrelated organisms may come to resemble each other because natural selection has favored similar morphologies and physiologies, beginning with very different materials. Such *convergence* is particularly striking in the marsupial mammals of Australia when they are compared with the placental mammals of the rest of the world. The marsupials and the placentals have been separated since the very origin of mammals (some believe they even descend from two different reptilian ancestors). Yet each group, independently, has developed remarkably similar forms. There are marsupial "wolves," marsupial insectivores, marsupial "bears," marsupial "mice," "rats," and "moles." However, the marsupials never succeeded in invading the air or the sea, and the closest they got to hoofed grazing mammals is the very distinctive kangaroo. On the other hand, selection can result in extreme divergence of closely related forms. Virtually all the differences between cows, goats, and deer have arisen in the last 10 million years—only about 10 percent of the total time since the origin of the mammals. It is this possibility of very rapid divergence of closely related forms that makes the evolution of cognition such a difficult problem. Our nearest nonhuman relatives are the chimpanzee and the gorilla, with whom we had a common ancestor around 10 million years ago. Our proteins are about 98 percent identical with those of chimpanzees and gorillas, so on this basis we might consider them close relatives. Yet a qualitative difference in cognition has arisen in hominid evolution that makes the cognitive difference between gorillas and chimpanzees trivial as compared to our cognitive distance from them. Moreover, what evidence we have from paleontology and archeology, from cranial capacity and tool making, shows that most of the difference has evolved in less than 200,000 years. The mere totaling up of the number of amino acid similarities or differences in proteins cannot tell us about *functional* or even morphological similarity between two forms, for two reasons. First, only a small number of amino acid substitutions at the active site of a protein can change its physiological specificity considerably. In hemoglobin, only one amino acid substitution at one end of the molecule changes the optimum environmental oxygen pressure for the molecule's oxygenation function. Second, single nucleotide substitutions in DNA regions that do not code for proteins at all, the "controlling elements," are sufficient to change completely the time and cellular location of the activation of genes.

An important consequence of nonrandom, natural selective divergence of species is that similarity of various traits in two species may differ widely. To say that we are "closely" or "distantly" related to chimpanzees and gorillas is to give a false impression of a uniformity in divergence that may lead to false inferences. The 20 million years of evolution that separate us from the chimpanzee (we are each 10 million years from our common ancestor) makes us rather distantly related, compared to, say, the relationship between dogs and wolves. Humans and chimpanzees are nevertheless very similar in their proteins, *on the average*, but vastly different in the sizes of their brains and in their ability to write books about each other.

2.2.3   Evolutionary Constraints

A third element in evolutionary reasoning accepts both the historical and the functional elements in the determination of similarity but emphasizes a set of general constraints on the possibility of change. For reasons that are not at all clear but must be related to the physically possible range of mutations that can occur from a given gene, there is tremendous "inertia" of form in evolution. *All* the vertebrates have only four limbs and none has ever succeeded in adding an extra pair in the billion years of evolution that have gone on since the origin of the fish. When birds arose from dinosaurs, they had to sacrifice their front limbs to make wings, as did bats. Yet, of course, animals can be constructed with more than four legs. Insects have six in addition to wings. On the other hand, all insects have six legs and none has ever acquired eight. That is reserved for a completely separate evolutionary line, the spiders and mites. When mammals reentered the sea to become seals and whales, they turned their limbs into flippers and flukes but maintained the same basic skeletal architecture that characterizes the legs of their terrestrial relatives. There appear, then, to be basic body plans, *Baupläne*, that are maintained through immensely long evolutionary periods despite dramatic changes in the life activity patterns of organisms and the functions of their parts. This means, in turn, that when new functions arise in evolution, they often do so through a process of recruiting previously existing organs or physiological activities. So, although natural selection modifies the similarity between organisms that would appear from purely historical relations, the existence of *Baupläne* shows that history constrains the outcome of natural selection. Evolution under natural selection is historically contingent. The available material upon which selection acts is itself the outcome of a previous historical process that in turn was a historically contingent process of selectively constrained change.

2.3   Problems of Reconstruction

2.3.1   Reconstruction of Relationships

As we see, reconstruction of the evolution of traits involves both historical and ahistorical causal elements. From the historical standpoint, it must be possible to describe the relevant characteristics of an ancestral species and of closely related collateral relatives. In turn, however, such a description requires two kinds of information. First, it must be possible to reconstruct lines of relationship of species in order to know which forms are truly ancestral and which are merely collateral relatives not in a direct ancestral line of living forms. Moreover, it must be possible to make inferences about the degree of genetic relationship of living species to know which are "close" and which are "distant" relatives. Second, for the characters of interest, we require a description of their state in the various living and extinct ancestral and collateral lines. This includes the possibility that the trait simply does not exist in some or all related lines, that it is a novelty and therefore has no observable evolutionary history. The temptation is strong to stretch the description of the trait so that at least some rudimentary manifestation can be seen in ancestors. But even when the character seems obviously present to various degrees in several species, it is by no means certain that we are dealing with the same character in the genetic, anatomical, and physiological sense. Is vocalization in apes and monkeys a rudimentary form of human speech, connected to speech by an unbroken line of neuro-anatomical transformation, or is it merely a superficial analogy with speech?

Unfortunately, the problems of drawing lines of ancestry and of proper description of traits in relatives are not independent. How do we decide whether two forms are closely or distantly related, except by using their manifest similarities and differences to infer their relationship? If we use brain size and form to infer relationship, we cannot then turn around and use the inferred relationship to make assertions about the evolution of brain size and structure. In the creation of a structure of inferred relationships we must try to find a set of characteristics of organisms that are evolutionarily independent of the traits whose evolution we want to reconstruct. So, we can use overall similarity in DNA or an average similarity in randomly chosen proteins to establish lines of relationship. These implied relationships can then be used to reconstruct brain evolution, on the reasonable grounds that overall DNA and protein similarity averages out particular functional changes and provides an estimate of average genetic similarity among organisms.

2.3.2   Reconstruction of Function and Changes

When we turn from the chronicles of events, the "begats" of evolutionary history, to causal stories involving function and natural selection, quite different problems arise. First, we must distinguish between forces that influenced the acquisition of characters and the functional forces that operate on them currently. That is, we must not confound past forces with current function. For example, no one would deny that an insect's wings are "for flying" in the sense that many insects do indeed depend upon them for flight and that in a normally winged species an individual with defective wings will not long survive. Yet wings could not have originated in evolution by natural selection for flight, because rudimentary wings provide no aerodynamic lift at all. Recent experiments strongly support the view that wings originated as thermoregulatory devices and only functioned as flying appendages when they reached a critical size. Yet the fact that rudimentary wings can serve as thermoregulatory devices does not exclude other possibilities for their origin. Perhaps they were used as mating signalers, or to repel competitors for food, or for any one or a combination of other functions that an imaginative mind can invent. The problem of origin is the problem of reconstructing the function of traits in long extinct forms living in long extinct environments together with other long extinct forms. Although we may exclude some explanations on purely mechanical grounds, we can choose among many allowable ones. Did the dinosaur *Stegosaurus* use the large leaflike plates along its back for physical defense, for appearing deceptively large to potential predators, for sexual attraction, for thermoregulation, for all four, for some at one time and others at another, or none of the above? We will never know.

The second problem is to detemine the possible selective forces operating even on modern forms that are accessible to observation and experiment. The ascertainment of function is not the same as the determination of natural selection. Selection occurs if there is difference in the probability of survival and reproduction of different forms. But it is not always obvious that the presence or absence of some function will have a significant influence on reproductive rates. The ability to create well-formed sentences is a characteristic of normal human cognition, whose social and individual functions seem manifold and obvious. Yet no one has ever measured the reduction, if any, of survivorship and reproductive rate consequent on the lack of this ability. Plausible stories about what *might* be the reproductive consequences of aphasia are not sufficient. The issue, after all, is not whether syntactic power *might* have been favored by natural selection (obviously it *might* have been), but whether, in fact, it was. There are two requirements for a demonstration of the efficacy of natural selection. First, there must exist contrasting groups, those possessing the trait and those without it, or those possessing the character to different degrees, in order to measure the reproductive effect of variation in the trait. One reason we cannot measure natural selection for syntactic ability is that there are too few individuals with defective syntactic abilities and, anyway, they have suffered traumas that interfere in themselves with survivorship and reproduction. Second, even when there are contrasting groups as part of the natural variation of the species, the differences in reproductive rate are likely to be small and thus difficult to measure. A 1-percent difference in reproductive rate between types represents an enormous evolutionary force that would result in quite rapid changes in the prevalence of a trait in a species. Yet to measure a 1-percent difference in reproductive rate requires immense numbers of observations. In human beings it would require the complete survivorship and reproductive histories, from birth, of about 100,000 individuals in the contrasting groups, an enormously costly enterprise that has never been carried out for any human trait. Third, even if there are demonstrated differences in reproductive rates of different types, those differences cannot be the cause of evolution unless the types differ *genetically*. If the differences in morphology, physiology, and behavior are not passed from parent to offspring, then differential reproduction cannot change the distribution of a trait in the population. Even though the strong may leave more offspring than the weak, if the offspring of the strong are no stronger than the average, then differential reproduction is irrelevant to the species composition. Unfortunately, it is extremely difficult to obtain evidence of the biological heritability of traits, especially behavioral traits, and most especially in humans. Evidence about inheritance comes from the similarity of biological relatives. But because many animals, certainly all mammals, have a family structure, offspring will resemble their parents both because of biological inheritance and because of environmental similarity. For behavioral traits there is the added complication of learned behavior. The problem is to distinguish between genetic similarity and similarity from environment and learning. This is impossible unless offspring can be raised apart from their parents in randomized environments. Though this is possible for a few domesticated or laboratory species, it cannot be done, for example, in humans. As a result, we simply do not know how genes are implicated, if at all, in most trait differences. There are a few "natural experiments" that make some inferences possible. For example, it is clear that differences in phonemic structure between, say, Slavic, Germanic, and Romance languages are not genetic since the offspring of Polish, German, and Italian speakers in North America can all speak unaccented American English. On the other hand, group differences in human stature have both genetic and environmental causes. The offspring of Japanese immigrants to North America are taller than their parents but shorter, on the average, than the North American average. Curiously, stature has increased again in the second generation.

Finally, we need to note a contradiction between the claim that a trait has been established by natural selection and the attempt to measure the actual force of that selection. When traits have been made the norm for a species by the force of selection, then we do not expect to find much variation for the trait, for selection will have eliminated the variant types. Yet the possibility of measuring the force of natural selection depends precisely on the availability of contrasting types whose reproductive rates are to be measured! Only rarely can we catch natural selection *in flagrante delicto*, in the process of causing the replacement of one form by another or changing the average value of a trait in a species. More often, the deed has already been done, leaving no trace of its action behind.

2.4 Specific Problems in the Evolution of Human Cognition

2.4.1 Human Relations and Ancestors

The first serious problem in the reconstruction of human cognitive evolution is that we do not have any close relatives, nor do we know who our ancestors were. Relationships among living forms can be judged on the basis of overall similarity in DNA sequence. It is possible to make use of DNA similarity because of a remarkably constant rate of divergence of DNA per unit of evolutionary time. In part, this rate constancy arises because not all changes in DNA are reflected in changes in proteins. Both within genes and in the spaces between genes on the chromosome there is DNA whose changes are functionally "silent." For such DNA, the divergence between species is simply the clocklike accumulation of mutation of no functional significance. But even for DNA changes that do matter to the anatomy and physiology of the organism, because some genes evolve slowly and others rapidly, the average over all genes is roughly independent of individual selection events.

On the basis of DNA similarity, it now seems clear that the two closest relatives of *Homo sapiens* are the chimpanzee, *Pan troglodytes*, and the gorilla, *Gorilla gorilla*. On the basis of the average rate of DNA divergence for a broad range of organisms, it is estimated that there was a common ancestral form of *Homo*, *Pan*, and *Gorilla* about 7 to 10 million years ago, so that 15 to 20 million years of evolution separate us from either the gorilla or the chimpanzee. (Paleontological evidence suggests a much older separation.) For comparison, this is roughly the evolutionary time separating giraffes and deer, whereas deer and moose are separated by less than a million years. The value of close living relatives in evolutionary reconstruction is that the close relatives will share characters or have close character similarity, in contrast to the differences that separate the relatives, as a group, from more distantly related forms. But a great deal of evolution separates us from the great apes, so a priori we cannot expect that we will share many characteristics with them that differentiate us and them, as a group, from other primates. Indeed, the classical taxonomy of the primates based on morphology places the chimpanzee and gorilla in the same family, *Pongidae*, as the orangutan; and somewhat older classifications put the *Pongidae* together with the gibbon in a single family.

A further difficulty about the relatives of *Homo* is that they are so few. Only two species form the group of our "close" relatives, and only three others, the orangutan, gibbon, and siamang, are included in our superfamily, the *Hominoidea*. All other primates, the monkeys, lemurs, and so on, are very far from us indeed. When there are so few forms that are even moderately related, it becomes very difficult to trace the successive changes of a trait. The evolutionary space is too sparsely populated to be able to connect the points sensibly. This contrasts sharply with the densely packed evolutionary space of many invertebrate fossils like snails, for which thousands or tens of thousands of fossil specimens of closely related species exist, all deposited in serially successive rock layers in the same locality. For such material, it is possible to distinguish rapid evolutionary changes from mere gaps in the fossil record. It is not surprising, then, that the theory of "punctuated equilibrium," the theory that evolution does often occur by rapid bursts of change separated by long periods of stasis, has been developed by invertebrate paleontologists!

In contrast to the paucity of living related species, there is a relative richness of fossil forms that seem to be relevant to human evolution. The oldest of these is about 4 million years old. Considerable intellectual blood has been spilt over the interpretation of the diverse collection of fossil remains. The discoverer of each claims it as a definitive human ancestor, while revisionist critics continue to reorganize the taxonomy of the remains. There is no general consensus, but a very conservative view is that the hominoid fossils belong to only two genera. The older genus, *Australopithecus*, runs from about 4 million to 1.2 million years ago, and the younger one, *Homo* (including us), begins about 2 million years ago and runs to the present. What is not clear, however, is whether *any* of these fossil forms is, in fact, a direct human ancestor.

It is important to understand that the appropriate metaphor for the evolution and diversification of a group of species is not a "tree" but a "bush." Beginning with a remote ancestor, a very large number of parallel lines and sublines evolve so that at any moment in time there may exist many species that are cousins and second cousins. Some of these family lines die out, whereas others give rise to yet further groups of cousins. If we then pass back along this bushlike array of collateral relatives, finding a form here and there as fossils, we cannot know how two forms are related. Most important, we cannot tell, if one form follows another in time, whether the older form is a direct parent or only an uncle or a cousin of a previous generation (a cousin once-removed). So, of all the human fossils, we do not know which, if any, was a direct ancestor. The only form we are sure of is one that is already indubitably human, like the Cro-Magnon forms of the Upper Paleolithic. But Cro-Magnon man is already us and so throws no light at all on our ancestors. The genus *Homo* consists essentially of three species: *H. habilis*, running from 2 million to 1.5 million years ago, with a cranial capacity of 750 cubic centimeters; *H. erectus*, running from 1.8 million to 300,000 years ago, with a cranial capacity of about 1000 cubic centimeters; and *H. sapiens*, starting around 400,000 years ago, with a cranial capacity of about 1300 cubic centimeters. All of these species have been placed in the genus *Homo* on the basis of purely morphological evidence, but quite independently all have been found in association with shaped stone tools. Such tools have not been found in association with any earlier fossils. Thus, the cognitive ability needed to manufacture tools appears suddenly about 2.5 million years ago as a novelty. It is true that a refinement of these tools is seen in later deposits. The earliest objects from Olduvai in Africa are stone cores that have been partly shaped by chipping off pieces to sharpen them. Then, at about 1.5 million years ago, there appear *at the same site* tools made from large stone flakes that had been chipped off larger stones. The flakes are worked on both surfaces and carefully chipped around the edges to make a variety of scrapers and cutters. These sophisticated flake tools coexisted with older cave tools for a half a million years, before the earlier types disappear from the record. The refinement of tools does not, of course, demonstrate biological evolution of their makers. The Arabic numerals represent a vast technological advantage over the Roman numerals, and even the refined and sophisticated Classical Chinese culture lacked a convenient method of multiplication and division. Yet we do not suppose that the technical progress in calculation is evidence of the biological evolution of cognitive ability.

When we consider other evidence of high cognitive function—language, planning, political organization, technology beyond stone tools—we have absolutely no evidence. Even fire does not seem to have been domesticated before 100,000 years ago, when our ancestors were already fully human and presumably had begun to feel the chill of advancing glaciers.

2.4.2   Homology and Analogy

To make any use at all of information from different species, we must be able to distinguish between characters that have only a formal or functional similarity and so are merely *analogous* between species, and those that are connected with each other by an unbroken line of inheritance in evolution and thus are truly *homologous*. The rear flipper of a seal and the tail fluke of a whale serve similar functions in swimming and are in the same terminal position in both animals, but the seal's rear flippers are modified hind legs, whereas the whale's flukes are appendages attached to the tail vertebrae. They are only analogous to each other. We cannot reconstruct the evolution of a seal's flippers from anatomical knowledge of whale flukes, but a great deal is to be learned about evolutionary origins from comparing them with dogs' legs, because both the seal's flippers and the dog's rear leg are derived from the same appendage in their common carnivore ancestor.

The problem of analogy and homology is particularly serious for cognition. What are we to take as the comparable characteristics in different species? What, indeed, is the mark of cognition and how are we to tell homology from analogy? On the one hand, if we are extremely loose in our definition of cognition, too many utterly unrelated organisms will appear to possess the trait. *Recognition*, for example, is not informative because every living organism has some form of recognition system that distinguishes one species from another, one family from another, one individual from another. There is a chemical recognition of opposite mating types in fungi; female insects recognize males of their own species; mice recognize their own newborns by odor; dogs know their masters by sight, smell, and sound. What about *communication*, then? But all sorts of animals communicate information about themselves and the outer world to other individuals. By movements of their bodies and wings, bees communicate the direction, distance, and amount of food sources to other bees in the hive. Birds give alarm calls at the approach of a predator. Other birds signal their feeding territories by song. Even *problem solving* is much too general a character to provide evolutionary hints, if we mean, by problem solving, the flexible construction of sequences of action in response to various situations, leading to an adaptive end. Squirrels are remarkable at finding their way along complex pathways and over obstacles to gather food, as anyone who has ever tried to keep a squirrel away from a bird feeder knows. Behavioral experiments have shown these small-brained rodents to be considerably better at solving the particular problem of finding their way around barriers to food than are large dogs. Even plants solve problems. Tropical vines, when they germinate from seed, find their way to tree trunks by being positively geotropic (hugging the ground) and negatively phototropic (heading toward dark objects as they grow). On reaching the tree trunk, they become negatively geotropic and positively phototropic and so climb the tree into the light. Particular organisms are good at solving particular problems, the problems that have been set by their condition of making a living. "Problem-solving ability" is too general a category to make homologous comparisons, and specific problem-solving abilities are too much contingent on the particularities of an organism's life history.

In contrast, we might define cognition in an extremely restrictive way—say, the ability to communicate the difference between past and future or the ability to make tools. However, these criteria are so human-centered that, in fact, no other species possesses them in even a rudimentary form, so that no evolutionary inferences are possible. In this case it is important to distinguish tool *making* from tool *use*. Other animals use tools. A finch in the Galapagos digs insects out of holes with a twig held in its beak, and thrushes break snails against stone "anvils." Hence, the fact that chimpanzees use sticks to dig cannot be taken as showing homology, although their peeling of twig tools with their teeth and hands does represent deliberate fashioning. On the other hand, only the genus *Homo* has ever used one tool to shape another into a form particularly suited to some function. Only *Homo* has manufactured the means of production; other animals use *objets trouvés*. The demonstration of homology of a particular trait for a particular pair of species requires an intimate knowledge of the developmental and anatomical basis of the trait in each species. It must be possible to make a convincing case, based upon anatomical, biochemical, and developmental detail, that the genetic basis of the trait has passed from a common ancestor into the two evolved forms. This is not an easy task for any trait, and for cognition, whose neuroanatomical basis is so poorly understood, it is a truly formidable one.

Finally, we must avoid the process of ad hoc adjustment of our definition of cognition so as to include just *Homo* and a few related genera, for then we will have invented a character that is, by definition, found exactly in *Homo* and genera X, Y, and Z and so has an arbitrarily determined set of evolutionary relationships. We must decide to begin with what is to delimit that "cognitive ability" whose evolution we want to study and then accept the possibility that it is a *de novo* state with no homologies in other known organisms.

A paradigm of the problem of homology and analogy in cognition is the question of the evolution of linguistic competence. Chimpanzees and gorillas vocalize, grunt, screech, hoot, and make a variety of lip, tongue, and mouth gestures that signal pleasure, anger, threat, and other internal states. Are these the rudimentary forms of speech? Are the grunts of Mr. Jiggs the primitive homologues of Hamlet's soliloquy?

The evidence that we have in this matter comes from the comparative neuroanatomy and experimental functional anatomy of the brain. Several areas of the human cerebral cortex are involved in speech. In the frontal lobe there is a motor area that is responsible for movements of the face, tongue, and larynx. Just adjacent is Broca's area, which seems to play a primary role in syntactic function. If Broca's area is damaged, a particular aphasia results in which speech and comprehension are possible but of a degenerate kind. Broca's aphasics can move their tongues, lips, and mouths on command but cannot respond to the sequence command, "Stretch out your tongue, then pout your lips, then open your mouth." They can create and comprehend simple declarative sentences in which object follows subject and in which adjectives occur. But they cannot comprehend passive constructions in which subject and object are in reverse order or use connective terms like *by, for, which, or,* and so on. They have the same problems in both written and spoken language.

Posterior to the frontal lobe, in the temporal lobe, is Wernicke's area, which is concerned with auditory inputs. Disturbances in this area interfere with auditory comprehension of speech, but not with hearing acuity. Finally, there are larger areas in the parietal and temporal lobes where electrical stimulation results in a variety of speech and comprehension disorders including misnaming, confused counting, and inability to repeat heard utterances. The major areas are connected to each other: the primary motor area is connected to Broca's area, which in turn is connected to Wernicke's area. If the latter connection is broken, there is no loss of comprehension or speech, but there is interference with the ability to repeat a heard utterance. Broca's and Wernicke's areas are also connected to the parietal and frontal regions with diverse functions.

If we turn to the lower primate brain, we find anatomical homologues to the human language areas and substantially the same connections between the different areas. Electrical stimulation studies show important similarities and differences, however. When the primary motor area in macaques is stimulated, vocalization is produced; when the same area is stimulated in humans, grunts and "vocalizations" are also produced. When the homologue of Broca's area is stimulated in monkeys, movement of the lips, tongue, and face are produced, but no vocalization. The homologue of Wernicke's area in monkeys mediates the distinction between self-produced and externally produced vocalizations. It is clear that speech is not simply vocalization writ large. The motor areas for the production of sound and the movement of lips, tongue, and mouth have remained more or less conserved. A region of the monkey brain also associated with muscles of the lips, tongue, face, and larynx became Broca's area, in which syntactic functions now reside. At the same time a temporal region associated with discriminately self-produced vocalization, Wernicke's area, became the center for auditory comprehension of phonemic differences and the syntactic structure of heard speech. The commissures connecting these regions have remained intact, coordinating heard speech with the organization of what is to be spoken. In sum, areas of the lower primate brain have been recruited from their former functions to serve the novel functions of speech. The maintenance of those original functions, while new ones were added, may have been made possible by the considerable increase in total brain volume and numbers of neurons.

The phenomenon of *recruitment* in the origin of new functions is widespread in evolution. Birds and bats recruited bones of the front limbs to make wings. In the bat, the wing is suspended from a long lower arm bone and four extremely long fingers. Birds, in contrast, have a greatly elongated wrist and one digit supporting a wing that is almost all feather. Sometimes recruitment results in the partial or complete loss of an old function. In birds, the original reptilian functions of the front limbs in terrestrial locomotion, digging, fighting, and limited manipulation of objects were either given up entirely or taken over by the beak. On the other hand, old functions may be taken over completely by yet other structures with no loss. The three inner ear bones of mammals were recruited from the skull and jaw suspension of their reptilian ancestors. The panda's thumb is really a wrist bone recruited for stripping leaves from bamboo. Given the general conservation of *Bauplan* that characterizes large groups of species, the recruitment of previously existing morphological features into new function is the only path open to evolution when functional novelties arise. Consequently, we should not expect to find homologous functions in the ancestral forms where the homologous organs still serve the original functions. It should not surprise us, then, if our nearest relatives do not have homologous cognitive functions.

The problem of homology is directly relevant to the experiments in training chimpanzees and gorillas to communicate with humans. There have been repeated claims that chimpanzees and gorillas have been taught to create syntactic structures, using computers to help them say things like, "Me pour water." Many arguments have been marshaled to call into question the claimed homology with human linguistic function. From an evolutionary standpoint, however, the possibility of teaching a gorilla to produce a sentence is not in itself critical evidence on the evolution of human speech. Dolphins have also been taught to distinguish sentences, for example, the difference between "Put the ball in the ring" and "Put the ring on the ball." Yet the *Cetacea*, the order to which dolphins belong, have been separate from the primates since near the beginning of mammalian divergence, and we are no closer to them evolutionarily than we are to mice. To show a homology between ape and human "language" rather than a mere analogy requires that equal energy and ingenuity be put into attempting to teach linguistic competence to cows, dogs, horses, and mice, as has been expended on the chimpanzee and gorilla. Only when a wide range of comparisons over the mammals is available will it be possible to judge the homology of the ape behavior to the human. The choice of our closest hominid relatives for the experiment is an anthropocentric bias. Given the neuroanatomical evidence and the results obtained with dolphins, it is not likely that the communication of primatologists with chimpanzees and gorillas is a reciprocal homologous process. What the trainers say to the apes is probably only analogous to what the apes "say" to the primatologists.

2.4.3   Function and Selection

Wherever cognition came from, one would like to make arguments about the forces of natural selection that established it. On the face of it, generalized problem solving and linguistic competence might seem obviously to give a selective advantage to their possessors. But there are several difficulties. First, there may have been no direct natural selection for cognitive ability at all. Human cognition may have developed as the purely epiphenomenal consequence of the major increase in brain size, which, in turn, may have been selected for quite other reasons. Perhaps larger brain led to greater hand-eye coordination and a consequent increase in hunting or fighting efficiency. Aristotle thought that the function of the brain was to cool the blood, and that indeed is one important function of the brain because it is so highly vascularized. Is it absurd to imagine that human brain size evolved largely in response to pressure for better thermoregulation? Perhaps, but *all* reconstructions of the selection of human brain size and structure are purely speculative. Second, even if it were true that selection operated directly on cognition, we have no way of measuring the actual reproductive advantages—and it must be a *reproductive* advantage —that accrued to the early hominids who had rudimentary linguistic competence. Third, any imaginative reconstruction of that advantage must show that individuals or family groups, rather than the species as a whole, had such an advantage. Natural selection operates within populations to increase the frequency of some types and decrease others through differences in reproductive rates of individuals. Unless a more cognitively competent individual or its immediate family leave more offspring than other families, selection will not increase the frequency of the selected character. Moreover, there is no necessary relation between the selective increase of a character in a species and any benefit to the species as a whole. Individuals who are more fertile will leave relatively more offspring than their less fertile conspecifics and will therefore increase in frequency within the species. But the total population size of the species will not thereby be increased, since population size is usually limited by food resources, space, predators, and so on, not by fertility. There is no general principle of natural selection that operates to benefit a species as a whole. Consequently, stories about how the species as a whole would be benefited by speech are not to the point.

Fourth, the claim that greater rationality and linguistic ability lead to greater offspring production is largely a modern prejudice, culture- and history-bound. It lays onto our primitive ancestors the view of an individualist, competitive, entrepreneurial society, that the smart and the articulate win power. Our hunting ancestors, living in small bands, may have had a social organization much more akin to that of the cooperative hunting bands of present-day hunters and gatherers, where bonds of mutual obligation result in widespread sharing of resources. It may have been that more adventurous and inventive Australopithecines actually had a *lower* probability of survival and reproduction than their stodgier and more risk-averse relatives. The problem is that we do not know and never will. We should not confuse plausible stories with demonstrated truth. There is no end to plausible story telling.

Suggestions for Further Reading

An extremely easy to read but quite sophisticated treatment of Darwinism, including cartoons and a certain raunchy humor, is Miller and Van Loon 1982. It contains material on the social history of Darwinism not usually found in textbooks. The best available short technical treatment of the genetic mechanisms of evolution is in Maynard Smith 1966. The best overview of general trends in the actual evolution of life is found in Simpson 1967. In this classic book the author does not concern himself with genetic mechanisms but offers an overview of the process as seen by a paleontologist. The last chapter contains one of many attempts to draw ethical conclusions from evolutionary facts. A series of articles on various topics in modern evolutionary research, written at the level of the nonexpert by leading experts on the subjects, is contained in the *Scientific American* collection (1978). When we turn to issues of human evolution in particular, the best summary of the paleontological evidence is given in Eldredge and Tattersall 1982. The present diversity within and between human groups, the degree to which these differences are influenced by genes, and a cautious view of the evolution of this diversity is contained in Lewontin 1982. Finally, Lumsden and Wilson 1981 is a well known, although failed, attempt to tell a convincing story about the evolution of human cognition and culture, despite the lack of any real evidence. It should be read as a cautionary tale.

Questions

2.1 If Darwin was correct that evolution occurs by the addition of large numbers of very small changes, so that evolution is quasi-continuous, how can we account for the appearance of qualitatively new features like human linguistic competence?

2.2 A simple and direct theory of the forces that give rise to various aspects of human cognition is the classical Darwinian view of natural selection. According to such a theory, individuals with, say, syntactic ability would leave more offspring, and therefore the ability would increase in the species as a whole. Leaving aside the problem of novelty and continuity raised in question 2.1, are there other problems with this explanation for the evolution of human syntactic capability? What alternative explanations besides direct natural selection for linguistic competence can you offer for its evolution?

2.3 At the beginning of our discussion of evolution, we noted that we may be interested either in the evolution of a trait or in the way in which the change of a trait influences the evolution of the organism as a whole. This chapter has emphasized the evolution *of* cognition. Can you speculate on the way in which human cognition has influenced human evolution in general? Has the possession of a cognitive ability influenced, say, stature, or the shape of the hand, or noncognitive psychic properties?

References

Eldredge, N., and I. Tattersall (1982). *The myths of human evolution.* New York: Columbia University Press.

Lewontin, R. C. (1982). *Human diversity.* San Francisco: W. H. Freeman.

Lumsden, C. J., and E. O. Wilson (1981). *Genes, mind and culture.* Cambridge, MA: Harvard University Press.

Maynard Smith, J. (1966). *The theory of evolution.* 2nd ed. Baltimore, MD: Penguin Books.

Miller, J., and B. Van Loon (1982). *Darwin for beginners.* New York: Pantheon.

Scientific American (1978). *Evolution.* New York: W. H. Freeman.

Simpson, G. C. (1967). *The meaning of evolution.* Rev. ed. New Haven, CT: Yale University Press.

Chapter 3
The Computer Model of the Mind
Ned Block

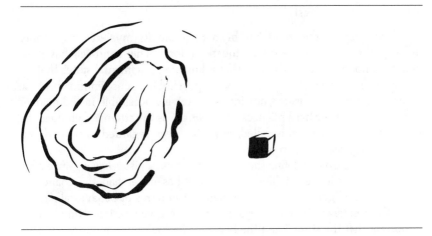

The computer model of the mind is the point of view that has guided research in cognitive science since it toppled the behaviorist paradigm in the 1960s. The basic idea is that the mind is the program of the brain and that the mechanisms of mind involve the same sorts of computations over representations that occur in computers. The purpose of this chapter is to explain what the computer model of the mind is, to give an idea of some of the considerations that have been raised for it and against it, and to explain aspects of the key ideas of computation and representation.

3.1 Machine Intelligence

Machine intelligence is of interest for two very different reasons. First, machines that can act intelligently would be very useful. Second, we can use machines to test our ideas about human intelligence. If we can turn a theory of a human mental competence into a program that gives the

I am grateful to Susan Carey, Jerry Fodor, and Stephen White for comments on an earlier draft. This work was supported by the National Science Foundation grant DIR8812559.

machine the detailed manifestations of that competence, our theory thereby gains some confirmation. In practice, the two enterprises overlap considerably, mainly because the best strategy for the project of making machines that can do intelligent things has turned out to be the strategy of trying to build ideas about how people think into machines. In this section we will start with an influential attempt to define *intelligence*, and then we will consider how human intelligence is to be investigated on the machine model. The last part of the section will discuss the relation between the mental and the biological.

3.1.1   The Turing Test

One approach to the mind has been to avoid its mysteries by simply defining the mental in terms of the behavioral. This approach has been popular among thinkers who fear that acknowledging mental states that do not reduce to behavior would make psychology unscientific, because unreduced mental states are not intersubjectively accessible in the manner of the entities of the hard sciences. *Behaviorism*, as the attempt to reduce the mental to the behavioral is called, has often been regarded as refuted, but it periodically reappears in new forms.

Behaviorists do not define the mental in terms of just *behavior*, since after all something can be intelligent even if it has never had the chance to exhibit its intelligence. Rather, they define it in terms of behavioral *dispositions*, the tendency to emit certain behaviors given certain stimuli. It is important that the stimuli and the behavior be specified nonmentalistically. The behaviorist cannot make use of a behavioral description like "throws," because the same series of motions that are a case of throwing given one mental cause could be a dance to get the ants off given another mental cause, or even a series of involuntary twitches given a nonmental cause. Thus, intelligence could not be defined in terms of the disposition to give sensible responses to questions, since that would be to define a mental notion in terms of another mental notion (indeed, a closely related one).

An especially influential behaviorist definition of intelligence was put forward by Turing (1950). Turing, one of the men who cracked the German code during World War II, formulated the idea of the universal Turing machine, which contains, in mathematical form, the essence of the programmable digital computer. Turing's version of behaviorism formulates the issue of whether machines could think or be intelligent in terms of whether they could pass the following test: a judge in one room communicates by teletype (this was 1950!) with a computer in a second room and a person in a third room for some specified period. (Let's say an hour.) The computer is intelligent if and only if the judge cannot tell the difference between the computer and the person. Turing's definition finessed the

difficult problem of specifying nonmentalistically the behavioral dispositions that are characteristic of intelligence by bringing in the discrimination
behavior of a human judge.

If Turing meant his test as a practical criterion of machine intelligence, it
is acceptable, but not enormously useful. If one wants to know whether a
machine does well at playing chess or diagnosing pneumonia or planning
football strategy, it is better to see how the machine performs in action
than to make it take a Turing test. For one thing, what we care about
is that it do well at detecting pneumonia, not that it do it in a way indistinguishable from the way a person would do it. So if it does the job, who
cares if it doesn't pass the Turing test? Whatever Turing really intended
his test to do, it has been widely taken as a proposal concerning the
meaning of *intelligence* in nonmentalistic terms—that is, a behavioristically acceptable conceptually necessary and sufficient condition for intelligence. This is how I will be construing Turing's proposal: as a behaviorist
definition of *intelligence*.[1]

So construed, there is a gap in the definition of *intelligence* in terms of the
Turing test: we are not told how the judge is to be chosen. A stupid judge,
or one who has had no contact with technology, might think that a radio
was intelligent. At the other extreme, a judge who was a leading authority
on genuinely intelligent machines might know how to tell them apart from
people; for instance, the expert may know that current intelligent machines
get certain problems right that people get wrong.[2] One response to this
objection is to make some sort of specification of the mental qualities of the
judge part of the formulation of the Turing test. For example, one might
specify that the judge be intelligent and knowledgeable, but not too

1. I am interpreting Turing this way because he is often so construed, and because this
makes Turing a useful behaviorist target, but George Boolos has convinced me that Turing
had something a bit different in mind. Turing was famous for having formulated a precise
mathematical notion that he proffered as a replacement for the vague idea of mechanical
computability. The precise notion (computability by a Turing machine) did everything one
would want a precise definition of mechanical computability to do, and one supposes that
Turing hoped that, similarly, the Turing test conception of intelligence would yield everything
one would want from a definition of intelligence without the vagueness and other
problematic features of the ordinary idea of intelligence. This is a more complex form of
behaviorism than the one I will be talking about, but I believe it succumbs to much the same
objections. The key question is, What is the replacement for? If it is supposed to be useful
for practical purposes, then I have no strong objection. But if it is supposed to be useful for
theoretical purposes, the proponent of the Turing test will have to confront the fact that
machines such as the Weizenbaum machine discussed below have been dead ends in
artificial intelligence research, not exciting beginnings. (See, for example, the section
"Mimicry versus Exploration" in Marr 1977.) Finally, if the replacement is meant to be
useful for conceptual clarification, then the refutation developed in the text applies.
2. Turing acknowledged a version of the latter but not the former point. He reacted to the
latter point by jettisoning the claim that being able to pass the Turing test is a necessary

knowledgeable. But including a specification of the mental qualities of the judge in the description of the test will ruin the test as a way of *defining intelligence* in nonmentalistic terms.

So defenders of a Turing test conception of intelligence are faced with a dilemma. Either they can specify the judge mentalistically, in which case they must give up behaviorism, or they can try to finesse the matter by stipulating who the judge is, in which case they run the risk of the judge being sufficiently knowledgeable or intelligent to tell the difference between smart machines and people or too ignorant or too stupid to reject mindless machines.

Focusing on the last possibility, notice that none of us is so clever that he or she can't be fooled by an unintelligent machine. This point is suggested by ELIZA, a very simple program that in one version imitates a psychiatrist (see Weizenbaum 1976). It employs a group of simple but effective strategies. For example, it looks for "key words" on a list supplied by the programmer—say, *I, you, alike, father,* and *everybody.* The words are ordered; for example, *father* comes before *everybody,* so that if you type in "My father is afraid of everybody," the machine will spit back one of its "father" responses, such as "WHAT ELSE COMES TO MIND WHEN YOU THINK OF YOUR FATHER?" If you type in "Everybody laughed at me," you will get one of its responses to *everybody,* such as "WHO IN PARTICULAR ARE YOU THINKING OF?" It also has techniques that simultaneously transform *you* into *I* and *me* into *you,* so that if you type in "You don't agree with me," it can reply, "WHY DO YOU THINK THAT I DON'T AGREE WITH YOU?" It also stores sentences containing certain key words such as *my.* If your current input contains no key words, but if you earlier said, "My boyfriend made me come here," the program will say, "DOES THAT HAVE ANYTHING TO DO WITH THE FACT THAT YOUR BOYFRIEND MADE YOU COME HERE?" It also has stock responses to "Parlez-vous français?" (or any other sentence with *français* in it), namely, "I SPEAK ONLY ENGLISH." If all else fails, the machine has a list of last-ditch responses such as "WHO IS THE PSYCHIATRIST HERE, YOU OR ME?"

ELIZA thus illustrates that a simple program can be extraordinarily successful in activities akin to passing the Turing test. It is certainly not

---

condition of intelligence, weakening his claim to: passing the Turing test is a sufficient condition for intelligence. He says,

> May not machines carry out something which ought to be described as thinking but which is very different from what a man does? This objection is a very strong one, but at least we can say that if, nevertheless, a machine can be constructed to play the imitation game satisfactorily, we need not be troubled by this objection. (1950, 435)

sophisticated or complex by current standards (there is a PC version that is only 200 lines in BASIC), yet it is as good at passing the Turing test as any program I know of. Imagine how convincing a program would be produced if the defense budget were devoted to this task for a year! But even if a high-budget government initiative produced a program that was superlative at passing the Turing test, if the program was just a bundle of tricks like ELIZA, with question types all thought of in advance, and canned responses placed in the machine, the machine would not be intelligent.

This point can be better appreciated by considering the ultimate in unintelligent Turing test passers, a hypothetical machine that contains all conversations of a given length in which the machine's replies make sense. Let's stipulate that the test lasts one hour. Since there is an upper bound on how fast humans can type, and since there are a finite number of keys on a teletype, there is an upper bound on the "length" of a Turing test conversation. Thus, there are a finite (though more than astronomical) number of different Turing test conversations, and *all* of them can in principle be *listed*.

Let's call a string of characters that can be typed in an hour or less a *typable* string. In principle, all typable strings could be generated, and a team of intelligent programmers could throw out all the strings that cannot be interpreted as a conversation in which at least one party (say, the second contributor) is making sense. The remaining strings could be stored in a hypothetical computer (say, with marks separating the contributions of the separate parties), which works as follows. The judge types in something. The machine locates a string that starts with the judge's contribution, spitting back its next element. The judge then types something else. The machine finds a string that begins with the judge's first contribution, followed by the machine's, followed by the judge's next contribution, and then the machine spits back its fourth element, and so on. (We can eliminate the simplifying assumption that the judge speaks first by recording pairs of strings; this would also allow the judge and the machine to talk at the same time.) Of course, such a machine is only logically possible, not physically possible. The number of strings is too vast to exist, and even if they could exist, they could never be accessed by any sort of a machine in anything like real time. But since we are considering a proposed definition of *intelligence* that is supposed to capture the concept of intelligence, logical possibility will do the job.

Note that the limitation to a Turing test of one hour is immaterial, since the procedure just described works for *any* finite Turing test.

The following variant of the machine may be easier to grasp. The programmers start by writing down all typable strings, call them $A_1 \ldots A_n$. Then they think of *just one* sensible response to each of these, which we

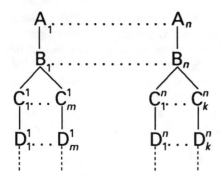

Figure 3.1
A conversation is any path from the top to the bottom.

may call $B_1 \ldots B_n$. (Actually, there will be fewer Bs than As because some of the As will take up the entire hour.) The programmers will have an easier time of it if they think of themselves as simulating some definite personality (say, my Aunt Bubbles) and some definite situation (say, Aunt Bubbles being brought into the teletype room by her strange nephew and asked to answer questions for an hour). So each B_i will be the sort of reply Aunt Bubbles would give to A_i. For example, if A_{73} is a request to solve a mathematical problem, B_{73} might be "Ask my nephew, he's the professor." Now we must consider the judge's replies to each of the Bs. The judge can give any reply up to the remaining length limit, so below each of the Bs there will sprout a vast number of Cs (vast, but fewer than the number of Bs, since the time remaining is less than an hour). The programmers' next task is to produce just one D for each of the Cs. Think of conversations as paths downward through a tree, starting with an A_i from the judge, a reply, B_i, from the machine, and so on. See figure 3.1. For each A_i–B_i–C^i_j that is a beginning to a conversation, the programmers must produce a D that makes sense given the A, B, and C that precede it.

The machine works as follows. The judge goes first. Whatever the judge types in (typos and all) is one of $A_1 \ldots A_n$. The machine locates the particular A—say, A_{2398}—and then spits back B_{2398}, a reply chosen by the programmers to be appropriate to A_{2398}. The judge types another message, and the machine again finds it in the list of Cs that sprout below B_{2398} and then spits back the prerecorded reply (which takes into account what was said in A_{2398} and B_{2398}). And so on. Though the machine can do as well in the Turing test as Aunt Bubbles, it *has the intelligence of a jukebox*. Every clever remark it makes was specifically thought of by one of the programmers as a response to the previous remark of the judge in the context of the previous conversation.

Though this machine is too big to exist, there is nothing incoherent or contradictory about its specification, and so it is enough to refute the behaviorist interpretation of the Turing test that we have been looking at.[3]

Note that there is an upper bound on how long any particular Aunt Bubbles machine can go on in a Turing test, a limit set by the length of the strings it has been given. Of course, real people have their upper limits too, given that real people will eventually quit or die. However, there is a very important difference between the Aunt Bubbles machine and a real person, namely, that it is very likely that real people have an infinite *competence* to go on. If humans were provided with unlimited memory and with motivational systems that overruled all other aims, they could go on forever (at least according to conventional wisdom in cognitive science). This is definitely not the case for the Aunt Bubbles machine. But this difference provides no objection to the Aunt Bubbles machine as a refutation of the Turing test conception of intelligence, because the notion of competence is not behavioristically acceptable, requiring as it does for its specification a distinction among components of the mind. For example, the mechanisms of thought must be distinguished from the mechanisms of memory and motivation. Competence really amounts to an idealization or abstraction from certain components of the mind.

"But," you may object, "isn't it rather chauvinist to assume that a machine must process information in just the way *we* do to be intelligent?" Such an assumption would indeed be chauvinist, but I am not assuming it. The point against the Turing test conception of intelligence is not that the Aunt Bubbles machine wouldn't process information the way we do but rather that the way it does process information is unintelligent despite its performance in the Turing test.

3.1.2   Two Kinds of Definitions of Intelligence

Let us now step back and ask how the kind of definition of intelligence involved in the Turing test conception of intelligence contrasts with other approaches to defining intelligence.

There are two kinds of definitions of water. One might be better regarded as a definition of the word *water*. The word might be defined as 'the

---

3. The Aunt Bubbles machine refutes something stronger than behaviorism, namely, the claim that the mental "supervenes" on the behavioral—that is, that there can be no mental difference without a behavioral difference. (Of course, the behavioral dispositions are finite—see the next paragraph in the text.) I am indebted to Stephen White for pointing out to me that the doctrine of the supervenience of the mental on the behavioral is widespread among thinkers who reject behaviorism, such as Donald Davidson. The Aunt Bubbles machine is described and defended in detail in Block 1978, 1981a and was independently discovered by White (1982).

colorless, odorless, tasteless liquid that is found in lakes and oceans'. In this sense of *definition*, the definition of *water* is available to anyone who speaks the language, even someone who knows no science. But one might also define water by saying what water really is, that is, by saying what physicochemical structure in fact makes something pure water. The answer to this question would involve its chemical constitution: H_2O. Defining a *word* is something we can do in our armchair, by consulting our linguistic intuitions about hypothetical cases or, bypassing this process, by simply stipulating a meaning for a word. Defining (or explicating) the *thing* is an activity that involves empirical investigation into the nature of something in the world.

What we have been discussing so far is the first kind of definition of intelligence, the definition of the word, not the thing. Turing's definition is not the result of an empirical investigation into the components of intelligence of the sort that led to the definition of water as H_2O. Rather, he hoped to legislate a certain way of thinking about machine intelligence by stipulating that the word *intelligent* should be used a certain way, at least with regard to machines. Quite a different way of proceeding is to investigate intelligence *itself* in the way physical chemists investigate water. We will consider how this is done in the next section, but first we should note a complication.

There are (at least) two kinds of kinds: *natural* kinds such as "water" or "tiger," and *functional* kinds such as "table" or "gene." A natural kind has a "hidden essence"; in the case of water, its molecules are H_2O, and in the case of tiger, it is a matter of its DNA structure. Simple functional kinds, by contrast, have no hidden essence. A certain sort of function, a causal role, is all there is to being a table. (Well, not quite: human purposes are relevant as well as causal role: a table must be made for or taken over for a familiar causal role (eating dinner on, and the like); if something is made for that function but doesn't fulfill it, then it is a *lousy* table.) Likewise, there is no hidden essence to being a gene. What makes a bit of DNA a gene is its function with respect to mechanisms that can read the information that it encodes and use this information to make a biological product. Even the pen I'm now writing with is a gene relative to a hypothetical creature whose "cells" contain reading mechanisms for which the design on the nib of my pen translates into instructions to build an organ or a limb.

Now intelligence is no doubt a functional kind, but it still makes sense to investigate intelligence—as with the gene—in the manner in which one investigates a natural kind such as water. The reason is that *human* intelligence (and the *human* gene) is a natural kind. Indeed, human intelligence—and the human gene as well—encompasses two types of natural kinds. First, there is a functional kind (in the sense used here of causal role): in the case of the gene this will include patterns of interaction with other genes. For example, part of the functional role of the blue eye gene is being recessive with respect to the brown eye gene. One can imagine a creature for whom the blue eye gene functions differently—say, it is dominant over brown. Second, there is the human physical realization of that function, the physical structure that has that function in us. In the case of the gene this is DNA. We can investigate the details of the function of human genes and also their physicochemical structures without being bothered by the fact that our results will not apply to the genes of all sorts of hypothetical creatures. Similarly, we can investigate the functional details and physical basis of human intelligence without attention to the fact that our results will not apply to other mechanisms of other hypothetical intelligences. Investigation of intelligence *in general* has been less fruitful than investigation of human intelligence. Moreover, we don't even know for sure that intelligence of a kind radically different from human intelligence can exist.

We now leave the topic of defining the word *intelligence*, moving to a discussion of defining or explicating the thing itself.

3.1.3 Functional Analysis

The paradigm of defining or explicating intelligence in cognitive science is a methodology sometimes known as *functional analysis*. (No close relation to the functional kinds just mentioned.) Think of the human mind as represented by an intelligent being in the head, a "homunculus." Think of this homunculus as being composed of smaller and stupider homunculi, and each of these being composed of still smaller and still stupider homunculi, until you reach a level of completely mechanical homunculi. (This picture was first articulated in Fodor 1968; see also Dennett 1974 and Cummins 1975.)

Suppose one wants to explain how we understand language. Part of the system will recognize individual words. This word recognizer might be composed of three components, one of which has the task of fetching each incoming word, one at a time, and passing it to a second component. The second component has a dictionary, that is, a list of all the words in the vocabulary, together with syntactic and semantic information about each word. This second component compares the target word with words in the vocabulary (perhaps executing many such comparisons simultaneously) until it gets a match. When it finds a match, it sends a signal to a third component, whose job it is to retrieve the syntactic and semantic information stored in the dictionary. Of course, this is only a small part of a model of language understanding; it is supposed to illustrate the process of explaining part of a cognitive competence via simpler cognitive competences, in this case the simple mechanical operations of fetching and matching.

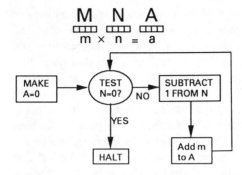

Figure 3.2
Program for multiplying. One begins the multiplication by putting a representation of the numbers m and n, the number to be multiplied, in registers M and N. At the end of the computation the answer, a, will be found in register A. See the text for a description of how the program works.

The idea of this kind of explanation of intelligence comes from attention to the way computers work. Consider a computer that multiplies the number m by the number n by adding m to itself n times. Here is a program for doing this. Think of m and n as represented in the registers M and N in figure 3.2. Register A is reserved for the answer, a. First, a representation of 0 is placed in register A. Second, N is examined to see whether it contains (a representation of) 0. If the answer is yes, the program halts and the correct answer is 0. (If n = 0, m times n = 0.) If no, N is decremented by 1 (so the value of register N is now n − 1), and m is added to the answer register, A. Then the procedure loops back to the second step. Register N is checked once again to see whether its value is 0; if not, it is again decremented by 1, and m is again added to register A. This procedure continues until N finally has the value 0, at which time m will have been added to the answer register exactly n times. At this point register A contains a representation of the answer.

This program multiplies via a "decomposition" of multiplication into other processes, namely, addition, subtraction of 1, setting a register to 0, and checking a register for 0. Depending on how these things are themselves done, they may be the fundamental bottom-level processes, known as *primitive processes*.

The cognitive science definition or explication of intelligence is analogous to this explication of multiplication. Intelligent capacities are understood via decomposition into a network of less intelligent capacities, ultimately grounded in totally mechanical capacities executed by primitive processors.

The concept of a primitive process is very important; the next section is devoted to it.

3.1.4   Primitive Processors

What makes a processor primitive? One answer is that for primitive processors, the question "How does the processor work?" is *not a question for cognitive science to answer*. The cognitive scientist answers "How does the multiplier work?" in the case of the multiplier described above by giving the program or the information flow diagram for the multiplier. But if certain components of the multiplier—say, the gates of which the adder is composed—are primitive, then it is not the cognitive scientist's business to answer the question of how such a gate works. The cognitive scientist can say, "That question belongs in another discipline, electronic circuit theory." We must distinguish the question of *how something works* from the question of *what it does*. The question of *what* a primitive processor does is part of cognitive science, but the question of *how* it does it is not.

This idea can be made a bit clearer by looking at how a primitive processor actually works. The example will involve a common type of computer adder, simplified so as to handle only one-digit addends.

To understand this example, you need to know the following simple facts about binary notation: 0 and 1 are represented alike in binary and normal (decimal) notation, but the binary representation that corresponds to decimal 2 is *10*.[4] Our adder will solve the following four problems:

$$0 + 0 = 0$$

$$1 + 0 = 1$$

$$0 + 1 = 1$$

$$1 + 1 = 10$$

The first three equations are true in both binary and decimal, but the last is true only if understood in binary.

The second item of background information is the notion of a *gate*. An *and* gate is a device that accepts two inputs and emits a single output. If both inputs are *1*s, the output is a *1*; otherwise, the output is a *0*. An *exclusive or* gate is a "difference detector": it emits a *0* if its inputs are the same (*1, 1* or *0, 0*), and it emits a *1* if its inputs are different (*1, 0* or *0, 1*).

This talk of *1* and *0* is a way of thinking about the "bistable" states of computer representers. These representers are made so that they are always in one or the other of two states, and only momentarily in between. (This is what it is to be bistable.) The states might be a 4-volt and a 7-volt potential. If the two input states of a gate are the same (say, 4 volts), and

4. The rightmost digit in binary (as in familiar decimal) is the 1s place. The second digit from the right is the 2s place (corresponding to the 10s place in decimal). Next is the 4s place (that is, 2 squared), just as the corresponding place in decimal is the 10 squared place.

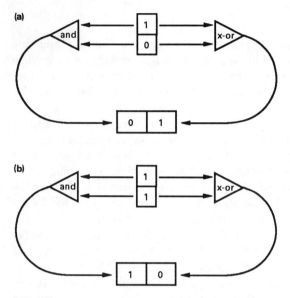

Figure 3.3
(a) Adder doing $1 + 0 = 1$. (b) Adder doing $1 + 1 = 10$.

the output is the same as well (4 volts), and if every other combination of inputs yields the 7-volt output, then the gate is an *and* gate, and the 4-volt state realizes *1*. A different type of *and* gate might be made so that the 7-volt state realized *1*. The point is that *1* is conventionally assigned to whatever bistable physical state of an *and* gate it is that has the role described in the sentence before last. And all that counts about an *and* gate from a computational point of view is its input-output function, not how it works or whether 4 volts or 7 volts realizes *1*. Note the terminology: one speaks of a physically described state (4-volt potential) as "realizing" a computationally described state (having the value *1*). This distinction between the computational and physical levels of description will be important in what follows, especially in section 3.3.3.

The adder works as follows. The two digits to be added are connected both to an *and* gate and to an *exclusive or* gate as illustrated in figures 3.3a and 3.3b. Let's look first at figure 3.3a. The digits to be added are *1* and *0*, and they are placed in the input register, which is the top pair of boxes. The *exclusive or* gate, which is a difference detector, sees different things and therefore outputs a *1* to the rightmost box of the answer register, which is the bottom pair of boxes. The *and* gate outputs a *0* except when it sees two *1*s, and so it outputs a *0*. In this way, the circuit computes $1 + 0 = 1$. For this problem, as for $0 + 1 = 1$ and $0 + 0 = 0$, the *exclusive or* gate does all the real work. The role of the *and* gate in this circuit is *carrying*, and that is illustrated in figure 3.3b. The digits to be added, *1* and *1*, are again placed in the top register. Now, both inputs to the *and* gate are *1*s, and so the *and* gate outputs a *1* to the leftmost box of the answer (bottom) register. The *exclusive or* gate makes the rightmost box a *0*, and so we have the correct answer, *10*.

The borders between scientific disciplines are notoriously fuzzy. No one can say exactly where chemistry stops and physics begins. Since the line between the upper levels of processors and the level of primitive processors is the same as the line between cognitive science and one of the "realization" sciences such as electronics or physiology, the boundary of the level of primitives will have the same fuzziness. Nonetheless, in this example it seems clear that it is the gates that are the primitive processors. They are the largest components whose operation must be explained, not in terms of cognitive science, but rather in terms of electronics or mechanics or some other realization science. That is, assuming that the gates are made in the common manner described in the next section. It would be *possible* to make an adder each of whose gates was a *whole computer*, with its own multipliers, adders, and normal gates. It would be silly to waste a whole computer on such a simple task as that of an *and* gate, but it could be done. In that case the real level of primitives would be, not the gates of the original adder, but rather the (normal) gates of the component computers.

Primitive processors are the only computational devices for which *behaviorism is true*. Two primitive processors (such as gates) count as computationally equivalent if they have the same input-output function (that is, the same behavior), even if one works hydraulically and the other electrically. But computational equivalence of *non*primitive devices is not to be understood in this way. Consider two multipliers that work via different programs. Both accept inputs and emit outputs only in decimal notation. One, however, converts inputs to binary, does the computation in binary, and then converts back to decimal. The other does the computation directly in decimal. These are not computationally equivalent multipliers despite their identical input-output functions.

What is the functional analysis of the human mind? What are its primitive processors? These are the questions that functional analysis of human intelligence aims at.

3.1.5   The Mental and the Biological

One type of electrical *and* gate consists of two circuits with switches arranged as in figure 3.4. The switches on the left are the inputs. When only one or neither of the input switches is closed, nothing happens, because the circuit on the left is not completed. Only when both switches are closed does the electromagnet go on, and that pulls the switch on the

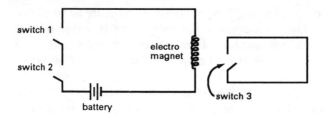

Figure 3.4
Electrical *and* gate.

Figure 3.5
Cat and mouse *and* gate.

right closed, thereby turning on the circuit on the right. (The circuit on the right is only partially illustrated.) In this example a switch being closed realizes *1*; it is the bistable state that obtains as an output if and only if two of them are present as an input.

Another *and* gate is illustrated in figure 3.5. If neither of the mice on the left (mouse$_1$ and mouse$_2$) is released into the part of their cages that have the cheese, or if only one of the mice is released, the cat does not strain hard enough to pull the leash. But when both mouse$_1$ and mouse$_2$ are released into the cheese part and are thereby visible to the cat, the cat strains enough to lift mouse$_3$'s gate, letting it into the cheese part of its box. So we have a situation in which a mouse getting cheese is output if and only if two cases of mice getting cheese are input.

The point illustrated here is the irrelevance of hardware realization to computational description. These gates work in very different ways, but they are nonetheless computationally equivalent. And of course, it is possible to think of an indefinite variety of other ways of making a primitive *and* gate. How such gates work is no more part of the domain of cognitive science than is the nature of the buildings that hold computer factories. This reveals a sense in which the computer model of the mind is profoundly *unbiological.* We are beings who have a useful and interesting biological level of description, but the computer model of the mind aims for a level of description of the mind that abstracts away from the biological realizations of cognitive structures. As far as the computer model goes, it does not matter whether our gates are realized in gray matter (which is actually gray only when preserved in a bottle), switches, or cats and mice.

Of course, this is not to say that the computer model is in any way incompatible with a biological approach. Indeed, cooperation between the biological and computational approaches is vital to *discovering* the program of the brain. Suppose one were presented with a computer of alien design and set the problem of ascertaining its program by any means possible. Only a fool would choose to ignore information to be gained by opening the computer up to see how its circuits work. No doubt, one would put information at the program level together with information at the electronic level, and likewise, in finding the program of the human mind, one can expect biological and cognitive approaches to complement one another.

Nonetheless, the computer model of the mind has a built-in antibiological bias, in the following sense. If the computer model is right, we should be able to create intelligent machines in our image—our *computational* image, that is. If we can do this, we will naturally feel that the most compelling theory of the mind is one that is general enough to apply to both them and us, and this will be a computational theory, not a biological theory. A biological theory of the *human* mind will not apply to these machines, though the biological theory will have a complementary advantage: namely, such a biological theory will encompass us together with our less intelligent biological cousins and thus provide a different kind of insight into the nature of human intelligence. (More on this in section 3.3.3.)

It is an open empirical question whether or not the computer model of the mind is correct. Only if it is *not* correct could it be said that psychology, the science of the mind, is a *biological* science. I make this obvious and trivial point to counter the growing trend toward supposing that the fact that we have brains that have a biological nature shows that psychology is a biological science.

3.2   Intelligence and Intentionality

Our discussion so far has centered on computer models of one aspect of the mind, intelligence. But there is a different aspect of the mind that we have not yet discussed, one that has a very different relation to the computer model—namely, intentionality.

For our purposes, we can take intelligence to be a capacity, a capacity to do various intelligent activities such as solving mathematics problems, deciding whether to go to graduate school, and figuring out how spaghetti is made. (Notice that this is not a behaviorist account of the sort that would be challenged by the Aunt Bubbles machine, because it is mentalistic. Solving, deciding, and figuring out are themselves mentalistic concepts, so an analysis of intelligence as a capacity to do such things is a mentalistic analysis, not a behaviorist analysis.)

Intentionality is aboutness. It is the property possessed most clearly by mental states or events such as beliefs, thoughts, or "cognitive perception" (for instance, in chapter 5 of Osherson, Kosslyn, and Hollerbach 1990, seeing that there is a cat on the sofa). Intentional states represent the world as being a certain way. For example, a thought might represent an earthquake as having an intensity of 6.1 on the Richter scale. If so, we say that the *intentional content* of the thought is *that the earthquake has an intensity of 6.1 on the Richter scale*. A single intentional content can have very different behavioral effects, depending on its relation to the person who has the content. For example, the fear that there will be nuclear war might inspire one to work for disarmament, but the belief that there will be nuclear war might influence one to emigrate to Australia. (Don't let the spelling mislead you: intending is only one kind of intentional state. Believing and desiring are others.) Intentionality is an important feature of many mental states, but it is controversial whether it is "the mark of the mental." Pain, for example, would seem to be a mental state that has no intentional content.

The features of thought just mentioned are closely related to features of language. Thoughts represent, are about things, and can be true or false; and the same is true of sentences. The sentence *Bruce Springsteen was born in the USSR* is about Springsteen, represents him as having been born in the Soviet Union, and is false. In the light of this similarity between the mental and the linguistic, it is natural to try to reduce two problems to one problem by reducing the content of thought to the content of language or conversely.

Before we go any further, let's try to see more clearly just what the difference is between intelligence and intentionality. That there is such a distinction should be clear to anyone who attends to the matter, but the precise nature of the distinction is controversial.

One way to get a handle on the distinction between intelligence and intentionality is to note that in the opinion of many writers on this topic, it is possible to have intentionality without intelligence. Thus, John McCarthy (1980) (the creator of the artificial intelligence language LISP) holds that thermostats have intentional states in virtue of their capacity to represent and control temperature. And there is a school of thought that assigns content to tree rings in virtue of their representing the age of the tree. (See the references in section 3.3.) But no school of thought holds that the tree rings are actually intelligent. An intelligent system must have certain intelligent capacities, capacities to do certain sorts of things, and tree rings can't do these things.[5]

Moreover, there can be intelligence without intentionality. Imagine that an event with negligible (but importantly, nonzero) probability occurs: in their random movement, particles from the swamp come together and by chance result in a molecule-for-molecule duplicate of you. The swamp creature will have all the capacities (behavioral capacities) that you have, and they will be produced by the same sort of physiological processes as occur in you. So it will arguably be intelligent. But there are reasons for denying that it has the intentional states that you have, and indeed, for denying that it has any intentional states at all. The swamp creature says, as you do, "Gorbachev influenced Thatcher on his trip to England." But unlike you, it has never seen Gorbachev or Thatcher (or anything else) on TV, or read about them in the papers. (It was created only seconds ago.) The swamp creature has had no causal contact of any sort with them or with any case of anyone meeting or influencing anyone. No signals from the Soviet Union or Britain have reached it in any way, no matter how indirectly. Its utterance is not in any way causally affected by Gorbachev, Thatcher, or England, or by Gorbachevian or Thatcherian or English states of the world, so how can it be regarded as being *about* Gorbachev or Thatcher or England? The swamp creature is simply mouthing words. Had its molecules come together slightly differently, it would be uttering "Envelopes sir tattoo Eisenhower on Neptune." Much more must be said to be convincing on this point, but I hope you can see the shape of the case to be made that the swamp creature has intelligence without intentionality.

The upshot is this: what makes a system intelligent is what it can do. What makes a system an intentional system is a matter of its states' representing the world—that is, having aboutness. Even if you are not convinced that either can exist without the other, you can still agree that intelligence and intentionality are very different kettles of fish.

Now let's see what the difference between intelligence and intentionality has to do with the computer model of the mind. Notice that the method of functional analysis that explains intelligent processes by reducing them to unintelligent mechanical processes *does not explain intentionality*. The parts of an intentional system can be just as intentional as the whole system. (See Fodor 1981 on Dennett on this point.) In particular, the component processors of an intentional system can manipulate symbols that are about just the same things that the symbols manipulated by the whole system

5. I should mention that functionalists (including myself) are more skeptical than proponents of the views just mentioned about the possibility of intentionality without intelligence. The functionalist point of view will be explained later.

are about. Recall that the multiplier of figure 3.2 was explained via a decomposition into devices that add, subtract, and the like. The multiplier's states were intentional in that they were about numbers. The states of the adder, subtractor, and so on, are also about numbers and are thus similarly intentional.

There is, however, an important relation between intentionality and functional decomposition. The level of primitive processors is the *lowest intentional level*. That is, though the inputs and outputs of primitive processors are about things, primitive processors do not contain any parts that have states that are themselves about anything. That is why the internal operation of primitive processors is in the domain of a "realization" science (such as electronics or physiology) rather than in the domain of cognitive science.

The explication of intentionality is more controversial (this is an understatement) than the explication of intelligence, but one aspect of the matter is relatively straightforward, namely, the explication of rational *relations* among intentional states. It is widely (but not universally) agreed that part of what it is for a state to have a certain intentional content is for it to have certain relations to other contentful states. Thus, if a person makes claims of the form "If x then y," but infers from this conditional and y to x, and never from the conditional and x to y, other things being equal it would be reasonable to conclude that the person's claims of this form do not express beliefs to the effect that if x, then y. This point is spelled out in the opening paragraphs of section 7.2.1 of Stich's chapter, especially in the *nehtfi* example. Let us explore the computer model of the mind's approach to relations among intentional states by returning to the adder depicted in figures 3.3a and 3.3b. The cognitive science account of these rational relations among intentional states hinges on the idea of the brain as a syntactic engine, which is the topic of the next section.

3.2.1   The Brain as a Syntactic Engine Driving a Semantic Engine

To see the idea of the brain as a syntactic engine, it is important to see the difference between the number 1 and the symbol (in this case a numeral or digit) *1*. (Note the use of roman type in referring to the number and italics in referring to the symbol, as is the convention in this book.) Certainly, the difference between the city, Boston, and the word *Boston* is clear enough. The former has bad drivers in it; the latter has no people or cars at all but does have six letters. No one would confuse a city with a word, but the distinction may seem less clear in the case of a symbol denoting a number and the number itself. The point to keep in mind is that many different symbols can denote the same number (say, *II* in Roman numerals and *two* in alphabetical writing), and one symbol can denote different numbers in different counting systems (as *10* denotes one number in binary and another in decimal).

With this distinction in mind, we can see an important difference between the multiplier and the adder discussed earlier. The algorithm used by the multiplier in figure 3.2 is *notation-independent*: "Multiply the number n by the number m by adding n to itself m times" works in any notation. And the program described for implementing this algorithm is also notation-independent. As we saw in the description of this program in section 3.1.3, the program depends on the properties of the numbers represented, not the representations themselves. By contrast, the internal operation of the adder described in figures 3.3a and 3.3b depends on binary notation, and its description in section 3.1.4 speaks of numerals (note the italic type). Recall that the adder exploits the fact that an *exclusive or* gate detects differences, yielding a *1* when its inputs are different digits, and a *0* when its inputs are the same digits. This gate gives the right answer all by itself so long as no carrying is involved. The trick used by the *exclusive or* gate depends on the fact that when we add two digits of the same type (*1* and *1* or *0* and *0*), the rightmost digit of the answer is the same. This is true in binary, but not in other standard notations.

The inputs and outputs of the adder must be seen as referring to numbers. One way to see this is to note that otherwise one could not see the multiplier as exploiting an algorithm involving multiplying numbers by adding numbers. But once we go inside the adder, we must see the binary states as referring to the *symbols themselves*. This fact gives us an interesting additional characterization of primitive processors. Typically, as we functionally decompose a computational system, we reach a point where there is a shift of subject matter from things in the world to the symbols themselves. The inputs and outputs of the adder and multiplier refer to numbers, but the inputs and outputs of the gates refer to numerals. Typically, this shift occurs when we have reached the level of primitive processors. The operation of the higher-level components such as the multiplier can be explained in two ways: (1) in terms of a program or algorithm manipulating numbers, or (2) in terms of the functional decomposition into networks of gates manipulating numerals. But the operation of the gates cannot be explained in terms of number manipulation; it must be explained in symbolic terms (or at lower levels—say, in terms of electromagnets). At the most basic computational level, computers are symbol-crunchers, and for this reason the computer model of the mind is often described as the symbol manipulation view of the mind.

Seeing the adder as a syntactic engine driving a semantic engine requires noting two functions: one maps numbers onto other numbers, and the other maps symbols onto other symbols. The symbol function is concerned with the numerals as symbols—without attention to their meanings. Here is the symbol function:

0, 0 → 0

0, 1 → 1

1, 0 → 1

1, 1 → 10

This symbol function is mirrored by a function that maps the numbers represented by the numerals on the left onto the numbers represented by the numerals on the right. This function will thus map numbers onto numbers. We can speak of this function that maps numbers onto numbers as the *semantic* function (semantics being the study of meaning), since it is concerned with the meanings of the symbols, not the symbols themselves. (It is important not to confuse the notion of a semantic function in this sense with a function that maps symbols onto what they refer to.) Here is the semantic function (in decimal notation—we must choose *some* notation to express a semantic function):

0, 0 → 0

0, 1 → 1

1, 0 → 1

1, 1 → 2

Notice that the two specifications just given differ in that the first maps italicized entities onto other italicized entities. The second has no italics. The first function maps symbols onto symbols; the second function maps the numbers referred to by the arguments of the first function onto the numbers referred to by the values of the first function. (A function maps arguments onto values.) The first function is a kind of linguistic "reflection" of the second.

The key idea behind the adder is that of a correlation between these two functions. The designer has joined together (1) a meaningful notation (binary notation), (2) symbolic manipulations in that notation, and (3) rational relations among the meanings of the symbols. The symbolic manipulations correspond to useful rational relations among the meanings of the symbols—namely, the relations of addition. The useful relations among the meanings are captured by the semantic function above, and the corresponding symbolic relations are the ones described in the symbolic function above. It is the correlation between these two functions that explains how it is that a device that manipulates symbols manages to add numbers.

Now the idea of the brain as a syntactic engine driving a semantic engine is just a generalization of this picture to a wider class of symbolic activities, namely, the symbolic activities of human thought. The idea is that we have symbolic structures in our brains, and that nature has seen to it that there are correlations between causal interactions among these structures and rational relations among the meanings of the symbolic structures. The primitive mechanical processors "know" only the "syntactic" form of the symbols they process (for instance, what strings of zeros and ones they see), and not what the symbols mean. Nonetheless, these meaning-blind primitive processors control processes that "make sense"— processes of decision, problem solving, and the like. In short, there is a correlation between the meanings of our internal representations and their forms. And this explains how it is that our syntactic engine can drive our semantic engine.[6]

The last paragraph referred to a correlation between causal interactions among symbolic structures in our brains and rational relations among the meanings of the symbol structures. This way of speaking can be misleading if it encourages the picture of the neuroscientist opening the brain, just *seeing* the symbols, and then figuring out what they mean. Such a picture inverts the order of discovery and gives the wrong impression of what makes something a symbol.

The way to discover symbols in the brain is to first map out rational relations among states of mind and then identify aspects of these states that can be thought of as symbolic in virtue of their functions. Function is what gives a symbol its identity, even the symbols in English orthography, though this can be hard to appreciate because these functions have been made rigid by habit and convention. In reading unfamiliar handwriting, we may notice an unorthodox symbol, someone's weird way of writing a letter of the alphabet. How do we know which letter of the alphabet it is? By its function! Th% function of a symbol is som%thing on% can appr%ciat% by s%%ing how it app%ars in s%nt%nc%s containing familiar words whos% m%anings w% can gu%ss. You will have little trouble figuring out, on this basis, what letter in the last sentence was replaced by %.

3.3   Functionalism and the Language of Thought

Thus far, we have examined the computer model of the mind's approach to intelligence, distinguished intelligence from intentionality, and considered

6. The idea described here was first articulated to my knowledge in Fodor 1975, 1980. See also Dennett 1981, to which the terms *syntactic engine* and *semantic engine* are due, and Newell 1980. More on this topic can be found in Dennett 1987 by looking up *syntactic engine* and *semantic engine* in the index.

the idea of the brain as a syntactic engine. But where is the computer model's account of intentionality? The idea of the brain as a syntactic engine is certainly *relevant* to explaining intentionality. But it is also relevant to explaining intelligence, since it is an account of how a symbol processor can have the capacity to emit sensible responses to stimuli. It is time to admit that although the computer model of the mind has a natural and straightforward account of intelligence, there is nothing natural or straightforward about its account of intentionality. We can easily understand how computers manage to have the intelligent capacities that they have—via the method of functional analysis. But as noted earlier, functional analysis does not explain intentionality. And the question of how computers manage to mean what they mean is one about which philosophers disagree at least as much as they do about human intentionality.

The computer model of the mind, with its commitment to a central role for symbol manipulation, is itself controversial even in the cognitive science community. A new biologically oriented group, the "connectionists" (see chapter 1 of this epilogue), rejects it. But the matters into which we now delve are ones on which even those who *accept* the computer model of the mind disagree. We cannot survey the field here. Instead, let us look at a view that represents a kind of orthodoxy, not in the sense that most researchers believe it, but in the sense that the other views define themselves in large part by their response to it.

The main tenet of this orthodoxy is that our intentional contents are simply meanings of our internal representations. As noted earlier, there is something to be said for regarding the content of thought and language as a single phenomenon, and this is a quite direct way of doing so. There is no commitment in this orthodoxy on the issue of whether our internal language, the language in which we think, is the same as or different from the language which we speak. Further, there is no commitment concerning a direction of reduction—that is, concerning which is more basic, mental content or meanings of internal symbols.

For concreteness, let us talk in terms of Fodor's (1975) doctrine that the meaning of external language derives from the content of thought and that the content of thought derives from the meanings of elements of the language of thought. According to Fodor, believing or hoping that grass grows is a state of being in one or another computational relation to an internal representation that means that grass grows. This can be summed up in a set slogans: believing that grass grows is having *Grass grows* in the "belief box," desiring that grass grows is having this sentence (or one that means the same) in the "desire box," and so on.

Now if all content and meaning derives from meanings of the elements of the language of thought, we immediately want to know how the mental symbols get their meanings.[7] This is a question that gets wildly different answers from different philosophers, all equally committed to the cognitive science point of view. We will look at just two of them, one in passing and the other—a quite different perspective—more seriously. The first point of view, mentioned earlier, takes as a kind of paradigm those cases in which a symbol in the head might be said to covary with states in the world in the way that the number of rings in a tree trunk correlates with the age of the tree (see Dretske 1981; Stampe 1977; Stalnaker 1984; Fodor 1987). On this view, the meanings of mental symbols are a matter of the relations between these symbols and the world.

The second approach is known as *functionalism* (actually, *functional role semantics* in discussions of meaning) in philosophy, and as *procedural semantics* in cognitive psychology and computer science. (See Block 1986 for a list of references to both literatures.) Functionalism says that what gives internal symbols (and external symbols too) their meanings is how they function. To maximize the contrast with the view described in the last paragraph, it is useful to think of the functionalist approach with respect to a symbol that does not (on the face of it) have *any* kind of correlation with states of the world—say, the symbol *and*. Part of what makes *and* mean what it does is that if we are sure of *Grass is green and grass grows*, we can infer *Grass is green* and also *Grass grows*. Or if we are sure that one of the conjuncts is false, we can conclude that the conjunction is false too. The meaning of *and* is a matter of its behavior in these and other inferences. The functionalist view of meaning applies this idea to all words. The picture is that the internal representations in our heads have a function in our deciding, deliberating, problem solving—indeed, in our thought in general—and that is what their meanings consist in.

This picture can be bolstered by a consideration of what happens when one first learns Newtonian mechanics. In my own case, I heard a large number of unfamiliar terms more or less all at once: *mass, force, energy*, and the like. I never was told definitions of these terms in terms I already knew. (If anything is clear from the failure of logical empiricism, there are no definitions of such "theoretical terms" in observation language.) What I did learn was how to *use* these terms in solving homework problems, making observations, explaining the behavior of a pendulum, and the like. In learning how to use the terms in thought and action (and in perception as well, though its role there is less obvious), I learned their meanings, and this

7. In one respect, the meanings of mental symbols cannot be semantically more basic than the meanings of external symbols. The name *Aristotle* has the reference it has because of its causal connection (via generations of speakers) to a man who was called by a name that was an ancestor of our external term *Aristotle*. So the term in the language of thought that corresponds to *Aristotle* will certainly derive its reference from and thus will be semantically less basic than the public language word.

fits with the functionalist idea that the meaning of a term just *is* its function in perception, thought, and action. (See chapter 6 by Carey for a discussion of the restructuring of concepts that goes on in learning a new theory.) A theory of what meaning is can be expected to jibe with a theory of what it is to acquire meanings, and so considerations about acquisition can be relevant to semantics.

An apparent problem arises for such a theory in its application to the meanings of numerals. After all, it is a mathematical fact that truths in the familiar numeral system *1, 2, 3,...* are preserved, even if certain nonstandard interpretations of the numerals are adopted. For example, *1* might be mapped onto 2, *2* onto 4, *3* onto 6, and so on. That is, the numerals, both "odd" and "even," might be mapped onto the *even* numbers. So how can the functional role of *1* determine whether *1* means 1 or 2? It would seem that all functional role could do is "cut down" the number of possible interpretations, and if there are still an infinity left after the cutting down, functional role has gained nothing.

A natural functionalist response would be to emphasize the *input* and *output* ends of the functional roles. We say "Two cats," when confronted with a pair of cats, not when confronted with one cat, and our thoughts involving the symbol *3* affect our actions toward triples in an obvious way in which they do not affect our actions toward octuples. The functionalist can avoid nonstandard interpretations of *internal* functional roles by including in the semantically relevant functional roles the external relations involving perception and action. In this way, the functionalist can incorporate the insight of the view mentioned earlier that meaning has something to do with covariation between symbols and the world.

The emerging picture of how cognitive science can handle intentionality should be becoming clear. Transducers at the periphery and internal primitive processors produce and operate on symbols so as to give them their functional roles. In virtue of their functional roles, these symbols have meanings. The functional role perspective explains the mysterious correlation between the symbols and their meanings. It is the activities of the symbols that give them their meanings, so it is no mystery that a syntax-based system should have rational relations among the meanings of the system's symbols. Intentional states have their relations in virtue of these symbolic activities, and the contents of the intentional states of the system—thinking, wanting, and so forth—are inherited from the meanings of the symbols. This is the orthodox account of intentionality for the computer model of the mind. It combines functionalism with a commitment to a language of thought. Both views are controversial, the latter especially, both in regard to its truth and in regard to its relevance to intentionality even if true. The next two sections will be devoted to arguments for and against the language of thought.

3.3.1 Objections to the Language of Thought Theory

Many objections have been raised against the language of thought theory. Let us look briefly at three such objections made by Dennett (1975).

The first objection is that we all have an infinity of beliefs (or at any rate a very large number of them). For example, we believe that trees do not light up like fireflies, and that this book is probably closer to your eyes than George Bush's left shoe is to the ceiling of the Museum of Modern Art gift shop. But how can it be that so many beliefs are all stored in the rather small belief box in your head? One line of response to this objection involves making a distinction between the *ordinary* concept of belief and a *scientific* concept of belief toward which one hopes cognitive science is progressing. Actually, given that we have only a glimmer of what a science of belief would be like, perhaps we should speak of a *protoscientific* conception of belief rather than a scientific conception. (I will speak this way in what follows.) For scientific purposes, we home in on cases in which our beliefs *cause* us to *do* something (say, throw a ball or change our mind) and cases in which beliefs are caused by something (as when perception of a rhinoceros causes us to believe that there is a rhinoceros in the vicinity). So the protoscientific concept of belief is the concept of a *causally active* belief. And it is only for these beliefs that the language of thought theory is committed to sentences in the head. As Fodor (1987) says, "No intentional causation without explicit representation." Thus, the response to the infinity objection is that on the protoscientific concept of belief, most people would not *have* the beliefs mentioned in the last paragraph until they read the examples.

Beliefs in the protoscientific sense are explicit, that is, recorded in storage in the brain. For example, you no doubt were once told that the sun is 93 million miles away from the earth. If so, perhaps you have this fact explicitly recorded in your head, available for causal action, even though until you read this paragraph, this belief hadn't been conscious for years. Such explicit beliefs have the potential for causal interaction and thus must be distinguished from cases of belief in the ordinary sense (if they are beliefs at all) such as the belief that trees do not light up like fireflies.

Being explicit is to be distinguished from other properties of mental states, such as being conscious. Theories in cognitive science tell us of mental representations about which no one knows from introspection, such as mental representation of aspects of grammar. If this is right, there is much in the way of mental representation that is explicit but not conscious, and thus the door is opened to the possibility of belief that is explicit but not conscious.

It is important to note that the language of thought theory is not meant to be a theory of all possible believers, but rather only of *us*. There may be

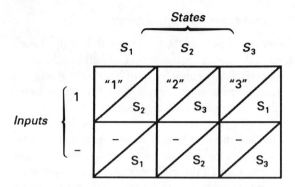

Figure 3.6
Finite automaton that counts "modulo" three.

creatures who can believe without any explicit representation at all, but the claim of the language of thought theory is that they aren't us. A digital computer consists of a central processing unit (CPU) that reads and writes explicit strings of zeros and ones in storage registers. One can think of this memory as in principle unlimited, but of course any actual machine has a finite memory. Now any computer with a finite amount of explicit storage can be simulated by a machine with a much larger CPU and no explicit storage (that is, no registers and no tape). The way the simulation works is by using the extra states as a form of memory. So, in principle, we could be simulated by a machine with no explicit memory at all.

Consider, for example, the finite automaton in figure 3.6. The table shows it as having three states. The states, S_1, S_2, and S_3, are listed across the top. The inputs are listed on the left side. Each box is in a column and a row and specifies what the machine does when it is in the state named at the top of the column, and when the input is the one listed at the side of the row. The top part of the box names the output, and the bottom part of the box names the next state. When the machine is in S_1, and it sees a 1, it says "1" and goes to S_2. When it is in S_2, if it sees a 1, it says "2" and goes into the next state, S_3. In that state, if it sees a 1, it says "3" and goes back to S_1. When it sees nothing, it says nothing and stays in the same state. This automaton counts "modulo" three; that is, you can tell from what it says whether it has seen a number of 1s divisible by 3. But what the machine table makes clear is that this machine need have no memory of the sort that involves writing anything down. It can "remember" how many 1s it has seen solely by changing state.

Suppose, then, that we are digital computers with explicit representations. We could be simulated by finite automata that have many more states than we do, and no explicit representations. The simulators will have just the same beliefs as we do, but no explicit representations (unless the simulators are just jukeboxes of the type of the Aunt Bubbles machine described earlier).

The machine in which remembered items are recorded explicitly has an advantage over a computationally equivalent machine that "remembers" by changing state, namely, that the explicit representations can be part of a combinatorial system. This point will be explained in the next section.

To sum up: The objection was that an infinity of beliefs cannot be written down in the head. My response was to distinguish between a loose and ordinary sense of *belief* in which it may be true that we have an infinity of beliefs, and a protoscientific sense of *belief* in which the concept of belief is the concept of a causally active belief. In the latter sense, I claimed, we do not have an infinity of beliefs.

Even if you agree with this response to the infinity objection, you may still feel dissatisfied because you wonder about the relation between the protoscientific concept of belief and the ordinary concept. It is natural to want some sort of reconstruction of the ordinary concept in scientific terms, a reconstruction of the sort we have when we define the ordinary concept of the weight of x as the force (in the sense of mechanics) exerted on x by the earth at the earth's surface. To scratch this itch, we can give a first approximation to a definition of a belief in the ordinary sense—as Dennett himself suggests—as anything that is either (1) a belief in the protoscientific sense or (2) naturally and easily deduced from a protoscientific belief.

A second objection to the language of thought theory is provided by Dennett's example of a chess-playing program that "thinks" it should get its queen out early, even though there is no explicitly represented rule that says anything like "Get your queen out early." The fact that it gets its queen out early is an "emergent" consequence of an interaction of a large number of rules that govern other matters. But now consider a human analogue of the chess-playing machine. Shouldn't we say that she believes she should get her queen out early despite her lack of any such explicit representation?

The reply is that in the protoscientific sense of belief, the chess player simply does not believe that she should get her queen out early. If this seems difficult to accept, note that there is no additional predictive or explanatory utility to the hypothesis that she believes she should get her queen out early beyond the predictive or explanatory utility of the explicitly represented strategies from which getting the queen out early emerges. Indeed, the idea that she should get her queen out early can actually conflict with her deeply held chess principles, despite being an emergent property of her usual tactics. If so, postulating that she believes that she should get her queen out early could lead to mistaken predictions of her behavior. In sum, the protoscientific concept of a causally active belief can be restricted to the strategies that really are explicitly represented, and not encompass any belief (in the loose and ordinary sense) that the queen should come out early.

Perhaps there is a quasi-behaviorist ordinary sense of belief in which it is correct to ascribe the belief that the queen should come out early simply on the basis of the fact that the chess player behaves as if she believes it. Even if we agree to recognize such a belief, it is not one that ever causally affects any other mental states or any behavior, so it is of little import from a scientific standpoint.

A third objection to the language of thought theory is provided by the "opposite" of the "queen out early" case, Dennett's "brother in Cleveland" case. Suppose that a neurosurgeon operates on a man's belief box, inserting the sentence "I have a brother in Cleveland." The patient wakes up, and the doctor asks, "Do you have a brother?" "Yes," the patient says, "in Cleveland." Doctor: "What's his name?" Patient: "Gosh, I can't think of it." Doctor: "Older or younger?" Patient: "I don't know, and by golly I'm an only child. I don't know why I'm saying that I have a brother at all." Finally, the patient concludes that he never really believed he had a brother in Cleveland but rather was a victim of some sort of compulsion to speak as if he did. The upshot is supposed to be that the language of thought theory is false, because you can't produce a belief just by inserting a sentence in the belief box.

The objection pinpoints a misleading aspect of the "belief box" slogan, not a problem with the doctrine that the slogan characterizes. Believing that I have a brother in Cleveland is a computational relation to a sentence, but this computational relation shouldn't be thought of as simply *storage* in the brain. Rather, it must include some specification of relations to other sentences to which one also has the same computational relation. This point holds both for the ordinary notion of belief and for the protoscientific notion. It holds for the ordinary notion of belief because we don't count someone as believing just because that person mouths words the way our neurosurgery victim mouthed the words "I have a brother in Cleveland." And it holds for the protoscientific notion of belief because the unit of explanation and prediction is much more likely to be groups of coherently related sentences in the brain than single sentences all by themselves. If one is going to retain the "belief box" way of talking, one should say that for a sentence in the belief box to count as a belief, it should cohere sufficiently with other sentences so as not to be totally unstable, disappearing on exposure to the light.

3.3.2   Arguments for the Language of Thought

So it seems that the language of thought hypothesis can be defended from these a priori objections. But is there any positive reason to believe it? One such reason is that it is part of a reasonably successful research program. But there are challengers (mainly, the connectionist program mentioned earlier), so a stronger case will be called for if the challengers' research programs also turn out to be successful.[8]

A major rationale for accepting the language of thought has been one or another form of *productivity* argument. The idea is that people are capable of thinking vast numbers of thoughts that they have not thought before—and indeed that no one may have ever thought before. Consider, for example, the thought mentioned earlier that trees do not light up like fireflies. Indeed, abstracting away from limitations on memory, motivation, and length of life, there may be no upper bound on the number of thinkable thoughts. The most obvious explanation of how we can think such new thoughts is the same as the explanation of how we can frame the sentences that express them: namely, via a combinatorial system. The number of sentences in the English language is certainly infinite. (See chapter 9 of Osherson and Lasnik 1990, especially example (2).) But what does it mean to say that sentences containing millions of words are "in principle" thinkable?

The explanation for the limitation on the actually thinkable sentences appeals to such facts as that were we to try to think sufficiently complicated thoughts, our attention would flag, or our memory would fail us, or we would die. And we can idealize away from these limitations, since the mechanisms of thought themselves are unlimited. But this claim that if we abstract away from memory, mortality, motivation, and the like, our thought mechanisms are unlimited, is a doctrine for which there is no direct evidence. The perspective from which this doctrine springs has been fertile, but it is an open question what aspect of the doctrine is responsible for its success.

After all, we might be finite beings, essentially. Not all idealizations are equally correct, and contrary to widespread assumption in cognitive science, the idealization to the unboundedness of thought may be a bad one. Consider a finite automaton naturally described by the table in figure 3.6.[9]

---

8. Note that the type of success is important to whether connectionism is really a rival to the language of thought point of view, As noted in chapter 1 of this epilogue, connectionist networks have been successful in discriminating mines from rocks. Of course, this sort of success does not suggest that these networks can provide models of higher cognition.

9. This table could be used to describe a machine that does have a memory with explicit representation. I say "naturally described" to indicate that I am thinking of a machine that does not have such a memory, a machine for which the table in figure 3.6 is an apt and natural description.

Its only form of memory is change of state. If you want to get this machine to count to 4 instead of just to 3, you can't just add more registers or more tape; you have to give it another state. You have to change the way the machine is built. Perhaps we are like this machine.

An extension of the productivity argument to deal with this sort of problem has been proposed by Fodor (1987) and by Fodor and Pylyshyn (1988). Fodor and Pylyshyn point out that someone who can think the thought that Mary loves John can also think the thought that John loves Mary. And likewise for a vast variety of pairs of thoughts that involve the same conceptual constituents but are put together differently. There is a *systematicity* relation among many thoughts that begs for an explanation in terms of a combinatorial system.

However, the most obvious candidate for the elements of such a combinatorial system in many areas are the external symbol systems themselves. Perhaps the most obvious case is arithmetical thoughts. Someone who is capable of thinking the thought that $7 + 16$ is not 20 is presumably also capable of thinking the thought that $17 + 6$ is not 20. Indeed, a person who has mastered the ten numerals plus other basic symbols of Arabic notation and their rules of combination can think any arithmetical thought that is expressible in a representation that person can read. (Note that false propositions can be thinkable—one can think the thought that $2 + 2 = 5$, if only to think that it is false.) One line of a common printed page contains eighty symbols. There are a great many different arithmetical propositions that can be written on such a line— about as many as there are elementary particles in the universe. How is it that we have so many possible arithmetical thoughts? The obvious explanation for this is that we can string together—either in our heads or on paper—the symbols (numerals, pluses, and so on) themselves, and simply read the thought off the string of symbols. Of course, this does not show that the systematicity argument is *wrong*. Far from it, since it shows *why* it is right. But this point does *threaten the value* of the systematicity argument considerably. For it highlights the possibility that the systematicity argument may apply only to *conscious* thought, and not to the rest of the iceberg of unconscious thought processes that cognitive science is mainly about. In other words, I am agreeing with Fodor and Pylyshyn that the systematicity argument shows that there is a language of thought. They are right that if connectionism is incompatible with a language of thought, so much the worse for connectionism. Where I am challenging them is on the issue of what the systematicity argument shows about the *extent* of the use of the language of thought in mental processes.

Much of the success in cognitive science has been in our understanding of perceptual and motor modules. (See chapters 4, 5, and 6 of Osherson and Lasnik 1990 on language processing, chapter 1 of "Visual Cognition" in

Osherson, Kosslyn, and Hollerbach 1990 on low-level vision, and chapters 1–5 of "Action" in the latter volume on motor control.) The operation of these modules is neither introspectible—accessible to conscious thought— nor influencible by conscious thought. These modules are "informationally encapsulated" (see chapter 6 of Osherson and Lasnik 1990; Pylyshyn 1984; Fodor 1983). The productivity in conscious thought that is exploited by the systematicity argument certainly does not demonstrate productivity in the processing inside such modules. True, someone who can think that John loves Mary can also think that Mary loves John. But we do not have access to such facts about pairs of representations of the kind involved in unconscious processes. We must distinguish between the conclusion of an argument and the argument itself. The conclusion of the systematicity argument may well be right about unconscious representations. That is, *systematicity itself* may well obtain in these systems. My point is that the systematicity *argument* shows little about encapsulated modules and other unconscious systems.

The weakness of the systematicity argument is that, resting as it does on facts that are so readily available to conscious thought, its application to unconscious processes is more tenuous. Nonetheless, as you can see by consulting the references in the previous paragraph, the symbol manipulation model has been quite successful in explaining aspects of perception and motor control. So although the systematicity argument is limited in its application to unconscious processes, the model it supports for conscious processes appears to have considerable application to unconscious processes nonetheless.

To avoid misunderstanding, I should add that the point just made does not challenge the thrust of Fodor's and Pylyshyn's critique of connectionism. If connectionism is to be a cognitive theory, it will have to accommodate the fact of our use of a systematic combinatorial symbol system in conscious thought. It is hard to see how it could do this without in one way or another being an implementation of a standard symbol-crunching model.

Fodor and Pylyshyn (1988, 44) counter the idea that the systematicity argument depends entirely on conscious symbol manipulating by noting that the systematicity argument appears to apply to animals. For example, the conditioning literature apparently contains no cases of animals that can be trained to pick the red thing rather than the green one but *cannot* be trained to pick the green thing rather than the red one.

This reply has some force, but it is uncomfortably anecdotal. Notoriously, the data scientists collect depend on their theories. We cannot rely on data collected in animal-conditioning experiments run by behaviorists—who, after all, were notoriously opposed to theorizing about internal states. There are well-known examples in the ethology literature of failure of systematicity in stimulus arrays (for instance, special responses to one combination of shapes but not to another). But these appear to be special cases, explainable in terms of genetic programming or the presence of one combination but not others in the environment. I know of no evidence that representation of thought and learning is not systematic in animals, but prudence suggests waiting for further research on this matter.

Another objection to the systematicity argument derives from the distinction between linguistic and pictorial representation that plays a role in the controversies over mental imagery. Many researchers feel that we have two different representational systems, a languagelike system—thinking in words—and a pictorial system—thinking in pictures. The fact about the animal studies pointed to by Fodor and Pylyshyn may reflect the properties of an imagery system shared by humans and animals, not a properly languagelike system. Suppose Fodor and Pylyshyn are right about the systematicity of thought in animals. That may reflect only a combinatorial pictorial system. If so, it would suggest (though it wouldn't show) that humans have a combinatorial pictorial system too. But the question would still be open whether humans have a *languagelike* combinatorial system that is used in unconscious thought. In sum, the systematicity argument certainly applies to conscious thought, and it is part of a perspective on unconscious thought that has been fertile, but there are difficulties in applying it to unconscious thought.

3.3.3 Explanatory Levels and the Syntactic Theory of the Mind

In this section let us assume that the language of thought hypothesis is correct, in order to ask another question: should cognitive science explanations appeal only to the syntactic elements in the language of thought (the 0s and 1s and the like), or should they appeal to the contents of these symbols as well? Stich (1983) has argued for the "syntactic theory of mind," a version of the computer model in which the language of thought is construed in terms of uninterpreted symbols, symbols that may *have* contents but whose contents are irrelevant for the purposes of cognitive science. This is a very controversial matter, one that I cannot discuss here in any detail. Instead, I will give a critique of an argument I derive from remarks in Stich 1983, though I cannot in good conscience ascribe the argument to Stich in the form in which I will discuss it. I will use a cartoon version of Stich's argument as a foil for introducing crucial issues about levels of explanation and description.

Let us begin with Stich's case of Mrs. T, a senile old lady who answers "What happened to McKinley?" with "McKinley was assassinated" but cannot answer questions like "Where is McKinley now?" and "Is he alive or dead?" Mrs. T's logical faculties are fine, but she has lost most of her memories and virtually all the concepts that are normally connected to the concept of assassination, such as death. Stich sketches the case so as to persuade us that though Mrs. T may know that something happened to McKinley, she doesn't have any grasp of the concept of assassination and thus cannot be said to believe that McKinley was assassinated.

The argument I will critique concludes that a purely syntactic account is superior to a content account. The syntactic approach is alleged to be superior in two respects. First, it can handle Mrs. T, who has little in the way of intentional content but plenty of internal representations to which we can attach no clear meaning. The same holds for very young children, people with weird psychiatric disorders, and denizens of exotic cultures. In all these cases cognitive science can (at least potentially) assign internal syntactic descriptions, but there are problems with content ascriptions (though, in the last case at least, the problem is not that these people have no contents but just that their contents are so different from ours that we cannot assign contents to them in *our terms*). In sum, the syntactic perspective is allegedly superior to the content perspective because it allows for the psychology of the senile, the very young, the disordered, and the exotic and thus is alleged to be far more *general* than the content perspective.

The syntactic perspective is also alleged to be superior because it allows more *fine-grained* predictions and explanations than the content perspective. To take a humdrum example, the content perspective allows us to predict that if someone believes that all men are mortal, and that he is a man, he can conclude that he is mortal. But suppose that the way this person represents the generalization that all men are mortal to himself is via a syntactic form of the type *All nonmortals are nonmen*; then the inference will be harder to draw. In general, what inferences are hard rather than easy, and what sorts of mistakes are likely, will be predictable from the syntactic perspective but not from the content perspective, in which all the different ways of representing one belief are lumped together.

The upshot of this argument is supposed to be that since the syntactic approach is more general and more fine-grained than the content approach, cognitive science would do well to scrap attempts to explain and predict in terms of content in favor of appeals to syntactic form alone.

But there is a fatal flaw in this argument, one that applies to many reductionist arguments. *If this argument were correct, it would undermine the syntactic approach itself.* This objection is so simple, fundamental, and widely applicable that it deserves a name; let's call it the *Reductionist Cruncher*. For example, suppose we can find a physicochemical account of the syntactic objects in our heads. Just as the syntactic objects on paper can be described in molecular terms, for example as structures of carbon molecules, so the syntactic objects in our heads can be seen from the viewpoint of chemistry and physics. But a physicochemical account of the syntactic objects in our heads will be more general than the syntactic account in just the same way that the syntactic account is more general than the content account. There are possible beings, such as Mrs. T, who are similar to us syntactically but not in contents. Similarly, there are possible beings who are similar to us in physicochemical respects but not syntactically. For example, creatures could be like us in physicochemical respects but not have physicochemical parts that function as syntactic objects—just as Mrs. T's syntactic objects don't function so as to confer content upon them. Further, the physicochemical account will be more fine-grained than the syntactic account, just as the syntactic account is more fine-grained than the content account. Syntactic generalizations will fail under some physicochemically specifiable circumstances, just as content generalizations fail under some syntactically specifiable circumstances. In sum, if we could refute the content approach by showing that the syntactic approach is more general and more fine-grained than the content approach, then we could also refute the syntactic approach by exhibiting the same deficiency in it relative to a still deeper theory. The Reductionist Cruncher applies even within physics itself. For example, anyone who rejects the explanations of thermodynamics in favor of the explanations of molecular statistical mechanics will be frustrated by the fact that the explanations of molecular statistical mechanics can themselves be "undermined" in just the same way by quantum mechanics.

The same point can be made in terms of the explanation of how a computer works. Compare two explanations of the behavior of the computer on my desk, one in terms of the programming language and the other in terms of what is happening in the computer's circuits. The latter level is certainly more general in that it applies not only to programmed computers but also to nonprogrammable computers that are electronically similar to mine (for instance, certain calculators). Thus, the greater generality of the circuit level is like the greater generality of the syntactic perspective. Further, the circuit level is more fine-grained in that it allows us to predict and explain computer failures that have nothing to do with program glitches. Circuits will fail under certain circumstances (such as overload, excessive heat or humidity) that are not characterizable in the vocabulary of the program level. Thus, the greater predictive and explanatory power of the circuit level is like the greater power of the syntactic level to distinguish cases of the same content represented in different syntactic forms that make a difference in processing.

However, the computer analogy reveals a flaw in the argument that the "upper" level (the program level in this example) explanations should be scrapped. The fact that a "lower" level like the circuit level is superior for some purposes does not show that "higher" levels such as the program levels are dispensable. The program level has its own type of greater generality—namely, it applies to computers that use the same programming language but are built in different ways, even computers that don't have circuits at all (but work, say, via gears and pulleys). Higher levels have their own utility, and the sensible policy is to retain and use all levels that are useful. Indeed, there are many predictions and explanations that are simple at the program level but would be absurdly complicated at the circuit level. Further (and here is the Reductionist Cruncher again), if the program level could be refuted by the circuit level, then the circuit level could itself be refuted by a deeper theory (for example, the quantum field theory of circuits).

The point here is not that the program level is a convenient fiction. On the contrary, the program level is just as *real* and *explanatory* as the circuit level.

Perhaps it will be useful to see the matter in terms of an example from Putnam (1975). Consider a rigid round peg 1 inch in diameter and a square hole in a rigid board with a 1-inch diagonal. The peg won't fit through the hole for reasons that are easy to understand via a little geometry. (The side of the hole is $1/\sqrt{2}$, which is a number substantially less than 1.) Now if we went to the level of description of this apparatus in terms of the molecular structure that makes up a specific wooden board, we could explain the rigidity of the materials, and we would have a more fine-grained under-standing, including the ability to predict the incredible case where alignment of molecules might be such as to allow the peg to actually go through the board. But the "upper" level account in terms of rigidity and geometry nonetheless provides correct explanations and predictions and applies more generally to *any* rigid peg and board, even one with quite a different sort of molecular constitution, say, one made of glass (a supercooled liquid) rather than wood.

It is tempting to say that the account in terms of rigidity and geometry is only an approximation and that the molecular account is the really correct one. (See Smolensky 1988 for a dramatic case of yielding to this sort of temptation.) But the cure for this temptation is the Reductionist Cruncher: note that from the point of view of an elementary particle account, the molecular account will seem only an approximation. In turn, the elementary particle account itself may seem only an approximation from the point of view of a still deeper theory. And so on, perhaps ad infinitum. The point of a scientific account is to cut nature at its joints, and nature *has real joints* at many different levels, each of which requires its own kind of idealization.

I have been talking as though there were just one content level, but actually there are many. Marr (1977) distinguished among three different levels: the computational level, the level of representation and algorithm, and the level of implementation. At the computational or formal level the multiplier discussed earlier is to be understood as a function from pairs of numbers to their products, say, from $\{7, 9\}$ to 63. The most abstract characterization at the level of representation and algorithm is simply the algorithm of the multiplier: Multiply the number n by the number m by adding m to itself n times. A less abstract characterization at this middle level is the program described earlier, a sequence of operations including subtracting 1 from the register that initially represents n until it is reduced to zero, adding m to the answer register each time. (See figure 3.2.) *Each of these levels is a content level rather than a syntactic level.* There are many types of multipliers whose behavior can be explained (albeit at a somewhat superficial level) simply by reference to the fact that they are multipliers. The algorithm mentioned gives a deeper explanation, and the program— one of many programs that can realize that algorithm—gives a still deeper explanation. However, when we break the multiplier down into parts such as the adder of figures 3.3a and 3.3b, we explain its internal operation in terms of gates that operate on syntax, that is, in terms of operations on numerals. Now it is crucially important to realize that the mere possibility of describing a system in a certain vocabulary does not by itself demonstrate the existence of a genuine explanatory level. We are concerned here with cutting nature at its joints, and *talking* as though there is a joint does not make it so. The fact that it is good *methodology* to look first for the function, then for the algorithm, then for the implementation, does not by itself show that these inquiries are inquiries at different levels, as opposed to different ways of approaching the same level. The crucial issue is whether the different vocabularies correspond to genuinely distinct laws and explanations, and in any given case this question will only be answerable empirically. However, we already have good empirical evidence for the reality of the content levels just mentioned—as well as the syntactic level. The evidence is to be found in this very book and its companion volumes, where we see genuine and distinct explanations at the level of function, algorithm, and syntax.

A further point about explanatory levels is that it is legitimate to use different and even *incompatible* idealizations at different levels (see Putnam 1975). It has been argued that since the brain is analog, the digital computer must be incorrect as a model of the mind. But even digital computers are analog at one level of description. For example, gates of the sort described earlier in which 4 volts realizes *1* and 7 volts realizes *0* are understood from the digital perspective as always representing either *0* or *1*. But from the point of view of the electronic level, values intermediate between 4 and 7 volts appear momentarily when a register switches between them. We abstract from these intermediate values for the purposes of one level of description, but not another.

3.3.4   Searle's Chinese Room Argument

As we have seen, the idea that a certain type of symbol processing can be what *makes* something an intentional system is fundamental to the computer model of the mind. Let us end this chapter with a discussion of a flamboyant frontal attack on this idea by Searle (1980). Searle's strategy[10] is one of avoiding quibbles about specific programs by imagining that cognitive science of the distant future can come up with the program of an actual person who speaks and understands Chinese, and that this program can be implemented in a machine. Unlike many critics of the computer model, Searle is willing to allow that perhaps this can be done. His claim is that *even if this can be done, the machine will not have intentional states.*

The argument is based on an example. Imagine yourself taking a job in which you work in a room (the Chinese room). You understand only English. Slips of paper with Chinese writing on them are put under the input door, and your job is to write sensible Chinese replies on other slips and push them under the output door. How do you do it? You act as the central processing unit (CPU) of a computer, following the computer program mentioned above that describes the symbol processing in an actual Chinese speaker's head. The program is written in English in a library in the room. This is how you follow the program. Suppose the latest input has certain unintelligible (to you) Chinese squiggles on it. There is a blackboard on your wall with a "state" number written on it; it says 17. (The CPU of a computer is a device with a finite number of states whose activity is determined solely by its current state and input, and since you are acting as the CPU, your output will be determined by your input and your "state.") You take book 17 out of the library and look up these particular squiggles in it. It tells you to look at what is written on your scratch pad (the analogue of the computer's internal memory), and given both the input squiggles and the scratch pad marks, you are directed to change what is on the scratch pad in a certain way, write certain other squiggles on your output pad, pushing the paper under the output door, and change the state board to 193. As a result of this activity, speakers of Chinese find that the pieces of paper you slip under the output door are sensible replies to the inputs.

But you know nothing of what is being said in Chinese; you are just following instructions (in English) to look in certain books and write certain marks. Searle argues that since *you* don't understand any Chinese, the system of which you are the CPU is a mere Chinese simulator, not a real Chinese understander. And since he rightly rejects the Turing test for understanding Chinese, he concludes that no symbol-manipulation theory of Chinese understanding (or any other intentional state) is correct. Thus, the conclusion of Searle's argument is that the fundamental idea of thought as symbol processing is wrong even if it allows us to build a machine that

10. I will be taking liberties with Searle's actual text, trying to get at the strongest form of the argument.

can duplicate the symbol processing of a person and thereby duplicate a person's behavior.

The best criticisms of the Chinese room argument have focused on what Searle—anticipating the challenge—calls the *systems reply*. (See the responses following Searle 1980, and the comment on Searle in Hofstadter and Dennett 1981.) The systems reply says that the whole system—man + program + board + paper + input and output doors— understands Chinese, even though the man who is acting as the CPU does not. If you open up your own computer, looking for the CPU, you will find that it is just one of the many chips and other components on the main circuit-board. The systems reply reminds us that the CPUs of the thinking computers we hope to have someday will not *themselves* think—rather, they will be *parts* of thinking systems. So why should we ascribe the CPU's (that is, your) lack of Chinese understanding to the whole system?

Searle's clever reply is to imagine the paraphernalia of the "system" *internalized* as follows. First, instead of having you consult a library, we are to imagine you *memorizing* the whole library. Second, instead of writing notes on scratch pads, you are to memorize what you would have written on the pads, and you are to memorize what the state blackboard would say. Finally, instead of looking at notes put under one door and passing notes under another door, you just use your *own body* to listen to Chinese utterances and produce replies. (This version of the Chinese room has the additional advantage of generalizability so as to involve the complete behavior of a Chinese-speaking system instead of just a Chinese note exchanger.) But as Searle would emphasize, when you seem to Chinese speakers to be conducting a learned discourse with them in Chinese, all you are aware of doing is thinking about what noises the program tells you to make next, given the noises you hear and what you've written on your mental scratch pad.

I argued above that the CPU is just one of many components. If the whole system understands Chinese, that should not lead us to expect the CPU to understand Chinese. The effect of Searle's internalization move— the "new" Chinese room—is to attempt to destroy the analogy between looking inside the computer and looking inside the Chinese room. If one looks inside the computer, one sees many chips in addition to the CPU. But if one looks inside the "new" Chinese room, all one sees is *you*, since you have memorized the library and internalized the functions of the scratch pad and the blackboard. But the point to keep in mind is that although the non-CPU components are no longer easy to see, they are not gone. Rather, they are internalized. If the program requires the contents of one register to be placed in another register, and if you would have done this in the original Chinese room by copying from one piece of scratch paper to another, in the new Chinese room you must copy from one of your mental analogues of a piece of scratch paper to another. You are implementing the system by doing what the CPU would do and also simulating the non-CPU components.

Keeping this point in mind, we can ask why we should suppose that a device that implements a Chinese-understanding system should itself be aware of doing anything, including being aware of understanding Chinese. Of course, if the implementer is you, you will be aware of following your memorized instructions, but why should you be aware of the Chinese understanding of the whole system? The burden of proof is on Searle to tell us why the implementer that is acting as the CPU of a system that understands Chinese should be aware of the Chinese understanding of the whole system just because this implementer is *also* implementing the non-CPU components.

The systems reply sees the Chinese room (new and old) as an English system implementing a Chinese system. What you are aware of are the thoughts of the English system, for example, your following instructions and consulting your internal library. But in virtue of doing this Herculean task, you are also implementing a real intelligent Chinese-speaking system, and so your body houses two genuinely distinct intelligent systems. The Chinese system also thinks, but though you implement this thought, you are not aware of it.

The systems reply can be backed up with an addition to the thought experiment that highlights the division of labor. Imagine that you take on the Chinese simulating as a 9-to-5 job. You come in Monday morning after a weekend of relaxation, and you are paid to follow the program until 5 P.M. When you are working, you concentrate hard at working, and so instead of trying to figure out the meaning of what is said to you, you focus your energies on working out what the program tells you to do in response to such an input. As a result, during working hours you respond to everything just as the program dictates. If someone speaks to you in English, you say what the program (which, you recall, describes a real Chinese speaker) dictates. So if during working hours someone speaks to you in English, you respond with a request in Chinese to speak Chinese, or even an inexpertly pronounced "No speak English" that was once memorized by the Chinese speaker being simulated, and which you the English-speaking system may even fail to recognize as English. Then, come 5 P.M., you stop working, and you react to Chinese the way any monolingual English speaker would.

Why is it that the English system implements the Chinese system rather than, say, the other way around? Because you (the English system whom I am now addressing) are following the instructions of a program in English to make Chinese noises and not the other way around. If you win Megabucks and quit your job, the Chinese system disappears. On the other hand, if the Chinese system is told he wins Megabucks, he will make plans in Chinese, but then when 5 P.M. rolls around, you quit for the day, and the Chinese system's plans are on the shelf until you come back to work. And of course you have no commitment to doing *whatever* the program dictates. If the program dictates that you make a series of movements that leads you to a flight to China, you can drop out of the simulating mode, saying "I quit!" The Chinese speaker's existence and fulfillment of his plans depend on your work schedule and your plans, not the other way around.

Thus, you and the Chinese system cohabit one body. In effect, Searle uses the fact that you are not aware of the Chinese system's thoughts as an argument that it has no thoughts. But this is an invalid argument. Real cases of multiple personalities are often cases in which one personality is unaware of the others.

Even if I am right about the failure of Searle's argument, it does succeed in sharpening our understanding of the nature of intentionality and its relation to computation and representation.

Suggestions for Further Reading

For an article-length treatment of the computer model of the mind, see Haugeland 1978; for a book-length treatment, see Pylyshyn 1984; and for an anthology, see Haugeland 1981. This anthology contains Haugeland 1978, Searle 1980, Marr's article on levels (Marr 1977), Putnam's paper about the round peg and square hole (Putnam 1975), Fodor 1980, and part of Dreyfus's well-known critique of the computer model (Dreyfus 1979). Block 1980, Rosenthal 1989, and Lycan 1989 contain many of the same papers, plus many excellent papers on reductive levels and functionalism. Block 1986 provides a recent review on functionalism, and chapter 3 of Fodor 1987 a critique.

On internal representation and its semantics, Fodor 1985 provides an excellent guide. Cummins 1989 is a readable book with chapters on all the major views. Haugeland 1989 looks at the major views from a phenomenological perspective. Putnam 1988 is a critique of the notions of meaning and content implicit in the computer model. See also the articles in the first section of Block 1980, especially Field 1978, which is the classic article on the relation between internal representation and functionalism. This book, and Lycan 1989 as well, contain sections on imagery as it concerns the issue of whether mental images are coded in representations like the 1s and 0s in computers, or in representations that are "pictorial."

References to work on connectionism are to be found at the end of chapter 1 of this epilogue. A critique of the computer model approach from the biological standpoint is provided in part 2 of Churchland 1986.

Philosophers are increasingly concerned with the reality of content and its role in cognitive science. The place to start is with Churchland 1981 and Stich 1983. Sterelny 1985 is an interesting review of Stich. Dennett 1987 takes a view somewhere between Churchland's eliminativism and the realism espoused here. The case against content from the point of view of issues in the philosophy of language is discussed in detail in Schiffer 1987, a difficult work. Horwich, forthcoming, argues that deflationary views of truth are irrelevant to these issues about content.

Discussions of the Turing test are to be found in Moor 1987 and Block 1980.

Questions

3.1 Recall the example of the molecule-for-molecule duplicate of you that happened by chance to come together from molecules from the swamp. You disapprove of the Supreme Court, and the swamp creature mouths all the same anti–Supreme Court slogans that you do. But as argued earlier, the swamp creature, having never read about the Supreme Court or heard anyone talk about it or anything of the kind, should not be regarded as having any intentional states that are *about* it. Still, all of the swamp creature's states are the same as yours "from the inside," so the question naturally arises, Is there some kind of content you share with it? Philosophers who answer yes have named the kind of content you (putatively) share with the swamp creature *narrow* content, and there is a raging debate about whether there is such a thing. The case against it is presented in Burge 1979, 1986, Putnam 1988, Pettit and McDowell 1986, and Stalnaker 1989. A defense is to be found in chapter 2 of Fodor 1987.

3.2 Our beliefs certainly influence what we do, and it seems that our beliefs do so in virtue of their content. If my belief that the American political system is rotten causes me to speak out, my action was due to the content of my belief. Had I believed our political system was great, I wouldn't have spoken. But how can content be causally efficacious when the primitive processors in our heads are sensitive only to the syntactic properties of representations, and not their semantic properties? The issue is further discussed in Lepore and Loewer 1987, Dretske 1988, and Block, forthcoming.

3.3 Suppose that you had an identical twin raised from birth with color-"inverting" lenses in his/her eyes. Isn't it possible that things you both call "green" look to him/her the way things you both call "red" look to you? If this sort of spectrum inversion is possible, does it show that there can be no computer model of this "qualitative" content? A good case for the possibility of spectrum inversion is provided in Shoemaker 1981. For the opposing view, see Dennett 1988 and Harman 1989; Block 1989 is a reply to Harman. For a comprehensive study, see Lycan 1987.

3.4 Schwartz (1988) argues for connectionism and against standard computational models on the ground that the brain is slow, squishy, and error-prone, whereas computers execute an intricate parallel dance of interlocking reliable processes. Does the point of section 3.3.3 work against Schwartz's argument? See Fodor and Pylyshyn 1988 on implementation theories and Pylylshyn 1984 on the notion of virtual architecture for the tools to use in thinking about this argument.

3.5 Many philosophers have followed Dennett (1969) in adopting an *evolutionary* approach to intentionality. Papineau (1984) and Millikan (1984) have argued that what makes the frog's fly representation represent flies is that this representation fulfills its biological function when flies are present. But if evolution is essential to intentionality, how could a computer, being a nonevolved device, have intentionality?

References

Block, N. (1978). Troubles with functionalism. In C. W. Savage, ed., *Minnesota studies in philosophy of science*, vol. 9. Minneapolis, MN: University of Minnesota Press. Reprinted in Rosenthal 1989 and Lycan 1989.

Block, N., ed. (1980). *Readings in philosophy of psychology*, vol. 1. Cambridge, MA: Harvard University Press.

Block, N. (1981a). Psychologism and behaviorism. *The Philosophical Review* 90, 5–43.

Block, N., ed. (1981b). *Readings in philosophy of psychology*, vol. 2. Cambridge, MA: Harvard University Press.

Block, N. (1986). Advertisement for a semantics for psychology. In P. A. French et al., eds., *Midwest studies in philosophy*, vol. 10. Minneapolis, MN: University of Minnesota Press.

Block, N. (1989). Inverted earth. In Tomberlin 1989.

Block, N. (forthcoming). Can the mind change the world? In G. Boolos, ed., *Essays in honor of Hilary Putnam.* Cambridge: Cambridge University Press.

Burge, T. (1979). Individualism and the mental. In P. A. French et al., eds., *Midwest studies in philosophy,* vol. 4. Minneapolis, MN: University of Minnesota Press.

Burge, T. (1986). Individualism and psychology. *The Philosophical Review* 95, 3–45.

Churchland, P. M. (1981). Eliminative materialism and the propositional attitudes. *The Journal of Philosophy* 78, 67–90.

Churchland, P. S. (1986). *Neurophilosophy: Toward a unified science of the mind-brain.* Cambridge, MA: MIT Press.

Cummins, R. (1975). Functional analysis. *Journal of Philosophy* 72, 741–765. Partially reprinted in Block 1980.

Cummins, R. (1989). *Meaning and mental representation.* Cambridge, MA: MIT Press.

Dennett, D. C. (1969). *Content and consciousness.* London: Routledge and Kegan Paul.

Dennett, D. C. (1974). Why the law of effect will not go away. *Journal of the Theory of Social Behavior* 5, 169–187.

Dennett, D. C. (1975). Brain writing and mind reading. In K. Gunderson, ed., *Minnesota studies in philosophy of science,* vol. 7. Minneapolis, MN: University of Minnesota Press.

Dennett, D. C. (1981). Three kinds of intentional psychology. In R. Healy, ed., *Reduction, time and reality.* Cambridge: Cambridge University Press.

Dennett, D. C. (1987). *The intentional stance.* Cambridge, MA: MIT Press.

Dennett, D. C. (1988). Quining qualia. In A. Marcel and E. Bisiach, eds., *Consciousness in contemporary society.* Oxford: Oxford University Press.

Dretske, F. (1981). *Knowledge and the flow of information.* Cambridge, MA: MIT Press.

Dretske, F. (1988). *Explaining behavior: Reasons in a world of causes.* Cambridge, MA: MIT Press.

Dreyfus, H. L. (1979). *What computers can't do.* New York: Harper and Row.

Field, H. (1978). Mental representation. *Erkenntnis* 13, 9–61. Reprinted in Block 1980.

Fodor, J. (1968). The appeal to tacit knowledge in psychological explanation. *The Journal of Philosophy* 65.20.

Fodor, J. (1975). *The language of thought.* New York: Crowell.

Fodor, J. (1980). Methodological solipsism considered as a research strategy in cognitive psychology. *The Behavioral and Brain Sciences* 3, 417–424. Reprinted in Haugeland 1981.

Fodor, J. (1981). Three cheers for propositional attitudes. In *RePresentations.* Cambridge, MA: MIT Press.

Fodor, J. (1983). *The modularity of mind.* Cambridge, MA: MIT Press.

Fodor, J. (1985). Fodor's guide to mental representation. *Mind* 94, 76–100.

Fodor, J. (1987). *Psychosemantics. The role of meaning in the philosophy of mind.* Cambridge, MA: MIT Press.

Fodor, J., and Z. Pylyshyn (1988). Connectionism and cognitive architecture: A critical analysis. *Cognition* 28, 3–71.

Harman, G. (1973). *Thought.* Princeton, NJ: Princeton University Press.

Harman, G. (1989). The intrinsic quality of experience. In Tomberlin 1989.

Haugeland, J. (1978) The nature and the plausibility of cognitivism. *The Behavioral and Brain Sciences* 1, 215–226. Reprinted in Haugeland 1981.

Haugeland, J., ed. (1981). *Mind design.* Cambridge, MA: MIT Press.

Haugeland, J. (1989). The intentionality all-stars. In Tomberlin 1989.

Hofstadter, D., and D. Dennett (1981). *The mind's I: Fantasies and reflections on mind and soul.* New York: Basic Books.

Horwich, P. (forthcoming). *The deflationary theory of truth.* Oxford: Basil Blackwell.

LePore, E., and B. Loewer (1987). Mind matters. *The Journal of Philosophy* 84, 630–641.

Lycan, W. (1987). *Consciousness*. Cambridge, MA: MIT Press.

Lycan, W., ed. (1989). *Mind and cognition*. Oxford: Basil Blackwell.

McCarthy, J. (1980). Beliefs, machines and theories. *The Behavioral and Brain Sciences* 3, 435.

Marr, D. (1977). Artificial intelligence: A personal view. *Artificial Intelligence* 9, 37–48. Reprinted in Haugeland 1981.

Millikan, R. G. (1984). *Language, thought, and other biological categories: New foundations for realism*. Cambridge, MA: MIT Press.

Moor, J. (1987). Turing test. In S. C. Shapiro, ed., *The Wiley encyclopedia of artificial intelligence*. New York: Wiley.

Newell, A. (1980). Physical symbol systems. *Cognitive Science* 4, 135–183.

Osherson, D. N., S. M. Kosslyn, and J. M. Hollerbach, eds. (1990). *Visual cognition and action: An invitation to cognitive science, volume 2*. Cambridge, MA: MIT Press.

Osherson, D. N., and H. Lasnik, eds. (1990). *Language: An invitation to cognitive science, volume 1*. Cambridge, MA: MIT Press.

Papineau, D. (1984). Representation and explanation. *Philosophy of Science* 51, 550–572.

Pettit, P., and J. McDowell (1986). *Subject, thought, and context*. Oxford: Oxford University Press.

Putnam, H. (1975). Philosophy and our mental life. In *Mind, language and reality: Philosophical papers*, vol. 2. London: Cambridge University Press. Reprinted in Block 1980 and in somewhat different form in Haugeland 1981. Originally published in *Cognition* 2 (1973) with a section on IQ that has been omitted from both of the reprinted versions.

Putnam, H. (1988). *Representation and reality*. Cambridge, MA: MIT Press.

Pylyshyn, Z. (1984). *Computation and cognition: Issues in the foundations of cognitive science*. Cambridge, MA: MIT Press.

Rosenthal, D. M., ed. (1989). *The nature of mind*. Oxford: Oxford University Press.

Schiffer, S. (1987). *Remnants of meaning*. Cambridge, MA: MIT Press.

Schwartz, J. (1988). The new connectionism: Developing relationships between neuroscience and artificial intelligence. *Daedalus* 117, 123–142.

Searle, J. (1980). Minds, brains, and programs. *The Behavioral and Brain Sciences* 3, 417–424. Reprinted in Haugeland 1981.

Shoemaker, S. (1981). The inverted spectrum. *The Journal of Philosophy* 74, 357–381.

Smolensky, P. (1988). On the proper treatment of connectionism. *Behavioral and Brain Sciences* 11, 1–23. See also the commentary that follows and the reply by the author.

Stalnaker, R. (1984). *Inquiry*. Cambridge, MA: MIT Press.

Stalnaker, R. (1989). On what's in the head. In Tomberlin 1989.

Stampe, D. W. (1977). Toward a causal theory of linguistic representation. In P. A. French, et al., eds., *Midwest studies in philosophy*, vol. 2. Minneapolis, MN: University of Minnesota Press.

Sterelny, K. (1985). Review of Stich, *From folk psychology to cognitive science: The case against belief*. *Australasian Journal of Philosophy* 63, 510–519.

Stich, S. (1983). *From folk psychology to cognitive science: The case against belief*. Cambridge, MA: MIT Press.

Tomberlin, J., ed. (1989). *Philosophical perspectives, IV: Philosophy of mind and action theory*. Atascadero, CA: Ridgeview.

Turing, A. M. (1950). Computing machinery and intelligence. *Mind* 59, 433–460.

Weizenbaum, J. (1976). *Computer power and human reason*. San Francisco: W. H. Freeman.

White, S. (1982). Functionalism and propositional content. Doctoral dissertation, University of California, Berkeley.

Contents of Volume 1

Language: An Invitation to Cognitive Science
edited by Daniel N. Osherson and Howard Lasnik

Contents of Volume 2

Index